MW01268624

The Centre and its Compass

STUDIES IN MEDIEVAL LITERATURE
IN HONOR OF PROFESSOR JOHN LEYERLE

The Centre and its Compass

STUDIES IN MEDIEVAL LITERATURE
IN HONOR OF PROFESSOR JOHN LEYERLE

EDITED BY

ROBERT A. TAYLOR

JAMES F. BURKE

PATRICIA J. EBERLE

IAN LANCASHIRE

BRIAN S. MERRILEES

STUDIES IN MEDIEVAL CULTURE XXXIII
WESTERN MICHIGAN UNIVERSITY
KALAMAZOO, MICHIGAN — 49008-3801
1993

Library of Congress Cataloging-in Publication Data

The Centre and its compass : studies in medieval literature in honor
  of Professor John Leyerle / edited by Robert A. Taylor . . . [et al.].
     p.   cm. -- (Studies in medieval culture ; 33)
   ISBN 1-879288-29-X. -- ISBN 1-879288-30-3 (pbk.)
   I. Taylor, Robert A. (Robert Allen), 1937- . II. Leyerle, John.
III. Series.
CB351.S83 vol. 33a
[PN681]
940.1 s--dc20
[809'.02]   93-12694
                                                CIP

Cover design by Linda K. Judy

Acknowledgements

It has been a joy to oversee the preparation of this volume at every successive stage, because of the enthusiastic commitment of all who participated.

The contributors took to heart our proposal that the articles embrace the diversity and richness of medieval culture itself; it is our hope that the breadth and originality of their scholarship may stand as a tribute to Professor Leyerle's own lifelong commitment to excellence.

Thanks must go as well to a number of colleagues whose names do not otherwise appear, but who have helped to assure the efficient realization and high quality of our project.

Tom Seiler, managing editor of Medieval Institute Publications, provided essential encouragement from the start, and continuing sage advice in matters editorial and psychological.

Juleen Audrey Eichinger, production editor of Medieval Institute Publications, offered heroic amounts of critical judgement, photographic memory, and an unforgiving eye, to polish our contributions to a sheen of clarity and consistency.

Jill Webster provided funding through the Centre for Medieval Studies to help with text processing and incidental expenses.

Karen Wagner took time from her graduate research to prepare the initial text entry, no small task in view of the number of disciplines and languages involved.

John Leyerle, through the variety and quality of his own editorial projects, provided a model of achievement toward which we might strive.

ACKNOWLEDGEMENTS

To ourselves as editors we reserve the right to proclaim our human fallibility through the presence of whatever imperfections may remain, for which we alone claim all credit.

ROBERT A. TAYLOR

Contents

CONTENTS

Preface

All medievalists in North America, and many beyond, owe a great debt to John Leyerle. As teacher, scholar, and administrator, John has been a leader in the rise and renewal of medieval studies on this continent in the past thirty years. To celebrate his sixty-fifth birthday and salute his many contributions to our common academic life, colleagues at the University of Toronto have assembled the essays in this volume as witness of gratitude, affection, and esteem.

John Leyerle came to medieval studies not by the usual route of the liberal arts but after a degree in electrical engineering from the US Naval Academy in Annapolis in 1949 and service with the US Navy at home and in Europe in the early 1950s. In 1954 he resigned from the services to undertake a course in medieval English language and literature at Oxford, where he studied with J. A. W. Bennett, Alistair Campbell, and J. R. R. Tolkien, proceeding on graduation to Harvard for graduate work with B. J. Whiting, Douglas Bush, and Francis P. Magoun, Jr. His Ph.D. thesis was an edition and study of Thomas Usk's *Testament of Love*. While enrolled at Harvard, John accepted the invitation of Jess B. Bessinger, Jr. to join the staff of the English Department at University College in the University of Toronto, where he quickly established a reputation as a dynamic teacher whose classes on Beowulf and Chaucer would inspire a generation of students attracted by his broad approach and fresh perspectives. John's innovative teaching prepared the way for a number of seminal papers, first delivered in Canadian and American universities and conferences and later published, and in some cases republished, that explored the structures of medieval poetry and the relationships of art and literary forms. His articles on interlace, the *rota/rosa* design, and the nature of the heroic remain vital studies that reflect the value of going outside the bounds of a single discipline. He has edited several volumes and journal collections on such diverse subjects as computing and Old English, marriage in the Middle Ages, chivalric literature, and medieval dance, and he is co-author of an introductory bibliography to Chaucer.

It was the need to cross over traditional disciplinary organization that similarly marked John Leyerle's influence on the development of medieval studies. At the University of Toronto he was the driving force in creating the Centre for Medieval Studies, which drew on faculty members from all departments and the well established Pontifical Institute to provide not only new graduate programs but a true center that promoted collaborative research among students and faculty and that attracted to Toronto medievalists from around the world. If interdisciplinary programs are a commonplace in the universities of the 1990s, they were not so in the 1960s, and it was John's vision and energy that helped persuade colleagues to enter into a new mode of pursuing the academic enterprise. He was supported early on by such scholars as Bertie Wilkinson, the Centre's first director, and Norman Zacour, both historians, and Father Laurence Shook of the Pontifical Institute of Mediaeval Studies, a colleague in English. The work flourished and the Centre remains today the choice of many of the best medieval students in North America and a model about which his advice is still often sought. John still teaches at the Centre and continues to work to place graduates in their first university jobs.

It was perhaps inevitable that John's administrative abilities would attract the attention of the wider community, and he was called to serve as Dean of Graduate Studies at the University of

Toronto from 1978 to 1984, Secretary-Treasurer (and founding spirit) of the Canadian Institute for Advanced Research from 1981 to 1985; and in 1988 he took on the onerous and politically sensitive post of Interim President of the Social Sciences and Research Council of Canada. In each rôle his skill at reorganization and innovation were manifest, and he earned new respect for humanities in a climate more favorable to science and technology.

John Leyerle is at heart a man of enterprise and throughout his career has undertaken many initiatives that succeeded to the benefit of the academy at large. The study of medieval theater has been much enhanced by the existence of the *Poculi Ludique Societas*, or *PLS*, once an acronym for "Professor Leyerle's Seminar," and he began several publications series at the University of Toronto, including *Toronto Medieval Bibliographies*, of which Professor Leyerle is General Editor, and *Visio*, a series devoted to the relation between art and literature, also under his editorship. A special talent has been his encouragement and support of the work of other, particularly younger, colleagues, such as the *Dictionary of Old English*, a project conceived by the late Angus Cameron, or the *Records of Early English Drama* led by Alexandra Johnston, which in both cases were helped into existence with John's advice and active involvement. There are many others, including the editors and contributors to this volume, who could recount similar tales of encouragement and aid. It was no surprise that Professor Joseph Strayer sought his collaboration in enlisting colleagues to contribute to the *Dictionary of the Middle Ages*, published by Scribners, a series that includes entries from no fewer than 115 faculty, graduates, and students of the University of Toronto. Beyond Toronto, John worked hard to help establish CARA (Committee on Centers and Regional Associations) and to promote the teaching of medieval culture through his active participation in a series of conferences under the continuing title of Teaching the Middle Ages. He was also a prime mover in the creation of the Medieval Academy Reprints for Teaching series (MART) that has been so beneficial to colleagues and students everywhere.

In recent years John has been a very successful fund-raiser, first for scholarly activities at the University of Toronto, especially in the humanities, and also for the Endowment Campaign of the Medieval Academy of America. Again there are lasting returns for colleagues and the wider profession, as well as a new sense of optimism that such projects engender.

In planning the present volume we have tried to encompass John Leyerle's broad academic interests and interdisciplinary approach to scholarship with a range of contributors from Canada, the United States, and abroad. The title, as some will recognize, comes from an article that John published in *Chronica* in 1970, devoted to a discussion of the place of medieval studies in the university setting, one of several papers he wrote on academic issues and their resolution. It is our hope that these essays capture some of the boldness and imagination that John Leyerle himself has shown throughout his career, and it is our wish that in them his central role in the furthering of our discipline may be suitably encompassed.

BRIAN S. MERRILEES

Tonic Accent, Codicology, and Literacy

LEONARD E. BOYLE O.P.

MS. Royal I. A. VIII in the British Library is a plain, small Vulgate Bible of the second half of the thirteenth century, with routine initials. Probably of Parisian origin, it certainly was in England well before 1300, when it was much used, was annotated heavily with cross-references in the margins, and was provided with line-numbering in fives in the center of each page of fifty-five lines between the two columns.

It is, in fact, unexceptional and commonplace as a Bible. What is interesting from my point of view is that at the end of the Bible, from folios 411–21, there is a short, unascribed treatise labelled "Correctorius biblie," which in fact is extant in four other copies, one of which, that of Canterbury (which I have not seen) is from about the year 1400 and is ascribed to Robert Grosseteste. If the ascription to Grosseteste proves to be acceptable—and certainly the purpose of the work is not at variance with his well-known pastoral concerns as bishop of Lincoln, 1235–53—then, on the authority of S. Harrison Thompson, it is probably to be dated to the last decade of his life.[1]

This little work, which is called "Correctorium tocius biblie" in most of the five manuscripts, covers all the books of the Bible

---

[1] S. Harrison Thompson, *The Writings of Robert Grosseteste, Bishop of Lincoln, 1235–1253* (Cambridge, 1940), pp. 127–28.

I

LEONARD E. BOYLE

and was intended, in general, to correct misspellings in copies of
the Bible and, in particular, to provide a guide to the pronunciation of difficult or unusual words. In most of the manuscripts—
but not in the British Library copy—an accent or tonic mark has
been placed in red above the correct syllable to be stressed (in the
British Library copy the mark is in black).

Sources are quoted to back up various decisions on where the
tonic accent should fall, predictably Bede but more interestingly
Marbod of Rennes (1035–1123: *Lapidarius*), Alexander de Villa
Dei (*Doctrinale*, c. 1200), Petrus de Riga (d. 1209), Alexander
Neckham (d. 1217), and John of Garland (his *Speculum* or *De
mysteriis ecclesiae*, written 1245). Although the use of Bede
prompts the authors of the catalogue of Royal manuscripts in the
British Library to conclude rather unhelpfully that "a reference to
Bede shows it was written after his date," the later sources seem
to place the date of composition firmly in the middle of the thirteenth century.[2] On occasion there are also quotations from
Vergil or Ovid to illustrate how proper tonic accent or syllable-
stress in tonic writing may be established from metre or rhyme.

This *Correctorium*, which thus appropriately accompanies a
copy of the Bible in the Royal manuscript, naturally begins its
survey of the Bible from Genesis and notes the difficult words
there such as *írrigans, bdéllum, virágo, déinde, deórsum, seórsum,
óbstetrix*, and *bíssinum*, placing a stress or tonic mark in each
case over the correct syllable. Then it moves on to Exodus (noting, for example, *accersítus* and *Pharáo*) and gradually works its
way through all the books of the Hebrew Testament before turning to the Four Gospels, the Acts of the Apostles, the letters of

[2]G. F. Warner and J. P. Gilson, *British Museum. Catalogue of Western
Manuscripts in the Old Royal and King's Collections*, 1 (London, 1921), p. 4. The
"Vocabularius tocius biblie" is fols. 411–21.

Paul, Hebrews, and Revelation. Some chapters are quite long, but most are rather short and summary. Thus the comment on Hebrews is just six lines and is almost totally taken up with Hebrew names.

What is particularly interesting about the *Correctorium* is that it is written for the *iunior lector* and that it was written by someone who was desirous of helping those "juniors" who were uncertain of where the tonic accent should fall in certain words: *cupiens prodesse pusillis*, as the author says.

There is, in fact, nothing new in this concern for the placing of tonic accents, as the following two examples illustrate. About 1140 the Cistercian monk Nicholas Maniacutia wrote a *Libellus de corruptione et correptione psalmorum* at the monastery of Tre Fontane in Rome. His main concern was the correction of the text of the Bible, and on this score he has an interesting account of a visit to the scriptorium at S. Martino on the Oppian Hill (near S. Maria Maggiore), where he asked a scriptor why he had chosen a particular word that was not commonly in copies of the Bible and received a splendid lesson in textual criticism: "because I found it in the Bible written in a large hand." But on many occasions Nicholas touches on the question of accentuation, and in one long passage, commenting on the phrase *Buccinate in neomenia tuba* in Psalm 80, he states with respect to *neomenia* that the Roman usage is to stress in the Greek fashion the penultimate, thus *neomenía* (and, likewise, *castimargía, theología, philosophía, epiphanía, ierarchía, letanía, ethimología, melancolía,* and *orthographýa*), where others prefer *neoménia* and so on.[3]

A century and a half later Bartholomew Cotton, the chronicler

---

[3]See V. Peri, "<Correctores immo corruptores>: Un saggio di critica testuale nella Roma del XII secolo," *Italia medioevale e umanistica* 20 (1947): 19–125, at p. 111.

3

and monk of Norwich, put together in 1291 "from the book of Brito" a dictionary of words in the Bible that frequently were mispronounced, and he did this for the benefit of his fellow monks. In each case he shows where the stress should come and in disputed cases—and there were some—lists different views. However, the only copy of this dictionary that I am aware of is to be found in Corpus Christi College, Cambridge, MS 460, fols. 86^r–141^r, a volume that also carries a copy of the *Vocabularium* above (fols. 1^r–24^v).[4]

Why this interest in accentuation where the Bible was concerned? Why append the "Correctorius tocius biblie" and Cotton's dictionary to that small Bible now in the British Library? Generally speaking it was probably out of respect for the text. For it was not sufficient just to have a correct text, which was Maniacutia's main concern. What was also required was a *rectus nomine prolatio* or proper pronunciation of the words, as Maniacutia terms it and as is splendidly illustrated by the *Correctorium* and by Cotton's dictionary in the Royal manuscript. More particularly, I suspect, the insistence on proper tonic accents owes much to the fact that monks and others had daily to read out or proclaim passages from the Bible in public, whether in chapter or in choir or in the refectory.

I am not speaking here, however, of the various rules about breaking up a sentence or punctuating it for a clear understanding

---

[4]For Cotton (d. 1298) see J. C. Russell, *Dictionary of Writers of Thirteenth Century England* (London, Institute of Historical Research: Special Supplement No. 3, Bulletin of Historical Research, 1936), pp. 22–23, who notes the Cambridge manuscript and quotes the title "Compilaciones de libro Britonis secundum ordinem alphabeti per Bartolomeum de Cottune" and the date 1291 from fol. 86^r. The "Book of Brito" may be the well-known *Summa Britonis* of William Brito, composed 1250–70, which survives in over 130 manuscripts; see *Summa Britonis sive Guillelmi Britonis Expositiones Vocabulorum Biblie*, ed. L. W. and B. A. Daly, 2 vols. (Padua, 1975).

of its meaning, whether in private reading or public. Donatus duly considers these under the general heading "De accentibus" and his pronouncements were repeated, with variations, all through the Middle Ages. In public reading in particular it was important not to destroy a sentence by pausing at the wrong time or by not raising the voice a little at the end when a sentence was interrogatory. But this is not at all the burden, as such, of the *Correctorium* and Cotton's dictionary. What they were concerned about was where the tonic accent comes or the main stress falls in words.

There is not much about this in Donatus and later grammarians, manualists, and stylists, presumably because it was taken for granted that everyone would automatically render *amaverant* as *amáverant* and not *amavérant*, or the infinitive *tribuere* as *tribú-ere* not *tribuére*, or *carmina* as *cármina* not *carmína*, from a knowledge of basic grammar and common usage. Possibly this is why Hildemar of Corbie (d. 850), in a letter to Bishop Ursus of Benevento, notes in passing, after a long discussion of pauses and voice-inflections in texts prepared for both public and private reading, that sometimes "for the sake of lazy readers" (*propter inertes lectores*) one finds in texts an indication of where the tonic accent falls in certain words, as in "édomo, édocet, sáturo, ímitor, álacer, quámdiu, híeremiás, isaiás, trucído, addícit, revéra, pudícus, ínlicit, íbidem," but adds significantly, "Haec vero adnotatio rarissime in libris invenitur veteribus."[5]

This may indeed be a very rare occurrence "in old volumes," but it is clear that by Hildemar's time there were some who were

---

[5]Texts of Donatus, Alcuin, Alexander, and others—including scholastics such as Albert, Aquinas, and Bonaventure—relative to punctuation are conveniently brought together in M. Hubert, "Corpus stigmatologicum minus," *Archivum Latinitatis Medii Aevi* 27 (1969–70): 5–171, with index in 39 (1973–74): 55–84. Hildemar is at pp. 82–84.

not as secure as he in matters of accentuation and who therefore had need of help with certain words, especially in texts destined for public reading. Infinitives such as *amare, monere, regere*, and *ducere* would not have caused any difficulty, but verbal forms such as *supárvenit, aperítur, áderant, révocat*, or *pértulit* could have invited such solecisms as *supervénit, apéritur, adérant, revócat*, or *pertúlit* from people who were not necessarily *inertes lectores*, much as they do today.

Hence it is not unusual to find, although I do not think that it has excited any interest among palaeographers or historians of literacy, that many manuscripts of the Bible and other texts are "scored" for public reading, that is, have tonic accents marked in certain words. Some samples from one splendid, comprehensive collection of facsimiles will suffice to illustrate the point. In R. A. B. Mynors' *Durham Cathedral Manuscripts to the End of the Twelfth Century* (Oxford, 1939), one finds many texts with tonic accents for the benefit of those who might be inclined, for example, to pronounce *párcere* as *parcére, mittére* (=*mitterunt*) as the infinitive *míttere*, or make a mess of *perpércerant*, as though it had the same tonic accent as *perpercérunt*. Some of the manuscripts are before 1096, others belong to the twelfth century. In each case there is a slender little stroke above the tonic mark that is clearly distinguishable from abbreviation sigla or other marks.

Before 1096

*MS. B. II. 22 (Mynors, plate 22): Augustine, *De civitate dei* e.g., lines 18: *párcere*; 19: *áppetit*; 23: *movérent*; 28: *perpércerant* (see 25: *perpercerunt* with no mark); 30: *immánitas*; 32: *pértulit, ímputant*; 34: *tribúere, contérere*; 38: *tribúere*; 40: *mendáciter, effúgerent*; and 43: *súbdolo*.

*MS. B. II. 9 (Mynors, plate 29): Gregory *Registrum* e.g., lines 9: *supérvenit, invíti*; 19: *prepóni*; 20: *monáchica*; and

22: *Próinde.*

*MS. B. IV. 4 (Mynors, plate 34): Ambrose, *In hexaemeron*
e.g., lines 15: *idéam*; 19: *Aristóteles*; and 36: *quibúsdam.*

*MS. B. I. 14 (Mynors, plate 21): Augustine, *In psalmos* e.g.,
lines a23: *Húcne*; b12: *exinániens*; b17: *témere*; b19: *precís-
us*; b21: *Déinde*; b26: *imperíti*; b27, 28: *períti*; b33: *aperítur*;
b35: *lánguidi*; and b40: *timére.*

*MS. B. IV. 14 (Mynors, plate 35): *Vita S. Nicholai Murri*
e.g., lines 4: *imperíto*; 6: *déinde*; and 23: *óppidi*

1096–1200

*MS. A. II. 1 (Mynors, plate 51): Puiset Bible (c. 1160) e.g.,
lines a2: *índia*; a9: *ínclitis*; 21: *cónsitum*; and b19: *áderant.*

*MS. A. III. 10 (Mynors, plate 45): Porretanus, *In psalmos*
e.g., lines a8: *ínfimis*; a29: *minúsve*; a31: *próinde*; a34:
trópicas; b4: *ácinum, révocat*; and b8: *indícit.*

All the same, given the undoubted presence of tonic accents
in works such as these, it is surprising that so little is said in rhetorical works or monastic rules and customs about tonic accentuation. Mostly these works are concerned with punctuation, as in the
famous lines by Alcuin about scribes and the importance of prop-
erly-punctuated texts as a protection for a monk who has to read
publicly in church: *ne vel false legat, taceat vel forte repente.*[6]
   There are of course passing remarks about accentuation in
these works, for example in the *Doctrinale* of Alexander de
Villadei, where the basic rules are set out in verse:

---

[6]Hubert, "Corpus stigmatologicum minus," p. 85.

7

Dictio, cui tantum duplex est syllaba, servat
accentum super primam, sit longa brevisve. . . .
Attrahit enclita vox accentum sibi vocis
premisse, quod eum finalis syllaba servat.
Accentum servat polysyllaba vox super illam
que preit extremam, si longa sit hec, aliter non.
Si brevis est, sedet accentus super antelocatam,
sive sit illa brevis, seu longa, tamen tenet illum.[7]

But much of the theory may have been beyond the capacity of many of those who had to read in public or who perhaps had difficulty in locating the long or short vowels in words of more than two syllables, or in words or verbs as declined, not to speak of enclitics. The safest thing was practice; and here the recitation of psalms, the repetition of prayers, and public reading by their seniors would have accustomed most young monks or clerics or friars to proper accentuation. Perhaps this is why few if any monastic or other rules have anything to say about tonic accent as such, though they have much to say about singing in choir, plain chant, and punctuation.

Yet clearly the going was not always easy for beginners. As usual, Humbert de Romanis, the fourth Master of the Dominican Order, is down to earth on this point and, in fact, provides the most explicit statement I am aware of on public reading, albeit in refectories. A reader reading publicly during meals, he writes, should be careful how he reads, not only with respect to punctuation and accentuation but also to the sense of what he is reading. If he has difficulties, he can consult beforehand with the *corrector mensae*, that official whose function it was to oversee readers and correct their pronunciation or accentuation where necessary. In fact, the better to fulfil that office, the corrector, in Humbert's

---

[7]Hubert, "Corpus stigmatologicum minus," pp. 122–23.

opinion, should see to it that his house is supplied with manuals on these and grammatical topics, as well as with *correctiones bibliae* and the like.[8]

Small, unpretentious works such as the *Correctorium* and Cotton's dictionary in the Royal manuscript had then a useful and valued place in medieval education. If they helped monks and friars and others to arrive at a general respect of *recta nominis prolatio*, they were of particular value when a text was being prepared for public reading, whether at source in a scriptorium or as the occasion arose. Then a slight but distinctive tonic mark over the proper syllable in insidious forms such as *temere* and *timere* would both guarantee the *recta nominis prolatio* and spare the blushes of the reader.

If, then, the alert palaeographer finds tonic accents in some text that he or she is studying in its full codicological setting, the chances are strong that the text in question was read publicly or at least was prepared at some point for public reading. Should the palaeographer-codicologist record the fact? After all, the basic function of palaeography is to address the text as it is transmitted in writing and to persuade it to communicate as it was meant to do. From this point of view the fact that a text is "scored" for public reading may seem a side issue. But from the point of view of circulation and literacy and use, it is hardly unimportant.

Any mark or sign or correction or illustration or erasure is part of the history of the transmission of the text, and should be recorded and, if necessary, justified or explained. This phenomenon—and it is widespread—of "scored for public reading" is one such mark or sign. It is surely part of the history of the text that someone actually read it, and read it publicly at that.

---

[8]*De officiis*, Ch. XXV, *De officio lectoris mense*, in Hubert, "Corpus stigmatologicum minus," pp. 138–39.

Marginal notations, interlinear notes and scuffed edges are generally signs that a given manuscript was heavily used or thoughtfully read. Signs of "scoring" or tonic marks are in the same class, but at a different level. They suggest that certain works did not just have a private circulation but also had a public audience—in monasteries or similar assemblies.

From this point of view a tabulation of "scored" texts might yield interesting results. Here in the Durham example given above one finds Augustine *De civitate dei*, Augustine on the psalms, Ambrose on the Hexaemeron, the *Registrum* of Gregory the Great, the life of Nicholas of Myra, patron of sailors, and, surprisingly, Gilbert de la Porée on the psalms. Everyone knows, of course, that the Bible or "Bibliotheca" was read publicly: the Puiset Bible of c. 1160 at Durham is a nice example. But what other books were read this way, or at least were prepared for such reading? And what was the relationship of this public reading to *Lectio divina*?

These are not idle questions. Public reading is an aspect of monastic and other (perhaps courtly) literacy that has not had much consideration, if any. It is an aspect that any and every palaeographer, in the guise of a codicologist, may very easily explore and record. By doing so the palaeographer—and any medievalist who has access to manuscripts or facsimiles—will not only learn much about medieval accentuation and the words that caused problems but will also begin to appreciate more fully the Latin language as it was lived and spoken and indeed cherished in the Middle Ages.

The Ritual Frame of *Peribañez*

JAMES F. BURKE

Lope de Vega's play *Peribañez*, which was probably written in 1604, is in many respects an excellent example of the dramatic talent of that prodigious playwright.[1] The structure of the work appears to reflect the same pattern present in its sister "social drama," *Fuente Ovejuna*, where an initial idyllic social situation is disturbed and disordered, and then is brought to harmonious resolution during the course of the action of the play.[2]

Peribañez is the story of a young and relatively wealthy farmer who marries a beautiful young girl. The action of the drama, drawn to some degree from historical happenings, would have taken place in August of 1406 or 1407. The play begins on their wedding day with an elaborate display of images of harmony certainly appropriate for the happy occasion. This felicitous situation is almost immediately disturbed when a local nobleman, the Comendador de Ocaña appears on the scene just as a spirited young bull is released into the streets of the village in celebration of the marriage. The beast charges the Comendador and knocks him from his horse. The initial horrified dismay of the rustic revelers

---

[1]Lope de Vega, *Peribañez y Fuente Ovejuna*, ed. Alberto Blecua (Madrid, 1981), p. 27.

[2]John Bryans, "Providence or Discretion in *Peribañez*," *Journal of Hispanic Philology* 2 (1977): 121–33, at p. 128.

turns to relief when the unconscious Comendador quickly revives. The play is launched on its course as the Comendador determines to possess the first thing that he sees when he recovers consciousness—the lovely new bride, Casilda.

After an initial lack of success in his amorous venture, the Comendador insists that Peribañez head a company of local recruits leaving to fight the Moors in Granada. But the young farmer, while in the studio of an artist in nearby Toledo to have refurbished a statue of the patron of the local guild, has seen there a portrait of his bride, commissioned by the Comendador and executed in secret. He immediately realizes what the Comendador is planning to do. Peribañez agrees to lead the group but insists that the Comendador personally gird on his sword for him. With this action and the resulting rank of captain, the young husband is no longer just a well-to-do farmer; now he has the necessary standing that entitles him to defend his honor. He leaves the village of Ocaña with his band of men and escorts them to Toledo, but under the cover of darkness he returns and enters his house secretly to confront the Comendador, who has also gained access with the help of a perfidious cousin and a servant. Peribañez rapidly dispatches the three of them. He returns with his young wife to Toledo, where they throw themselves upon the mercy of King Enrique III. The monarch, upon hearing their story, gives Peribañez a full pardon, confirms him in the rank of captain, and grants him a license to bear arms. The queen bestows upon Casilda four dresses from her wardrobe so that the young wife may attire herself in a fashion suitable to the new status of her husband. The initial harmony and order that prevailed at the beginning of the play appear to have been reestablished.

But as Robin Carter has demonstrated, there is a series of incongruities in the drama that suggests that *Peribañez* in reality demonstrates the reverse of a proper restoration of order and is a

kind of "reflection of a *continuing* disorder."[3] Although Peribañez probably had a proper legal right to kill the Comendador, that
right would not have allowed him to deal so summarily with the
other two men who had offended him. King Enrique, known as
the "justice-giver," does pardon him, an action that should absolve
the young farmer from his crime.

The symbols on the king's new *pendón*, which decorates the
audience chamber where Peribañez and his wife come to plead
their cause, strongly support Enrique's role as *justiciero*. On one
side there is depicted a hand holding a sword underscored by the
legend "Enrique Justiciero," while on the other side the image of
the crucified Christ with the words "Juzga tu causa" (line 2985;
an echo of Psalm 83:22) seems iconically to reinforce this idea.

But Enrique III is the grandson of Enrique II, who gained the
throne after years of struggle by stabbing and killing the legitimate King Pedro I on the field of Montiel. Lope has made sure
that his public remembered this fact by having Peribañez recount
the story to his wife toward the beginning of the play. The final
words of the story, "le dio la daga / que agora se ha vuelto cetro"
(lines 983–84) make absolutely clear to any audience or reader the
brutal process by which the dagger, instrument of regicide, has
become the royal scepter.[4]

In the last scene of the play, just before Peribañez and Casilda
appear, the king and queen are discussing their young son who
will soon reign as Juan II. Enrique says of him:

> Guárdalo Dios; que es un divino espejo,

---

[3]Robin Carter, "*Peribañez*: Disorder Restored," in *What's Past is Prologue: A Collection of Essays in Honour of L. J. Woodward*, ed. Salvador Bacarisse et al. (Edinburgh, 1984), p. 27.

[4]All quotations from the play are taken from the Blecua edition.

donde se ven agora retratados,
mejor que los presentes, los pasados.   (lines 2937–39)

Considering the violent origins of the dynasty, this statement rings as ironic; the child as *speculum* would mirror, as Carter has pointed out, not the image of the ideal prince but that of the murderer and usurper of the throne.[5] But if the play does present a kind of "continuing disorder," as Carter believes, how does one reconcile this flux with the imagery of harmony that begins the play and seems to reappear at the end with the confirming of Peribañez's knightly status and the bestowing of gifts from the queen's wardrobe?

Judson Allen has explained an important characteristic of medieval poetry that makes it different from later varieties. For any medieval poem "one must expect parallels which exist outside the poem but are no less present to it than Gloucester is to Lear." These are "the whole world of beasts, and histories, and other books, and philosophy, and God." But in a play such as *King Lear* the "analogies work within the world of the play."[6] Allen sees Shakespeare as having accomplished what most critics of Golden Age Spanish drama observe in the works of playwrights from this period. The writer placed within the confines of the play all the thematic material that he wished an audience to accept as pertinent and important for the dramatic situation.

I think that Lope in *Peribañez* followed a scheme that adheres more to the medieval mode of procedure than that of the Renaissance and post-Renaissance. He conceived a dramatic plot with seeming incongruities and contradictions that can be understood

---

[5]"*Peribañez*," p. 23.

[6]Judson Boyce Allen, *The Ethical Poetic of the Later Middle Ages: A Decorum of Convenient Distinction* (Toronto, 1982), p. 151.

as properly ordered only if seen as set against another parallel system of a broader, more universal nature. This system would have been perceivable, in part, even to the most rustic of his audience, while his educated public would have been aware of a great deal more. Some aspects of the system are so subtle that only explanations given by modern anthropological critics in regard to certain basic operations of Hispanic culture appear to offer clues as to their meaning. My contention is that Lope sensed the importance of such motifs and linked them to the action of the play by means of framing situations that enclose and demarcate the actions in the drama.

In regard to its temporal setting, the play takes place just before August 15, the Feast of the Assumption of the Virgin (line 496). This is a time of fullness and harvest in the Castilian *meseta*, when the crops sown in the spring begin to come to their full maturity. The situation of Peribañez and Casilda, two young people just beginning their married life, seems to stand in ironic counterpoint to the ripeness implied by the season.

The time of year is also indicated in the incident having to do with the statue of the patron of the guild in Ocaña that Peribañez takes for repairs to Toledo. The patron is San Roque (St. Roch), whose feast day is August 16. Lope presents the cult of San Roque as in full flower, but, of course, this is anachronistic, as devotion to the saint did not really begin in earnest until the mid- to late-fifteenth century, well after the action of the play supposedly took place.

San Roque was best-known as a protector against the plague; however, as Louis Réau has indicated, his powers were rapidly extended in rural communities in the late Middle Ages to farm animals and to the crops.[7] His role in the play, one that reinforces

---

[7]Louis Réau, *Iconographie de l'art chrétien*, 3 vols. (Paris, 1959), 3:1157–58.

the sense of security and well-being that prevailed at the beginning, does not figure until after the serious problem has begun.

Bryans sees the newlyweds' idyll as edenic in nature, with elements such as mountains and torrents—normally taken as hostile to man—disposed as friendly to the young couple in the song early in the first act.[8] For him the context is suggestive of that which preceded the fall of man, an event seen as "re-presented," perhaps, in the play in the tumble by the Comendador from his horse.

The youth of mankind is symbolically alluded to in another fashion, and this is with a constant series of references to the spring and various ritual happenings that occur then. Casilda tells her husband that she prefers him to all the flowering herbs of St. John's Day (lines 96–100), the feast that was viewed in the Middle Ages as ending the springtime "season of love." She calls him "hornazo en Pascua de Flores" (line 109), "cirio pascual" (line 116), and "mazapán de bautismo" (line 117), images that all harken back to Easter. At the beginning of the song that follows there is an allusion to "el mayo garrido" (line 127), May, the month traditionally known for its dedication to the goddess of love.[9]

But in the midst of these images Casilda also refers to Peribañez with a term that, in effect, sets the context for one of the major frames in the drama. She says "Pareces en verde prado / toro bravo y rojo echado" (lines 111–12). Immediately thereafter, the *novillo* that will occasion the fall of the Comendador comes tearing through the streets of the village. Peribañez is a young bull *in bono* whose positive image is promptly countered by that of the *novillo* and, as I shall suggest further along, by the one of

---

[8]"Providence or Discretion in *Peribañez*," pp. 126–65, esp. 128–29.

[9]Julio Caro Baroja, *La estación de amor: fiestas populares de mayo a San Juan* (Madrid, 1979).

the Comendador himself, who is also in the play a kind of taurine figure.

The cult of the bull, with its wealth of symbolic associations, is a very ancient one in the Iberian Peninsula and throughout the Mediterranean basin. As the second sign in the zodiac, the bull ruled the season during which the lushness of spring replaced the barrenness of winter. In the Middle Ages the precession of the equinoxes had caused the zodiacal year to begin with Aries on March 13, which meant that the reign of Taurus was April 13 to May 13. Although the calendar had been adjusted with the Gregorian reforms in 1582, the old associations would still have been vivid when Lope wrote his play.

Right in the middle of the medieval Taurus came May Day, with its wealth of erotic associations. The Church in Spain countered May Day with May 3, Cruz de Mayo, which effectively replaced the phallic maypole with the Cross of Christ. The negative aspects of Taurus were dealt with by associating the bull with the Feast of St. Mark on April 25, which was a christianization of the Roman Robigalia, a celebration designed to protect the crops from harm.[10]

The bull that charges through the streets of Ocaña is not one escaped from his pen or let loose to chase the adventurous youths of the town. He is a *toro nupcial*, as is made clear in the song that the *músicos* sing in Act III. "El novillo de tu boda / a tu puerta me cogió" (lines 2721–22). This *toro nupcial* was a wedding guest of great vintage in Spain, as his presence is alluded to many times in medieval literature. The best explanation of the meaning of this bull has been given by the scholar Alvarez de Miranda:

> Varias fiestas populares . . . reiteraban bajo diversas combi-

---

[10]Julio Caro Baroja, *Ritos y mitos equívocos* (Madrid, 1974), pp. 77–78.

> naciones los mismos o parecidísimos elementos rituales. El
> común denominador de todos ellos lo constituye la asociación
> del toro y la mujer . . . esterilidad, nupcialidad y virginidad.
> El eje del binomio toro-mujer se evidencia en la esfera ritual,
> lo mismo que en la mítica, como una intuición de los proces-
> os de la generación y de la fecundidad.[11]

The bull as an ancient emblem of fertility in Iberia is present at weddings in the form of the charging animal with whom, of course, the young men in attendance could spar. Peribañez himself asks Casilda if she would like to see him contend a bit with the creature. "¿Tú quieres que intente un lance?" (line 208). Her reply alludes to another aspect of the mythology of this symbol-ridden beast: no recently married man should have anything at all to do with the horns of a bull. Of course, very soon such an unfortunate association will almost occur, since the Comendador will, in effect, attempt to place the horns onto the young husband.

Another way in which the ferocious and lusty bull was presented as properly christianized throughout much of central and southwestern Spain is probably alluded to in the play. The village priest is present with the newlyweds at the beginning of the drama. When the young bull comes charging through the streets, the priest decides to ascend to the roof, thereby distancing himself, the sign of the Church, from this raging symbol *in malo*. Costanza, one of the farm girls, urges the priest to say a prayer in order to calm the beast. But the priest refuses, declaring ". . . que hay novillo / que no entiende bien latín" (lines 200–01). What seems to be no more than a joke may well be a reference to another of the semi-religious folk customs by means of which the Spanish attempted to turn the image of the ferocious bull *in bono*.

---

[11]Angel Alvarez de Miranda, "Cuestiones de mitología peninsular ibérica," vol. 2 of *Obras*, 4 vols. (Madrid, 1959), pp. 181–210, esp. 205.

In villages where there was a Guild of St. Mark, the group would, on the eve of the feast of the Saint, go out and choose a fierce bull from among the cattle. They would call him Marcos and beseech him to come to them. The suddenly tamed animal would comply, and they would lead him in procession to the village, where the women would adorn his horns with flowers and wreaths and the whole group would proceed to the church, where all would attend the Solemn Vespers of St. Mark's.[12] The following is a description of such a ceremony from 1608: ". . . empiezan las vísperas con mucha solemnidad, á las cuales asiste el toro quietamente, con mucho sosiego y reposo, como si fuera una persona que tuviera entendimiento."[13] This bull, who almost seems to possess human understanding, might also be said to understand Latin, if indeed the animal did seem to appreciate the significance of Vespers. But the *novillo* that comes raging through the streets of Ocaña is no such tamed bull, and the priest is more than aware of this fact.

After the *novillo* causes the fall of the Comendador, Bartolo, another of the farmers present, curses the animal, and there is another implication as to how the temporal framing of the play is structured.

> ¡Oh, mal hayas, el novillo!
> Nunca en el abril llovioso
> halles yerba en verde prado
> más que si fuera agosto.   (lines 230–33)

The animal is exiled from his symbolic domain, the lushness of April, to the harsh dryness of the Castilian August. But the pre-

---

[12]Caro Baroja, *Ritos y mitos*, pp. 84–88.

[13]Ibid., p. 88.

sentation of August in this manner reverses the positive aura of the Assumption and San Roque and all that which the era of Virgo, beginning on August 13 in the Middle Ages, would have carried. The action of the play is framed not only by its setting in real time but also by constant allusion to the spring season. Bartolo's words confirm the meaning of both time periods *in bono et in malo* and thereby demonstrate to us what was a major concern of the playwright in this drama, the constant oscillation and interplay of positive and negative aspects that characterized the baroque Christian worldview.

Alison Turner has recognized that the Comendador, who launches forth after Casilda, replaces the charging *novillo*.[14] An animal bull is supplanted by a human one. Peribañez early in the play asks to borrow from the Comendador rich hangings to decorate his wagon for a trip to Toledo for the celebrations of the Assumption (lines 865–74). He receives them and, after the trip and still unaware of the designs of the nobleman, decorates the walls of his home with them. When he realizes the Comendador's intention, he immediately takes down the hangings, which metaphorically could have served the nobleman—now designated as charging bull—as a cloak and disguise:

> Vine yo, súpelo todo,
> y de las paredes bajas
> quité las armas, que al toro
> pudieran servirle de capa.   (lines 3060–63)

J. E. Varey has observed that the actions of the bullish Comendador are themselves framed, in that at the end of the play, after he has been wounded by Peribañez, he is placed emblemlike in a chair

---

[14]"The Dramatic Function of Imagery and Symbolism in *Peribañez* and *El Caballero de Olmedo*," *Symposium* 20 (1966): 174–91, esp. 177.

(stage direction between lines 2853 and 2854), a positioning that mirrors his place at the beginning of the play after he is thrown from his horse (stage direction between lines 289 and 290).[15] In this final position he repents before he dies for what he has done.

> Señor, tu sangre sagrada
> se duela agora de mí
> pues me ha dejado la herida
> pedir perdón a un vasallo.   (lines 2854–57)

There are, thus, two major framing circumstances in the play, the first the temporal one, and the second the positioning of the Comendador. The first shows the symbolism, both positive and negative, inherent in the two periods of time important for the drama, the spring and the August harvest season, and suggests the bull as symbol *in bono et in malo*. The second frame demarcates the actions and attitudes of the Comendador; at the beginning he is ready to launch out on his trajectory of evil (*taurus in malo*), while at the end he has realized his error and has repented. What, then, is the significance of the action sequence, that which gives body to the play, which these two sets of frames enclose?

Critics would have no difficulty in accepting that a medieval or Renaissance play might reflect certain patterns founded in what Wlad Godzich has termed a culture of *memoria*, "all the explanatory regresses that provide the members of a particular collectivity with a hold on their lived experience and distinguish them from their neighbors."[16] *Peribañez* involves a series of images and

---

[15]J. E. Varey, "The Essential Ambiguity in Lope de Vega's *Peribañez*: Theme and Staging," *Theatre Research International* 1 (1975): 157–78.

[16]Wlad Godzich, Foreword to *From Topic to Tale: Logic and Narrativity in the Middle Ages*, by Eugene Vance (Minneapolis, 1987), p. xiv.

happenings in which the important symbol of the bull is seen in a positive and negative light as the action of the play progresses. Is there in Hispanic culture some form of ritual action or process, drawn perhaps from the culture of *memoria*, which can clarify what the various sequences of the work mean and how they finally signify?

Manuel Delgado Ruiz has studied the *fiesta de toros* in Iberian culture and has demonstrated that this event and the broad field of associated taurine symbolism that accompanies it reflect and regularize within popular culture certain universal problems of humankind as they are formulated within Hispanic civilization.[17] He believes that the modern bullfight is an evolution from an ancient ritual process by means of which the community controlled the physical force and sexual vigor of its young men and integrated them, suitably civilized, into the social fabric. During his youth the male was encouraged, often by the women in the household, to develop his strength and to some degree his aggressive stance and may even have been compared to a young bull by being called *torito*. Such a male, when mature, would represent a danger to the social order were he not eventually to submit to the forces of civilization and domestication.

The basic ritual process of domestication begins when a figure, frequently taurine in appearance and representing the unbridled male instinct, suddenly launches itself upon the community, which reacts in panic to this violent intrusion. A woman appears as a lure for the figure, and there is often an allusion to the story of Eve. After the figure has been enticed into some variety of entanglement or trap and disposed of, it is clear that the forces that disturbed the social order, an order dependent upon patterns of

---

[17]Manual Delgado Ruiz, *De la muerte de un dios: la fiesta de los toros en el universo simbólico de la cultura popular* (Barcelona, 1986).

feminine restraint and domestication, have been neutralized.

The character who counters the disturbing intruder is always an *actant* who is in some respect feminine or who bears certain feminine attributes. The *vaquilla*, a young male dressed as a bull who appears in the streets of certain Spanish villages on feast days insulting passers-by and attacking women, is an example of one of the negative figures. He is confronted by and put in his place by *la dama*, another young male clothed as a woman.[18] The *matador* with his glittering *traje de luces* is the epitome of such a figure in the highly ritualized *corrida*, which is the highest artistic representation of the sequence described above.

The wedding ceremony can also be seen as related to this process. Here the young man is forced to relinquish the freedom of his bachelorhood in order to integrate himself into the structure of married life.[19] The agent who effects this change is, of course, the priest, another male who has been feminized in order to serve the needs of society.

Again the problem in *Peribañez* is that, although harmony appears to be restored at the end, the recuperative process by which this happens involves certain actions (such as the killing of the minor characters and the pardoning by a king called the justice-giver, who is only third in a dynasty established by regicide) that prevent us from seeing the play as uniformly conceived in terms of the principle, order disturbed → order restored. The discordant elements in the work seem to reflect the conflicting factors in the seasonal frame that circumscribe the action sequences within it.

---

[18]*De la muerte de un dios*, p. 120.

[19]Delgado Ruiz says "El varón acabará tomando conciencia, acaso en la misma noche nupcial, de que ha sido objeto de un engaño y de que ha sido obligado a retornar a un grave cuadro de restricciones en el campo de la instintividad" (*De la muerte de un dios*, p. 172).

I think that an explanation of the contradictory nature of certain aspects of the play derives from the fact that the action of *Peribañez* is, in effect, a *mise-en-scène* of the ritual process described by Delgado Ruiz. The play shows that although the rite may finally be effective, its course does not always run smoothly and is subject to a series of variations and turns.

Peribañez, designated as *toro bravo* by his bride early in the drama, follows her advice and does not get involved with the *novillo*.[20] By this and by his acceptance of his role as husband, he demonstrates that he has accepted his place in the civilized order. The necessary allusion to the story of Eve comes immediately afterwards, in lines 398–99, when Peribañez reminds his wife of the injunction of Genesis 3:16 "Ya sabes que la mujer / para obedecer se casa." It is clear that Casilda is able to accept her part in reversing the action of Eve by being the dutiful wife, and the fact that the marriage is celebrated near the Feast of the Assumption, the most important dedicated to the Virgin, the New Eve, underlines this point.

When the Comendador sees Casilda and decides to possess her, he shows that he is unwilling to honor the rules of society and thus will be launched into the course of the ritual process and metamorphosed into a metaphorical bull. He must perforce be controlled, something eventually realized by Peribañez when he fatally wounds the nobleman with his sword.

A form of symbolic feminization of the young husband comes just before his confrontation with the Comendador, when he secretly enters his own house. He hides in the *gallinero*, the chicken coop, an enclave where the rooster rules over twenty or

---

[20]Peter Evans, "*Peribañez* and Ways of Looking at Golden Age Dramatic Character," *Romanic Review* 74 (1983): 136–51, esp. 145, believes that by his decision not to spar with the bull, Peribañez shows that his "brío" is now part of his bachelor past.

thirty hens (lines 2760–67). Delgado Ruiz points out that in Spain the rooster is often substituted for the bull in the role of dominant symbolic male that must be subjugated.[21]

Peribañez plaintively laments the fact that while his cock is able to watch over these twenty to thirty hens, he is incapable of defending properly even one. "No puedo yo guardar una, / ¡y quieres tú guardar tantas!" (lines 2770–71). His problem is the Comendador, whom the play now transforms into a marauding rooster through the mention of a heraldic red crest that emblazoned the front of his tunic.

> No duermo yo, que sospecho,
> y me da mortal congoja
> un gallo de cresta roja
> porque la tiene en el pecho.   (lines 2772–75)

All of this affects the young husband to such a degree that he almost breaks down in tears.

> Gana me da de llorar;
> lástima tengo de verme
> en tanto mal. . . .   (lines 2796–98)

But his weakness, his moment of feminization, lasts but a moment, and he rapidly reassumes the role of aggressive male to kill the Comendador, the cousin, and the servant.[22]

The plot of *Peribañez*, as a reflection of the ritual process, may have been even understood by the playwright as reflecting a

---

[21]*De la muerte de un dios*, p. 144.

[22]Peter Evans thinks that the Comendador is Peribañez's double and that in resorting to the violence of killing him, his other self, the young farmer has destroyed the remnant of his own heroic instincts ("*Peribañez*," p. 146).

long-range process in the history of the state. King Pedro I, killed at Montiel, had been known as "el cruel" because of the often brutal actions that he took in defense of his throne. Enrique of Trastámara, who stabbed him and succeeded to the throne as Enrique II, was the forebear of the dynasty that was still ruling Spain when Lope de Vega was writing his dramas.[23]

For those monarchs who descended from Enrique III, it would have been preferable to see the killing of Pedro el cruel in terms other than regicide. Could Lope de Vega have been suggesting that the actions of Peribañez in dealing with the Comendador were analogous to those of Enrique of Trastámara in stabbing Pedro el cruel?

The child who would reign as Juan II, father of the great Isabel, had been born two years before the time of the play in the city of Toro, a fact that could certainly have been known to Lope.[24] Although the name of the city derives from the phrase *campus Gothorum*, folk etymology would doubtless have connected the name with the animal. If the dramatist was viewing the actions of Enrique II as within the ritual context, then the reference to young Juan as *speculum* to his ancestors would have positive connotations. This king born in the city of the bull, and those of his family who came after him, would, across a course of history already clear to the playwright, exercise as positive a role for Spain, the macrocosm, as Peribañez did for his household, the microcosm. In such a case the contradictions noticed in the play

---

[23]Enrique was the grandfather of Isabel. Juana, the daughter of Isabel and Fernando, married Philip the Fair of Burgundy, and the Trastámara bloodline was continued by their son Carlos. Historians, of course, generally call the dynasty, after Carlos inherits the throne, the "House of Austria."

[24]*Enciclopedia universal ilustrada Europeo-americana*, 70 vols. (Madrid, 1928), vol. 20, p. 30.

would largely vanish, and it would be possible to see the work and its elements as coming to harmonious resolution.

I propose that *Peribañez* should be understood in line with the medieval practice that imagined a structure or structures as parallel to the principal line of action of a work. This is the ritual frame that in this play involves the contrast in the meaning of the seasons and the bull as a symbol of instincts that must be controlled. Once this secondary anatomy is taken into account, much of what appeared contentious in the drama is, in fact, relevant to and in line with theories that pertained in regard to the ordering of dramatic works in the Spanish Golden Age. *Peribañez* may, on its surface level, convey a sense of "continuing disorder," but it is a flux that must be understood as ultimately framed and controlled by processes greater than the immediate occurrences in the drama.

Chaucer's Boethius and Thomas Usk's *Testament of Love*: Politics and Love in the Chaucerian Tradition[1]

DAVID R. CARLSON

I. USK AND THE CHAUCERIAN TRADITION

> And gret wel Chaucer whan ye mete,
> As mi disciple and mi poete:
> For in the floures of his youthe
> In sondri wise, as he wel couthe,
> Of Ditees and of songes glade,
> The whiche he for mi sake made,
> The lond fulfild is overal:
> Wherof to him in special
> Above alle othre I am most holde.
> For thi now in hise daies olde
> Thow schalt him telle this message,
> That he upon his latere age,
> To sette an ende of alle his werk,
> As he which is myn owne clerk,
> Do make his testament of love,
> As thou hast do thi schrifte above,
> So that mi Court it mai recorde.

---

[1]John Leyerle first interested me in the *Testament of Love* when I had the good fortune to participate in his graduate seminar on Chaucer at the University of Toronto. Most immediately, I am grateful to him for allowing me to use his own unpublished work on Usk, from which I have borrowed much. My debts to him are more extensive, of course; I hope the present paper can do his teaching some of the credit it deserves.

Near the end of the *Confessio Amantis*, in its first recension, Venus takes her leave of Amans in a passage including this "Chaucer Greeting."[2] Gower's deletion of the greeting from subsequent versions of the *Confessio* has abetted speculation about a deterioration of relations between the two most prominent English poets of the high Middle Ages.[3] No matter its later expunction, however, the greeting itself has considerable interest, as perhaps the earliest document to recognize Chaucer, publicly, as an eminence in English literature. It is analogous to the "Shake-scene" passage in Greene, in other words: a statement by someone in a position to know (though by no means a disinterested witness), implying that Chaucer had earned a literary reputation already.[4] In addition, the passage may refer to other evidence on this same issue: the early development of Chaucer's reputation as a writer.

It is possible that Gower had nothing specific in mind when he asked Chaucer here to make "his testament of love." It has also been suggested that Gower's remark was a gibe against the still unfinished state of Chaucer's *Legend of Good Women*, a "penance" set Chaucer by the God of Love, possibly as early as the mid-1380s, parallel to Amans' "schrifte" in the *Confessio Amantis*.[5] A

---

[2]*Confessio Amantis* 8.2941*–2957*, ed. G. C. Macaulay, *The English Works of John Gower*, EETS es 81–82, 2 vols. (London, 1900–01); on the date of the first recension see Macaulay, 1:xxi–xxii, and John Fisher, *John Gower: Moral Philosopher and Friend of Chaucer* (New York, 1964), pp. 116–27.

[3]See Fisher, *John Gower*, pp. 26–34.

[4]Quoted and discussed, e.g., in Samuel Schoenbaum, *William Shakespeare: A Documentary Life* (Oxford, 1975), pp. 113–17.

[5]Quotation is from the Prologue to *The Legend of Good Women*, F 479, G 469; see also Fisher, *John Gower*, pp. 235–50. All references to and quotations from Chaucer's writings, made parenthetically in the paper, are to the texts in *The Riverside Chaucer*, 3rd ed., Larry D. Benson, Gen. ed. (Boston, 1987).

third possibility, not exclusive of the second, is that Gower's phrase alluded to Thomas Usk's work of this name, *The Testament of Love*, a prose piece of self-consciously Chaucerian aspirations, completed probably by June 1385 and certainly by the time Gower was finishing his first version of the *Confessio Amantis* in about 1390.[6] If Usk's *Testament* was circulating as Chaucerian—or even possibly as Chaucer's—already by 1390 or so, Gower may have meant to suggest that Chaucer had better do something to rectify the impression of himself that Usk's writing would have fostered.

Whether or not Gower linked Usk's *Testament* with Chaucer, and whether or not Gower's remark in the *Confessio Amantis* alluded to a prevalent association of Usk with Chaucer already in the late fourteenth century, others afterwards made the connection unequivocally. Thomas Thynne had *The Testament of Love* printed among Chaucer's works in 1532, and for three and one-half centuries thereafter it was part of the canon. The reasons for Thynne's attribution are not clear. The praise of his contemporary, John Leland, however, who described Thynne as one "qui multo labore, sedulitate, ac cure usus in perquirendis vetustis exemplaribus," and the picture of his motives and methods in his son Francis' *Animadversions uppon Chaucers Workes* (1598) as those of a man who with "laborious care" and "love . . . to Chaucers learnynge" searched "all the libraries of Englande for Chaucers works" and "was fully furnished with multitude of Bookes," suggest that Thynne probably had more than venal reasons for attributing the *Testament* to Chaucer.[7] Gower's remark may have

---

[6]This possibility was raised by J. A. W. Bennett, *Selections from John Gower* (Oxford, 1968), p. 172.

[7]On the Thynne edition see James E. Blodgett, "William Thynne (d. 1546)," in *Editing Chaucer: The Great Tradition*, ed. Paul G. Ruggiers (Norman, Okla., 1984), pp. 35–52. Leland's praises are quoted from his life of Chaucer in the

DAVID R. CARLSON

played a part in the initial attribution, and it did help authorize the attribution during the period begun in 1598, with the Speght edition of Chaucer, which included the first biography published with the works, when the *Testament* was taken to be an important autobiographical source of information about Chaucer.[8] Harris Nicolas did not question the attribution, even after he demonstrated in 1844 that the official documents of Chaucer's career belied the references in the *Testament*; only in 1866, in the preface to a German translation of the *Canterbury Tales*, did Wilhelm Hertzberg first argue that Chaucer had not written the *Testament*; and, according to Lounsbury, "it is entirely within bounds to say that three-fourths of the biographical sketches of the poet's life, which

---

Commentarii de scriptoribus Britannicis, repr. in Eleanor Prescott Hammond, *Chaucer: A Bibliographical Manual* (New York, 1908), p. 4; Francis Thynne's praises are quoted from his *Animadversions*, ed. G. H. Kingsley, rev. ed. by F. J. Furvinall, EETS os 9 (London, 1875), pp. 4–6, 8–9, and 56–57. It is noteworthy that Francis Thynne troubled to distinguish "Chaucers proper woorkes" from "the adulterat and suche as were not his, as the Testamente of Cresside [and] the Letter of Cupide" (*Animadversions*, p. 57). On Francis' work on Chaucer see my "The Writings and Manuscript collections of the Elizabethan Alchemist, Antiquary, and Herald Francis Thynne," *The Huntington Library Quarterly* 52 (1989): 214-15; for evidence that William Thynne exercised a like discrimination see Thomas R. Lounsbury, *Studies in Chaucer*, 3 vols. (1892; repr. New York, 1962), 1:435–36.

[8]Although the "Chaucer Greeting" was deleted from Gower's revisions of the *Confessio Amantis* after 1390, it occurs in both of the printed editions of writings of Gower that William Thynne could have known: Caxton's of 1483 and Berthelette's of 1532 (see Macaulay, *John Gower*, 1:clxviii–clxix; and Fisher, *John Gower*, pp. 12–14); the greeting is also discussed as evidence for the relationship between Chaucer and Gower by Francis Thynne in his *Animadversions*, pp. 13–14. Fisher, *John Gower*, pp. 16–17 and 323 n. 32, suggests that "Berthelette, [William] Thynne and Leland were in communication while these two editions [sc. Berthelette's of Gower and Thynne's of Chaucer] and Leland's *Commentaries* were being prepared"; see also the comments of Lounsbury, *Studies in Chaucer*, 1:146–47. On the Speght edition see Derek Pearsall, "Thomas Speght (ca. 1550–?)," in *Editing Chaucer*, pp. 71–92; its life of Chaucer is reprinted in Hammond, *Chaucer: A Bibliographical Manual*, pp. 19–35.

have appeared up to 1880, and perhaps to the present time," which was 1892, treated the *Testament* as if it were by and so about Chaucer. The attribution was only finally laid to rest in 1893, when Skeat published his discovery of an acrostic in the *Testament* spelling out the name of Thomas Usk.[9]

Mistaken as attribution of the *Testament* to Chaucer now appears to be, the fact that it began as early as it did, and persisted as long as it did, indicates that there is something appropriate about it. Thynne and others later took the *Testament* to be Chaucer's work; perhaps Gower and Chaucer saw Chaucerian qualities in it already in the fourteenth century; more certainly, Usk himself intended it to be Chaucerian. In the *Testament* he advertises his literary affiliations with Chaucer. He drew on Langland's *Piers Plowman*, too, but Usk saw fit to lionize only Chaucer in the *Testament*, as if he has a special interest in associating himself with Chaucer.[10] From this perspective the *Testament* has the same implication as the "Chaucer Greeting" in the *Confessio Amantis* of a few years later: by its uses of Chaucer's name and writings, it bespeaks the importance for English literature's development that Chaucer was acquiring already in the fourteenth century.

This importance was at least as much extrinsic as intrinsic, not only a matter of the felicities of Chaucer's writing but also a matter of the success that Chaucer and his literary labors enjoyed immediately, at court and in the city of London. As John Burrow

---

[9]On this history of the Chaucer legend based on Usk's *Testament* see, esp., Lounsbury, *Studies in Chaucer*, 1:180–204; Skeat published the acrostic in "The Author of 'The Testament of Love'," *The Academy* 1088 (March 1893): 222–23; see also Skeat's *Chaucerian and Other Pieces, Being a Supplement to the Complete Works of Geoffrey Chaucer* (Oxford, 1897), pp. xix–xx.

[10]Usk's praise for Chaucer is quoted below, p. 47. Usk drew on *Piers Plowman* B XVI or C XIX for the image of the Tree of Charity developed in *Testament* 3.5–3.7; see Skeat, *Chaucerian and Other Pieces*, p. 483.

remarked, the "rapid spread of Chaucer's reputation cannot be ascribed simply to the force of his genius."[11] Usk depended on Chaucer—on specific writings of Chaucer's as well as on the model of Chaucer's career as a writer in general—for shaping his own literary work. No doubt, in view of the circumstances in which he was writing, Usk's motive for using Chaucer as a literary source and model was mercenary above all. Chaucer was favored by persons by whom Usk hoped also to be favored, and Chaucer's literary work contributed something to the success he enjoyed; for currying favor in the metropolis or in royal and aristocratic circles, writing in the Chaucerian vein, with specific links to Chaucer, the nearer the better, must have seemed to Usk more likely to yield success than any alternative. Usk was the first to try to use Chaucer in this way. For him, as for others later— Thomas Hoccleve, for example—the emergent Chaucerian tradition would have been comparatively lucrative.[12]

However simple his motive for it, Usk's dependence on Chaucer is in literary terms still complex. Usk's allegorical exposition of the nature of love is rich and involved. For the knowledge of Boethius' *Philosophiae consolatio* that informs the *Testament*, Usk seems to have relied in some degree on Chaucer's recent English translation, from which he took phrases and more. Chaucer's Englished *Boece* was probably also the inspiration for Usk's notion of a sophisticated, artful prose, as well as for his effort to augment philosophical English with the translations from Anselm that make up a portion of the *Testament*. In addition, Usk drew on Chaucer's Boethius in the sense that he took over and developed certain reformulations of key Boethian concepts—*imperitans*

---

[11]"The Audience of Piers Plowman," *Anglia* 75 (1957): 377.

[12]See my "Thomas Hoccleve and the Chaucer Portrait," *The Huntington Library Quarterly* 54 (1991): 283–300.

Amor, above all—that Chaucer had articulated in the *Troilus and Criseyde*. With the *Testament*, Usk had, in effect, already done what Gower asked Chaucer to do in about 1390. Usk worked with tools largely provided him by Chaucer, and Usk's *Testament* does in some sense complete, or, to borrow Gower's phrase, "sette an ende of," a particular line of thought about love—a line of thought running back to Boethius—evident in Chaucer's *Troilus*.

Finally, Usk was indebted to Chaucer for the peculiar notion of literature's social function embodied in the *Testament*. For Chaucer as for Usk, literature was meant to be not immediately political but a relief or escape from politics—an attitude with, of course, inescapable political implications. Both Chaucer and Usk were deeply enmeshed in the politics of the day; paradoxically, it might seem, both produced literature that pretended to stand apart from or above the day-to-day antagonisms that are politics in inequitable societies. From the perspective of politics, the point of apolitical writings—as well as anti-political writings, which are only less subtle and efficient about doing the same job—is to impute a freedom from political worries to writer and audience, and to create and foster it. Such writings "originate in the need to prove that crude practical considerations have been dispensed with, to prove, in particular, that one can spend one's time on the useless, in order to improve one's position in the social hierarchy, increase one's social honour, and, finally, strengthen one's power over others." Literature thus "turns against utility," but "for the sake of a mediated utility:" implicitly denying a need to worry about keeping or gaining political advantage could be useful as a way to insinuate possession of an unassailable political advantage already, and to extend it.[13]

---

[13]These comments derive from Thorstein Veblen, *The Theory of the Leisure Class* (1899); the quotation is from Theodor Adorno, "Veblen's Attack on Culture," in *Prisms*, trans. Samuel Weber and Shierry Weber (Cambridge, Mass., 1981), p. 76.

Unlike Gower and Langland, Chaucer never devoted a work or a major portion of a work to open, direct discussion of class relations, social conditions, the nature of kinship, or local or international affairs.[14] Chaucer's work is always political nevertheless, in the sense that his elision of overt political discussion would have flattered his audience, by encouraging it to imagine itself safe and untroubled, if only for the moment. Without ever spelling the point out—spelling it out tends to spoil the effect—Chaucer's apolitical writings always seem to intimate that, for those privileged to have access to it, literature was, and formed part of, a realm of pleasurable, personal fulfillment, beyond political strife. Somewhat clumsily, Usk makes the Chaucerian point explicit, that the political should be subordinate to the personal, by detailing his own conversion from public affairs to personal *amours* and their literary exposition. The *Testament* talks politics explicitly, but its purpose in doing so is to show that politics should be kept subordinate to the personal and the private. No matter that it has political motives and points to make, then, the *Testament*'s focus is on an apolitical topic, love, and above all on love as private devotion and romance. "This book shal be of love," Usk announces in his prologue, "and the pryme causes of steringe in that doinge, with passions and diseses for wantinge of desyre."[15]

---

[14]The Melibee is the possible exception (see, for example, Gardiner Stillwell, "The Political Meaning of Chaucer's *Tale of Melibee*," *Speculum* 19 (1944): 433–44), but it is often read as a parody of political discussion. Nonetheless, Chaucer repeatedly goes out of his way to ridicule, in passing, popular participation in decision making and mass opinion, as in The Clerk's Tale (lines 995–1001), for example, or The Nun's Priest's Tale (lines 3394–97).

[15]*Testament*, 1.Pro.81–83. This and subsequent references to the *Testament*, which will be made parenthetically in this essay, are to the text edited and printed by Skeat, in *Chaucerian and Other Pieces*, pp. 1–145. The social dimension of

II. USK AND CHAUCER'S BOECE

Even in its subjugation of matters of politics to matters of love, however, the *Testament of Love* reacts to public, political conflicts in which Usk had a part. Usk was an activist and agitator of some sort, before he turned to literature. A scrivener by trade, certainly by October 1381 and possibly as early as July 1376, Usk involved himself with the party of John Northampton, a populist, militant mayor of London from October 1381 to October 1383, who employed Usk nominally as a scrivener.[16] In fact, Usk was

---

Usk's writing, touched on here, has been discussed recently also in a very good paper by Paul Strohm, "Politics and Poetics: Usk and Chaucer in the 1380s," in *Literary Practice and Social Change in Britain, 1380–1530*, ed. Lee Patterson (Berkeley, 1990), pp. 83–112, esp. 97–106, which comes to a perhaps somewhat different conclusion about the politics of the *Testament* and the uses to which Usk put Chaucer. Strohm represents the *Testament* as given over wholly to factional politicking, rather than as an effort to rise above politics; and he suggests that what Usk learned from the example of Chaucer's career was how to participate in factional politics: "While his reference to Chaucer seems literary rather than political, it probably carries a political charge. For he would have known Chaucer as a successful adherent of the very faction to which he wished to belong, and his mention of Chaucer within a work so calculated to advance factional aspiration cannot be politically innocent. A speculative, but I believe wholly reasonable, conclusion is that Chaucer's career embodied for Usk a source of inspiration and precedent in two respects: he was a literary artist, and also an artist who had thrived in the service of faction" (p. 107).

[16]The biographical sketch that follows is based principally on Leyerle's unpublished notes, which are in turn based on a thorough re-examination of the original documents. Usk's biography has recently been discussed by Strohm, "Politics and Poetics," esp. pp. 85–90; see also the earlier discussion of Ramona Bressie, "The Date of Thomas Usk's *Testament of Love*," *Modern Philology* 26 (1928): 17–29. The tendency in these discussions to treat Northampton and Brembre as co-equally oligarchic factionalists—as if there was nothing for someone like Usk to choose between them—is probably mistaken; see the cautionary remark of Rodney Hilton, "Feudalism in Europe: Problems for Historical Materialists," *New Left Review* 147 (1984): 91: "The manipulation involved in buying a product

active—more active than published records indicate—in organizing and spreading the sedition that Northampton encouraged when
he failed to win re-election to a third term as mayor in October
1383.[17]

Usk was occupied with political agitation on Northampton's
behalf from October 1383 to about mid-February 1384, when the
new mayor, Nicholas Brembre, moved decisively to suppress his
opposition, and Usk's name disappeared from the records for a
time. He may have been among those who fled London following
the riots of 11 February. In any event, Usk was arrested and imprisoned for his role in the sedition on about 20 July 1384. By the
end of the month, however, when Brembre put a petition to the
king for process of law against Northampton and several of his
supporters, including Usk, Usk seems to have turned traitor
against Northampton and his party. The factor that enabled

---

cheap and selling it dear on the market was not strictly analogous to the exercises
of non-economic coercion by the landowner to extract feudal rent from the peasant,
but it created similar antagonisms. Social conflict in medieval towns often seems to
be no more than factional struggle within oligarchies, but it often involved the
mobilization of the resentment of the middle stratum of master craftsmen against
town governments run by merchant capitalists."

[17]The most comprehensive document is the record of Northampton's trial before
the king in August 1384, preserved among the *Coram rege* rolls, in London, PRO,
KB 27/507, mm. 40–43d, portions of which have been published in E. Powell and
G. C. Trevelyan, *The Peasants' Rising and the Lollards* (London, 1899), pp. 27–38,
and in Ruth Bird, *The Turbulent London of Richard II* (London, 1949), pp. 134–40.
Leyerle has found that Bird's excerpts represent the document's contents faithfully,
although her transcriptions of letters and particular words are often erroneous; and
that, although Powell and Trevelyan transcribe accurately, they are less careful
about the document's contents. They often acknowledge omitting material, by the
use of ellipses (which can represent from four to five hundred words), but, just as
often, they have not marked their omissions; names and lists of names are
prominent among the passages that they omit without note, and the complete
document implicates Usk in wrongdoing extensively and regularly.

Brembre to move against Northampton at this point was probably Usk's *Appeal*, a detailed account of conspiracy and subversion, written by an insider, which was introduced as evidence at the trial that began before the king at Reading on 15 August 1384.[18]

On the basis of Usk's *Appeal*, with the corroboration of other testimony, Northampton and his most prominent supporters were condemned; but on 26 September 1384 their sentences were commuted to banishment from London at "the urgent prayer" of John of Gaunt.[19] On behalf of the other, temporarily ascendant, party of Brembre, the king pardoned Usk at the same time; and from the summer of 1385 Usk received a series of royal preferments, including appointment as Sergeant-at-Arms to the king by May 1386 and appointment as Undersheriff of Middlesex in September 1387, until Thomas of Woodstock staged his *coup d'état* against his nephew Richard in December 1387. As a servant to the king and the king's familiar, Nicholas Brembre, and, more importantly perhaps, as the betrayer of John Northampton to the benefit of Brembre's party in the London troubles of 1383–84, Usk was arrested on 28 December 1387. He was tried before the Merciless Parliament on 3 March 1388 and was beheaded, with Brembre, the following day. His head was set up above Newgate "volucrum rostribus lacerandum."[20]

The latest datable reference in the *Testament of Love* is to

---

[18]The *Appeal* survives, somewhat damaged, as London PRO, E 163/5/28; it is edited in R. W. Chambers and Marjorie Daunt, *A Book of London English 1384–1425* (Oxford, 1931), pp. 22–31.

[19]Reginald Sharpe, ed., *Calendar of Letter-Books Preserved among the Archives of the Corporation of the City of London at the Guildhall: Letter-Book H* (London, 1907), p. 307.

[20]May McKisack, ed., *Historia sive Narracio de Modo et Forma Mirabilis Parliamenti*, Camden Miscellany 14, Camden 3rd Series 37 (London, 1926), p. 20.

Richard's pardon of Usk, on 24 September 1384; none of Usk's subsequent preferments is mentioned, nor any later event; so it appears probable that Usk wrote it between the end of September 1384, when he was pardoned, and the end of June 1385, when he began to be preferred.[21] This was at a time when Geoffrey Chaucer—a colleague of Usk's local patron Brembre and a favorite of Usk's royal benefactor Richard—had finished the *Boece* and was well along with a draft of the *Troilus and Criseyde*, if he had not already finished it.[22] The disruption of life in the city wrought by Usk and his collaborators between October 1383 and February 1384 was so extensive, and Usk's subsequent role in the affair must have been so notorious, that civic-minded Londoners like Chaucer or Gower were likely to have known of Usk, and perhaps of the *Appeal* or the *Testament of Love*, even had they not come more directly into contact with him. The "philosophical" Ralph Strode, friend of Chaucer and Gower, lost his position as Common Sergeant of the Corporation of London in 1382, largely as a result of Northampton's election to the mayoralty; Gower wrote knowingly of Brembre and the events leading up to the execution of Brembre and Usk in the *Vox clamantis* and the *Cronica tripertita*; and Chaucer, as Comptroller of Customs, had been a colleague of Brembre, who was Collector of Customs throughout Northampton's mayoralty 1381–84, until he defeated Northampton

---

[21]The reference to Usk's pardon occurs in the *Testament* 2.4.120–24.

[22]The consensus presently is that the *Boece* was written in the late 1370s or early 1380s and the *Troilus* c. 1382–85; see *The Riverside Chaucer*, pp. 1003 and 1020. Dating the *Troilus* depends in part on dating the *Testament*, which is the crucial external attestation. The *Troilus* must have been finished and available first, in some form or other, even if not its final form; however, the notion that Usk saw Chaucer's poem unfinished, in an early draft or some other pre-publication state, supposes nearer relations between Chaucer and Usk, and better access, than the evidence warrants.

in the disputed election of October 1383.[23] If Chaucer or Gower took a side in the London troubles of 1383–84, either would have probably inclined towards the party of Brembre, whom Usk benefitted by his *Appeal* and whose patronage Usk enjoyed from September 1384 until they were executed together in 1388. There is no reason to suppose, however, that Chaucer and Usk had met or were familiars, or to imagine that Chaucer meant to help Usk in any way. Nonetheless, Usk knew at least something of Chaucer's writings and Chaucer's career in literature; he had access to the most recent of Chaucer's works—the *Boece* and the *Troilus*—both of which he used in the *Testament*.[24]

At the time of the composition of the *Testament*, Usk seems to have felt that he had not had what was due him for his part in the troubles and that he was still open to charges of opportunism; so on both counts, he needed to put his actions in the most favorable light possible. From this perspective the *Testament* is Usk's apology: a complicated explanation for his public behavior, set in the context of an allegorical explication of the nature of love, meaning to exonerate him but finally deny that politics was or should be of much consequence. For framing this apology, Usk suggestively chose to follow the model of Boethius' *Philosophiae consolatio*. In both the *Consolatio* and the *Testament*, a sapiential figure visits an unjustly imprisoned man in order to explain the prisoner's circumstance and to console him: Love to Usk as *Philosophia* to Boethius. More specifically, Usk likewise seems to have followed Boethius for the plan of the *Testament* and for cer-

---

[23]See Fisher, *John Gower*, pp. 61–62; Skeat, *Chaucerian and Other Pieces*, p. xxiii; and, for Gower's writings on the troubles, see *Cronica tripertita* 1.154–59 and *Vox clamantis* 5.835 ff.

[24]Skeat, *Chaucerian and Other Pieces*, pp. xxv–xxvi, pointed out that Usk also took over almost *verbatim* a long passage from *The House of Fame*, lines 269–359.

tain details of situation and exposition. Neither Usk nor Boethius is capable of recognizing the woman, described in allegorical detail, who appears to him (*Testament* 1.2.17–53; *Phil. cons.* 1.pr.1–1.pr.4); and both Love and *Philosophia* begin their instruction by examining their disciples' misfortunes (*Testament*, esp. 1.3, 1.5–7; *Phil. cons.* esp. 1.pr.4) and their disciples' misapprehension of what has happened (*Testament* 1.8–1.10; *Phil. cons.* 1.pr.5–2.m.8). The third book of the *Philosophiae consolatio* describes a *summum bonum*, initially in terms of what it is not (3.pr.1–3.m.8), and then in positive terms (3.pr.10–3.m.12), beginning with the lyric "O qui perpetua mundum ratione gubernas" (3.m.9); the second book of the *Testament of Love*, which likewise contains a significantly placed "Latin song" (2.2), similarly describes the possibility of a *summum bonum*, first again in terms of what it is not (2.4–2.11), and then in positive terms, of Usk's "Margarite perle" (2.12–2.14). From such a point, both Usk and Boethius proceed to discussions of the nature of evil (*Testament* 3.2.1–135, 3.6–3.7; *Phil. cons.* 4.pr.1–4.m.5) and of the relationship between free will and divine providence (*Testament* 3.2–3.5, 3.8; *Phil. cons.* 4.pr.6–5.pr.6). Boethius' work ends summarily, with *Philosophia*'s brief injunction to have faith in the *summum bonum* and to live the good life (5.pr.6); in the *Testament of Love*, the completion of Love's cure is done in more celebratory and metaphorically more satisfying (if not rhetorically more effective) terms: Love enters and inhabits Usk (3.7.160–64), and he can now finish her talk for her (3.8–3.9.51).[25]

In view only of such broad structural parallels, it would be difficult to say what Boethius Usk had worked with, since several

---

[25]The correspondence between the plans of the *Testament* and the *Philosophia consolatio* is least precise in these sections because, in place of Boethius' discussion, Usk used instead material from Anselm's *De concordia* to fill this slot in the expositional framework provided by Boethius.

different versions would have been available to him in 1384–85: the original Latin, probably in a late medieval "vulgate" version instead of the ancient text, perhaps glossed with one or some combination of the several current commentaries; or one of the French translations; or Chaucer's recent English version. But the verbal choices Usk made when incorporating specific Boethian matter into the *Testament* suggest that he preferred Chaucer's English *Boece* to the other materials in circulation.[26]

W. W. Skeat documented instances of verbal borrowing from the *Boece* in the *Testament of Love*, of translations peculiar to Chaucer, and of phrases not occurring in the Latin original.[27] It may be that he tended to exaggerate the extent of the verbal debt. Moreover, since Skeat's time, many of Chaucer's seemingly characteristic departures from the Latin have been shown to result from his use of secondary materials in Latin and French, specifically the French translation by Jean de Meun, written before 1305, *Li livres de confort de philosophie*, and the Latin commentary of Nicholas Trivet, written before 1307, *Explanatio librorum Boetii de Consolatione philosophica*.[28] Comparison of these materials with Usk's work, however, indicates that he did not use them as

---

[26]See the remarks of Ralph Hanna III and Traugott Lawler, in *The Riverside Chaucer*, pp. 1003–04, noting further the existence of manuscripts combining more than one such version, as, for example, manuscripts juxtaposing Jean de Meun's French translation, a Latin "vulgate" text, and Trivet's commentary. Rita Copeland's discussion of the production and reception of Chaucer's translation, *Rhetoric, Hermeneutics, and Translation in the Middle Ages* (Cambridge, 1991), pp. 142–45, sheds much light on the conditions of Usk's use of the *Boece*.

[27]Skeat, *Chaucerian and Other Pieces*, pp. xxv–xxvi.

[28]Chaucer's use of Jean de Meun's translation was first detailed by John Livingston Lowes, "Chaucer's *Boethius* and Jean de Meun," *Romanic Review* 8 (1917): 338–400; and his use of Trivet's commentary was first detailed by Kate O. Peterson, "Chaucer and Trivet," *PMLA* 18 (1903): 173–93.

Chaucer did and tends to confirm his debt to the *Boece* for his borrowings from the *Philosophiae consolatio*. The treatment of a passage from 2.pr.3 by Jean de Meun, Nicholas Trivet, Chaucer, and Usk exemplifies equally well the nature of Chaucer's borrowings from the ancillary materials, Usk's independence of them, and Usk's dependence on Chaucer:

> Boethius, *Phil. cons.* 2.pr.3.44–46:
> An tu in hanc vitae scaenam nunc primum subitus hospesque venisti?

> Jean de Meun, *Confort* 2.pr.3.45–46:
> Es tu ores premierement venus soudainz et hostes en la cortine et l'ombre de ceste vie?

> Trivet, *Explanatio* ad 2.pr.3 (fol.31ʳ):
> *An tu*, O Boeci, *in hanc vite scenam*, id est habitationem transitoriam—scena enim tabernaculum significat—*nunc primum subitus*, improvisus, *hospes venistis*, ut scilicet sic ignorare debeas que in ista vita geruntur?

> Chaucer, *Boece* 2.pr.3.79–81:
> Artow now comen first, a sodeyn gest, into the schadowe or tabernacle of this lif?

> Usk, *Testament* 2.10.95-97:
> Art thou now come first in-to the hostry of this lyfe, or els the both of this worlde? Art thou now a sodayn gest in-to this wrecched exile?

For rendering Boethius' apparently difficult *scaenam* ("theatre" or "stage" in classical usage), Chaucer took *schadowe* from Jean de Meun's *ombre* and *tabernacle* from Trivet's *tabernaculum*. Usk does not seem to have been similarly dependent on any secondary materials. His most evident debt is not to the *Consolatio* but to the *Boece*, for the phrase *sodayn gest*; and he may have also taken the general point of his remark from the *Boece* as well. Usk went often, perhaps regularly, to the *Boece* for phrases in this way.[29]

Certainly, Usk preferred English to Latin or French—witness his remarks in its favor in the *Testament*, or his choice of it for making his *Appeal* against Northampton, at a time when juridical documents in it were rare.[30] Usk was also a confident (if not

---

[29]Jean de Meun's translation is quoted from the edition of V. L. Dedeck-Henry, "Boethius' *De consolatione* by Jean de Meun," *Mediaeval Studies* 14 (1952): 165–275. An edition of Trivet's commentary has not been published; Leyerle, from whose notes the present example is taken, refers to the MS. Vat. lat. 562; other manuscripts are listed by Pierre Courcelle, *La Consolation de Philosophie dans la tradition littéraire* (Paris, 1967), pp. 412–13. Usk's dependence on Chaucer for Boethius seemed so complete to Skeat that he concluded (*Chaucerian and Other Pieces*, p. xxvi): "I see no reason for supposing the author [of the *Testament*] anywhere troubled himself to consult the Latin original;" some, Leyerle among them (see esp. J. A. W. Bennett, *Middle English Literature*, ed. Douglas Gray, [Oxford, 1986], pp. 347–48), have found Skeat's claim exaggerated, but Usk's use of the *Boece* has also been independently reconfirmed recently by Hanna and Lawler, *The Riverside Chaucer*, p. 1003.

[30]See *Testament* 1. Pro.22–38, e.g., "Let than clerkes endyten in Latin, for they have the propertee of science, and the knowinge in that facultee; and let Frenchmen in their Frenche also endyten their queynt termes, for it is kyndely to their mouthes; and let us shewe our fantasyes in suche wordes as we lerneden of our dames tonge." Strohm, "Politics and Poetics," p. 98 n.20, suggests that the *Appeal* "is obviously designed for high accessibility." Of the four surviving English documents concerning the London troubles of 1383–84 (discussed by R. W. Chambers, *On the Continuity of English Prose* [London, 1932], p. cxi n.3), three are Brembre's proclamations as mayor *ad populum* (printed in Chambers and Daunt, *London English*, pp. 31–33) and so only the fourth—Usk's *Appeal*—is a court document. The Exchequer file that contains the *Appeal* (PRO, E 163/5/28) also contains records in Latin of the three inquisitions held by Brembre between January and August 1384; and the major legal document of the affair, the record of the August 1384 trial (in PRO KB 27/507, mentioned above, n. 17) is likewise in Latin. Edward III's "Statute of Pleadings," allowing that pleas "soient pledez, monstretz, defenduz, reponduz, debatuz et juggez en la lange engleise" but also "qils soient entreez et enroullez en latin" (36 Ed. III, st.1, c.15; ed. *Statutes of the Realm*, vol. 1 [1810; repr. London, 1963], pp. 375–76, dates only as recently as 1369.

altogether competent) Latinist, however: large sections of the third book of the *Testament* are made up of English renditions of passages from Anselm's *De concordia praescientiae et praedestinationis et gratiae Dei cum libero arbitrio*—a work of abstruse, professional philosophy.[31] For both his preference for English and his belief that English was an appropriate philosophical vehicle, Usk's chief debt was again to Chaucer's *Boece*. At the time, the *Boece* was the only model available for Usk on which he might base his own experiment in using English as a philosophical language, for translating Anselm or for expressing original thought. The *Boece* should also have confirmed Usk in his prejudice in favor of English, not only by showing it to be an appropriate language for philosophy but also by advancing the spread of English into areas until recently reserved for Latin or French. Increasingly, the polyglot culture of Gower and his audience was disappearing, while Usk's linguistic preference was spreading; to its spread, Chaucer's monolingual, English literary work contributed—not least significantly the *Boece*.

III. USK'S LOVE, PHILOSOPHIA, AND FORTUNA

Usk's debt to Chaucer extends beyond the *Boece* to the *Troilus and Criseyde* as well, from Chaucer's version of the letter of Boethius to his reinterpretation of Boethian ideas incipient in the *Troilus*. In the *Testament*, in addition to perhaps a dozen quotations from Chaucer's poem, there is also explicit reference to

---

[31]See esp. Stephen Medcalf, "Transposition: Thomas Usk's *Testament of Love*," in *The Medieval Translator*, ed. Roger Ellis (Cambridge, 1989), pp. 181–95; also, Margaret Schlauch, "Thomas Usk as Translator," in *Medieval Literature and Folklore Studies*, ed. Jerome Mandel and Bruce A. Rosenberg (New Brunswick, N.J., 1970), pp. 97–103. Usk's use of Anselm was first detailed by George Sanderlin, "Usk's *Testament of Love* and St. Anselm," *Speculum* 17 (1942): 69–73.

"the boke of Troilus"—the title that Chaucer seems to have preferred. The character Usk raises with Love, his interlocutor, the problem of responsibility for evil, given divine foreordination of events. To his interrogation, Love replies:

> I shal telle thee, this lesson to lerne. Myne owne trewe servaunt, the noble philosophical poete in Englissh, whiche evermore him besieth and travayleth right sore my name to encrese (wherfore al that willen me good owe to do him worship and reverence bothe; trewly, his better ne his pere in scole of my rules coude I never fynde)—he (quod she), in a tretis that he made of my servant Troilus, hath this mater touched, and at the ful this question assoyled. Certaynly, his noble sayinges can I not amende; in goodnes of gentil manliche speche, without any maner of nycete of storiers imaginacion, in witte and in good reson of sentence he passeth al other makers. In the boke of Troilus, the answere to thy question mayst thou lerne. (3.4.248–59)

Love's reference seems to be to Troilus' soliloquy in the fourth book; but Usk's debt to the *Troilus* is not to the discussions of free will and providence mentioned here, only to be passed by. Rather, Usk's debt is to Chaucer's adaptation of the Boethian conception of love, as Love's remark about Chaucer suggests ("his better ne his pere in scole of my rules coude I never fynde"). In other words, Usk owes to Chaucer both his familiarity with Boethius' work and the particular form that his broader Boethian outlook takes; the peculiar reading of Boethius made flesh in the *Testament* derives from or runs parallel to one sketched out by Chaucer in the *Troilus and Criseyde*.[32]

---

[32]It is in the *Retractions* (1086) that Chaucer calls it "the book of Troilus," as Usk does here. For a list of Usk's quotations from the *Troilus* see Skeat, *Chaucerian and Other Pieces*, p. xxvii. The most telling among them may be the quotation of *Troilus* 3.1656–59, Pandarus' response to Troilus' description of the "glade

Usk's most consequential departure from the Boethian model
that he chose for framing the *Testament of Love* was his replace-
ment of *Philosophia* with Love. The change meant that love was
philosophy for Usk: Love does for Usk what *Philosophia* did for
Boethius, offer consolation in the form of a perspective that
makes present misfortune seem bearable or even worthwhile. Love
maintains that persistence in her service can free Usk from the
kind of misfortune and suffering that he is presently experiencing:

> Continuaunce in thy good service, by longe processe of tyme
> in ful hope abyding, without any chaunge to wilne in thyne
> herte, this is the spire. Whiche, if it be wel kept and gov-
> erned, shal so hugely springe, til the fruit of grace is plen-
> tuously out-sprongen. . . . And so, by processe of growing,
> with thy good traveyle, it shal in-to more amd more wexe, til
> it be found so mighty, that windes of yvel speche, ne scornes
> of envy, make nat the traveyle overthrowe: ne frostes of
> mistrust, ne hayles of jelousy right litel might have, in
> harming of suche springes. Every yonge setling lightly with
> smale stormes is apeyred; but whan it is woxen somdel in
> gretnesse, than han grete blastes and weders but litel might,
> any disadvantage to them for to werche.   (3.5.12–26)

Love also promises Usk a better outcome for his affairs: "Sorowe
and joy kyndely moten entrechangen their tymes," she says; "thy
sorowe in-to wele mot ben chaunged" (2.9.175–78). Even if Usk

---

nyght," his first night of love with Criseyde: "he / That ones may in hevene blisse
be, / He feleth other weyes, dar I leye, / Than thilke tyme he first herde of it seye."
Love's description of the rewards that Usk can win by persevering in his love for
his Margarite concludes with the same remark: "He that is in heven felith more
joye, than whan he firste herde therof speke" (*Testament* 2.9.116–17). The
quotation suggests that Usk attended with particular care to this portion of the
Troilus, where the interpenetration of romantic experience and religious conceptions
is especially striking.

does not meet with joy in this life, "yet shal the passion of thy martred lyfe ben written, and rad toforn the grete Jupiter, . . . and ever thou shalt forward ben holden amonge al these hevins for a knight" (2.9.106–13).

Love's consolation comes to rest, however, on her important and unusual assertion that even an opportunity to love is already in itself a greater gift than anyone deserves; for the gift of a chance to love, "continuaunce in good service" is owed as thanks, without regard for any additional rewards:

> Thou that were naked of love, and of thy-selfe non have mightest, it is not to putte to thyne owne persone, sithen thy love cam thorow thy Margaryte-perle. *Ergo*, she was yever of the love, although thou it use; and there lente she thee grace, thy service to beginne. She is worthy the thank of this grace, for she was the yever. Al the thoughtes, besy doinges, and plesaunce in thy might and in thy wordes that thou canst devyse, ben but right litel in quytinge of thy dette; had she not ben, suche thing hadde not ben studyed. So al these maters kyndly drawen hom-ward to this Margaryte-perle, for from thence were they borowed; al is hoolly her to wyte, the love that thou havest; and thus quytest thou thy dette, in that thou stedfastly servest. (3.7.135–45)

Through such persistent "service . . . art thou able right sone to have grace," Love explains (3.7.148–49); nonetheless, "retribution of thy good willes . . . bereth not the name of mede, but only of good grace; and that cometh not of thy desert" (3.7.112–14):

> Thus thy ginning and ending is but grace aloon; and in thy good deserving thy dette thou aquytest; without grace is nothing worth, what-so-ever thou werche. Thanke thy Margaryte of her grete grace, that hiderto thee hath gyded, and praye her of continuaunce forth in thy werkes herafter; and that, for no mishappe, thy grace overthwartly tourne.
> (3.7.150–56)

Just as *Philosophia* offered Boethius the perspective of philosophy and philosophical understanding as consolation for his suffering, so Love here offers Usk the perspective of persistent love and an understanding of love's properties as consolations for his: grace of love will be the end of his suffering; perseverance in love even while suffering for it is part of the debt owed love for the chance to love; and love itself is a gift, for which thanks are due. But at the same time that Love thus plays the part of *Philosophia* to Usk's Boethius, she makes it equally clear that she has also taken the part of *Fortuna*. Not only is she now responsible for consoling Usk; after a fashion, she was also responsible for having caused his misfortune in the first place.

Love repeatedly asserts that Usk never "chaunginge herte haddest in my service" (2.4.119); she maintains that, even when Usk served the causes that later resulted in his suffering, "in thy hert thou wendest to have ben there thou shuldest" (2.4.105–06). Love assents to Usk's claims on his own behalf

> that ye knowe your-selfe that I in my conscience am and
> have ben willinge to your service, al coude I never do as I
> shulde; yet forsothe, fayned I never to love otherwyse than
> was in myn herte; and if I coude have made chere to one and
> y-thought another, as many other doon alday afore myn eyen,
> I trowe it wolde not me have vayled. . . . Trewly, there ye me
> sette, by acorde of my conscience I wolde not flye, til ye and
> reson, by apert strength maden myn herte to tourne.
>
> (1.2.158–70)

Usk would have it both ways about his dealings with the Northampton faction, in other words. On the one hand, he maintains that his betrayal of Northampton was well intentioned and that he came to speak out against him and his supporters "for no harme ne malice of tho persones, but only for trouthe of my sacrament of ligeaunce, by whiche I was charged on my kinges behalfe" (1.6.164–66).[33] On the other hand, Usk wants also to maintain that his service to Northampton was equally well intentioned and in fact resulted in good.[34] But in the course of his discussions with Love, Usk is taught to recognize that "thilke service was an enprisonment, and alway bad and naughty, in no maner to be desyred" (2.10.136–38). Of course, Usk the character finds the contradiction that Usk the author puts here: if even as Northampton's man he had always been Love's true servant, as both he and Love say that he has been, then why has his service resulted in "enprisonment," suffering, and misfortune? Love summarizes the problem for him:

> Thou woldest conclude me, if thou coudest, bycause I brought thee to service; and every of my servantes I helpe to come to this blisse, as I sayd here-beforn. And thou saydest thy-selfe, thou mightest nat be hoplen as thou wenest, bycause that vertue in thee fayleth; and this blisse parfitly without vertue may nat be goten; thou wenest of these wordes contradiccion to folowe.   (2.11.110–16)

Love resolves Usk's dilemma by arguing that "suche maner badnesse, whiche is used to purifye wrong-doers . . . is good"

---

[33]See also 1.6.82–87: "Than, lady, I thought that every man that, by any waye of right, rightfully don, may helpe any comune wele to ben saved; whiche thing to kepe above al thinges I am holde to mayntayne, and namely in distroying of a wrong; al shulde I therthrough enpeche myn owne fere, if he were gilty and to do misdeed assentaunt."

[34]See 1.8.81–88: "whyle I administred the office of commen doinge, as in rulinge of the stablisshmentes amonges the people, I defouled never my conscience for no maner dede; but ever, by witte and by counsayle of the wysest, the maters weren drawen to their right endes. And thus trewly for you, lady, I have desyred suche cure; and certes, in your service was I nat ydel, as fer as suche doinge of my cure streccheth;" see also 1.6.53–61.

(2.13.17–19): although his "misgoinges" in love "be nat worthy to thilke blisse, . . . yet [they] somwhat must ben cause and way to thilke blisse" (2.4.31–32). Most simply, she argues that the contrast between bliss and misfortune makes bliss seem more valuable, just as "after grete stormes the weder is often mery and smothe" (1.5.87–88), and since "if a man . . . thilke blisse in haste folowed, so lightly comminge shulde lightly cause going" (3.5.88–90).[35] More tellingly, Love also makes a case that the misgoing in well-intentioned love that leads to suffering can be a step towards finding the bliss of properly directed love. The "parfit blisse" of love "is desyred in every mannes herte, be he never so moche a wrecche; but every man travayleth by dyvers studye, and seketh thilke blisse by dyvers wayes;" even among those firmly fixed in Love's service, "yet her erroneous opinions misturne it by falsenesse of wening" (2.4.2–10). Seeking after bliss "out-forth" leads only to disillusionment. Love says:

> By queynt thinges blisse is desyred; and the fruit that cometh
> of these springes nis but anguis and bitter; al-though it be a
> whyle swete, it may not be with-holde; hastely they departe;
> thus al-day fayleth things that fooles wende. Right thus hast
> thou fayled in thy first wening. (2.8.119–23)

But then the disillusionment that inevitably comes of such an "out-waye-goinge" (2.8.126) may prompt lovers to look "in-forth" for fulfillment:

> He that out-forth loketh after the wayes of this knot [of bliss],

---

[35]See also 2.11.130–35: "'Now,' quod she, 'be nat wroth; for there is no man on-lyve that may come to a precious thing longe coveited, but he somtyme suffre teneful diseses: and wenest thy-selfe to ben unliche to al other? That may not ben. And with the more sorowe that a thing is getten, the more he hath joye the ilke thing afterwards to kepe.'"

> his conning with whiche he shulde knowe the way in-forth,
> slepeth for the tyme. Wherfore he that wol this way knowe,
> must leve the loking after false wayes out-forth, and open the
> eyen of his conscience, and unclose his herte. Seest nat, he
> that hath trust in the bodily lyfe is so besy bodily woundes to
> anointe, in keping from smert (for al-out may they nat be
> heled), that of woundes in his true understanding he taketh no
> hede; the knowing evenforth slepeth so harde: but anon, as in
> knowing awake, than ginnith the prevy medicynes, for heling
> of his trewe intent, inwardes lightly helen conscience, if it be
> wel handled. Than must nedes these wayes come out of the
> soule by stering lyfe of the body; and els may no man come
> to parfit blisse of this knotte. And thus, by this waye, he shal
> come to the knotte, and to the parfit selinesse that he wende
> have had in bodily goodes outforth.   (2.11.13–28)

At the end of the second book—before she lies down to rest
for a while—Love concludes her account of the process whereby
her true servants fall prey to "fayned love," find it "anguis and
bitter," and so come to more "parfit selinesse," with a parable.[36]
It concerns:

> an innocent [who] walkid by the way in blyndnesse of a
> derke night; whom mette a woman (if it be leefly to saye) as
> a strumpet arayed, redily purveyed in turninge of thoughtes
> with veyne janglinges, and of rest inpacient, by dissimulacion
> of my termes.   (2.14.7–13)

Usk was "this innocent, . . . a scoler lerninge of my lore, in seching
of my blisse;" he was "in derknesse of many doutes" and "forsothe,
suche oon may lightly ben begyled" (2.14.16–22). Usk did succumb
to the strumpet of "fayned love"—a phrase that occurs also at a
critical point near the end of the Troilus and Criseyde, though the

---

[36]It derives from Proverbs 7:7–22.

"fayned love" at issue here is evidently Usk's political involvement with Northampton—"in whiche thing thou hast founde mater of mokel disese" (2.14.28– 31). But, Love explains, "be the burthen never so greet," "my foundement endureth" (2.14.64–65). Through this experience of "misgoinge," Usk was prepared to love better; and Love, having explained that her service was a necessary precondition for his suffering, and that his suffering was a necessary part of his service, can now console him:

> Truste wel to me, and I wol thee not fayle. The leving of the first way with good herte of continuance that I see in thee grounded, this purpose to parfourme, draweth me by maner of constrayning, that nedes muste I ben thyne helper. Although mirthe a whyle be taried, it shal come at suche seson, that thy thought shal ben joyed.   (2.14.87–92)

Much as submission to *Fortuna*'s sway in the Boethian world often leads to misfortune, so in the world of Usk's *Testament*, admission to Love's service entails misgoing and suffering in love. But whereas in Boethius causing suffering is the function of *Fortuna* and offering consolation is the function of *Philosophia*, in the *Testament*, both of these are the functions of Love: she causes Usk's suffering when he loves wrongfully and then consoles him for it with an education in rightful love.[37]

IV. MARGARITE, LOVE, RELIGION, AND ROMANCE

Love is still more complicated in the *Testament*, however,

---

[37]Usk knows these two faces of Love even before she appears to him, as his initial complaint makes clear: "Remembraunce of love lyth so sore under my brest, that other thought cometh not in my mynde but gladnesse, to thinke on your goodnesse and your mery chere; ferdnes and sorowe, to thinke on your wreche and your daunger" (1.1.56–60).

than this combination of danger and the potential for causing suffering characteristic of the Boethian *Fortuna* with the hope for consolation characteristic of the Boethian *Philosophia*, the things that Usk's allegorical figure has and does. Its depiction involves also delineating varieties of love within the general concept, and the relations among them. The account that Love gives of Usk's misgoing and return to the right way of love—her account of her dual functioning as Fortune and Philosophy in his career—includes an explanation for Usk's public doings: his political activity was a kind of love, perhaps, but a misguided, ill-conceived love. The account of Usk's suffering and consolation also describes the course of Love's mediation between Usk and someone (or something) whom Usk names Margarite, whom he also loves but with a love always characterized as rightful. Love specifies that Usk's misgoing was his involvement in the political program of John Northampton and that his return to the right way was his abandonment of politics in favor of the apolitical, higher affairs of the heart that his love for Margarite represents. Usk's love for his Margarite is complicated, incorporating both religion and romance, in a way evidently indebted to a medieval tradition that reached Usk through Chaucer's *Troilus*.[38]

---

[38]Much of the material concerning the character Margarite discussed below was treated by C. S. Lewis, in *The Allegory of Love* (Oxford, 1936), pp. 223–27. The best discussion of the allegory of love in the *Testament* remains that of S. K. Heninger, Jr., "The Margarite-Pearl Allegory in Thomas Usk's *Testament of Love*," *Speculum* 32 (1957): 92–98, who stresses the fundamental point that religion and romance are complementary, according to the *Testament*: "Usk has thus resolved the dilemma of carnal *versus* spiritual love": he "binds the two worlds together, makes them interpenetrable" (p. 98); for Usk Lady Love "governs the realms of both sacred and profane love" (p. 96). See also Renzo Donati, "The Threefold Concept of Love in Usk's *Testament*," in *Genres, Themes, and Images in English Literature From the Fourteenth to the Fifteenth Century*, ed. Piero Boitani and Anna Torti (Tübingen, 1988), pp. 59–72. The "Robertsonian" analysis of Edmund Reiss, "The Idea of Love in Usk's *Testament of Love*," *Mediaevalia* 6 (1980):

By these means, Usk's political activity is dismissed as an abuse of Love, as if politics ought properly to be kept subordinate to higher callings, specifically romance and religious devotion. There is nothing to indicate that political considerations were in fact ever secondary to Usk; here too the effort to paint politics as secondary serves Usk's rehabilitation, with the suggestion that he sees things differently now, and better, in a way no longer threatening to those who had so far kept him from criminal prosecution. The claim advanced is that Usk is out of politics, finally. For reasons of policy, however, the *Testament* means to make Usk's love for Margarite an acceptable, higher alternative to the misguided loves in civic affairs that he had pursued earlier.

Margarite is first mentioned in Usk's complaint against her absence, with which the *Testament* proper begins: "From my comfort I ginne to spille, sith she that shulde me solace is fer fro my presence," he says; "blisse of my joye, that ofte me murthed, is turned in-to galle, to thinke on thing that may not, at my will, in armes me hente" (1.1.8–12). If it is clear enough in this passage, as elsewhere, that Margarite is a proper name for an actual woman, one with arms and so on—"a womanly woman in her kynde, in whom . . . of answeringe shappe of limmes, and fetures so wel in al pointes according, nothing fayleth" (2.12.114–17)— soon enough it also becomes apparent that she is also something more than a woman. In the course of this same initial complaint, Usk points out the "oon vertue of a Margarite precious is, amonges many other, the sorouful to comforte" (1.1.23–25). The assimilation nascent at this point—of Usk's "womanly woman," named Margarite, to the "Margarite" proper, or pearl—is used

---

261–71, has to find an opposition between human romance (a bad thing) and divine love (a good thing) and a progression away from the first towards the second; and so it does less justice to Usk's allegory.

later in the *Testament* to attribute to her various supernatural powers: as the jewel, she is "so good and so vertuous, that her better shulde I never finde, al sought I ther-after to the worldes ende" (1.3.81–82); she "moder is of al vertues," "endelesse vertue and everlasting joy," and a "ful vessel of grace" (2.12.50–70); and she enjoys "knowing of devynly and manly thinges joyned with studie of good living" (3.1.54–55).[39]

The cumulative effect of Usk's persistent attribution of both divine and human qualities to his Margarite is an equation of religion and romance in his love for her. When, for example, Usk asserts that "bothe professe and reguler arn obediencer and bounden to this Margarite-perle as by knotte of loves statutes and stabblisshment in kynde" (3.1.130–32), it is not possible to decide whether the properly religious terms used here—"professe" (one who has made a profession of religious vows), "reguler" (a member of a religious order observing a rule), and "obediencer" (a member of a conventual establishment charged with any duty or obedience)—are to be taken literally and Margarite figuratively (religious take vows to Margarite as to a saint or to God); or whether they should be taken metaphorically and Margarite literally (all lovers are obligated to Margarite, by virtue of her special place in the amatory order of things); or some combination. Religion and romance fuse.

The imbrication of the divine and the human that characterizes Margarite figures also in Usk's characterization of the lady Love.

---

[39]The divinized nature of Usk's Margarite is already fixed when, in an early chapter, Usk likens himself to the man in the Gospel of Matthew (13:45) "that sought the precious Margarytes, and whan he had founden oon to his lyking, he solde al his good to bye that jewel" (1.3.84–85). "My moeble is insuffysaunt . . . to make th'eschange"; but "the vertue" of this jewel Margarite "out of this prison may me deliver, and naught els, and if I be not ther-throw helpen, I see my-selfe withouten recovery," says Usk, incorporating in Margarite a Christ-like grace and mercy (1.3.131–40).

It seems from some of her remarks that Love embodies God's love and religion. She likens herself to the "good shepherde," for example, who searches for his "sperkelande sheep, that arn ronne in-to wildernesse:" "for everich of my folke, and for al tho that to me-ward be knit in any condicion, I wol rather dye than suffre hem through errour to ben spilte" (1.2.74–87). Not only "kinde I was to Paris," Love says, but also, "most of al, maked I not a loveday bytwene God and mankynde, and chees a mayde to be nompere, to putte the quarel at ende?" (1.2.91–96); she says later that "somtyme . . . I bar both crosse and mytre, to yeve it where I wolde; with me the pope went a-fote; and I tho was worshipped of al holy church" (2.2.35–38).

Much of the advice that Love gives, however, casts her clearly in the role of courtly love or romance. For example, when she says that she teaches "my servaunts . . . to make songes of playnte and of blisse, and to endyten letters of rethorike in queynte understondinges, and to bethinke hem in that wyse they might best their ladies in good service plese," in order to show how she has "in curtesye made hem expert" (1.2.129–42), it is clear that she speaks of human romance, as a courtly kind of love. She stands for an ennobled ideal of courtly love: in addressing poetic "plaintes" to his Margarite, Usk is to "beware of thy lyfe, that thou no wode lay use, as in asking of thinges that strecchen in-to shame. . . . Freel-witted people supposen in suche poesies to be begyled; in open understandinge must every worde be used" (3.7.52–58). Only the simple suppose that the accord of two hearts in love "may not be, but the rose of maydenhede be plucked"; "do way, do way," Love chides, "they knowe nothing of this" (1.9.89–90). Nevertheless, as definitely as her ideals are honest and chaste, just so definitely does Love embody romance in passages such as these.

Love offers more capacious conceptions of herself as well, as a love that comprehends all varieties of love and is insinuated in all realms of experience, including religion and romance and a good deal else besides. Love's Latin song at the beginning of the second book of the *Testament* recalls the song of Boethius' *Philosophia* "Felix nimium prior aetas" (2.m.5), in that it is Love's lament for "the clips of me, that should be his [sc. man's] shynande sonne" (2.2.15); it also recalls the "O qui perpetua mundum ratione gubernas" (3.m.9), in that the song is a sort of catalogue of the things that Love is responsible for as the *mobile* of much of the universal order. Formerly, she used to be sought out "in heven on highe, above Saturnes sphere, in sesonable tyme." But these days, she says, she is wrongly supposed to dwell "in celler with wyne shed; in gernere, there corn is layd covered with whete"; "in purse, with money faste knit"; "in presse, among clothes layd, with rich pelure arayed"; and "in stable among hors and other beestes, as hogges, sheep, and neet" (2.2.23–31). Not only did she once animate "al holy church," "in pleasaunce bothe of God and of the people," though the people have since turned to "symonye," "voluntarie lustes," and "ribaudye"; likewise, she once implanted "reignatif prudence" in rulers, when "kinges baden me their crownes holden," though now "that governaunce fayleth." She "the law . . . set as it shuld," though now "among legistres there dar I not come"; she infused relations "amonges cosinage" and "kinrede," where too now "dar I not come, but-if richesse be my mene"; and she propagated an ideal of "gentilnesse," since also degenerated, into the empty, fallacious notion of "linage" based on "the vertues of . . . auncestres" (2.2.35–133).

In this song, Love presents herself as the embodiment of a comprehensive range of loves, including the love between God and his church, the church and his people, elements of society, members of families, and men and women in love: as she had claimed earlier, also, this Love has "caused worthy folk to voyde vyce and shame," "holde cytees and realms in prosperite," "worthyed kinges in the felde," and "honoured ladyes in boure," all at once (1.2.108–12). Elsewhere, however, Love singles out two of her responsibilities, for divine and for romantic love, to suggest that, of all the varieties of love that she encompasses, these two are the highest. Love speaks of "a melodye in heven, whiche clerkes clepen 'armony'; but that is not in brekinge of voice, but it is a maner swete thing of kyndely werching, that causeth joyes out of nombre to recken" (2.9.8–11); "al sugre and hony, al minstralsy and melody ben but soot and galle in comparison, by no maner proporcion to reken, in respect of this blisful joye" (2.9.37–40). This harmony exists in only two kinds of relationships, Love says, the relationship among the elements of the cosmos and the relationship between men and women in romance: "this armony, this melody, this perdurable joye may nat be in doinge but betwene hevens and elementes, or twey kyndly hertes ful knit in trouth of naturel understonding, withouten weninge and disceit" (2.9.40–43). Apprehension of the cosmic harmony is the greatest experience to which a person can aspire: "more soverain desyr hath every wight in litel heringe of hevenly conninge than of mokel material purposes in erthe"; and to this, the ambition of Love's servants is comparable: "right so it is in propertee of my servauntes, that they ben more affiched in steringe of litel thinge in his desyr than of mokel other mater lasse in his conscience" (2.9.25–39). "No tonge may telle, ne herte may thinke," Love claims, "the leest point of this blisse" (2.9.103–04).

Love thus presents the divine love that pervades the universe and romantic love between human beings as pre-eminent among the range of loves that she comprehends. They are her highest callings, uniquely alike in embodying the difficult to apprehend, ineffable "armony" that she speaks of here as "what hath caused any wight to don any good dede" and a source of "endelesse joye" (2.9.70–71, 2.9.99). These two varieties of love become in-extricably assimilated to one another in the *Testament*, by virtue of the particular qualities that Love attributed to them, as well as the admixture of human and divine characteristics in Usk's Margarite. "Margarite, a woman, betokeneth grace, lerning, or wisdom of God, or els holy church" (3.9.102–103), Usk says in the end; she must be both womanly and the divine, and Usk's love for her must be both romance and religion.

The love that mediates between God and individuals in relig-ion, and between human beings in romance, as also between social groups, members of families, and the rest, is a single love here, comprehended in the single figure of lady Love in the conception that Usk adumbrates in the *Testament*. The diversity of the natures, however, between which this single figure mediates, seems in Usk's work to entail a comparable diversity in the experiences of love that these diverse natures have. To the extent that they are imperfect, their experiences in love will be imperfect and will involve suffering; to the extent that they are perfect or perfectible, their loves too will be perfectible and a source of consolation. So when with good intentions, but wrongfully, Usk involved himself in the imperfect political projects of John Northampton, his love was a "misgoinge" and form of misfortune; and so when Usk loves well his "womanly woman" Margarite, or the Margarite-pearl that she also is, his love is a straight way to bliss. It is not simply that when love is romance Love acts as the Boethian *Fortuna* in Usk's allegory, and when love is religion Love acts as *Philosophia*. In view of the complex nature of Margarite and the complex nature of Love herself, in relation to both of whom Usk experiences both suffering and consolation and in both of whom romance and religion are effectively amalgamated, the knitting up of two human hearts in romance is also an at least potential source of consolation in the *Testament*, just as is God's love. Whether Love shows her servant Usk the face of *Philosophia* or the face of *Fortuna* depends finally not on whether he chooses romance or religion. Both can be sources of suffering and consolation alike in the *Testament* (where only the loves of political activism are without redeeming consolations). It depends instead on the particular qualities that Usk shows or fails to show in pursuit of a particular desire. He is bound to see each of Love's faces from time to time, even after his initial misfortune has taught him the value of higher loves, since his human nature remains imperfect, since his life in the world remains volatile, and since God allows humankind the possibility of eventual perfection.

V. USK AND CHAUCER'S TROILUS

There is about Usk's Love something of the Empedoclean Ølλότηo, an all-encompassing, all-harmonizing force. Usk's ultimate source, Boethius, expounds the concept in the *Philosophiae consolatio*, especially in the eighth metre of the second book, detailing the influence of *regens et imperitans Amor*: "Hanc rerum seriem ligat / Terras ac pelagus regens / Et caelo imperitans Amor" (2.m.8.13–15); and its principal exponent in the high Middle Ages was Dante, with "l'amor che move il sole e l'altre stelle." Usk's Love claims for herself a similar breadth and a similarly pervasive influence; but Usk's conception is not so clearly Dantesque in its definition of relations between romance and religion. For Dante, loving Beatrice was an education in ways of loving God, in such a way that Beatrice leading Dante to his vision of God at the end of the *Paradiso* is more than a metaphor; it is also the reenactment of an actual interior process. "I mie' disiri," Beatrice tells Dante when they are reunited in the earthly paradise, "ti menavano ad amar lo bene / di là dal qual non è a che s'aspiri"; when he looks into her eyes here, as lovers are wont to do, he sees an image of Christ.[40]

Usk does not so emphatically make of romance a propaedeutic for religion. Instead, he presents the possibilities of romance and religion, and of suffering and consolation in them, in ways that are more closely akin to what Chaucer does in the *Troilus and Criseyde*.[41] The *Troilus* addresses similar questions, of love's properties and, in the end, of the relations between romance and religion. The conception of love adumbrated in the *Troilus* is as capacious as that spelled out in greater detail in the *Testament*. Here too, "in this world no lyves creature / Withouten love is worth, or may endure" (3.13–14); Chaucer's poem, too, incorporates the Boethian metre on *imperitans Amor*, putting a free, verse translation of it in his protagonist's mouth, in which the powers of an all-pervasive Love are enumerated:

> Love, that of erthe and se hath governaunce,
> Love, that his hestes hath in hevene hye,
> Love, that with an holsom alliaunce
> Halt peples joyned, as hym lest hem gye,

---

[40]The most pertinent of the fragments of Empedocles are edited and translated in G. S. Kirk and J. E. Raven, *The Presocratic Philosophers* (Cambridge, 1957), esp. pp. 327–31. The lines from Dante referred to are *Paradiso* 33.145 and *Purgatorio* 31.22–24 and 31.118–23.

[41]The view of love in the *Troilus* espoused here derives from Leyerle's discussion in "The Heart and the Chain," in *The Learned and the Lewed: Studies in Chaucer and Medieval Literature*, ed. Larry D. Benson (Cambridge, Mass., 1974), esp. pp. 124–42 (e.g., p. 137: "The poem shows the continuity as well as the progression from worldly to divine love"); see also Bonnie Wheeler, "Dante, Chaucer, and the Ending of *Troilus and Criseyde*," *Philological Quarterly* 61 (1982), esp. pp. 115–16. Leyerle's "The Heart and the Chain," p. 134, also contains the suggestion, developed herein, that Usk depended on the *Troilus* for the conception of love worked out in the *Testament*: "The knot of the heart, without its sexual implications was borrowed from the *Troilus and Criseyde* by Thomas Usk and used in his *Testament of Love* as the central metaphor for stable, binding love."

Love, that knetteth lawe of compaignie,
And couples doth in vertu for to dwelle,
Bynd this acord, that I have told and telle.

That, that the world with feith which that is stable
Diverseth so his stowndes concordynge,
That elementz that ben so discordable
Holden a bond perpetuely durynge,
That Phebus mote his rosy day forth brynge,
And that the mone hath lordshipe over the nyghtes:
Al this doth Love, ay heried be his myghtes! —

That, that the se, that gredy is to flowen,
Constreyneth to a certeyn ende so
His flodes that so fiersly they ne growen
To drenchen erthe and al for evere mo;
And if that Love aught lete his bridel go,
Al that now loveth asondre sholde lepe,
And lost were al that Love halt now to-hepe.

So wolde God, that auctour is of kynde,
That with his bond Love of his vertu liste
To cerclen hertes alle and faste bynde,
That from his bond no wight the wey out wiste;
And hertes colde, hem wolde I that he twiste
To make hem love, and that hem liste ay rewe
On hertes sore, and kepe hem that ben trewe!

(3.1744–71)

Chaucer likewise endows this capacious love in the *Troilus* with some of the qualities of Boethian *Fortuna* and Boethian *Philosophia*: romance brings Troilus consolation and suffering by turns; and then, in the end, Troilus' apprehension of the heavenly "armonye"—a key term in Usk, too—enables him to put romance in perspective, so bringing him to consolation again. Chaucer assimilates Fortune to love in the *Troilus* by making the operations of Fortune over the course of a romance the prime matter of his narrative: his stated purpose is to tell of Troilus "*In lovynge*, how his aventures fellen / Fro wo to wele, and after out of joie" (1.3–4; emphasis mine). In the *Troilus*, as in the *Testament* also, politics is significant as background, in the form of the story of the fall of Troy.[42] Here also it remains in the background, functioning only to shed light on the apolitical romance at the core of the work, in which exemplification of the effects of Fortune is concentrated. In the *Troilus*, good and bad fortune affects lovers above all, not kings or civic agitators.

Chaucer also assimilates philosophy to love in the *Troilus*, most clearly in the love that consoles Troilus at the end of the poem. Translated "up to the holughnesse of the eighthe spere" and there "herkenyng armonye / With sownes ful of hevenyssh melodie" (5.1809, 5.1812–13), Troilus can appreciate the difference between human romance and divine love, that the one is transitory, because of human imperfection, while the other need not be. This is not to say that romance is without its joys or consolations, which Chaucer depicts feelingly, especially in the third book of the *Troilus*, often using quasi-religious terms. But for Troilus, following his bitter experience of the imperfection of human romance, with his apprehension of the heavenly harmony —the divine love that pervades the cosmos—he

> fully gan despise
> This wrecched world, and held al vanite
> To respect of the pleyn felicite
> That is in hevene above; . . .
>
> . . . .
> And dampned al oure werk that foloweth so,

---

[42]See McCall, "The Trojan Scene in Chaucer's *Troilus*," *ELH* 29 (1962): 263–75.

DAVID R. CARLSON

The blynde lust, the which that may nat laste,
And sholden al oure herte on heven caste.
(5.1816–19, 5.1823–25)

"Repeyreth hom fro worldly vanyte," Chaucer finally enjoins the
"yonge, fresshe folkes" in his audience; "and thynketh al nys but
a faire, / This world that passeth soone as floures faire" (5.1837,
1840–41). Christ, by contrast with a human lover like Criseyde,
can be constant:

For he nyl falsen no wight, dar I seye,
That wol his herte al holly on hym leye.
And syn he best to love is, and most meke,
What nedeth feynede loves for to seke?
(5.1845–48)

The relationship between religion and romance implied in
Chaucer's story of Troilus seems to be that of the tradition of
monastic theology, as represented by Hugh of St. Victor, for example, or the Cistercian Fathers: that once the possibilities of imperfect human love have been exhausted, by experience of its
limits and its failures and reflection on them, the soul must turn to
divine love for fulfillment, as Troilus sees at the end of Chaucer's
poem.[43] In the *Testament*, Love uses comparable terms to ex-

---

[43]See esp. Hugh's *Quid vere diligendum sit* 1.1–1.3, ed. R. Baron, *Hughes de
Saint-Victor: Six opuscules spirituels* (Paris, 1969); Bernard of Clairvaux, *De
diligendo Deo*, esp. 8.24 and 15.39, ed Jean Leclercq and H. M. Rochais, *S.
Bernardi Opera*, vol. 3 (Rome, 1963); and William of St. Thierry, *De natura et
dignitate amoris* 1–7 and *De contemplando Deo* 6–8, both ed. M.-M. Davy, in
Guillaume de Saint-Thierry: Deux traités de l'amour de Dieu (Paris, 1953).
Chaucer's friend John Clanvowe made the basic point repeatedly in his devotional
tract *The Two Ways*, ed. V. J. Scattergood, *The Works of Sir John Clanvowe*
(Cambridge, 1975), that divine love "shal not passe as worldy love dooth, but it
shal laste evere with outen ende" (lines 812–13; see also lines 28–35 and 422–44).

plain Usk's experience to him: reflection on the failure of his political involvement led him to look again to his higher, potentially more stable, love for Margarite and the Margarite-pearl, and to value it properly. Chaucer differs from Usk perhaps in linking romance with *Fortuna* and religion with *Philosophia* more regularly, whereas Usk's conception is more catholic, providing for sins and suffering in the course of a strictly religious love, and for the simply romantic consolations of love between human beings.

In neither Usk's *Testament* nor Chaucer's *Troilus* is the relationship between religion and romance spelled out in as much detail or in quite the same terms as it is in Dante's work. Nevertheless, the equation of romance and religion with which the *Testament* ends—"Charite is love, and love is charite"—echoes Troilus' exclamation "O Love, O Charite!" at the beginning of the hymn to "Benigne Love, thow holy bond of thynges" (3.1254– 74). In a passage from Chaucer's poem such as this account of the first night of love of Troilus and Criseyde, the conjunction of romantic experience and religious conception is such as to suggest that Chaucer, like Usk, was working with a concept that comprehended both religion and romance:

> Of hire delit or joies oon the leeste
> Were impossible to my wit to seye;
> But juggeth ye that han ben at the feste
> Of swich gladnesse, if that hem liste pleye!
> I kan namore, but thus thise ilke tweye
> That nyght, bitwixen drede and sikernesse,
> Felten in love the grete worthynesse.
>
> O blisful nyght, of hem so longe isought,
> How blithe unto hem bothe two thow weere!
> Why nad I swich oon with my soule ybought,
> Ye, or the leeste joie that was theere?
> Awey, thow foule daunger and thow feere,

And lat hem in this hevene blisse dwelle,
That is so heigh that al ne kan I telle!

(3.1310–23)[44]

The notion that even this night combines both "drede and siker-
nesse" suggests also how love can be both Fortune and Philosophy in the *Troilus*, as it is in the *Testament of Love*. Although, in
Chaucer and Usk, the love that mediates between lovers, between
God and creation, or between human beings, seems to be always
one love, Love's servants like Troilus and Usk, in an imperfect
world, are more or less imperfect in pursuing their desires, and so
find love to be at once Fortune and Philosophy.

The conceptions of love articulated in Usk's *Testament of Love*
and in Chaucer's *Troilus and Criseyde* are fundamentally similar,
then, and similarly devolve from a realignment of central concepts
of Boethius' *Philosophiae consolatio*: in the *Testament* and in the
Troilus, there is a single love, which comprehends both romance—
naturally the more inclined towards mutability—and religion—
likewise only imperfectly realized in this world but in the end the
ultimate consolation—and which thereby subsumes the functions
of both Boethius' Fortune and Boethius' Philosophy, inflicting
suffering on her servants when they love improperly and offering
consolation when they love well. Where Chaucer made narrative of
it, Usk personified and allegorized this common conception,
returning it to the setting of a Boethian fiction, of philosophical
dialogue between a sapiential figure and an imprisoned man.

Usk saw Chaucer's *Troilus* before finishing the *Testament*; he
must have been indebted to the *Troilus* for the reformulation of

---

[44]Usk's final equation comes at *Testament* 3.9.108. The long passage quoted
from the *Troilus* (3.1310–23) is discussed by Peter Dronke, "The Conclusion of
Troilus and Criseyde," *Medium Aevum* 33 (1964): 47–52, esp. 51.

Boethian ideas that he presents, much as he must have been more concretely indebted to Chaucer's *Boece* for his familiarity with the Boethian original. Usk may in fact have had a quadruple debt to Chaucer: for the nature of his *Troilus*-like reading of Boethius, in which an all-embracing love, both romance and religion, is also both fortune and philosophy; for a chance to use Boethius' *Philosophiae consolatio* in English translation; for the formal possibility of a non-devotional, English *Kunstprosa*, just then opened to persons like Usk by the unique precedent of Chaucer's *Boece*; and, finally, for the perversely political, anti-political bent of his writing, for the overt rejection of public action in favor of private, personal fulfillment that the *Testament* describes. Usk entered Chaucer's debt—however many the ways—for reasons of policy of his own, giving evidence by writing the *Testament* that he had abandoned politics, with its inevitable disruptions, for love-literature in the Chaucerian vein. Once he had betrayed Northampton, Usk's well-being, and then his life, depended on the favor of members of circles into which Chaucer and Chaucer's largely a-political writings had already come, into which Chaucer and Chaucerian writing might have helped Usk to advance. How successful Usk's literary effort was is impossible to gauge, there being no evidence; but probably it did not do him much good, as he did not live long after writing the *Testament*.

Gower moved in these same circles. By virtue of his intimacy with Chaucer and Chaucer's writings, Gower was well placed to perceive the Chaucerian aspirations of a piece like the *Testament of Love*, and to comment tellingly on them, perhaps even to the point of bidding Chaucer, ironically, to do what Usk had already essayed on Chaucer's behalf. But Gower's remark, particularly as it could be understood from early in the sixteenth century at the latest, combined with Thynne's attribution of the work to Chaucer and the acceptance of the attribution even after it was shown that the biographical data would not fit, all attest that much of the credit for the *Testament of Love* must be accrued to Chaucer himself. In its depiction of love, and the relations among love, politics, and literature, the *Testament* was in a nascent Chaucerian tradition—for good and for ill.

The Antwerp *Landjuweel* of 1561:
A Survey of the Texts

In the early afternoon of 3 August 1561, a spectacular procession entered Antwerp through the Keizerspoort, passing slowly to
the Grote Markt, where the *magistraten* of the city waited to receive the visitors. The tail of the procession reached the market
square twelve hours later, at about 2 a.m. According to contemporary reports, there were about 1400 horsemen, brilliantly clothed,
twenty-three *praalwagens* or exceptionally elaborate wagons with
scenes, and about two hundred other wagons, richly decorated;
also heralds, standard-bearers, trumpeters, drummers, footmen,
and children.

The occasion was a grand regional festival and competition of
theatrical rhetoric, or rhetorical drama, known as a *Landjuweel*
("regional jewel," referring to the prizes offered and, no
doubt—bearing in mind the participants' love of word-play—to
the presumed importance and quality of the occasion). The participants were members and associates of "chambers of rhetoric" of
Brabant, cultural societies drawn from the dominant groups of the
large and small towns of the Netherlands—master craftsmen, merchants, and entrepreneurs such as, at a somewhat later date, look
complacently at us from the group portraits of Frans Hals. By another word-play, members from these chambers were known as
rederijkers—a corruption of the French *rhétoriqueurs*, with the
convenient implication of *rijk aan rede*, "rich in expression."

The Antwerp *Landjuweel* was the seventh and most elaborate of a cycle of festivals of these chambers, starting at Mechelen in 1515 and continuing every seven years until that held in Diest in 1541. A twenty-year gap reflects a period of intermittent and disruptive warfare, and the 1561 event is presented as a celebration of peace and brotherhood; as the most important Antwerp chamber, *De Violieren* (violets), had been the leading prize winner at Diest, it was—as was the custom—their responsibility to organize and host the *Landjuweel* that followed.

Some of the preliminary documents and almost all the plays and other set pieces presented on this occasion were printed by "Willem Siluius" in the following year, in a commemorative volume edited by Willem van Haecht of *De Violieren*. This essay, a preliminary account of the 1561 event, is based largely on the van Haecht/Siluius volume, now in the Museum of Flemish Literature, Antwerp.[1]

The organizing began in proper fashion early in 1561. First, permission to hold the *Landjuweel* had to be requested of Philip II through his Regent, Margaret of Parma. In their letter, the Council of Antwerp points out that these festivals are "à grand prouffit des Villes et Franchises ou est le dict Landjuweel," and that the city hopes in this way to more than recoup the expenses incurred in taking part in the previous six festivals of the cycle. The identification of Antwerp's administration with the activities of the city's chambers of rhetoric is noteworthy—these events, and the regular annual processions or *ommegangen*, are to some extent used as a means of advertising the home-town as a suitable place for trade and investment, and the city administration helps to underwrite expenses.

---

[1] *Spelen van sinne vol scoone moralisacien wtleggingen ende bediedenissen*, etc. (Antwerp, 1562).

The letter to Philip also included, for his approval, a list of twenty-four possible topics for the *Spel van sinne*, or allegorical play (what has come in English to be called a "morality"), which was the most prestigious item in the *Landjuweels*. Philip—or his representative—turned down all those that might tend to political or religious controversy, and left the organizers to choose one of the following: (1) Which brings more wisdom: experience or learning? (2) What stimulates people most to practice the arts? (3) Why does a rich avaricious person desire more riches? Considering the traditional interests of the chambers, it is not surprising that, from among these rather unstimulating topics, they chose the second.

Philip also included in his reply a specific warning against dealing with matters of religion or making any comments that might tend to bring scorn or disrepute upon any of his servants or officers. Although peace had been declared and established, there was still considerable tension, with a strong but suppressed presence in the town of Lutherans, Calvinists, and Anabaptists. Indeed, within a few years religious and economic tensions would lead again to open conflict within the city, until a form of order was reimposed by imperial troops under the Duke of Alva.

Official sanction having been received, the next step in organizing the *Landjuweel* was to issue a formal invitation (the *Charte* or *Caerte*), in 143 lines of verse. This was sent to the large and small chambers in all the towns in the Duchy of Brabant. Citing the Apostles as a group of men who came together willingly and parted peacefully, the chamber of *De Violieren*, now flourishing in the time of peace, invited their brother artists (in a broad sense) to come to Antwerp for the love of Rhetoric. Each chamber would be expected to take part in or present the following items: the presentation on arrival, the entry, a banner with the chamber's device, a tableau to do with peace, a Prologue of two hundred lines on a set theme, an *Esbatement* or light-hearted play of four hundred to five hundred lines, the procession to church, followed by a new *Spel van Sinnen* more or less seven hundred lines long on the set theme mentioned above, and, finally, a *Factie*—a short cheerful play followed by a dance-song.

In noting each category and outlining the definition and requirements of each, the *Charte* also itemized the prizes: a variety of small silver figures designed by the Antwerp architect Cornelis Floris—a Saint Luke (patron saint of the *Violieren*), an ox (his animal), a violet, a garland of roses, etc. There would also be prizes for the best actor,

> Daer hen die toehoerders meest in verhueghen
> Met goey contenantien, en minst fauten smal.   (fol. Bi^b)

> (Who most pleases the spectators, with good facial expressions, with the fewest little mistakes);

also for the best *Sot* (Fool) *in woorden in wercken* (in words [and] in action). The *Charte* ends with the wish that all participants will behave as brothers and that, in particular, they will accept the results of the lottery that will decide the order in which the chambers are to appear.

Inserted as a fold-out plate in the volume (between fols. Div and Ei) is a *figure* that, we are told, was printed at the head of the invitations. Raised up in the center sits Retorica, holding a scroll in her left hand, with an olive branch in her right—her overall pose is strikingly reminiscent of Christ the Judge in representations of the Last Judgement. On the platform below her stand, on her right, Prudentia and, on her left, Inventio; Prudentia has a snake coiled about her right arm (wisdom) and a mirror in her left (self-knowledge); Inventio carries a large book (presumably representing authority and precedent) and a pair of compasses (indicating the craftsmanlike care required of the "rhetorician").

74

In the top corner of Retorica's right (the reader's left), LVX shines from a cloud, while in the opposite bottom corner TENE-BRAE is a pit emitting smoke. From the side of light, three figures approach the dais: PAX with an olive branch; CHARITAS with children, a dove on her hand and holding a flaming heart; and RATIO with a rod. Staggering despairingly towards the darkness are IRA, screaming and gesticulating; INVIDIA, directly balancing CHARITAS by literally "eating her heart out"; and DIS-CORDIA. Before the dais sits the winged ox of Saint Luke, crowned with the three violets of *De Violieren* and supporting a shield. Above and to each side of the dais are the arms of the Empire and of Antwerp. Large claims are implied here for the nature, influence, and central importance of rhetoric in the lives of individuals and of communities. The prerequisites for the practice of rhetoric are wisdom, self-knowledge, learning, and technical skill; and its consequences are so far-reaching that comparisons with the Day of Judgement are not thought to be hyperbolic.

In Silvius' commemorative volume, the *Charte* is preceded by an introduction *Totten goetwillighen Leser* (To the benevolent Reader) (Aii[b]–Aiv[a]). This introduction sets out to put *onse duvtse Retorijcke* (Our 'Dutch' Rhetoric) in an historical context. The writer praises the early native practitioners for their achievements, which came mainly from their inborn talents rather than from having learned anything from Greece and Rome. In order, however, to stimulate contemporary writers of plays (both edifying and entertaining) to even greater achievements, he proceeds to give an account of the origins and development of the classical forms and their physical settings, illustrated by a cutaway picture of an amphitheatre or *Theatrum*.

Coming to the present, the writer comments that wise princes have taken note that "no entries of great lords, festivals of shooting guilds (a characteristic feature of south Netherlands social life for centuries), ceremonious processions, annual church festivals, etc., are complete where the arts (i.e., of rhetoric, represented by the chambers) are lacking" (Aiv^a). This writer clearly recognizes and accepts as self-evidently desirable that public events of this kind, whatever their ostensible religious or cultural function, are to a considerable degree political or ideological instruments.

After the text of the *Charte* comes a description of the formal entry into Antwerp of the fourteen chambers of rhetoric participating in the *Landjuweel* itself (the chambers from the smaller towns took part in a *Haechspel*; see below). Using a typical freight of references to Apollo, the Muses, a new Parnassus arising in Antwerp, etc., the writer notes that the festivities include *Comedien / Ebatementen / Moralen als inde Poetijcsce punten* (allegorical representations in tableau form) / *Epigrammen baladen Retrograden* (verses that may be read both forward and backward) *en Deuijsen* (in this case, the elaborate pictorial devices representing the various chambers).

Apart from the hosts, *De Violieren*, the participating chambers in the *Landjuweel* are *De Goudbloeme* (marigold) of Antwerp; *De Olijftak* (olive branch), Antwerp; *Der Vreuchdenbloeme* (flower of joy), Bergen-op-Zoom; *Die Pionie* (peony), Mechelen; *Den Groeyende Boom* (the growing tree), Lier; *Die Lisbloeme* (iris), Mechelen; *De Cauwoerde* (gourd, colocynth), Herentals; *De Goudbloeme*, Vilvoorden; *Die Leliebloeme* (lily), Diest; *Die Lelikens wten Dale* (lily-of-the-valley), Sout-Leeuwen; *Die Christus ooghe* (Christ's-eye), Diest; *Die Roose* (rose), Leuven; *Den Vierighen Doern* (fiery thorn), S'Hertogenbosch; and *Het Marien Cransken* (Mary's Garland), Brussels.

Next there follows a description of the entry of the chambers into Antwerp (fols. Bii^b–Biv^a). The writer (in the first person) notes in each case the number of horsemen, their costume or livery, the wagons, and the characteristic saying of the Fool: e.g., the Fool of *De Violieren, Ick ben soo fray ick en kenne my seluen niet* (I'm so frisky I don't know myself). Most of the wagons are referred to as being *opt antijcx* (in the antique style); one of the most elaborate wagons was that of *Die Pionie*, Mechelen:

> seuen welghecierde antijxe speelwaghens met personagien / waer af dleste punt soo constich ende excellentelijck ghemaect ende toegherust was / datment onghepresen niet en behoort voorby te gaen / wesende eenen os daer eenen S. Lucas op sat / . . . S. Jan Euangelist met sijnen arent beneuen hem / noch sesthien andere hubsche waghens bouen viercant ghemaect seer plasantelijck / elcx verciert met viii diueersse schoone blasoenkens / ouerdect met root laken / ende Guldebroeders daerop houdende een paer toortssen / ende vierpannen achter uit stekende. . . .

> (seven well-decorated antique-style playing-wagons with [allegorical] personages, of which the last tableau was so skillfully and excellently presented and fitted out that one ought not to leave it unpraised, being an ox with a St. Luke sitting upon it and St. John the Evangelist with his eagle; another sixteen fine wagons made square above very attractively, each adorned with eight different scutcheons, draped in red cloth; and guild-brothers on [each] holding a pair of [hand-] torches, and [larger] torches sticking out at the rear. . . .)

There follows (fol. Biv[b]) a summary of the leisurely but ceremonious preliminary proceedings. On 4 August, the day after the formal entry, lots are drawn to decide upon the order of playing; this is done in the presence of the chief men of the town and the *Hooftmannen / Princen / Dekens / ende facteurs* of the chambers (the *facteur / factor* of a chamber was the stage-master, organizer and chief writer, usually employed on contract).

On 5 August, the chambers took part in a *solemnelen ende figuerlijcken kerkganck* (a ceremonious procession to church, with emblematic/allegorical shows); and, in the afternoon, *De Violieren* put on a play of welcome (see details below). On the 6th, the Fool of the *Violieren* invited the Fools of the other chambers to join him on the *scena oft speelhuys* (scena or playhouse; see below), to come and drink *de langste toghe* (the longest swig—apparently a comical drinking competition), and where they also "carried out and presented many ridiculous farcical actions (*cluchten*)."

On 8 August, the *Olijftak* of Antwerp presented the first *spel van sinne* with their answer to the set question, "What is it that most stimulates people to practice the arts?" Their answer was *Den gheest God's* (the spirit of God). For the convenience of the reader, all the answers of the chambers (in effect, the titles of their longer allegorical plays) are listed at this point, including "love," "truth," "hope of undying glory in heaven and on earth," etc.

On the facing page (Ci^a) appears *De figure van tSpeeltanneel*, a picture of the playing space that was the setting for most of the official activities of the *Landjuweel*. It consists of a raised stage with, at the rear, a structure explicitly based on the classical *scena*: divided horizontally in the proportion of 2:1 (lower:upper), with three openings (separated by pilasters) below and above, both central openings being curtained. Above the upper level is inscribed the motto of *De Violieren, wt ionsten versaemt* (gathered together out of goodwill), and above that sits Rhetoric within a circle inscribed with the vowels A E I O V. This stage was set up *op die groote merct* (in the great marketplace; fol. Bii^b).

There follows a list of prizes: for *tschoonste ende triumph-antste incomen* (the finest and most spectacular entry), a prize each for the best of the larger towns and of the smaller ones; *tfiguerlijcste ende dmoralijcst incomen bediedende "hoe datmen wt Ionsten sal versamen ende minnelijck scheyden"* (the most expressive and effectively moralized/allegorized entry explaining "how people shall gather together out of goodwill and part lovingly"); the *schoonste Blasoen oft deuijse* (finest scutcheon or device); the *schoonsten ende solemnelijcsten kerkganck* (the finest and most ceremonious church-going); the *schoonste en triumphantste vieren* (the finest and most spectacular "celebration"—this refers to the decoration of the inns in which the various chambers were separately lodged[2]); *beste Ebatement*; the *spel van sinne*; *de Prologhe / inde welck ghestelt wort "Hoe orboirlijck den menschen sijn, Cooplieden die rechtueerdelijck handelen"* (the Prologue, in which is put forward "How profitable to people are merchants who act justly"); *de beste personagie* (best performance by an actor); *'t Poëtijckelijck punt* (poetical allegory); and *innocentelijcst oft onnooselijcst den sot te maken* (most naively or stupidly playing the fool).

The preliminary material in the volume continues (Ci[b]–Cii[a]) with—under the *blasoen* of *De Violieren*—a fourteen-line "retrograde" in which, phrase by phrase, each line may be read forward or backward. This is a poem of welcome as from the Prince of the host chamber, Melchior Schets, and its headman, Stralen. The device and poem were printed and "strewn in great numbers at the time of the entry of the chambers and also at the time of performances during the whole festival." The retrograde also "stood written in large capital letters on the gallery of the *Heeren* (prominent persons, VIPs), and was read in various ways." The hosts were clearly proud of this piece of high artifice, which began with a play on the motto of *De Violieren* and ended with the first of many couplings of *Ionste* (goodwill) and *Conste* (art, skill), suggesting that the practice of rhetoric plays an important part in the establishment and maintenance of peace (cf. the olive-branch and scroll held by Rhetoric in the picture on the *Charte*).

The play of welcome followed the entry, the drawing of lots,

---

[2]J. J. Mak, *De Rederijkers* (Amsterdam, 1944), p. 95.

and the churchgoing, and was put on by *De Violieren* on the afternoon of 5 August. It begins with a substantial prologue: three nymphs (clad in white, red, and purple, and carrying violets of these colors) decide it is time to seek out Retorica; they find her in a cold swoon but protected in the lap of Antwerpia; they appeal to Pallas, Apollo, and Mercury, each of whom in turn throws down an arrow from the clouds, respectively Sciencia, Inventia, and Eloquentia (*stralen*, "arrows," is a play on the name of the chamber's *Hooftman*). Retorica is aroused from her cold and moribund state by the warmth of the arrows (*stralen* may also mean "rays," but they are clearly shown as arrows in the accompanying illustration), but she eventually speaks only in response to one of the nymphs thanking God.

After thanking Antwerpia and the *Violierkens* for keeping her alive, Retorica asks what year it is and comments that she has been in great sickness for twenty years (that is, since the last *Landjuweel* in Diest in 1541). Antwerpia points to the *ghereetscappe excellent* ("excellent tools," glossed in the margin as *Mechanische instrumenten*) with which she has been active in the meantime (few opportunities are missed to point out Antwerp's economic busyness). As a sign of gratitude Retorica presents Antwerpia with a treasure-chest, the *schat der Rhetorijcken*, and takes up residence with her. The nymphs conclude the prologue by welcoming all the participating chambers by name.

The play of welcome itself now follows, preceded by a note to the reader explaining the appropriateness of the subject matter. After noting that the chamber organizing the *Landjuweel* is permitted to compete for the highest prize (*De Violieren* did not do so on this occasion), he goes on to say:

> om dat zy opt seuenste doordeel niet alleen en heeft / kiest-
> men van elcke Camere eenen of twee Facteurs oft Compon-
> isten diet oordeelen op haren eedt ende en is daer om den

oordelaers het oordeel van Tmolus tusschen Apollo ende den
veltgodt Pan niet voorghehouden geweest / sonder oorsake.

(so that they should not make judgements on their own on the
seventh [festival], one or two Factors or Composers are chos-
en from each Chamber, who judge on their oath, and it is
therefore not without cause that the judgement of Tmolus between Apollo and Pan, god of the wilds, was presented.)

This lively piece, written by Willem van Haecht, is in three
scenes. Pan, speaking coarsely and egotistically, insists on a contest with the courteous and eloquent Apollo. Tmolus is unable to
dissuade Pan, and presides over the contest, observed by *Bot*
(Bud), *Ruyt* (Reed), and Midas, uncritical supporters of Pan, and
by *Oprecht Verstandt* (Upright Understanding). Apollo is adjudged the winner, and Midas expresses his disgust and disagreement, then finds that he has sprouted ass's ears (on these stages,
one of the traditional appurtenances of the Fool). Then follows a
longer comic scene of Midas at the barber's, trying to get a hair-
cut without displaying his ears. In the short final scene, Understanding, supported by the chastened Bud, suggests to the assembled *rederijkers* and others that, unlike Midas, they should be dis-
criminating spectators. The play therefore entertainingly offers advice to the spectators, to practitioners of the art of rhetoric (the
crudely "natural" behavior and performance of Pan is contrasted
with the polished and eloquent craftsmanship of Apollo), and to
the judges (Tmolus' fairness and courtesy are exemplary) in the
competition that is about to get under way.

Before that can happen, however, there is yet another tone-
setting preliminary, in the form of a dramatic Prologue, also written by van Haecht for the *Violieren*. As the set theme for the Prologues to be put on in the competition is the praise of the just
merchant, the *Violieren* will present a Prologue *tot lof der Ouer-*

heyt / des Eersamen Raedts / ende der goeder Ghemeynten (in praise of the [imperial] Authority/Lordship, the honorable Council [of Antwerp] and the worthy citizenry). This piece is not a drama, but a carefully constructed three-part oration on the ideal balance of power and consequent peace and prosperity. This ideal collaboration is emphasized in the choice of names (*Beminde Ouerheydt*, "Beloved Authority"; *Wijsen Raet*, "Wise Council/Counsel"; *Goetwillighe Ghemeynte*, "Well-disposed Citizenry"); in the content (the appeal to classical and other examples, good and bad, and to the topos of the "body politic"); and in the medium itself (in much of the piece, the personages speak in incomplete sentences that need to be completed through the collaboration—in patterns of rhyme and rhythm—of one or more of their colleagues; this feature is not uncommon in *rederijker* plays, but is especially appropriate here).

On the 6 and 7 August were the Fools' Day and the welcoming banquet, and the competition itself began on the 8th. But not quite: the two other Antwerp chambers, *De Olijftak* and *De Goudbloeme*, appeared first, after agreement had been reached that only the *buyten Cameren* (chambers from outside) would be eligible for the prize for the *spel van sinne*; they *hebben alleen ter eeren der stadt van Antwerpen ende wt liefde hen spelen eerst ende voor dandere gheexhibeert* (only put on their plays first and before the others in honor of the city of Antwerp and out of love).

The printed volume includes in these two cases the texts of the *Presentacie* (with the accompanying device); the *spel van sinnen* and the *Prologhe* (printed *after* the main allegorical play). The other twelve chambers also presented a *poetijckelijk punt* (with a full-page illustration in each case) and a *Factie*. There is no sign or mention of the *Esbatementen* (light-hearted pieces) after the *Charte* and the list of prizes in the preliminary documents (which notes that six prizes were awarded to the *Esbate-*

menten, more than for any other category). Kruyskamp, noting that the *Facties* are not mentioned in the prize-list but *are* printed, suggests three possible explanations for the omission of the texts of the *Esbatementen*: they were played, but were disapproved of by the authorities; they were played, but the award of prizes caused disagreement among the chambers; they were not played, and the prizes were given to the *Facties* instead.[3]

Let us now finally consider the dramatic and other pieces that were presented in the above categories on this occasion, starting with the *Presentacie*. Each chamber presents the hosts, *De Violieren*, with a banner or device (illustrated in the volume), which will be hung up in the *Violieren*'s regular meeting-room; the presentation of the banner is accompanied by the recitation of a *refrein* in a set form: four thirteen-line stanzas, each using four rhymes in various acceptable combinations (i.e., variations on the rondel form), the fourth stanza being addressed to the "Prince"—in this case, appropriately the traditional title of the patron of the chamber. These poems point out and interpret the important features of the visiting chamber's device, and express their joy at being gathered together in peace in the name of Rhetoric. Most of them incorporate and expand upon a version of *De Violieren*'s motto *Wt Ionste Versaemt*, "gathered together out of goodwill."

The *poetijckelijk punt* is also a combination of the visual and the written or recited, but on a more elaborate scale. A *punt* (literally "point") is in effect a moral, religious, or political statement in the form of a tableau or dumb-show, scriptural or allegorical, such as were presented by chambers of rhetoric as part of the annual *omnegangen* or processions. Such tableaux on wagons are referred to in van Haecht's description of the Entry, and the *punt* entered by a

---

[3]C. Kruyskamp, *Het Antwerpse Landjuweel van 1561* (Antwerp, 1962), p. xv.

chamber in this category of the competition was most probably presented on a wagon; each chamber put this on *voor zijn logijs . . .*
sdaechs eer zy speelden / waer af zy den sin ende bediedinghe met
vier xiiij regulen pronuncieerden (outside their lodging . . . as the
first item on the day they played, the meaning and significance of
which they recited in four fourteen-line stanzas).

To judge from the illustrations in the printed volume, each
punt in the competition was "framed" within a small stage, ac-
commodating about half a dozen *personagien*. Some, however,
appear to be larger—the *punt* of the Brussels *Marie Cransken* appears to require a stage of double width, while that of the *Pioen*
bloeme of Mechelen is exceptionally high, to accommodate the
large tree under which Orpheus is sitting. Some are quite simple
in their presentation, while others—such as those of the *Marie*
Cransken and the *Lelie van Dalen* of Sout-Leeuwen, are visually
complex and crowded and may have been a combination of
human actors, models, and painted cloths.

The first prize for the *poetelijck punt* on this occasion went to
Sout-Leeuwen for a detailed presentation on the nature and conditions of Concordia and Discordia. The visual complexity of this
punt is recognized in the accompanying verses, which take the
form of a dialogue in which speaker A comments that *Tdunct my*
een bedietsel van vremde manieren (it seems like a strange busi-
ness to me).

After the *punt*, each chamber presented its *Spel van sinne* and
Prologhe, each on its set theme. The themes are abstract, suiting
the allegorical mode so highly valued by the *rederijkers*, and were
played on the official *Speeltanneel* in the Great Market to an audience that would have included non-members and passers-by, as
well as visiting guildsmen. Within this very broad and elastic
genre of allegorical drama, however, the plays collected here
show a considerable range in theatricality and dramatic interest, in
tone and in clarity or subtlety of argument.

The chamber of Sout-Leeuwen won the prize for the *Prologhe* with a clever and eloquent piece that presents Christ as the *Rechtueerdich Coopman*, or Just Merchant, who brings his ship full of spiritual food to the aid of *Behoeflijcke nature*, Needy Nature, and who ends by appealing to the many just merchants of *dese stadt* (this city) to carry out their functions to the benefit of the materially poor.

The *Spel van sinne* put on by *De Roose* of Leuven was adjudged the best in this most prestigious category. In a dramatic "frame," Longing Heart is desperate to know the answer to the set question—"What is it that most stimulates mankind to practice the arts?"—and is consoled by the spirit of Wisdom, in the shape of an angel carrying Mercury's winged scepter, who shows him the answer in *figuerlijck* form: Mankind, a young man, is awakened and urged to practice the arts by Natural Inclination and Desire to Know; but he drives Labor away and falls into idleness until he is rescued by Hope of High Position and Fear of Bad Name, who show him a convincing dumb-show in which Honor, enthroned, is surrounded by Philosophers, Poets, Ambassadors, and other honorable persons. The answer to the question is *Lot eere ende prijs* (Praise, honor, and commendation). The fall and recovery of the central character is, of course, the basic shape of "moralities," and the theme and treatment in this case are generally reminiscent of John Redford's *Wit and Science* (1541).

The *Charte* (fol. Bi^a) announced that the *Facties* would be played *Achter straten. . . met een vrolijck rellen* (on the street. . . with cheerful chatter); this is confirmed in the *Factie* of the Diest chamber *De Christus ooghen* (Aaaii^a), when *Thooft vol sorghen* (Head full of cares) comments that there are at the festival

> Veel wonderlijcke vreemde sotte bollen
> Wt alle plaetsen om te spelen haer rollen
> Al ist op gheen stellagie

(many wonderful and strange fools from everywhere, to play
their roles, even if it isn't on a stage).

These short pieces include, among others, a condensed morality (Vi-
voorden), a light-hearted pastoral (Sout-Leeuwen), a pleasant farce
('sHertogenbosch), and an amusing fantasy (Diest). They are all
immediately followed by songs, with direct address to the audience.
Indeed, direct address is frequent in all the dramatic categories.

The *Landjuweel* was brought to an end on 23 August with the
prizegiving and a play of farewell by *De Violieren*, involving Antwerpia, Retorica, Musica, *Menich constich gheest* (Many skillful
spirits), and *Minnelijck scheyden* (friendly parting). Retorica and
Musica consent to stay on in Antwerp for the *Haechspel* that is
about to follow, also hosted by *De Violieren*. The *Haechspel*,
which began with the formal entry on 24 August, was arranged on
similar lines to the *Landjuweel*, and was intended to be *van
minder costen / maer niet altijt van minder conste* (of less
expense, but not always of less artistry), for the benefit of the
smaller chambers, four of whom took part on this occasion. The
texts—again excluding the *Esbatementen*—are also printed in the
commemorative volume.

After more than a month of feasts, processions, recitations,
dramatized idealism, and street-level farce, *De Violieren* wish a
safe journey to the last of their guests, repeating the refrain that
the arts of rhetoric are stronger than envy and discord, and that
Altijt verdrijft sy gramschap / daer sy logeert wel (she always
drives out anger, where she is well established). Brave words, but
this was the last *juweel* of any standing. Never an institution in
the northern Netherlands, this kind of festive competition was
never again, even in the south, to enjoy the esteem and the wide
public of the 1561 Antwerp event. War, religious strife, economic
uncertainties, and changing tastes were, in the end, more than a
match for Retorica in these forms.

From Text to Text and From Tale to Tale: Jean Froissart's *Prison amoureuse*

LAURENCE DE LOOZE

If Guillaume de Machaut is considered the greatest French poet of the fourteenth century, surely Jean Froissart, though remembered today primarily for his prose *Chronicles*, holds second place. First among Machaut's disciples, Froissart is both very similar to and very different from his mentor. In a series of major courtly *dits*, which includes, above all, the *Espinette amoureuse*, the *Prison amoureuse*, and the *Joli Buisson de Jonece*, Froissart reworks the clerkly stance of Machaut's narrators.[1] Whereas Machaut depicted the difficulty of combining the crafts of poetry and love, Froissart, especially in the *Espinette amoureuse*, portrays the two as mutually exclusive. In Froissart, the courtly poet puts his craft in the service of his patron rather than of love. As Daniel

---

[1] All three have been well edited by Anthime Fourrier, who dates the *dits* as follows: the *Espinette amoureuse* (ed. Fourrier [Paris, 1972]; hereafter EA) between 1365 and 1371; the *Prison amoureuse* (ed. Fourrier [Paris, 1974]) late 1371–early 1372; and the *Joli Buisson de Jonece* (ed. Fourrier [Geneva, 1975]; hereafter JB) sometime after 30 November, 1373. In the *Joli Buisson de Jonece* Froissart himself lists his major poetic works as follows: "Voirs est q'un livret fis jadis / Qu'on dist *l'Amoureus Paradis* / Et ossi celi del *Orloge*, / Ou grand part del art d'Amours loge; / Apriés, *l'Espinete amoureuse*, / Qui n'est pas al oÿr ireuse; / et puis *l'Amoureuse Prison*" (lines 443–49). Some critics would be inclined also to include the *Paradis d'amours* among the list of Froissart's principal *dits*.

Poirion has elegantly observed, Froissart is willing to sing of summer in the middle of winter if his patron willed it.[2]

My focus in this essay is the *Prison amoureuse*. I argue that in it Froissart puts forth the process of literary composition as a potentially endless cycle of intertextual rewriting, one which includes both what we now consider "creative" and what we label "critical." Derivative of Machaut's *Voir Dit* yet central in every way to Froissart's literary corpus, the *Prison amoureuse* tells of a correspondence between the narrator Flos (evocative of Froissart) and his patron Rose (evocative of Wenceslas of Luxemburg), who consults him on an amorous matter. As in the *Voir Dit*, letters and poems exchanged between the two correspondents form the scaffolding for the narrative whole. We also find the sort of thematization of bookmaking that figures so prominently in Machaut's *Voir Dit*: just as in the *Voir Dit* the narrator is ordered to write the *Voir Dit* by his correspondent, Toute-belle, so in the *Prison amoureuse* the narrative is made into a book at the request of the narrator's patron, Rose. Also in Froissart's work, as in Machaut's, the correspondents exchange not only letters but poems along with them.

Despite these similarities, there are considerable differences between Froissart's *Prison* and Machaut's *Voir Dit*, as Anthime Fourrier noted in the introduction to his edition of the *Prison amoureuse*. First, both correspondents in the *Prison* are men. Thus, what Fourrier calls "une banale histoire d'amour" in Machaut's *Voir Dit* is turned, in Froissart, into an "amitié littéraire."[3] Froissart no longer feels himself obliged to associate *ars poetica* and *ars amoris*, and the love interest therefore recedes greatly.

---

[2]Daniel Poirion, *Le Poète et le prince* (Paris, 1965), p. 210.

[3]*Prison amoureuse*, ed. Fourrier, p. 16. All textual citations are from this edition. Verses are cited by line number; letters are cited by letter number, followed by line number, then page number. All translations are my own.

88

The most marked difference between Froissart's *Prison* and Machaut's *Voir Dit*, however, is the way in which the *Prison* thematizes not only bookmaking and writing, as did Machaut, but also the processes of interpretation and glossing—what today we would call "literary criticism."[4] Froissart presents literature as deeply hermeneutic and as necessarily intertextual. As will be the case in his subsequent writing of chronicles, everything depends not on the basic events (which in the chronicle are already given by history and, in the *Prison amoureuse*, greatly determined by the model, the *Voir Dit*) but on the interpretation given them. Douglas Kelly has quite rightly argued that "the structure [of the *Prison amoureuse*] resembles to an extraordinary degree the fine interlocking of adventure, vision, and exposition in the *Queste del saint graal*," with the result that "one must regard Flos' exposition as one does the hermits' interpretations in the *Queste del saint graal*."[5] The salient difference is, of course, that whereas in the *Queste* there is always a right and a wrong interpretation, in the *Prison amoureuse* Froissart argues for a multiplicity of equally plausible readings. Nevertheless, I would concur with Kelly and argue here, as I have elsewhere with respect to the *Queste*, that the explications *are* the story as much as, and perhaps more than, the events they seem to explicate.[6]

Whereas Guillaume de Machaut—in such works as the *Voir Dit*, the *Remede de Fortune*, and the *Jugement* poems—tended to portray

---

[4]On the function of "glossing" in the *Prison amoureuse* see also the complementary discussion by Claire Nouvet, "Pour une économie de la dé-limitation: La *Prison amoureuse* de Jean Froissart," *Neophilologus* 70 (1986): 341–56, esp. 344–46.

[5]Douglas Kelly, *Medieval Imagination: Rhetoric and the Poetry of Courtly Love* (Madison, Wis., 1978), pp. 155 and 163.

[6]Laurence N. de Looze, "A Story of Interpretations: the *Queste del Saint Graal* as Metaliterature," *Romanic Review* 76 (1985): 129–47, esp. 133–34.

himself as having, at best, limited success with women, Froissart portrays himself as having none whatsoever. In both the *Prison amoureuse* and his earlier *Espinette amoureuse*, Froissart's first-person narrator is not merely a feeble lover; he is no lover at all. It is perhaps no surprise, then, that in his last great courtly *dit*, *Le Joli buisson de jonece*, Froissart makes what Michelle Freeman has called a "farewell to poetry" that is, at the same time, a farewell to erotic love and a turning toward *caritas*.[7] In the *Prison amoureuse* itself he depicts the narrator as jealous not because the lady he wants may have other men but because she might have other (men's) poems; he is miffed when she sings another's *virelay* (421–80).

This comical vexation announces one of the dominant concerns of the *Prison amoureuse*: how to control the dissemination and distribution of the literary text. One aspect of this concern is an obsession with closure—textual, thematic, and physical. Another is a deep awareness that literary creation flourishes between the two extremes of the text that is not disseminated and the text whose dissemination is subject to no controls. Here Froissart again evokes Machaut's *Voir Dit*, in which the narrator tries to maintain a certain openendedness in constructing a "livre ou je met toutes mes choses" yet laments uncontrolled dissemination.[8] For example, Machaut's narrator rails that he cannot pull his life together while his life-works manuscript is in more than twenty pieces.[9]

---

[7]Michelle A. Freeman, "Froissart's *Le Joli Buisson de Jonece*: A Farewell to Poetry?" in *Machaut's World: Science and Art in the Fourteenth Century*, ed. Madeleine Pelner Cosman and Bruce Chandler (New York, 1978), pp. 235–47.

[8]Paulin Paris, ed., Guillaume de Machaut, *Le Livre du Voir-Dit* (1875; repr. Geneva, 1969), p. 259.

[9]". . . mais il est en plus de .xx. pieces" (Paris, p. 69; discussed in Sarah Jane Williams, "An Author's Role in Fourteenth-Century Book Production: Guillaume de Machaut's 'livre ou je met toutes mes choses'," *Romania* 90 [1969]: 442–43).

As if to emphasize this tension between too-tight closure and openendedness bordering on lack of order, many of the major scenes of narrative composition and interpretation in the *Prison amoureuse* take place within the open-ended space of a lay. After Flos has written the first three sections of the lay, the composition is interrupted by the arrival of the book of Rose's dream that Rose has written. Flos proceeds to write a gloss on the dream and only after a period of many months and over a thousand verses of poetry interspersed with letters does he return to finish the remaining nine sections of the lay. Moreover, Froissart cleverly allows the length of time it takes Flos to write this lay to evoke the length of time it took to write the *Prison amoureuse* story; having mentioned a nine-month silence on the part of Flos, Froissart makes his oft-quoted pronouncement that a lay took six months to write.[10]

The acts of writing books and enclosing them in glosses take place within the confines of two halves of a lay, which is part of a larger reflection on closure and enclosure, both literary and literal. Froissart evinces an awareness that one must strike a balance between the text so tightly enclosed that it cannot be opened and the work so open that dissemination is uncontrolled. The concern is a recurrent one in the fourteenth century. Dante, for example, ends his *Commedia* with the vision that the quires of his book will be drawn together in one volume bound by love, so that the leaves will not be lost.[11] Machaut also depicted the fear of

---

[10]"D'un lay faire c'est .I. grans fes, / Car qui l'ordonne et rieule et taille / Selonc ce que requiert la taille, / Il y faut, ce dient li mestre, / Demi an ou environ mettre" (To make a lay is a great feat, for he who composes, or orders, or forms it, according to what its form requires, he needs, as the experts say, half a year or thereabouts; 2199–2203).

[11]"Nel suo profondo vidi che s'interna, / legato con amore in un volume, / ciò che per l'universo si squaderna. . ." (Dante Alighieri, *The Divine Comedy*, ed. and trans. Charles S. Singleton, vol. 3, *Paradiso* [Princeton, 1975], 33.85–87).

uncontrolled dissemination in the *Voir Dit*: as his life came apart
so did his manuscript, parts of it circulating separately or being
reproduced without authorization.[12] Chaucer too will admonish
his *scriveyn* not to take liberties with his texts.[13]

In the *Prison amoureuse* the superabundance of *coffrets*,
folios, envelopes, sacks, and tomes into which letters, poems, and
manuscripts are put is itself notable. Though indicative of daily
realia, this literal *emboîtement* of texts, and Froissart's repeated
mention of it, also draws our attention to the text-within-a-text
structure that characterizes the *Prison amoureuse* as a whole. In
fact, the book becomes a kind of super-*coffret*, containing within
it all the poems and letters as well as the many *coffrets* of the
story. Significantly, the final book of the *Prison amoureuse* will
not be placed in a container when it is sent. Froissart's only worry
is that perhaps, after having worked so hard on the book, his
"painne ne fust veüe" (labor might not be seen; 3894)—a reference that could refer either to the danger of loss (lack of enclosure, random dissemination) or to the failure to open the work
(the prison, the *coffret*).[14]

If the danger of enclosure is that what is enclosed may never

---

[12]The *Voir Dit* narrator twice makes reference to his lords' pressure to see
excerpts from his correspondence with Toute-belle (Paris, pp. 189 and 202); when
the manuscript of the *Voir Dit* is in Toute-belle's possession he specifically asks
"que vous le monstrez à meins de gens que vous pourrez" (ibid., p. 276).

[13]"Chaucers Wordes unto Adam, His Owne Scriveyn," in Larry D. Benson, ed.,
The Riverside Chaucer, 3d ed. (Boston, 1987), p. 650.

[14]Moreover, there is an equivalence established between the composition of the
lay and the composition of the *Prison amoureuse* at Rose's order. A lay, Froissart
tells us, takes six months to compose; this is precisely how long Rose gives Flos to
compile the *Prison amoureuse*: "je vous donne jour que dou faire .VI. mois apriés
le datte de ches lettres" (To do it I am giving you six months from the date of
these letters; Letter X, 26–28, 164).

be seen, its extreme opposite is also evoked by Froissart. Like Guillaume de Machaut, who depicted the dangers of uncontrolled dissemination in the *Voir Dit* through the narrator's disquietude regarding the component letters floating among the nobility, Froissart also depicts the act of despoiling an author of his texts, but in a somewhat different way. The tension between poet and public takes on sexual overtones in Froissart and hints at the sort of conflict between male and female that he developed in detail in his earlier *Espinette amoureuse*. In a scene often praised as an example of "medieval realism," the *Prison amoureuse* narrator comes across his Lady out for a walk. As he chats with her, she and her maidens open a sack that hangs from his belt and rob him of Rose's letters and poems. Whether anecdotal or not, this scene adheres to a code of the eroticized literary work: text elides sex as the "stripping" (pointedly enough, the verb used is *desrober*, 1107) of the narrator becomes purely literary, a textual emasculation. Opening the narrator's "pouch" causes an unintended dissemination of the texts he carries and the spilling of distinctly literary seed; the scene ends with the Lady cutting a poem away from the missive that contains it—castration, if you will, at the level of lettricity.

The *Prison amoureuse* thus is strung between two poles: at one extreme *(en)closure*, which implies the unseen, hidden, inaccessible, and at the other extreme complete *openness*, with its connotations of dissemination and the dangers of indiscriminate scattering. Concern over the enclosed or disseminated textual selves is surely a reflection of the most obvious instance of enclosure in the whole work: Rose's captivity in prison. The prison is interpreted allegorically, however, as nothing other than Rose's estrangement from his Lady (Letter IX, 61–64, 152)—in other words, as the *Roman de la Rose*, but with the man having become the "rose" this time. For what was the *Roman de la Rose* about if not the forcing open of a closed tower in which a rose was imprisoned? This association is strengthened by Rose's own dream in the *Prison amoureuse*. Already in prison, he dreams that he is put in prison by allegorical personages—a dream in which he thus effectively becomes the Rose of the *Roman de la Rose* and which repeats yet again the *emboîtement* technique so central to the Froissartian work as a whole.

Froissart might then be said to retranslate the "poetics of propagation" that Jean de Meun set forth in his section of the *Roman de la Rose* back into a realm of purely literary potency. If storming the tower that holds the *Roman*'s Rose symbolizes sexual intercourse and hints at the promise of offspring, for Froissart the opening of objects that enclose literary texts—whether *sacoche*, *coffret*, or *livre*—promotes the begetting of literary offspring, that is, new poetic works. The price of this literary propagation is, however, a cutting away, a castration, the very elision, in other words, of sexuality. In this light, Froissart's *Prison amoureuse* is ideologically as well as chronologically perfectly situated midway between his *Espinette amoureuse* and the *Joli Buisson*. In the former work the narrator's beloved makes clear her lack of interest in the narrator's love suit by ripping a patch of hair from his head, a mock-tonsuring with overtones of castration; and the latter work closes, as mentioned previously, by overtly substituting Christian *caritas* for erotic *cupiditas*.

What we witness in Froissart's works, then, is a major shift in mentality from the insistence, which dates back to the troubadours and classical poets, on an association of erotic talent and poetic craft. The alliance between procreation and literary creation that an author such as Jean de Meun was so concerned to maintain gives way in Froissart to a conscious *elision* of the former in favor of the latter. A cycle of purely literary propagation is privileged, divorced now from any myth of the writer's sexual fecundity. As Chaucer will also do, Froissart depicts poet-personages as finding their inspiration not in their ladies' eyes but in books, particularly old ones.

Nowhere is this bookish stance more in evidence than in Froissart's formation of new narratives from Ovidian materials. In the *Prison amoureuse* it is Rose who charges Flos with the composition

> d'un petit dittié amoureus, qui se traitast sus aucune nouvelle matere qu'on n'aroit onques veü ne oÿ mise en rime, tele com, par figure, fu jadis de Piramus et de Tysbé, ou de Eneas et de Dido, ou de Tristran et de Yseus. . . .
>
> (Letter V, 44–48, 82)

> (of a little *dittié* about love that would treat of some new matter that one had never seen or heard put into rhyme, such as, for example, was formerly [made] about Piramus or Thisbe or Aeneas and Dido, or Tristan and Iseut. . . .)[15]

The composition of this *dittié* reflects in miniature the view of poetic composition that Froissart proclaimed in the opening lines of the *Prison amoureuse* and that Daniel Poirion has seen as emblematic of Froissart's view: the poetic process as service to one's lord.[16] At the beginning of the *Prison amoureuse* the lord whom Froissart obeys is the God of Love; here, however, Flos obeys a more earthly patron. Like Froissart's Flos, Flos' own protagonist,

---

[15]This passage displays, self-consciously, an awareness of what we would call the intertextual nature of all literary creation in the very fact that some *new* matter that had never been seen or heard of before should nevertheless be seen as a reworking of elements already familiar from pre-existing narratives.

[16]"Je voel servir de franc voloir / Celi qui tant me poet valoir, / A cui j'ai fait de liet corage / Seüreté, foi et hommage: / Amours, mon signeur et mon mestre" (23–27; see also 5–8).

LAURENCE DE LOOZE

Pynoteüs, is himself a poet and an amalgamation of both Pygmalion and Orpheus. The *bricolage* technique that characterizes Froissart's manner of working up a poetic narrative also characterizes Flos' work. Flos/Froissart creates a patchwork narrative out of Ovid's tales of Pyramus and Thisbe, Pygmalion, Orpheus, and others.[17]

Pynoteüs, a young poet, is in love with Neptisphelé and she with him. When she is devoured by a lion (Pynoteüs finds only her belt and bloodstains) he convokes all the beasts and threatens them with death should the guilty party not come forward. The lion declares itself responsible and gets devoured in turn by the other beasts. But this punishment does not, of course, restore Neptisphelé to life, for which reason Pynoteüs, after considering and then rejecting an Orphean descent into hell, fashions an *ymage* of his beloved to which Phoebus gives the kiss of life in answer to Pynoteüs' prayers.

It is worthwhile to consider some of the ways the Froissartian obsession with *emboîtement* and enclosure of the work comes into play again here. As evidence of the quantitative importance of the Ovidian tale and the subsequent interpretations it is given,

---

[17]See the seminal essay by Douglas Kelly, "Les Inventions ovidiennes de Froissart: réflexions intertextuelles comme imagination," *Littérature* 41 (1981): 82–92, to which I am greatly indebted. Also useful to me have been: Kevin Brownlee, "Ovide et le Moi poétique 'moderne' à la fin du Moyen Age: Jean Froissart et Christine de Pizan," in *Modernité au moyen âge: Le défi du passé*, ed. Brigitte Cazelles and Charles Méla (Geneva, 1990), pp. 153–73; Sylvia Huot, "The Daisy and the Laurel: Myths of Desire and Creativity in the Poetry of Jean Froissart," *Yale French Studies*, special issue (1991): 240–51; and Michel Zink's "Froissart et la nuit du chasseur," *Poétique* 41 (1988): 60–77. Sylvia Huot, in *From Song to Book: The Poetics of Writing in Old French Lyric and Lyrical Narrative Poetry* (Ithaca, 1987), pp. 312–14, discusses the correspondences between the elements of the Pynoteüs-Neptisphelé tale and various Ovidian stories. In addition to those to which I refer in my discussion she considers the myths of Apollo and Coronis, of Galatea, of Daphne, of Leucote, and the ways in which Pynoteüs is similar to both Apollo and Apollo's son Aesculapius.

Fourrier has pointed out that they make up more than half of the *Prison amoureuse*.[18] The qualitative importance is equally notable. The tale of Pygmalion is contained in the very discourse of Orpheus himself in Ovid's *Metamorphoses* (Book X), as Fourrier attentively notes, and in Froissart's *Prison amoureuse* it is precisely upon opening a book of Ovid's tales that the narrator "finds" the Pynoteüs myth.[19] Ovid appears as one who puts things in books: *Ovides le met en son livre* (Ovid puts it in his book; 1991). The terms that Flos/Froissart uses to describe the discovery of the tale are also quite revealing:

> Adont tournai sus une *glose*
> Qui nous approeve et nous acorde,
> Si com Ovides le recorde,
> Les *oevres* de Pynoteüs,
> Qui par grant art et non par us
> Fist l'ymage parlans et vive. . . .   (1295–1300, my emphasis)

> (Then I turned to a *glose* that shows and confirms for us, just as Ovid records it, the works [*oevres*] of Pynoteüs, who, by means of great skill [*art*] and not as was customary, made the speaking and living image. . . .)

Given Froissart's fondness for witticisms, the *oevres* of the poet-artist Pynoteüs likely connote not only physical acts but also poetic and artistic achievements. Similarly, the Ovidian *glose* where Flos claims to have found the story may be understood as Ovid's own work, a work based on Ovid, or an exposition of Ovid. As we shall see below, Froissart would not have made the sharp distinction we do between "creative writing" and expository interpretation.

---

[18]*Prison amoureuse*, ed. Fourrier, p. 14.

[19]Ibid., p. 19.

The *glose* thus gives rise to a new literary work; a passage in an Ovid manuscript becomes expanded into a book in its own right. One literary work spawns another, with an almost geometric increase in size each time. If each passage of Ovid can become a complete book, Ovid as a source is virtually inexhaustible. The literary game may have been even more sophisticated for the more initiated among Froissart's audience: those who knew their Ovid probably would have known or at least suspected that there was, in fact, no Pynoteüs and Neptisphelé story, as such, in Ovid. They would have recognized the story as an intertextual amalgamation of Pyramus', Pygmalion's, and Orpheus' experiences into a single, unified narrative.

Like Jean de Meun and Guillaume de Machaut before him, Froissart uses his Pygmalion-like tale, buttressed by Pyramus, Thisbé, Phaeton, and Orpheus, to meditate on the limits of art. Reflecting Froissart's, and Machaut's, awareness that only the compilation and synthesis of experience in book form ensures its preservation, Pynoteüs learns that all art is synthetic. He learns that creation and destruction are two opposing movements and that only the former should be indicative of the artist. In the tale of Pynoteüs there is also movement from destruction to creation. (If ripping open a *sacoche* is contrary to the synthetic processes of art, ripping open people is even more so; in Flos' Ovidian tale blood is spilled, not poetry.) When Pynoteüs gets a life for a life, he learns that not even the supreme castigation of the lion will bring back Neptisphelé; the only hope for fulfilling Pynoteüs' wish for his beloved is through art and a process not of destruction but of (re)creation and (re)collection.[20] The heavily ironic sense of the poet's

<hr />

[20]Sylvia Huot, "The Daisy and the Laurel," p. 249. In *From Song to Book*, p. 312, Huot notes that, though "Pynoteus appears as a Pyramus figure in the first part of the story . . . there are crucial differences. . . . For one thing, Pyramus is guilty of misreading the signs; Thisbe is not in fact dead. Also, although his suicide does

JEAN FROISSART'S PRISON AMOUREUSE

futile accomplishment (*ouvra li poëtes*) in having the lion devoured or the rhyme of *trop grant membre* with *ramembre* in the
following passage is perfectly characteristic of Froissart:

> Tout ensi ouvra li poëtes,
> De s'amie prist la vengance;
> Et non pour quant li aligance
> De sa dolour n'est pas venue
> Pour la mort de la beste mue:
> Encor y a un trop grant membre,
> Car a toute heure li ramembre
> De la belle. . . .   (1587–94)

> (Thus the poet brought about all this; he took vengeance for
> his beloved; but for all that the alleviation of his grievance
> was not forthcoming because of the death of the savage beast:
> there are still too many factors, for at every moment he
> remembers his beautiful lady. . . .)

Pynoteüs' proposed solution of an Orpheus-like descent into Hell
proves to be no solution at all, as anyone who has read Ovid (much
less Boethius' reworking of the tale in the *Consolatio Philosophiæ*,
Bk. III, Met. 12) is aware: rather than bringing Euridyce back to
the world of the living, Orpheus loses her for all time.

The Pygmalion solution is better: a different way to *oevrer*,
one of not tearing apart but gathering together.[21] The *ymage*

---

result in the creation of a monument to their love—the blood-darkened mulber-
ries—Pyramus himself is entirely unaware that he has produced it. He thus consti-
tutes a purely negative model of the lover-reader or lover-writer, and must be transcended."

[21]On the relationship between the Pygmalion power of creating a living being
through art and the nature of charged language, of which poetry is but a part, see
E. H. Gombrich, *Art and Illusion: A Study in the Psychology of Pictorial Representation* (Princeton, 1960), pp. 111–12.

Pynoteüs fashions is of water and earth, a *mixtion* (1694):

> [Pynoteüs] Oevre une ymage a grans bracies:
> D'aige et de terre muiste et mole
> Ordonne et taille et fet le mole. . . .   (1717–19)

> (With movements of his arms [Pynoteüs] makes a sculpture
> [*ymage*]: from water and moist, soft earth he gives form to
> and shapes the mold. . . .)

This confection produces a Neptisphelé look-alike, which, with
the requisite supernatural assist, comes to life as Phoebus kisses it
with his warm rays. Whether or not we choose to see in this creation of life from earth a reflection of the Christian view of creation, Pynoteüs' sculptural technique certainly recalls Froissart's
own artistic technique of *bricolage*. Moreover, what is Phoebus if
not a writer himself whose book is the Earth itself?

> Mes, las, la Terre en quoi tu oevres
> Et escrips lettres et signaus
> Generaus et especiaus . . .   (1889–91)

> (But, fatigued, the Earth in which you operate [*oevres*] and
> write letters and signs, both of a general and a particular
> nature . . .)

and Phoebus' works surpass the talents of earthly poets:

> Tes merveilles innumerables
> Sont si grandes et si notables
> Que bouce ne le poroit dire
> Ne mains volumer ne escrire.   (1908–11)

> (Your innnumerable marvels are so great and so notable that
> a mouth would not be capable of telling them nor hands of
> putting them in writing or making a [manuscript] volume of
> them).

Flos/Froissart exalts himself, albeit obliquely, as an artist who accomplishes the impossible. He manages to tell of Phoebus' ineffable deeds, to write of them, and to put them in a book (in a book within a book, in fact). Finally, the Pynoteüs tale ends with Pynoteüs' preference for the artistic reproduction over the original product. At no point, after all, does the "real" Neptisphelé return: the maiden whom Pynoteüs returns to her father is an artistic look-alike (re)worked and (re)awakened by Pynoteüs' love. Love and craft are joined in the "classical" manner, the transforming power of the former being handed over to the transforming power of the latter as the crafted object replaces the "real" woman.

The Pynoteüs narrative could serve as almost a textbook illustration of current theories that regard literary creation invariably as the result of a rewriting of earlier literature. When Flos declares himself satisfied as an artist with the book he has made "de la plus *nouvelle* matere que j'aie trouvé entre les *anchiienes* hystores" (from the *newest* material that I found among *ancient* stories; Letter VI, 7–8, 103, emphasis mine) is this not an acknowledgement of what is now called intertextuality? The seemingly oxymoronic use of new and old points up literarity while being, nevertheless, almost banally accurate: for what does *tro[u]ver* imply if not a new confection of the materials provided by literary tradition, a constant "making new" of the discourses that intertextuality puts at the poet's disposal? This cycle of literary creation as rewriting continues when Flos advises Rose on the latter's love affair, having *ymaginé* the responses of his patron's Lady (Letter VI, 17, 104), and calls upon Rose to *gloser* what he has written. Though the immediate referent is Flos' advice on love, what Rose in fact glosses is the Pynoteüs treatise: for Flos' Ovidian work inspires a dream that Rose then writes as a book. This dream, highly allegorical, is seen by Rose as having been an interpretation of sorts of Flos' Pynoteüs narrative. But now this new book of Rose's dream itself requires a gloss—namely that of a learned explication—such as only Flos can supply because his understanding is "grans et ymaginatis" (Letter VIII, 22–23, 149). Moreover, Flos, aware that Rose's dream is a reading of his Pynoteüs tale, offers yet an "aultre exposition." Finally this interpretation, an allegorical response to Pynoteüs that differs from Rose's dream-response, will itself need to be augmented when Rose's Lady requests an interpretation of one part, the story of Phaeton's chariot, that has gone largely unglossed. Flos' reading of the Phaeton episode will therefore propose yet a third allegorical gloss.

The writerly process comprises here the complete cycle of composition and interpretation, the two functions being deeply intertwined and presented as corresponding parts of a creative whole. What we deem literary creation is portrayed precisely as a reworking and reinterpretation of earlier literary models, principally of Ovid and Machaut. The reception of the literary work is depicted as an interpretive reutilization. The new-old literary work (as Froissart would have it) provokes a new narrative—a meta-narrative, a work that is a new narrative but also a reception and a gloss of the previous one—in the form of Flos' book of Pynoteüs; but this narrative also needs in its turn to be retold, which is what takes place in meta-meta-narrative fashion when Rose metamorphoses it into an allegorical dream-book. The chain of literary production is thus: Ovid's written tale → Flos' book about Pynoteüs → Rose's allegorical dream also written as a book.

Given that the *Prison amoureuse* forms the central portion in the two manuscripts of Froissart's courtly poetry, this incessant bookmaking and rewriting that is at the center, physically and thematically, of the *Prison amoureuse* is, in fact, the center of the center, a book encased first in the shell of the framing lay that is enclosed in the *Prison amoureuse* book, which in turn is enclosed in

the manuscript collection.[22] Moreover, this lay in which the narrative is encased itself forms a circle: indeed, Froissart's lay self-
consciously insists upon the fact that the final strophe of the lay,
according to the rules of composition, dovetails back into the first:

> C'est d'un lay la certainne taille.
> Et ossi li vers darreniers,
> Qui dou congnoistre est coustumiers,
> Vous porra monstrer et aprendre
> Ou le premier ver porés prendre,
> Car d'otel taille et d'otel fourme
> Est li darrains, qui bien l'enfourme,
> D'otel matere et d'otel vois,—
> Sans nul reditté toutes fois,—
> Comme est dou lay li vers premiers:
> C'est uns rieules tous coustumiers.   (3504–14)

> (This is the sure form of a *lai*. And also the last verse, if one
> is used to knowing, will be able to show and teach you where
> you can find the first verse, for the last is of the same shape
> and form, if one forms it well, and of the same nature and
> voice—without, nevertheless, being a repetition of the first
> poem—as is the first verse of the lay. It's an entirely habitual
> rule.)

Just as an old Ovidian narrative can provoke an endless series
of new tales, so one explication can give rise to successive ones,
through a process of endless augmentation—that is, by a combination of what poststructuralist literary theoreticians like to call
supplément and *différance*. Rose asks Flos for an explication of

---

[22]Huot, *From Song to Book*, p. 302. The two "complete works" manuscripts of
Froissart's poetry are Paris, Bibliothèque Nationale f.fr. 830 and 831. Though the
two manuscripts are quite similar, there are reasons for preferring f.fr. 831 (see
Fourrier's description and explanation in EA 9–14).

his dream-book; Flos gives one, then a second, which is really an interpretation of the text the dream-book has already interpreted, and finally a third when Rose's Lady asks that the interpretation be augmented by a more detailed gloss of one particular section. The novelty of the *Prison amoureuse* is that it depicts literary interpretation as theoretically an endless cycle that continues the production of the narrative fiction. The schema of interpretation is much the same as that for the composition of the fictions: Flos' first explication → Flos' second explication → Flos' third explication. Each new interpretation is the result of a re-reading, a new intellectual fertilization, a new discourse fashioned intertextually out of the tools supplied by what one has already read.

It is important to note, however, that the distinction between literary creation and literary interpretation as two distinct activities would not have been adhered to by Froissart and his contemporaries. This cycle of reading, responding, and rewriting extends endlessly far back into the past (Ovid's tales are, at least putatively, part of an "always already" existing mythology) and can also be projected endlessly far into the future. What we separate into creative and analytical writing (a distinction that some critics in recent years, particularly Derrida, have refused to make) would have been subsumed for medieval peoples under a process of *alieniloquium*, that is, according to a consistent substitution of terms such as characterized both translation (*translatio*) and allegory.[23]

---

[23]See Isidore of Seville's definition of allegory: "Allegoria est alieniloquium. Aliud enim sonat, et aliud intelligitur" (*Etymologiarum sive Originum*, ed. W. M. Lindsay, 2 vols. [Oxford, 1911], I.37.22). See also Douglas Kelly, *"Translatio studii*: Translation, Adaptation, and Allegory in Medieval French Literature," *Philological Quarterly* 57 (1978): 287–310: "There are three prominent modes of *translatio* in medieval French: translation as such, including scribal transmission; adaptation; and allegorical or extended metaphorical discourse" (p. 291). And "Allegory itself is the combination of an extended literal discourse and a parallel reading. The second or parallel reading may be discursive and expository, or

Both are products of *imaginatio*, as Douglas Kelly has pointed out.[24] Flos specifically states that he explicates Rose's book with the aid of God "et d'une ymagination que j'ai eü," "and of an inspiration [*ymagination*] I had" (Letter IX, 16–17, 151; see also pp. 153 and 154). In his reading of the dream-book, the bed, so central to the erotic life and the procreative process, is interpreted as the *locus* of thought (*Douce pensee*) ready to be reawakened by Justice, Pité, and Raison. It is the interpretation that gives meaning (and new meanings) to what would otherwise simply be, in Kelly's words, "incomplete, substantially empty marvels."[25]

Froissart, like a post-structuralist critic, overtly recognizes that the explicative process does not end with the writing of the first gloss and that there are equally valid, though mutually conflicting, interpretations. Froissart demonstrates that just as individual features of Ovid can be expanded into whole books in an almost limitless fashion, so each element of his interpretations can be amplified and glossed *ad infinitum* in a continual deferral of a meaning.[26] The multiplicity of the text becomes a multiplicity of in-

---

merely another mode of representation" (p. 298).

[24]Kelly, *Imagination*, p. 164.

[25]Ibid., p. 166.

[26]"Si les [=the letter] lisi encor de rechief et y vi, che me samble, aultre matere que ceste ne soit que je vous ai exposee . . . et bien vous en croi, car les pensees et ymaginations que on a as coses enclinent les corages en diverses mervelles; dont, en lisant ces lettres, je me repris et jettai ailleurs mon avis et ymagination sus aultre fourme et bien propisce a ceste matere et selonc le teneur des lettres que dou tamps passé m'avés envoiies et par les queles je m'avisai que ceste aultre exposition j'escriroie et le vous envoieroie, ensi que j'ai fait, a fin que vous aiiés avis sus l'un et l'autre pourpos, et le plus agreable retenés pour vous ou tous deus" (Thus I read it again from the beginning and saw—so it seems to me—a subject different from the one I set forth for you . . . and I certainly believe you about that [the fact that you don't know to whom else to turn for an explication], for the thoughts and

terpretations, each of which may illuminate different aspects of the work. That Flos/Froissart gives free choice to his reader suggests that we are deep into the archaeology of reader-response aesthetics as well as of metafiction: the text means different things to different readers, even to the same reader at different times.

In sum, in the *Prison amoureuse* composition and interpretation turn out to be two ends of the same pole. All composition is intertextual rereading, which is also to say that it is interpretive rereading. Just as medieval writers do not rewrite or translate slavishly, but rather gloss and embroider, so also their practices of glossing are expansions and retellings as much as pure "interpretation." An Ovidian story gives rise to Rose's allegorical dream, which he rewrites as a book. In this configuration of Ovid, Rose, and dream allegory we have the *Roman de la Rose* refigured—reinterpreted, that is, even before Flos begins his triple series of interpretations. But as in the *Queste del saint graal* the interpretations *are* the events, though in the *Prison amoureuse* these interpretations are singularly writerly. The complete cycle of tale telling and textual production is therefore: . . . Ovid's "original" work → the Ovidian *glose* where the narrator "finds" the Pynoteüs tale → Flos' book of Pynoteüs → Rose's allegorical dream/book → Flos' book/gloss on Rose's allegorical dream/book → Flos' reinterpretation of his own interpretation → Flos' amplification and reinterpretation at the request of a reader (Rose's Lady). . . .

In glossing and reglossing what has been left unsaid previous-

---

imaginings [*ymaginations*] that one has about things tend [people's] temperaments toward different ideas. So, upon reading your letter I thought about it again and took a different direction, one more fitting for the subject, especially given what you say in the last letter you sent. On that basis, then, I decided to send you in writing this second interpretation I came up with so that you will have both of them and you will be able to accept either the one you like best or both, if you prefer; Lettre IX, 105–21, 153–54).

ly, the writing process draws new texts and new tales out of what has been left out of the previous text, out of the white "between the lines," as the critic Gerald Bruns has put it.[27] This is, of course, an old strategy in medieval literature, going back to the epic, in which a continuator characteristically declares the completed text incomplete with the claim that the earlier author has left out the best part. By declaring the former ending point a beginning and closure a lack of closure, one continually opens new spaces for more writing. Froissart presents us with but a few links of the process, set within the circular structure of the lay.

The foregoing analysis of Froissart's *Prison amoureuse* is by no means exhaustive. It serves to show, however, a remarkable rapprochement between the late fourteenth-century view of the literary process and current critical approaches. Though the terms are different—Froissart speaks of *gloses*, whereas contemporary critics are wont to toss around such terms as *intertextual rewriting*—both would deny the kind of sharp separation between literary creation and interpretive analysis for which New Critics, for example, might have argued. For both there is a sliding scale from what we conventionally call fiction to analysis; most writing, however, falls somewhere in between the two extremes and contains elements of both. Finally, Froissart denies that any one interpretation can have a Hirschian "validity" or primacy and instead displays a preference for multiple and mutually irreconcilable readings of a work—especially when the patron has requested the extra expositions.[28]

Among the principal elements that I, like Froissart himself,

---

[27]Gerald L. Bruns, "The Originality of Texts in a Manuscript Culture," *Comparative Literature* 32 (1980): 113–29, esp. 123.

[28]See E. D. Hirsch, *Validity in Interpretation* (New Haven, Conn., 1967).

have not specifically addressed is the matter of the political situation in the 1370s that forms part of the subtext to this work. Let me make clear that I accept the view that Froissart cleverly flattered his patron, Wenceslas of Luxemburg, by hinting at him in the personage of Rose, the patron figure of the narrative. The principal point of contact between the narrative and history is the fact that Wenceslas was himself held prisoner for something like Rose's nine or ten months in love's prison. Rose's silence can therefore be seen as a touching reference to Wenceslas' captivity.[29]

Here the similarity ends, however. There is no reason to assume, as has occasionally been done, that Rose's letters and poems of the *Prison amoureuse* were actually penned by Wenceslas himself.[30] Froissart would have learned from reading Ma-

---

[29]Wenceslas was captured at the battle of Baesweiler, then imprisoned from late August 1371 until July of the following summer. See *Prison amoureuse* 2128. If the composition of a lay took six months, as Froissart claims, and one accords four or five months for the writing of all the intervening material, then it is not wrong to attribute to Froissart a clever paralleling of Rose's silence, Flos' writing activities, and the time Wenceslas spent in captivity.

[30]This has been most recently—and perhaps most forcefully—argued by William W. Kibler, "Poet and Patron: Froissart's *Prison amoureuse*," *L'Esprit Créateur* 18 (1978): 32–46. Though open to criticism, Kibler's discussion serves as an important corrective to the excesses of some recent critical trends that would deny any reference to an external "real" world, even when such allusion is painfully obvious. Nevertheless, Kibler charges across the delicate line that separates the fictional characters Flos and Rose from the historically real Froissart and Wenceslas. A literary creation stretched over the bare facts of a historical configuration does not make it exactly synonymous with the "real" lived events, especially when the names are changed. Thus Kibler's statement (p. 35) that "toward the end of the *Prison amoureuse* itself Duke Wenceslas instructs Froissart" to pull together the letters and poems they have written is circular in its argumentation. For it is the fictional character Rose who instructs the narrator Flos here, the names "Wenceslas" and "Froissart" never being used. One cannot take as one's assumption that Flos and Rose are really Froissart and Wenceslas, reascribe the names, and then use the reascribed form to prove as one's conclusion that the

chaut's *Voir Dit*, in which the letters and poems attributed to his correspondent, Toute-belle, were almost assuredly penned by the author himself, how to invent a correspondence. And he was surely clever enough to construct his narrative in such a way that it would seem to parallel the historical reality of Wenceslas' captivity, thereby flattering and consoling his patron much as Machaut did his own in the *Confort d'ami*. Moreover, Froissart claims, in both his "Dit dou Florin" and his *Chroniques*, that his *Méliador* contains the entire corpus of Wenceslas' poetic production.[31] Must we not then discount all of Rose's poems in the *Prison amoureuse* that do not figure there? Finally, many of Wenceslas' supposed poems are included as being by Froissart himself in the two manuscripts of his complete works.

I would argue that the political situation is only alluded to in order to be cleverly elided. Though the allusion is there, it would have been tantamount to trivializing Wenceslas' captivity to reduce his very real imprisonment to the gaity of Rose's detention at the hands of comely allegorical personifications. I propose instead that the allusion, taken together with the refusal to make the correspondence specific, is part and parcel of a late fourteenth-century courtly aesthetic that sought to avoid the vicissitudes of social and political events. I would argue, in other words, that though intellectuals still paid lip service to what Judson

---

correspondence is really between Wenceslas and Froissart. Similarly flawed is the argument that just because some lyric poems known to be by Froissart are not included in the relevant section of his complete works manuscripts, B.N. f.fr. 840 and 841, this somehow means that poems that *are* included in those sections can be dismissively declared not to be by Froissart (Kibler, pp. 34–35, n. 7). See also the enlightening discussion by Claire Nouvet, "Pour une économie," pp. 352–55.

[31]See "Le Dit dou Florin," in Auguste Scheler, ed., *Oeuvres de Froissart: Poésies*, vol. 2 (Brussels, 1871), pp. 291–302; and Kervyn de Lettenhove, ed., *Oeuvres de Froissart*, vol. 11 (Brussels, 1870), p. 85.

Boyce Allen has called an "ethical poetic," they in fact wanted to avoid the hard ethical problems posed by the question of literature's relationship to the real world.[32] The *Prison amoureuse* seems to me an excellent case in point. Not only does Froissart show himself highly skilled in the art of turning one thing into another by glossing it as something entirely unrelated, but he skillfully avoids any of the burden that would result from allowing the "real" Wenceslas and "real" captivity to erupt into the comely space of his courtly narrative. What, then, could be more significant than his redefinition of his patron's very real exile and captivity in terms of a psychomachiac love battle in which one becomes metaphorically taken prisoner? Like Machaut in the *Jugement dou roi de Navarre* and Boccaccio in his *Decameron*, who all too conveniently manage to both bring up and then turn their backs on the ills of the plague, Froissart actively embraces a poetic that is increasingly skillful at an art of interpretation that can turn anything into anything else and that is concerned at all cost to avoid whatever might resemble what we would now call a sort of *littérature d'engagement*.

---

[32]Judson Boyce Allen, *The Ethical Poetic in the Later Middle Ages* (Toronto, 1982).

The Question of Authority and The Man of Law's Tale

PATRICIA J. EBERLE

In October 1386, Chaucer attended his first and only meeting of Parliament.[1] As it happened, this parliament marked the beginning of the series of constitutional crises during the reign of Richard II, which culminated in the deposition of the king in 1399. The 1386 crisis, like that of 1399, was seen by contemporary observers as a controversy turning on the question of authority, particularly the question of the nature and limits of the authority of the king.

The meeting of what was called by some contemporaries the "Wonderful Parliament" took place in an atmosphere of tension and widespread fear. France had assembled its largest invasion fleet yet, and English troops along the southern coast were being maintained with difficulty by loans and levies on the maritime counties. In his opening address, Chancellor Michael de la Pole called for the largest subsidy ever requested. Parliament responded by renewing the criticisms of the government made the previous year, when a commission had been appointed to investigate the income and reduce the expenses of the Crown. That commission had never func-

---

[1] On Chaucer's attendance at Parliament see M. Galway, "Geoffrey Chaucer, J.P. and M.P.," *Modern Language Review* 36 (1941): 1–36 and F. R. Scott, "Chaucer and the Parliament of 1386," *Speculum* 18 (1943): 80–86.

tioned, and now the Lords were supporting the Commons' demand for the dismissal of the Treasurer as well as the Chancellor himself. Richard II reacted to these criticisms by attempting to dissolve Parliament, and, when the members refused to disband, he departed for the royal palace at Eltham, leaving the Chancellor to preside in his place.[2] His refusal to preside was apparently designed as a practical demonstration of royal authority: it demonstrated the king's refusal to be held accountable to Parliament for management of Crown revenues and, at the same time, made the Chancellor, as representative of the Crown, immune to impeachment.

The consequences of his refusal to meet with Parliament must have taken Richard by surprise. He had commanded that a delegation of knights attend him at Eltham; instead, he was confronted by Thomas of Woodstock, Duke of Gloucester, and Thomas Arundel, Bishop of Ely, who bore a message from Parliament that went beyond criticism of the uses of Crown revenues and challenged the very foundations of royal authority. It was a formal

---

[2]For a fuller account of the Parliament of 1386 see J. J. N. Palmer, "The Parliament of 1385 and the Constitutional Crisis of 1386," *Speculum* 46 (1971): 477–90; Anthony Tuck, *Richard II and the English Nobility* (London, 1973), pp. 104–11; and J. S. Roskell, *The Impeachment of Michael de la Pole, Earl of Suffolk, in 1386 in the Context of the Reign of Richard II* (Manchester, 1984). Like the fourteenth-century chronicles that provide the primary sources, these accounts differ in some details: Tuck, apparently interpreting a passage in Henry Knighton (*Chronicon*, ed. J. R. Lumby, 2 vols., Rolls Series [London, 1889]), says that Richard did not attend the opening of Parliament at all; but the passage in question merely says that "for the greater part" (*pro majore parte*, 2:215), the king remained at Eltham; Roskell (following the anonymous *Continuatio Eulogii Historiarum*) provides the basis for my account of Richard's departure, after his attempt to dismiss Parliament. The main point in both accounts, as in the message delivered by Gloucester and Arundel, is that the king refused to preside. The pivotal importance of this parliament has long been recognized by modern historians; for a succinct review of Richard's reign that treats this parliament as a "watershed" see Caroline Barron, "The Art of Kingship: Richard II, 1377–1399," *History Today* 35 (June 1985): 31–37.

statement of Parliament's claims to exercise an authority of its own, an authority not derived from the Crown and, in some instances, even superior to the authority of the king himself. Nothing quite like it had ever been prepared by an English Parliament before, and Richard II was not mistaken in regarding it as revolutionary in its implications.

The fullest account of this statement and the king's reply is preserved in the Latin Chronicle of Henry Knighton, a source that has been largely overlooked by Chaucerians.[3] The wording of the statement offers valuable evidence that Chaucer and his fellow members of Parliament were alive to the question of authority and that they saw very clearly the relevance of this question to the constitutional crisis of 1386.

The statement begins by asserting that the king is required, "on the basis of an ancient statute," to summon a meeting of Parliament every year. (In fact, there were two such statutes, one from 1330 and another from 1362, but they were notoriously dif-

---

[3]For the text of the statement and the king's reply see *Chronicon*, ed. Lumby, 2:216–20. On the sources, reliability, and method of composition of this chronicle see V. H. Galbraith, "The Chronicle of Henry Knighton," in *Fritz Saxl, 1890–1948; A Volume of Memorial Essays from his Friends in England*, ed. D. J. Gordon (London, 1957), pp. 136–45. After a detailed study of what he argues is the author's autograph manuscript (Cotton Tiberius C. VII), Galbraith assigns a date of c. 1390 for this section of the text. In his account of the chronicle sources for the Parliament of 1386, John Taylor credits Knighton with offering "the fullest account" and "transcribing a selection of the official documents," including, presumably, the statement presented by Gloucester and Arundel; see *English Historical Literature in the Fourteenth Century* (Oxford, 1987), pp. 205–07. For a general assessment of the value of Knighton's chronicle as a whole in the context of other chronicles of Richard II's reign see Antonia Gransden, *Historical Writing in England II: c. 1307 to the Early Sixteenth Century* (London, 1982), pp. 159–81. The fullest treatment of The Man of Law's Tale in light of the Parliament of 1386 appears in Paul A. Olson, *The* Canterbury Tales *and the Good Society* (Princeton, 1982), pp. 159–81. A new edition is forthcoming, *The Chronicle of Henry Knighton, 1337–1396*, ed. G. H. Martin, Oxford Medieval Texts series.

ficult to enforce against the king's will.) The statement also claims the existence of another "ancient statute" (this time fictitious) that gave Parliament the power to disband itself "if the king, of his own will . . . should absent himself from parliament for a period of forty days or more." If the king hoped to make his departure a demonstration of his own authority, the framers of the Parliamentary statement were turning it into an opportunity to subordinate the king to the power of law.

Parliament's self-assertiveness becomes still stronger in the main body of the statement, which outlines its aim to extend its powers so as to claim three new kinds of authority. First, Parliament claims authority to consider matters concerning "the estate and governance of the king and kingdom"; this is a assertion of the right to take the initiative in all matters affecting the Crown and the whole state of the realm. Second, it claims authority "to manage and dispose the affairs of the realm so that, for the sake of the common good, all financial obligations incumbent on the king and kingdom may be made as light as possible"; this is a claim to exercise authority over such fiscal matters as taxation and the expenditures of the Crown. Third, it claims authority to identify "enemies of the kingdom" and to deal with these enemies "in whatever manner seems most expedient"; this is a claim to judge and sentence those accused of treason. In these three areas, the statement thus makes sweeping claims for what we would now call investigative, fiscal, and judicial authority, claims that far exceeded the actual powers of Parliament at the time.[4]

In view of these sweeping claims to Parliamentary authority,

---

[4]Only the Ordinances of 1311 had ever attempted to extend the authority of Parliament to any comparable extent, and these Ordinances had been declared null and void in 1322 by the Statute of York; see May McKisack, *The Fourteenth Century, 1307–1399*, The Oxford History of England, vol. 5 (Oxford, 1959), pp. 12–30 and 71–73.

it is not surprising that Richard II described this statement as constituting a threat to "mount a revolt" against his authority (*contra nos insurgere moliuntur*). In the context of the impending French invasion, however, it is surprising that he threatened to seek aid from the king of France, whom he referred to as "our cousin" and, if necessary "to submit to him rather than succumb to our own subjects" (*nos ei submittere potius quam succumbere subditis nostris*). Perhaps it was this threat that prompted the still stronger claim for Parliament as the source of the supreme legal authority in the realm. The claim is so revolutionary that it deserves quotation at length:

> On the basis of an ancient statute, and from the experience of a lamentable event in history not long past [a reference to the deposition of King Edward II in 1327] they maintained that if, either because of evil counsel or . . . his own willfulness, the king should alienate himself from his people, and should be unwilling to be governed and ruled by the laws . . . and praiseworthy customs of the realm, being guided by the good counsel of the lords and magnates, but instead, on the basis of his own foolish opinions, should stubbornly insist upon making his own individual will the basis of his rule, then it is lawful, on the basis of the common . . . consent of the people of the kingdom, to depose the king from his royal throne and to raise to the throne someone else of royal blood.[5]

---

[5]The full quotation is as follows: "Habent enim ex antiquo statuto et de facto non longe retroactis temporibus experimenter, quod dolendum est, habito, si rex ex maligno consilio quocunque vel inepta contumacia aut contemptu seu proterva voluntate singulari aut quovis modo irregulari se alienaverit a populo suo, nec voluerit per jura regni et statuta ac laudabiles ordinationes cum salubri consilio dominorum et procerum regni gubernari et regulari, sed capitose in suis insanis consiliis propriam voluntatem suam singularem proterve exercere, extunc licitum est eis cum communi assensu et consensu populi regni ipsum regem de regali solio abrogare, et propinquiorum aliquem de stirpe regia loco ejus in regni solio sublimare" (*Chronicon*, ed. Lumby, 2:219).

As Knighton's Chronicle makes clear, this confrontation between king and Parliament was seen by both sides as raising fundamental issues. The opposition between these two views of authority is clear. For the framers of the 1386 Parliamentary statement, the supreme authority was vested in the laws made by the consent of the people through their representatives; for Richard II, the supreme authority was the will of the king himself.

This confrontation between the king and parliament addresses what a number of historians of medieval political thought consider to be a central issue for the period as a whole. J. H. Burns, in his introduction to *The Cambridge History of Medieval Political Thought, c.350–c.1450*, describes this issue as, "the exercise of authority in *gubernatio*, which in turn was seen as being indissolubly connected with *jurisdictio*, 'laying down the law'."[6] In the most general sense, the question of authority was thus a question not merely about power itself but about the right to power, the right of one person to have power over another, at any level in society. This question gave rise to a wide variety of answers about the origin and nature of legitimate authority, which can be classified, using the terminology of the historian Walter Ullmann, as falling into two broad categories, "ascending" and "descending" views of authority.[7] The conflict between Richard II and the 1386 Parliament can be seen as a conflict between views belonging to these two opposed categories. The Parliamentary statement represents an "ascending" view of authority, in which authority arises in the people, who, through their representatives, have power to

---

[6](Cambridge, 1988), p. 6.

[7]For an account of this classification see Walter Ullmann, *Principles of Government and Politics in the Middle Ages* (London, 1961), pp. 19–26. For a re-assessment of Ullmann's schema, noting its limitations as well as its value, see Burns, *Cambridge History*, pp. 3–7.

bind the king to the laws they make as well as the power to de-
pose a king who refuses to be bound by the law. Richard II's response represents the "descending" view of authority, in which
authority granted the king by the grace of God descends to his
subjects through the will of the king, who has the power to punish
or put to death those subjects who rise against him.[8]

Knighton's account gives less space to Richard II's "descending" view of authority than it does to the "ascending" view of the
Parliamentary statement of 1386.[9] A fuller elaboration of
Richard's view appears in other texts, the most valuable for this
purpose being those works dedicated to or commissioned by the
king himself. The most relevant of these is the first version of the
Confessio Amantis by John Gower (1392), a work commissioned
by Richard II and dedicated to him in language expressing a view
of obedience to authority that is clearly the view of the king
himself. Gower describes his poem as

A bok for king Richardes sake,

---

[8]For the view that Richard's actions were motivated consistently by this
descending view of authority see R. H. Jones, *The Royal Policy of Richard II*
(Oxford, 1968). For a contrary view about the importance of patronage as a motive
behind the actions of both Richard II and his opponents see Tuck, *Richard II*. The
view suggested here is less about motives than about the argument over the source
and nature of authority that emerged in 1386. Whatever its political and economic
causes, this argument informed a number of conflicts in the reign and reappeared
clearly in 1399, most clearly in Articles 16 and 17 of the charges brought against
Richard II after his deposition, which allege that he said that "the laws were in his
own mouth . . . and that he alone could change or establish the laws of the realm,"
and that no statutes could bind him (*English Historical Documents*, vol. 4, ed. A.
R. Myers [London, 1969], p. 410).

[9]As Barron points out, Richard's response to the Parliamentary statement of
1386 was not confined to these remarks recorded by Knighton; she argues that
from this point onwards "Richard worked to rebuild the authority of the Crown"
("The Art of Kingship," p. 31).

To whom belongeth my ligeance,
With al myn hertes obeissance
In al that evere a liege man
Unto his king may doon or can:
So ferforth I me recomande
To him which al me may comande.
Preyende unto the hihe regne
Which causeth every king to regne,
That his corone longe stonde.[10]

The central tenets of Richard II's "descending" theory of authority are emphasized here by rhyming words. "Ligeance" (originally a word referring to a feudal tie that binds two ways) is here rhymed with "obeissance," a tie that binds only one way, committing the subject to obey the will of the king.[11] The link made in these lines between "ligeance" and unconditional "obeissance" is the result of a fundamental assumption of the "descending" theory, an assumption reinforced by the identical rhyme of the "regne" of God (the "hihe regne") and the "regne" of the king. As obedience to God is unconditional, obedience to the king whose reign God has established should be unconditional also. Gower's dedication thus rephrases St. Paul's well-known words, "The powers that be are ordained of God" (Rom. 13:1) in a way that was designed to

---

[10]Ed. G. C. Macaulay, *The English Works of John Gower*, 2 vols., EETS es 81, 82 (London, 1900–01; repr. 1957), Prologue, lines 24*–33*. For a detailed discussion of the dedication to Richard II in the first version of the *Confessio* see Peter Nicholson, "The Dedications of Gower's *Confessio Amantis*," *Mediaevalia* 10 (1984): 159–80.

[11]Not everyone in Richard II's England was willing to accept Gower's equation between "ligeance" and "obeissance." At the 1386 Parliament the mercers' guild presented a petition objecting that its members should not be commanded by their "ligeaunce" to do things that they believe are unlawful or even unnecessary; see *Middle English Dictionary*, ed. Sherman M. Kuhn and John Reidy, Part L.4, (Ann Arbor, Mich., 1972), *s.v.* ligeaunce.

reflect Richard II's view of the divine basis of his own authority.

Unlike Gower, Chaucer did not dedicate any of his major works to Richard II. He did receive the benefits of royal patronage: he was appointed Controller for the Port of London (1374–86) and Clerk of the Kings Works (1389–91). He also received annuities from the royal exchequer, both under Richard II (1394–99) and under Henry IV (1399–1400).[12] But we have no clear evidence that this patronage was connected with his poetry. Until quite recently, in fact, the general view has been that unlike Gower and Langland, Chaucer kept his political and his poetic careers at some distance from one another.[13] In the past five years, however, four books have all argued, in different ways, for the importance of the social and political context of the age of Richard II to an understanding of Chaucer's works.[14] In this

---

[12]For an account of Chaucer's public career see F. R. H. Du Boulay, "The Historical Chaucer," in *Geoffrey Chaucer*, ed. Derek Brewer (Athens, Ohio, 1975), pp. 33–57. In a review of the implications of the records for Chaucer's political stance ("Chaucer and Ricardian Politics," *Chaucer Review* 22 [1988]: 171–84), S. Sanderlin argues that Chaucer was a "cautious nonpartisan" and that his resignation from his controllerships following the Parliament of 1386 marked "the first stage in his withdrawal from the political scene."

[13]Very few direct and unambiguous references to Richard II appear in Chaucer's works. A balade, entitled in modern editions "Lak of Stedfastnesse" (dated 1397–99, on the basis of Shirley's statement that it was made in the "last years" of the poet's life), contains an envoy to "King Richard." The Prologue to *Astrolabe* (begun c. 1391) has a curious reference to the king: Chaucer tells "little Louis," his son, that if he finds anything of value in the treatise to "preie God save the king, that is lord of this langage," lines 56–57. All references to Chaucer's works are taken from *The Riverside Chaucer*, 3rd ed., Larry D. Benson, Gen. ed. (Boston, 1987).

[14]Olson, *The* Canterbury Tales *and the Good Society*; Joseph Hornsby, *Chaucer and the Law* (Norman, Okla., 1988); Paul Strohm, *Social Chaucer* (Cambridge, 1989); and Peggy Knapp, *Chaucer and the Social Contest* (New York and London, 1990).

essay I want to add further support for this approach to Chaucer
by suggesting that The Man of Law's Tale can be seen as a
reexamination of the controversy over the question of authority,
as it was formulated in repeated confrontations between Richard II
and his opponents, beginning in 1386.

Chaucer's Man of Law's Tale is the story of the trials of the
virtuous and long-suffering Custance, a woman who is presented
as the very model of obedience to authority.[15] Although she is
the daughter of the emperor of Rome, the most powerful secular
authority in her world, Custance in her own right is entirely
without power; she is deprived of some of the most basic rights
accorded to all medieval men and women, even to those of
humble birth. One of these rights was the right to form contracts,
including especially the most common contract, the contract of
marriage. In Chaucer's England, both canon law and common law
agreed that the basis of a valid marriage is the consent of both
parties, but in the world of The Man of Law's Tale, Custance is
denied this fundamental right.[16] Custance is given in marriage on
the basis of a treaty made by her parents and her future husband,
the Sultan of Syria, arrangements that involve, as the tale specifies, the mediation of the Pope as well as "al the chirche, and al

---

[15]Most readers of the story have seen Custance, like Griselda, as a model of
obedience; see the notes to The Man of Law's Tale in *The Riverside Chaucer* for
detailed references. For Olson, Custance represents the model of "what rule should
be," in the view of the Man of Law (*The* Canterbury Tales *and the Good Society*,
p. 93). For the view that Custance represents *constantia*, an aspect of *justitia*, see
Joseph E. Grennen, "Chaucer's Man of Law and the Constancy of Justice," *JEGP*
84 (1985): 498–514.

[16]For an account of the importance of consent in the canon law of marriage see
Harold J. Berman, *Law and Revolution: The Formation of the Western Legal
Tradition* (Cambridge, Mass., 1983), pp. 226–30. For the law of marriage in medi-
eval England as reflected in some of Chaucer's tales see Hornsby, *Chaucer and the
Law*, pp. 56–68.

the chivalrie" (MLT, line 235). Although everyone else of any importance seems to have been consulted in making the marriage arrangements, Custance's own views are not taken into account. We hear nothing about her feelings until the arrangements for the marriage have already been made and she is on the point of leaving Rome for Syria to meet her future husband for the first time. The lines describing her preparations for departure make clear that she is being married not only without her explicit consent but also against her will:

> Custance, that was with sorwe al overcome,
> Ful pale arist, and dresseth hire to wende;
> For wel she seeth ther is noon oother ende.   (lines 264–66)

In distilled form, these three lines convey the essence of Custance's character. It is not merely, as the lines suggest, that Custance accepts this marriage as inevitable, making virtue of necessity, as Theseus advises Emily in The Knight's Tale (line 3042). Her actions and speeches throughout the tale make clear that she herself advocates a view of authority that justifies her own disenfranchisement. In her first direct speech in the story, her farewell speech to her parents, she takes a rigidly hierarchical view of authority. She describes herself to her parents as "thy wrecched child Custance" (line 274) and sees herself as occupying the lowest level in the hierarchy, subordinate to her parents, whom she addresses as "my soverayn plesance / Over alle thyng" (lines 276–77), as well as to the higher authority she calls "Crist on-lofte" (line 277). When she describes her reaction to her parents' plans for her marriage, she makes clear that she views her own suffering, and even her own life, as of no importance in comparison with the will of her human and divine superiors:

> "Allas, unto the Barbre nacioun
> I moste anoon, syn that it is youre wille;

But Crist, that starf for our redempcioun
So yeve me grace his heestes to fulfille!
I, wrecche womman, no fors though I spille!
Wommen are born to thraldom and penance,
And to been under mannes governance." (lines 281–87)

The underlying assumption about the nature of authority conveyed by this speech can be paraphrased in the words of a legal maxim found in the *Digest* of Justinian and widely cited in the later Middle Ages as the expression of an absolutist view of political authority. This legal maxim, "The will of the prince has the force of law," is echoed in Custance's assumption that since it is the "will" of her father, she "must" leave for Syria.[17] When she says that the "will" of her father reflects the "heestes" or commands of Christ, her reasoning reflects another legal maxim, "all power is from God" (*omne potestas a Deo*) ultimately derived from St. Paul's Epistle to the Romans.[18]

As Custance's speech suggests, this view of authority has what might be called a "religious" as well as a "political" dimension. Her view that "wommen are born to thraldom and penance" attests not only to her acceptance of the authority of her father's will as

---

[17]"Quod principi placuit legis vigorem habet," *Digesta*, 1.4.1pr. (cf. *Institutiones* 1.2.6). For some discussion of the uses to which this maxim was put in later medieval political theory see K. Pennington, "Law, Legislative Authority and Theories of Government, 1150–1300" in Burns, *The Cambridge History*, pp. 424–47.

[18]"Let every soul be subject to higher powers: for there is no power but from God: and those that are, are ordained of God" (Romans 13:1–3; Douay-Rheims version). On the importance of this passage as "the most important Biblical statement of the duty of Christians to submit to secular power" see D. E. Luscombe and G. R. Evans, "The Twelfth-Century Renaissance," in Burns, *The Cambridge History*, pp. 316–17. For a discussion of this and other Biblical passages as a basis for the "descending" theory of authority see Walter Ullmann, "The Bible and Principles of Government in the Middle Ages," *La Bibbia nell' alto medioevo*, Settimane di Studio del Centro Italiano di Studi sull'alto medioevo (Spoleto, 1963), 181–227.

an expression of the will of God but also to her acceptance of the view of women presented in the Biblical account of the Fall as she interprets it. Later on in the story, she refers directly to the Biblical account of the Fall when she says that "thurgh wommanes eggement" or instigation, "Mankynde was lorn, and damned ay to dye" (lines 842–43). According to her interpretation of the story of the Fall, women bear the primary responsibility for bringing sin and death into the world, so it is only fitting that they are born to penance and the absolute obedience of a slave. Custance's unquestioning faith in this interpretation of the Biblical account of the Fall thus constructs an authoritative foundation for her unquestioning obedience to the patriarchal power structure.[19]

In both its religious and political implications, Custance's first speech provides a clear statement of the "descending" view of authority, the view that authority is vested in the will of superiors, who transmit to those below them the authority of the will of God. Her view of authority is the counterpart of the "descending" view of King Richard II, with the important difference that in her case this view is being articulated by someone who sees herself as the lowest link in the chain of command. Custance is thus the ideal subject as envisioned by Richard II's "descending" view of authority, a subject who not only obeys the will of the authorities as the will of God but cannot even contemplate any alternative to obedience.

In the course of The Man of Law's Tale, Custance makes several speeches on the question of authority, elaborating on the view presented in her first speech and adapting it to the increasingly difficult circumstances in which she finds herself. These speeches have no counterpart, either in the primary source for the

---

[19]For a reading of The Man of Law's Tale as providing support to the patriarchal power structure as Chaucer's Lawyer perceives it see Carolyn Dinshaw, *Chaucer's Sexual Poetics* (Madison, Wis., 1989), pp. 88–112.

tale, an episode from the Anglo-Norman *Chronicle* (c. 1334) of world history from the Creation to the early fourteenth century, written by the Dominican friar Nicholas Trevet (or Trivet), or in the most important analogue, the story of Constance as it is told in Book II of John Gower's *Confessio Amantis*. The view of authority in these speeches represents an important change in the character of the heroine and in the meaning of Chaucer's version of the story. Most studies of The Man of Law's Tale follow the lead of the important research done by Margaret Schlauch on the sources and analogues.[20] Schlauch emphasizes the similarities among the versions of Trevet, Gower, and Chaucer and their resemblances to the general story type she calls "The Accused Queen," a story type that has affinities with two narrative genres, the saint's legend and the sentimental romance.[21] I would like to take a different approach here and explore the affinities this story type has with another kind of narrative, the kind Brian Tierney calls the story of "origins." As Tierney defines it, a story of origins is a story told in order to lend legitimacy to a particular view on the question of authority.[22] Chaucer's The Man of Law's Tale, I want to suggest, can be read as a similar kind of story of "origins," a story that rewrites the view of the heroine found in his sources in order to

---

[20]*Chaucer's Constance and Accused Queens* (New York, 1927); the substance of her argument is repeated in her essay "The Man of Law's Tale" in *Sources and Analogues of Chaucer's* Canterbury Tales, ed. W. F. Bryan and Germaine Dempster (1941; repr. New York, 1958), 155–206.

[21]The genre of the tale is defined as a hagiographical romance by Paul M. Clogan, "The Narrative Style of *The Man of Law's Tale*," *Medievalia et Humanistica* ns 8 (1977): 217–33; this definition is accepted as the generally shared view by Helen Cooper in *Oxford Guides to Chaucer: The Canterbury Tales* (Oxford, 1989), pp. 126–27.

[22]*Religion, Law, and the Growth of Constitutional Thought, 1150–1650* (Cambridge, 1982), pp. 34–39.

offer a reexamination of the "descending" view of the question of authority that she represents.[23]

Tierney describes the story of origins as related to a tendency in medieval political thought to found a theory of political authority on a hypothesis about its beginnings in a primitive state. The hypothesis is typically put in the form of a narrative borrowed or adapted from other texts, often texts that are not themselves directly concerned with the question of authority. According to Tierney, one of the most popular texts was the little narrative that appears at the beginning of Cicero's *De inventione* (c. 87 B.C.). Cicero's story describes the period before rhetoric was discovered as primitive in the extreme, "a time when people wandered at large in the fields like animals." In this primitive time, the only authority was the rule of force in the service of desire: "They did nothing by the guidance of reason but . . . through their ignorance and error, blind and unreasoning passion satisfied itself by misuse of bodily strength." The decisive change that marked the end of this primitive state of affairs and the beginning of civilization as we know it, occurred with the appearance of a great man, a man in whom wisdom was united with eloquence. This man, Cicero says, summoned the people together to listen to a plan he had for their benefit. And when, by his eloquence he had persuaded them to listen to the wisdom of his plan, "he transformed them from wild savages into a kind and gentle folk."[24]

---

[23] As a rewriting of a political story of origins, The Man of Law's Tale has much in common with the type of story described by Judith N. Shklar, "Subversive Genealogies," *Daedalus* (Winter 1972): *Myth, Symbol, and Culture* (Cambridge, Mass., 1972), 129–54. I owe this reference to Lee Patterson.

[24] *De inventione* in *Cicero II: De Inventione, De Optimo Genere Oratorum, Topica*, ed. and trans. H. M. Hubbell, Loeb Classical Library (Cambridge, Mass., 1949; repr. 1976), I.1.2.

Viewed as a "story of origins," the story of Constance has some basic similarities with Cicero's story. All three versions of the story, by Trevet, Gower, and Chaucer, present it as the story of the origins of Christian rulership in Saxon England, and all the main events of the plot are designed to further this purpose. Constance is responsible for the conversion of Alla, the pagan Saxon king of Northumbria; she marries Alla and bears him a son, Moris, who succeeds her father and is named "the most Christian emperor," thus linking the Roman empire with the English royal line. In this story, Christianity serves the function of rhetorical eloquence in Cicero's story of origins: it transforms the Saxon people from a primitive state of savagery into a civilized state; and, as in Cicero, those who are not yet civilized are presented as acting out of passion under the sole authority of the rule of force.

The savagery of non-Christians receives repeated emphasis in all versions of the story and is reinforced by the three-part structure of the plot, based on Constance's three voyages. In the Saracen kingdom, where Constance lands first, the Sultan's mother uses a wedding feast as the occasion for a bloodbath, slaughtering not only her guests, the Christians in Constance's entourage, but also all of her own countrymen who have converted to Christianity, including her son. The mother-in-law Constance encounters after her second voyage, although more civilized in some respects, is only somewhat less savage. The unregenerate pagan mother of the Saxon king Alla demonstrates her civilized literacy by forging letters that deceive not only the king's subordinates but also the king himself. But she uses this skill to arrange the destruction of her own family, to set adrift her newborn grandchild as well as her despised Christian daughter-in-law, Constance. When, at the end of her last voyage, Constance comes ashore in Christian Rome once more, the difference in her treatment is striking. Although the Roman senator and his wife do not know who she is, they welcome her and her child into their home and treat her as a member of their family, demonstrating, as they do so, the obvious superiority of Christian civilization, in which authority is used to nurture rather than destroy, even at the level of the family unit. The denouement of the story arises from a deftly turned coincidence, a practical demonstration of the superiority of the Christian deity to savage pagan mothers-in-law, in the matter of plot construction: despite all their efforts to destroy her, Constance survives and is reunited with King Alla when he makes a pilgrimage to Rome to do Christian penance for the death of his mother, whom he had executed for her unjust and savage treatment of Constance. This reunion not only confirms the Christian conversion of England but leads to the close association of England with the Christianized Roman empire, since the child of Alla and Constance is to become the "most Christian" emperor.

In comparison with Cicero's story of the origins of all civilization, this story of the origins of Christian civilization in England is not only much longer but also much more complex. Both the length and the complexity attest to the ways in which Christian premises can complicate a story of origins. In this story it is not the effort of one man of wisdom and eloquence but the effort of divine providence that brings Christian rulership to England. Repeatedly, at every key turn in the plot, the point is made that just as God guides her rudderless ship so it is divine guidance that governs the course of events.[25] As a "story of origins," the story of Constance thus reinforces the underlying assumption of the "descending" theory of authority, that all power is from God, in a way that has special relevance for the authority of the Christian rulers of England.

---

[25]For a discussion of the importance of the image of the rudderless ship in the tale see V. A. Kolve, *Chaucer and the Imagery of Narrative: The First Five Canterbury Tales* (Stanford, 1984), pp. 297–358.

A second premise that adds to the length and complexity of the Constance story as a story of origins is the Christian view of the natural world as not merely uncivilized in Cicero's sense of the term but "fallen," a term that involves more than the mere absence of civil order. Because this world is "fallen," it is subject to the ongoing efforts of Satan to make humans the instruments of his power. All the wicked pagans in the story are described as under the influence of Satan, and Satan's efforts to thwart the plan of divine providence thus become an important counterplot competing with the main plot of the story.

The view of the world as "fallen" adds further reinforcement to the "descending" theory of authority, by justifying the need for a ruler with divine authority and by making obedience the religious duty of the subject. One of the most influential formulations of the Christian view of the "descending" theory of authority, St. Augustine's discussion of "subjection" in Book 19 of *The City of God*, makes clear the significance of the Fall for the question of authority. Augustine argues that, to a rational creature created in God's image, "subjection" is not natural but a punishment; the suffering involved in "subjection" to authority arises precisely because it goes against human nature. "Subjection," however, involves not only a punishment but also a remedy for sin; as the first sin arose from the refusal to obey the authority of God, so the remedy for sin is the discipline of obedience to authority.[26] Chaucer's Custance invokes this Augustinian view of authority and subjection when she says that she must obey her father's commands because women are born to "thralldom and

---

[26]Augustine, *The City of God*, vol. 6: Books XVIII.36–XX, ed. and trans. W. C. Greene, Loeb Classical Library, (Cambridge, Mass., 1960; repr; 1969), XIX.15. For a discussion of the sources and influences of this Augustinian view of authority and subjection see R. A. Markus, "The Latin Fathers," in Burns, *The Cambridge History*, pp. 92–122, esp. 108–11.

penance" and to be under the "governance" of men. And when she accepts without question the command of the Sultan's mother to set her adrift in a rudderless boat, not questioning its justice but instead praying to the Cross for grace to amend her own sinful life, Custance is accepting the Augustinian view that obedience, even to an authority that is manifestly unjust, is both a punishment and remedy for the sin of the subject.[27]

These fundamental Christian premises are important in all three versions of the story of Constance, but they are treated rather differently in each version. In Trevet's version, the fallen state of human nature is clearly evident in the behavior of Constaunce's enemies, who repeatedly attempt to thwart the plans of divine providence, but Constaunce herself does not invoke the Fall as providing a rationale for absolute obedience to authori-ty.[28] Unlike Chaucer's Custance, Trevet's heroine is not notable for her submission to the powers that be. On the contrary, she is independent and remarkably outspoken; from the first, her force-ful words gain her a considerable measure of personal authority. In the founding role it ascribes to the power of Constaunce's words, Trevet's version is the closest of the three to Cicero's story of origins. Trevet introduces Constaunce as a precocious thirteen-year old who has mastered the seven liberal arts together with several languages, as well as the fundamentals of Christian

---

[27]For a more detailed discussion of this view of sin and punishment, as applied to The Man of Law's Tale, see Patricia J. Eberle, "Crime and Justice in the Middle Ages: Cases from the *Canterbury Tales* of Geoffrey Chaucer," in *Rough Justice: Essays on Crime in English Literature*, ed. Martin L. Friedland (Toronto, 1991), pp. 19–51.

[28]All references to Trevet's version are based on the edition of this section of his *Chronicles* by Margaret Schlauch in *Sources and Analogues*, pp. 165–81. An edition of the full text of the *Chronicles* for The Chaucer Library is being prepared by Robert M. Correale. Translations from the Anglo-Norman are my own.

doctrine. When Saracen merchants arrive at her father's palace and try to persuade her to buy their exotic wares, she responds by persuading them to accept her Christian faith. Later, when she arrives in England, she is able to speak to the Saxon constable in his own language, and she is so well-spoken that the constable takes her for a princess from some Saxon kingdom overseas. Her mastery of Saxon as well as the Christian faith is so complete that she is able to instruct the constable's wife in all the fundamentals of the faith. Trevet's Constaunce has a well-founded confidence in her own abilities that contrasts markedly with Chaucer's heroine. When, for example, the constable's wife tells Trevet's Constaunce that she is "without equal in virtue on this earth," Constaunce does not deny the truth of this praise but urges her to convert to Christianity so that she can partake of some of this virtue herself.[29] After her conversion, when a blind Briton asks the constable's wife to perform a miracle and heal him, Constaunce encourages her, saying, "Don't hide the power that God has given you."[30] The Christian faith that Trevet's Constaunce professes evidently serves to empower women, not to prescribe for them the "thralldom and penance" that Chaucer's Custance takes as her divinely appointed lot.

The sin of Eve, which looms so large for Chaucer's Custance as the origin of the Fall, is never even mentioned in Trevet's account of Constaunce's Christian beliefs. In instructing the constable's wife, Trevet's Constaunce does mention the fallen condition of this world and the story of the Flood as God's punishment of a sinful world, but she never expresses any feeling of her own

---

[29]"'. . . [V]ous etez en terre sauntz peer en vertue.' E Custaunce lui respount: 'A ceo poez vous venir, si crere voudrez en celi dieu quest seignur de toute vertue'" (Schlauch, *Sources*, p. 169).

[30]"'Ne mucez pas, dame, la vertue qe dieu te ad done'" (p. 170).

personal sinfulness or of the especially sinful nature of womankind. Trevet's Constaunce is closer in spirit to Saint Cecilia in The Second Nun's Tale—forthright, self-confident, and empowered by her faith in God to speak out against those who wrongly attempt to force her to submit. When the Saxon knight makes an attempt on her virtue, she does not hesitate to rebuke him in forceful language; she tells him that "he is like a dog, who after the holy sacrament of his baptism wants to return to his own excrement."[31]

Trevet's version of the story of the origins of Christian authority in England must have been especially welcome to princess Marie, a daughter of Edward I who had entered holy orders and for whom Trevet wrote his *Chronicles*.[32] His story adapts the "descending" view of authority in a way calculated to appeal to a nobly born, well-educated, and religious woman. If "all power is of God," then God can grant power even to a woman, and a woman of noble birth, good education, and a strong commitment to the Christian faith can play a founding role in the course of English history.

Gower's version of the story makes an important change in the character of Constance by omitting all references to her eloquence and education.[33] All of the conversions in the story are caused

---

[31]"qil estoit com cheen, que apres si seinte sacrement de son baptesme voleit retourner a son merde" (p. 171).

[32]For an account of the *Chronicles* as a whole see Ruth Dean, "Nicholas Trevet, Historian," in *Medieval Learning and Literature: Essays Presented to Richard William Hunt* (Oxford, 1976), pp. 339–49.

[33]*Confessio Amantis*, Book II, lines 587–1598; all citations are from the edition of Macaulay. Gower's version is presented as a story against "Detraction," a branch of the sin of Envy, but its role as a "story of origins" also receives attention. Gower's Constance is described as one "Be whom the misbelieve of Sinne / Was left, and Cristes feith cam inne / To hem that whilom were blinde" (II, lines 1569–71).

not by the eloquence and wisdom of Constance but by "grace," the power of the God in whom she puts her faith. It is not Constance herself but "grace of Goddes pourveance" (*CA* II, line 753) that enables her to convert the constable's wife. And the conversions of many of the other Saxons, including King Alla, occur in reaction to the miracle that takes place during the trial of Constance for murder, when her false accuser is struck down by the hand of God. Although Constance is a powerful instrument for conveying the teaching of God, the cause is not her own power but God's power working through her. On her own, she is only a helpless and fearful woman. When she finds herself in the midst of the bloodbath created by the Sultan's mother, she cannot control her tears (II, lines 702–03); when she awakens to find the bloody body of the constable's wife next to her in bed, she swoons (II, lines 846–47); on both occasions she is nearly, Gower says, "ded for feere" (II, lines 696, 846). In contrast, Trevet's Constaunce never sheds a tear, and confronted with the feast turned bloodbath, she spends all her efforts in refuting the attempts of the Sultan's mother to persuade her to convert to the Moslem faith.

As we have seen, Gower began his *Confessio Amantis* by endorsing strongly the "descending" theory of authority associated with Richard II. But in his tale of Constance, as in many of the other tales in the *Confessio*, he interprets the "descending" theory in a way that is calculated to emphasize not the ruler's absolute authority over those beneath him but his absolute dependence on and duty of obedience to the God who is above him as the source of his power.[34] By reshaping Trevet's version of the story of the origin of Christian rulership in Saxon England so that the key fig-

---

[34]On the relevance of this tale, and of the *Confessio Amantis* as a whole, to the instruction of rulers, see Russell A. Peck, *Kingship and Common Profit in Gower's Confessio Amantis* (Carbondale and Edwardsville, Ill., 1978), esp. pp. 62–69.

ure is a helpless woman who, through the grace of God, plays a founding role, Gower makes the tale an *exemplum* of his own interpretation of the "descending" theory. The conclusion to the *Confessio* as a whole makes clear how Gower's interpretation differs from the "descending" theory he implicitly attributes to Richard II in his Prologue. He began the *Confessio* professing his subjection to the will of Richard II and he concludes it professing his subjection to the will of God as

> . . . thilke lord in special
> As he which is of alle thinges
> The creatour, and of the kinges
> Hath the fortunes upon honde,
> His grace and mercy forto fonde
> Upon mi bare knees I preye,
> That he my worthi king conveye,
> Richard by name the Secounde. . . . (VIII, lines 2980*–87*)

Richard II's view of the divine sanction for his authority is here transformed into a reminder of the king's complete dependence on the "grace" of the "lord" who has created him and who continues to hold his "fortunes" in his hand. The story of the origins of Christian rulership in England, as Gower tells it in his version of the story of Constance, is thus designed to set a precedent for later English kings. In the context of a work dedicated to Richard II, the image of a rudderless boat (*absque gubernaculo*, as a Latin sidenote to II, lines 655–56 describes it) serves as a striking reminder to the king that the supreme *gubernator* or helmsman is God.

Chaucer's The Man of Law's Tale, like Gower's and Trevet's versions, emphasizes the role of divine providence in his story of origins, but his image of divine authority is markedly different. The God of The Man of Law's Tale is a God of power whose justice is inscrutable. Chaucer's Man of Law also sees the story as part of God's predestined plan, but he repeatedly calls attention to human inability to understand the plan or comprehend its justice. Part of that plan is written, the Man of Law asserts, in the "large book" (line 190) we call the heavens, where the death of every man is foreordained, but very few can read this book and none can understand it. When he goes on to explain his views on the movements of the heavens, the Man of Law describes a world where power is exercised without regard for, even in opposition to, the natural desires of individuals. In standard medieval accounts of Ptolomaic cosmology, for example in the treatise *On the Sphere* (c. 1250) of Sacrobosco, the movements of the heavenly spheres were seen as an example of the concord of contrary forces.[35] The outermost sphere, the *primum mobile*, by moving in a contrary direction to the other spheres beneath, was believed to produce the famous "harmony of the spheres." This harmony, also called *discordia concors*, was looked up to as a model for all forms of earthly harmony, political and social as well as musical. In a remarkable departure from this standard view, the Man of Law delivers a highly rhetorical denunciation of the *primum mobile* as the very image and source of willful violence, exercised against the natural tendencies and desires of its subjects below:

> O firste moevyng! Crueel firmament,
> With thy diurnal sweigh that crowdest ay
> And hurlest al from est til occident
> That naturelly wolde holde another way. . . .   (lines 295–98)

In the Man of Law's view it is the movement of the "cruel" *primum mobile* that dooms Custance's marriage from the start and

---

[35]For a translation and discussion of the significance of this work see Lynn Thorndike, *The Sphere of Sacrobosco and its Commentators* (Chicago, 1949). The two motions are discussed in the Proemium and again in chap. 2.

sets her on her long journey of suffering.[36]

The story of origins he tells may have beneficial consequences for the course of history as a whole, but the Man of Law chooses repeatedly to emphasize the suffering it causes to individuals, especially to Custance herself. The Augustinian view of "subjection" as involving suffering because it is contrary to nature receives repeated emphasis in this version of the story. But contrary to Augustine's view, and even to the view of Custance herself, the suffering in this story does not seem to serve as a remedy for sin. Despite, or perhaps because of, her own repeated references to the inherent sinfulness of womankind and her own personal sins, we are never given evidence that Custance has any sin that needs a remedy. The Man of Law himself does not see her as suffering punishment for her sins, but as emblematic of the suffering that is inherent in the state of this world as a whole. A number of passages adapted from Pope Innocent III's treatise *On the Miseries of the Human Condition*[37] are put in the Man of Law's mouth as expressions of his view of the world, a world where suffering is the norm and "sodeyn wo" always follows hard upon "worldly blisse" (lines 421–22).

In this version of the tale Custance is an emblem of this woe. In Trevet's version, onlookers may weep at her departure but Constaunce herself remains dry-eyed; in Gower, Constance weeps at moments of crisis; but in Chaucer's version she is described as

---

[36]For a detailed analysis of the full passage in which the Man of Law denounces the heavens, blaming them for the doomed marriage between Custance and the Sultan, see Chauncey Wood, *Chaucer and the Country of the Stars: Poetic Uses of Astrological Imagery* (Princeton, 1970), pp. 219–34.

[37]For an edition of this text and an analysis of the glosses based on it see Lotario dei Segni (Pope Innocent III), *De miseria condicionis humane*, ed. Robert E. Lewis, The Chaucer Library (Athens, Ga., 1978).

a "woful" object of pity from beginning to end. When we first see
her depart from Rome she is a "woful faire mayde" (line 316). By
the time she reaches England, she is a "woful womman" (line
522), so full of "wo" that when the Saxon constable discovers her
the only act of "mercy" she requests is to be put out of her misery,

> The lyf out of hir body for to twynne,
> Hire to delivere of wo that she was inne.   (lines 517–18)

When at last she is reunited with her husband, King Alla, the Man
of Law emphasizes that sudden woe once again overtakes her, and
her husband dies soon afterwards. For the Man of Law the bleak
moral of the tale is the transitory nature of all human happiness:

> But litel while it lasteth, I yow heete,
> Joye of this world, for tyme wol nat abyde;
> Fro day to nyght it changeth as the tyde.   (lines 1132–34)

In this world, the ultimate authority belongs to Death, who is
described as an absolute sovereign who "taketh of heigh and logh
his rente" (line 1142); it is worth noting in passing that, as the
embodiment of absolute authority in the extreme, Death imposes
his "rente" or taxes on his all subjects without their consent.

Just as the world of The Man of Law's Tale is more decidedly
"fallen" than it is in the other versions of the tale, so the role of
divine providence is decidedly more inscrutable. It is not merely,
as in Trevet and Gower, that God manages to preserve Custance
through her trials; the Man of Law repeatedly emphasizes that the
trials visited on Custance are also expressions of God's will.
When Custance is put to sea in her rudderless boat for the second
time, she herself views this trial as an expression of the divine
will, saying "Lord, ay welcome be thy sonde!" (line 826). The
Saxon constable, whom she has converted to Christianity, shows

that he is also converted to her view of divine authority when he obeys what he thinks is the command of his king as an expression of the will of God himself.

Although he obeys this sentence, the constable does question the justice of this kind of authority:

> "O myghty God, if that it be thy wille,
> Sith thou art rightful juge, how may it be
> That thou wolt suffren innocentz to spille,
> And wikked folk regne in prosperitee?"   (lines 813–16)

Earlier in the tale, the Man of Law as narrator raises a similar question when he attempts to explain why, when the Sultan's mother was able to kill so many innocent Christians at the feast, Custance managed to be preserved. His reply begins confidently enough, only to end by revealing his inability to give a satisfactory answer to the larger question about the justice of divine authority:

> God liste to shewe his wonderful myracle
> In hire, for we sholde seen his myghty werkis;
> Crist, which that is to every harm triacle,
> By certeine meenes ofte, as knowen clerkis,
> Dooth thyng for certein ende that ful derk is
> To mannes wit, that for oure ignorance
> Ne konne noght knowe his prudent purveiance.
>
> (lines 477–83)

In this passage, the Man of Law's God appears as the embodiment of the idea of absolute authority as envisioned by the "descending" view of Richard II. The supreme authority is not obedient to any law but acts as he "liste"; the will of this lord has the force of law. Since their own "ignorance" is so far inferior to the "prudent purveiance" of their ruler, his subjects have no right to be consulted or offer their consent.

This view of divine providence, as operating arbitrarily and incomprehensibly, undermines a central premise of Trevet's version of the story of origins in a way that raises serious questions about the "descending" view of authority that the story seems to endorse. In Trevet's account, divine providence confers authority on an exemplary young woman, of great piety and force of character, enabling her to abolish the unjust rule of force and bring moral order to the realm. In Chaucer's version, the example set by the heroine is problematical. She is an example not of authority but of obedience to authority, unquestioning and absolute obedience founded on the conviction of her own sinfulness and of the divine authority of all those set above her. In Chaucer's version, moreover, Custance's Christian submissiveness does not always serve the interests of moral order in the world at large; sometimes it leads to acquiescence in the unjust use of authority. For example, King Alla, before his conversion, is presented as someone who is careful to question appearances; he does not accept the claim of the Saxon knight that Custance is guilty of murder but insists that the knight put his charges to the test of a formal oath. Once King Alla has converted to Christianity, however, he seems to lose this healthy distrust of questionable appearances. When he receives a letter (forged by his mother) with the highly questionable news that his wife is "an elf" who has given birth to a monster, he does not even think of inquiring further into the matter. Instead, he takes the unwelcome news as evidence of the will of God and he accepts God's will in submissive language of the sort we have learned to expect from Custance:

> "Welcome the sonde of Crist for everemoore
> To me that am now lerned in his loore!
> Lord, welcome be thy lust and thy plesaunce;
> My lust I putte al in thyn ordinaunce."   (lines 760–63)

It is not only the power of Satan that assists Alla's mother in her evil designs on Custance and her new child; it is also the newly acquired Christian faith of Alla and the constable, which leads them to accept the forged letters without question as an expression of the will of the powers that be and, thus, as an expression of the "ordinaunce" of God.

The recurrent pattern of unquestioning submission to absolute authority that appears in Chaucer's version of the story, and in Chaucer's version alone, is thus closely linked to another distinctive feature of Chaucer's version, its repeated emphasis on the suffering of the heroine and of all who share her faith. In this version, the arrival of Christian rulership in England comes about as a result of suffering, and this suffering is a direct consequence of the Christian attitude of unquestioning submission to secular authority as if it were the authority of God himself. This point is worth emphasizing. Custance's submission to the authority of God is what preserves her from death at various points in the story, but her suffering originates in her unquestioning submission to secular authority, beginning with the authority of her father the emperor.

In some political theories, the suffering created in the individual subject by submission to authority is justified by virtue of a greater good, the moral order of the whole that it makes possible. This is the view of Theseus in The Knight's Tale. In The Man of Law's Tale, however, submission is presented as making it possible for those who are wicked to gain authority and use it to create disorder and injustice. We have already seen how Chaucer adds speeches emphasizing the Christian submission of the constable and King Alla to the letters forged by Alla's wicked mother. What Chaucer omits from his account of Custance's unjust exile from England serves to demonstrate further his interest in the consequences of submission to authority. In Trevet's account, the people of Saxon England, when they learn that their beloved Queen Constaunce has been exiled without due cause, stage a public demonstration that amounts to a rebellion against the king's authority.

> As the king was making his way by day through cities and towns in England, there came to meet him men and women, children and old people, and they reviled him with words and gestures of outrage, throwing at him and his followers filth and excrement and large stones, and women and children out of scorn lifted up their garments and showed him their buttocks.[38]

The means they choose to express their dissent may not be dignified, but they do demonstrate Trevet's conviction that exile without due cause violated a fundamental right of English people (a right guaranteed by the famous clause 39 of Magna Carta) and his belief in the right of the people to refuse to submit to any authority that is manifestly unjust. By contrast with this vivid description of a popular protest movement in his source, Chaucer's description of the Christian submission of two men of power, to highly questionable charges against a woman they know and respect, is the more remarkable. In Chaucer's version, the effect of conversion to Christianity is to render people entirely submissive to authority, even when it is manifestly unjust.

With its emphasis on the unjust suffering caused by unquestioning submission to secular authority, Chaucer's version of the Constance story thus serves to undermine the "descending" theory of authority its sources recommend. Moreover, although Chaucer's Custance seems unable to envision anything other than the

---

[38]"Et com ly rois erra soun chemyn par cites e viles, de iour, en Engletere, luy vindrent encountrauns hommes e femmes, enfauntz e veilars, e le reuilerent de crie e ledengge, gettauntz sur lui et les seuns tay e ordure e grosses peres, e femmes e enfauntz deuestuz par despyt luy moustrerent lour derere. . ." (Schlauch, *Sources and Analogues*, p. 176).

"descending" view that puts her in the helpless posture of unquestioning submission, his Man of Law is aware of a possible alternative, the "ascending" view of authority advocated in the Parliamentary statement of 1386.

The Man of Law's view on the question of authority emerges in the course of his conversation with the Host that precedes his tale and provides the occasion for its telling. The Host speaks first, in keeping with his role as authority figure in the tale-telling contest:

> "Sire Man of Lawe," quod he, "so have ye blis,
> Telle us a tale anon, as forward is.
> Ye been submytted, thurgh youre free assent,
> To stonden in this cas at my juggement.
> Acquiteth yow now of youre biheste;
> Thanne have ye do youre devoir atte leeste."
>   "Hooste," quod he, "*depardieux*, ich assente;
> To breke forward is nat myn entente.
> Biheste is dette, and I wole holde fayn
> Al my biheste, I kan no bettre sayn.
> For swich lawe as a man yeveth another wight,
> He sholde hymselven usen it by right;
> Thus wole oure text."   (lines 33–45)

A number of those who have commented on this passage have called attention to the fact that both the Host and the Man of Law use legal terminology and legalistic arguments. But no one to my knowledge has pointed out that the debate about the origin and limits of the authority of the Host over the tale-telling contest echoes in a playful way a similar and more serious debate in English constitutional history, the ongoing debate between Richard II and his opponents that first became apparent in the Parliament of 1386.[39]

---

[39]In addition to the references given in the notes in *The Riverside Chaucer* see Hornsby, *Chaucer and the Law*, pp. 33–34.

At the heart of the debate between the Host and the Man of Law is a controversy over the origins of the Host's authority, in the "forward" or agreement made by the Canterbury pilgrims on the eve of their departure from the Host's tavern at Southwark. The Host's words here echo the terms of the agreement as described in the General Prologue. On the evening of their departure, the Host proposes to the pilgrims assembled in his tavern that, for their common benefit, they agree unanimously, "by ooon assent," to accept his authority. The Host's view of authority appears in the words he uses to describe the obedience of his pilgrim subjects. They are, he says, to "stonden at my juggement" and "for to werken as I shal . . . seye. . ." (GenPro, lines 777–79). The pilgrims agree to accept what would have been called his *jurisdictio*—a term that includes what we would now call "executive" and "legislative" as well as "judicial" authority—before they know the specific form that his authority will take. Not until they have given him their "assent" does the Host recount the rules of the tale-telling game they have authorized him to create. These rules make clear that he has arrogated to himself considerable fiscal authority. Before they grant their assent, he claims that his plan is only to amuse them and will cost them nothing (line 768), but once granted authority, he proceeds to make rules that will subserve his own economic interests as innkeeper, at the expense of the pilgrims. The prize he assigns the winner is a supper at his own inn at a price he will set himself, to be paid for by a collection taken from the other pilgrims, who will also pay for their own suppers at the same time. In order to reinforce his authority and further his economic interests still more, the Host stipulates that if anyone contests his judgement at any time (line 805), that person "shal paye al that we spenden by the weye" (line 806).

The political implications of this agreement are conveyed by the words Chaucer applies to him, calling him not only "juge" of the contest but also the "governour" or ruler of the pilgrim company in all other matters as well. All the pilgrims, he says, swore oaths that to be "reuled . . . at his devys / In heigh and lough" (lines 816–17); that is to say, the pleasure of the Host will have the force of law in all things for the whole community of pilgrims. Throughout *The Canterbury Tales*, the pleasure of the Host does, in fact, appear to be the supreme authority. Harry selects the first teller by lot, then abandons even this pretence of fairness or consistency and calls on whomever he pleases to tell the rest of the tales; the announced criteria for judging the tales are replaced by Harry's own personal pleasure, and he arrogates to himself a new power he did not specify in the original agreement, when he cuts short a tale like Sir Thopas that he does not like. In practice, throughout the frame of *The Canterbury Tales* as well as in the theory he articulates in his exchange with the Man of Law, the Host's view of his authority over the pilgrims is thus a variant of the "descending" theory of authority of Richard II.

In his reply to the Host, the Man of Law endorses a view of authority that has a good deal in common with the "ascending" view of the 1386 Parliamentary statement. Although the Man of Law begins by announcing his assent to the Host's request, the rationale he offers for his "assent" involves a rather different interpretation of the original agreement behind the tale-telling contest and the nature of the authority the agreement conferred on the Host. The Man of Law sees the tale-telling agreement not as an irrevocable and unlimited submission of his will to the will of the Host but as a contract that binds all parties equally. In agreeing to keep his "biheste," he refers not to the personal authority of the Host but to the authority of the principle on which all contract law is founded, the principle of good faith, as expressed in the legal maxim *pacta sunt servanda* that he translates freely as "Biheste is dette."[40] To this fundamental principle of contract law he adds another, a principle that he takes to be equally fundamental: "swiche lawe as a man yeveth another wight, / He sholde hymselven usen it, by right; / Thus wole oure text" (lines 43–45). In acknowledging the binding force of the tale-telling contract, the Man of Law argues that the Host as "governour" is equally bound, both to the contract and to the underlying legal principles on which it is based.

When the Man of Law concludes his reference, "Thus wole oure text," he may be referring to the *Digest* of Justinian, since his version of the principle that "the laws bind the lawgiver" closely resembles the statement of this principle that appears as the rubric to the second section of Book II. It is far more likely, however, that by "oure text" he means another work, the treatise *On the Laws and Customs of England* usually called simply "Bracton," from the great thirteenth-century English jurist who is credited with the primary role in its compilation. Bracton was designed as a textbook for the study of English legal practice and theory, and the large number of English manuscripts extant suggest that it was widely used in this way.[41] Chaucer's Man of Law, who, as a Sergeant of the Law, is a member of the elite order of justices regarded as experts in English common law, might well refer to Bracton as "oure text," the basic work of reference for his order. Bracton makes reference to the principle that "laws bind the lawgiver" in an argument having some notable similarities with the controversy between the Host and the Man of Law.

---

[40]On the origins of this maxim of canon law in penetential discipline see Berman, *Law and Revolution*, p. 247.

[41]For a brief discussion of Bracton's influence on the legal profession see Bryce Lyon, *A Constitutional and Legal History of Medieval England*, 2nd ed. (New York and London, 1980), pp. 290–91, 435–36.

The quotation of the maxim "laws bind the lawgiver" appears in the section of Bracton discussing the nature of the royal authority.[42] In the course of this discussion Bracton makes reference to a famous text from civil law, the so-called *lex regia*, which provided an explanation of the origins of the legal basis of the authority of a ruler. According to the *lex regia*, the authority of the Roman emperor must have originated in a founding grant of plenary power from the Roman people. In both the *Institutes* and the *Digest* of Justinian, this founding grant is assumed to be irrevocable, and the *lex regia* supports the "descending" theory of authority, by providing justification for the principle "What pleases the prince has the force of law." Bracton turns the civil law interpretation of the *lex regia* on its head and offers an interpretation of the *lex regia* that is influenced by his own view of the proper role of royal authority in English government. In his view, the *lex regia* shows the importance of *lex* (derived from *ligare*, "to bind") as an ongoing and mutual bond between the ruler and his people. The consent of the people to the founding *lex regia* sets a precedent for all future legislation: all subsequent laws also require their consent. Law is not, Bracton says, "whatever has been rashly put forward by the will of the ruler" but what "has been rightly decided with the counsel of his magnates, after deliberation and consultation, with the addition of the authority of the king." In Bracton's view *lex facit rex* (law makes the king); the "law" in question here is not only the founding *lex regia*, but also the coronation promises that each English king makes to uphold the laws of the land. The principle that "laws bind the lawgiver" is the key link in this chain of arguments designed to re-

---

[42]*Bracton De Legibus et Consuetudinibus Angliae/ Bracton on the Laws and Customs of England*, 4 vols., ed. George E. Woodbine, trans. Samuel E. Thorne (Cambridge, Mass., 1968–77), 2:305; the discussion appears in the section with the rubric "For what purpose a king is created; of ordinary jurisdiction."

interpret texts of civil law in such a way as to provide justification for Bracton's view of English constitutional practice.[43]

Following a logic similar to Bracton, the Man of Law uses the principle that the "laws bind the lawgiver" as a way of limiting the Host's claims to absolute authority and asserting the ongoing legal authority of his own power of assent. The Man of Law's own views on authority and subjection are thus very different from the views of the abjectly submissive Custance, and it should now be possible to see his tale as a continuation of his argument with the Host over the question of authority. The tale of Custance is a tale told to win a contest, a contest in which the Host is to serve as sole judge. As we have seen, the Host is a judge who does not rule according to law but according to his own will. It is only fitting, then, that when the Man of Law looks around for precedents for his story, he fastens on the group of tales that he calls "The Seintes Legende of Cupide" (line 61) and that modern readers know as Chaucer's own *Legend of Good Women.* This group of tales is told to please the God of Love, a judge who is as arbitrary and absolute a ruler as the Host. Like the Host, the God of Love believes in ruling according to the "descending" theory of authority, that is, according to the dictates of his own will.[44] The God of Love sets Chaucer the task of supporting his view of

---

[43]This account of Bracton's views on kingship in this section of the work is based on Fritz Schulz, "Bracton on Kingship," *English Historical Review* 60 (1945): 136–76; and Brian Tierney, "Bracton on Government," *Speculum* 38 (1963): 295–317. Other passages in Bracton can be interpreted to endorse other views of royal authority, and the analysis here is not meant to go beyond the specific passage in question.

[44]The discourse of Alceste condemning "wilfulhed" as the essence of tyranny and describing the "office" of a king as maintaining "justice" and "equite" (*LGW* G, lines 353–97) is a criticism of the "descending" view of authority she attributes to the God of Love as ruler.

authority by telling stories of good women who are uniformly submissive to his will. In invoking these stories of good women as a precedent for his story of Custance, the Man of Law not only suggests a parallel between his heroine and the "saints" of Cupid but also a similarity in the views of authority endorsed by the Host and the God of Love. The Man of Law's Tale, like the stories in the *Legend of Good Women*, only appears to support the view of authority endorsed by the authority figure at whose command it is told; in fact, as we have seen, by making the long-suffering Custance an example of the ideal subject in the "descending" theory of authority, The Man of Law's Tale emphasizes repeatedly that complete submission to absolute authority is not a model for ideal governance, but a kind of martyrdom to a flawed ideal.

Taken together, then, the Man of Law's Prologue and Tale offer a critique of the "descending" theory of political authority, a critique that takes the form of a discussion of the meaning of two rather different but interrelated stories of origins, the story of the origins of the Host's role as ruler in the tale-telling contest and the story of the origins of Christian rulership in England. Both stories are fictitious, but in raising the question of authority they raise a serious issue that affected the facts of political life in Richard II's England.

There is no need to insist that The Man of Law's Tale comments directly on specific political events, still less that one can see, by analyzing the tale, exactly where Chaucer himself stood in the confrontation between the king and Parliament in 1386. What can be suggested, however, is that both Chaucer and his immediate audience were very much alive to issues turning on the question of authority and aware of the many and complex arguments that could be made on this question. They were also aware of a commonplace of medieval political theory, that the question of authority was not merely a question about the authority of a ruler over his subjects; both "ascending" and "descending" theories addressed themselves not only to the issue of kingship but to a wide variety of kinds of authority, the authority of a parent over a child, of a husband over a wife, of the head of a household over his *familia*, of the king over his kingdom. The question of authority is repeatedly debated throughout the period, in a variety of contexts; behind many of the citations in the *Middle English Dictionary* for what might be called "keywords" in this semantic field—words such as *ligeaunce, obeissaunce, sovereignitee, subjeccioun, submissioun*, as well as *auctoritee* itself—may be sensed an ongoing debate among Chaucer's contemporaries over issues like those raised in The Man of Law's Tale.[45]

This kind of analysis could, of course, be extended to many other of the *Canterbury Tales* as well. Long ago, G. L. Kittredge persuaded many people that four of the tales turned on a debate about sovereignty in marriage; since then, a number of other tales have been seen as thematically related to what is now called "the Marriage Group."[46] In fourteenth-century England, however, marriage seems to have been less a matter for debate than the issue of sovereignty itself and the question of authority which lay behind that issue.[47] If what is suggested here has been persua-

---

[45]On the notion of "keywords" that serve as focal points for conflicting ideologies in a given culture see Raymond Williams, *Keywords: A Vocabulary of Culture and Society* (New York, 1976), pp. 9–24.

[46]For a bibliography of studies on "the Marriage Group" see John Leyerle and Anne Quick, *Chaucer: A Bibliographical Introduction*, Toronto Medieval Bibliographies, 10 (Toronto, 1986), pp. 147–49.

[47]For a discussion of the problem of sovereignty, focusing on the debates over the nature of the papal monarchy see Michael J. Wilks, *The Problem of Sovereignty in the Later Middle Ages*, Cambridge Studies in Medieval Life and Thought, 2nd

sive, it may be time to rethink the so-called "Marriage Group" and reconsider it as a group of tales related by an interest in the question of authority as it was understood in the age of Richard II. Considered from that perspective, many other tales can be added to the group. The "descending" view of the question of authority appears in stories of submission and rebellion, to husbands, to parents, or to rulers (The Knight's Tale, The Physician's Tale, and The Clerk's Tale, for example); the "ascending" view of authority typically appears in stories concerning the making and breaking of agreements and promises at various levels of society (such as The Franklin's Tale, The Shipman's Tale, The Wife of Bath's Tale). An awareness of the importance of the question of authority in the age of Richard II should make it possible to find a variety of interconnections among the *Canterbury Tales* that have not been fully appreciated. "Auctoritee," as Chaucer and his audience understood the term, encompassed a wide range of assumptions about politics, religion, literature, and gender, and then, as now, all of these interrelated assumptions were matters of controversy.

---

series, 9 (Cambridge, 1963). On the political uses of the metaphor of marriage see Wilks, "Chaucer and the Mystical Marriage in Medieval Political Thought," *Bulletin of the John Rylands Library* 44 (1961–62): 489–530.

The Scribe and the Late Medieval Liturgical Manuscript: Page Layout and Order of Work[1]

ANDREW HUGHES

PREAMBLE

Before better answers to important questions can be found, it may be necessary to answer questions of little importance in themselves. First the latter questions must be identified and asked.[2] Although interesting per se, the minutiae of manuscript production ought to be studied as evidence for dating, localizing,

---

[1] The following abbreviations are used in text and citations: BA=Biblioteca Apostolica, Vatican City; BL=British Library; BM=Bibliothèque municipale; and BN=Bibliothèque nationale, Paris.

Within this essay, these words have specific meanings:

runover: this refers to the end of a text or chant written as an incomplete line that does not begin at the left-hand margin, as at the end of this definition. Runovers are sometimes carried to a partially empty line above as well as to a line **disjunction:** this will refer to the place where the text | below. beginning at the left margin meets a runover, where the sense is not continuous.

[2] Much of the more informed reworking of this article from its original form is due to the comments of an anonymous reader, from whom I learned many things I had not been able to learn about elsewhere. Indeed, I have used some of those comments almost verbatim, since the wording was often so clear.

and relating sources, or for identifying scriptoria.[3] Some minutiae, to my surprise, have hardly ever been discussed in print, and
others have not been discussed systematically. Still others are
well-known, and I refer to them briefly in this study.[4] Because I
wished in this study to examine as wide a selection of scribal
habits as possible, I set aside any thoughts of choosing manuscripts known to be related. I also avoided any attempt at the
higher purpose of showing relationships among manuscripts or
identifying origins. Since my sources are mostly quite unrelated,
observations about them can be of no direct help in dating or
placing. Although not a major purpose of this study, I occasional-

---

[3]Léon Gilissen demonstrates how this process could work in "Un élément
codicologique trop peu exploité: la réglure," *Scriptorium* 23 (1969): 150–62.

[4]Late medieval treatises dealing with scribal procedures include Johannes
Gerson (1363–1429), *De laude scriptorum*, pp. 423–34 in *L'Oeuvre doctrinale*, vol.
9 of *Oeuvres complètes*, ed. P. Glorieux (Paris, 1973), a work that appears to be
entirely theological rather than technical; and Johannes Trithemius (1462–1516), *De
laude scriptorum*, ed. Klaus Arnold, trans. Roland Behrendt (Lawrence, Kan.,
1974), from which edition citations, by chapter, are taken in this essay. See also
Stanley Morison, *A Fifteenth-Century Modus scribendi from the Abbey of Melk*
(Cambridge, 1940). Invaluable as reference books are the bibliographies by
Leonard E. Boyle (*Medieval Latin Paleography: A Bibliographical Introduction*,
Toronto Medieval Bibliographies 8 [Toronto, 1984]) and Laurel Braswell (*Western
Manuscripts from Classical Antiquity to the Renaissance* [New York, 1981]); Bras-
well's work is an annotated bibliography. Modern discussions of general use are
Stephen J. P. van Dijk, "An Advertisement Sheet of an Early Fourteenth-Century
Writing Master at Oxford," *Scriptorium* 10 (1956): 47–64 and plates 8–11; Stanley
Boorman on Preparation and Copying under "Sources" in the *New Grove Diction-
ary of Music and Musicians*, ed. Stanley Sadie, vol. 17 (London, 1980), pp. 591–
671, which includes a facsimile of the manuscript that van Dijk discusses in "An
Advertisement," viz., Bodleian MS. e mus. 198*, fol. 8; Michel Huglo, "Règlement
du XIIIe siècle pour la transcription des livres notés," in *Festschrift Bruno Stäblein
zum 70. Geburtstag*, ed. Martin Ruhnke (Kassel, 1976), pp. 121–33; Raffaele
Arnese, *I Codici notati della biblioteca nazionale di Napoli*, Biblioteca de biblio-
grafia italiana 47 (Florence, 1967), intro.; and Donald Jackson, *The Story of
Writing* (New York, 1981), esp. pp. 50–101.

ly comment about how my observations might help in the dating or placing of manuscripts.

Anyone who has followed a complex book from typescript to print must admire the skills of the designer, who visualizes in advance the layout, the effect of various type-styles, and the placing of illustrations. If the job is done well, the reader may not give the designer a second thought. For certain types of medieval manuscript, few scholars have given the designer (substitute "the design process" or "execution") even a first thought, at least in print. Given a traditional format or a good exemplar, an experienced scribe would have made many decisions about the layout almost without thought: these would be transmitted to the next stage of production in the form of cues and by the layout of what had already been written.[5] The well-known sequence of events in the writing of a medieval manuscript is: 1) the ruling of the pages; 2) the writing of the main text, and cues; and 3) the addition of the initials, illuminations, and other colored material.

This sequence was adequate for the copying of continuous undifferentiated text. For the intricately complex Antiphonals and Breviaries of the later Middle Ages, however, additional stages in production and extra flexibility in execution were required. Liturgical books of the earlier Middle Ages were the Lectionary (containing only the readings), the Collectar (prayers), the Cantatorium (chants and their music), the Benedictional (blessings), and

---

[5]Denis Escudier, "Les manuscrits musicaux du Moyen Age (du IXe au XIIe siècles)," *Codicologica* 3 (1980): 34–45, esp. n. 2, maintains that matters such as format and binding are determined by the fact that liturgical books are used in choir: format here surely means size rather than layout of the page. I thank Prof. Leonard Boyle for directing me to this article.

the Ordinal (instructions about the performance). Each is self-contained and, like other similar books, presents continuous text, set off into "paragraphs" by colored initials. The liturgical process of combining separate books into a single book, the Breviary for the Office, the Missal for Mass, has been well explored.[6] The codicological process of conflating separate books has not. By the thirteenth century most liturgical books contained many kinds of texts, differing in length from a single word to many lines, with or without musical notes, differing in function from instruction to spoken text, and differing in the size of the script. I shall deal mainly with the most complex of liturgical books.

The Different Kinds of Text

Breviaries of the thirteenth to the fifteenth century include the following genres: lessons, chapters, blessings, dialogues, rubrics, responsories, antiphons, invitatories, and sometimes hymns.[7] Each is different in style and length and formal repetition: a benediction may be only a single sentence; different kinds of rubric may vary considerably in length; a lesson may occupy more than a column. Each may be only a brief incipit, because its complete text ap-

---

[6]Pierre Salmon, *L'Office divin au moyen âge*, Lex Orandi (Paris, 1967); Stephen J. P. van Dijk and Joan Hazelden Walker, *The Origins of the Modern Roman Liturgy* (London, 1960), esp. p. 226; and Stephen J. P. van Dijk, *Sources of the Modern Roman Liturgy*, 2 vols. (Leiden, 1963). Andrew Hughes provides a comprehensive survey, touching on many points discussed more fully here and explaining some of the terminology adopted, in his *Medieval Manuscripts for Mass and Office: A Guide to Their Organization and Terminology* (Toronto, 1982).

[7]It is not necessary here to know in detail what these sections, genres, and texts are, and no further descriptions will be given unless necessary: many well-known books give excellent descriptions. The terminology used in this article is mostly standard, although some terms not in frequent use have been introduced in order to avoid ambiguity. Hughes, *Medieval Manuscripts* (n. 6 above), may be consulted.

pears elsewhere. Each text or incipit is identified with its name, which may be given in full or abbreviated. Many of these genres have subsections that must be distinguished:

- with lessons, chapters, prayers: introductory and closing formulas such as *In illo tempore*, *Tu autem*, and *Per Christum.*
- with antiphons and invitatories: psalm-tones and termination formulas (EVOVAE).
- with responsories: repetenda, verse, repetenda cue, and often a doxology.

In musical items the distinction is usually made by some form of capital letter with an identifying abbreviation; in non-musical items the capital letter alone is the usual method.

Of this bewildering array of differentiated texts, some require smaller script or a musical stave, some require space for initials at the margin, some require space to be left for paraphs or colored capitals within the writing area, and all require identifying abbreviations and highlights. In a manuscript in which chant is to be provided for the sung texts, the scribe may have to enter the syllables so that there will be enough space to add the pitches above. From the textual point of view the spacing is irrational. Sometimes the "unsightly" text spaces were filled with decorative ornament, usually red.

Distinguishing the Different Texts

The content of individual books differs according to Use and date. Methods of scribal execution differ in minute but significant detail, and it is mainly such differences that I shall discuss. In matters of overall layout—the color and size of script, and the position of elements on the page—a rather uniform method of preparing liturgical books emerges from the thirteenth to the sixteenth century, to the general principles of which all well-produced books conform.[8] In such books several methods of distinguishing the various kinds of texts occur:

a) different colors are used. Instructions are conventionally written in red, hence the usual name "rubric," or in black and underlined, usually in red. Only black and red are used for words (that is, text or rubrics), but even this distinction necessitates a qualification to process 2) above, the writing of the main text, since it is usually assumed that all writing in black was completed before red material was added. This assumption must be questioned. Another use for red is in manuscripts transmitting the chants on staves: the latter are almost invariably drawn in red and thus involve a separate process.[9] Most

---

[8]Huglo, "Règlement" (n. 4 above). See p. 122 for the increasing assertions of uniformity and, especially, the different degrees of centralization (and the frequency of general chapter meetings) associated with the monastic and regular orders up to the thirteenth century. Well-known instructions for the careful and consistent writing of liturgical manuscripts emanated from most of the important orders, for example the following, from the Dominicans (cited from van Dijk, *Sources* [n. 6 above], 1:118; see also Huglo, "Règlement," pp. 124–25):

> In antiphonariis et gradualibus et aliis libris cantus. fiant note quadrate cum quatuor lineis debito modo distantibus. ne nota hinc inde comprimatur ab eis.
>
> Nullus scienter litteram aut notam mutet. sed teneantur littera et note et virgule pausarum.
>
> Puncta etiam directiva posita in fine linearum ad innuendum ubi prima nota sequentis linee debeat inchoari. diligenter a notatoribus observentur.
>
> Antequam legatur vel cantetur de cetero in quocumque libro de novo scribendo. prius liber bis ad correcta exemplaria corrigatur.

The book trade, too, stimulated uniformity of layout; see Malcolm B. Parkes, "The Influence of the Concepts of *ordinatio* and *compilatio* on the Development of the Book," in *Medieval Learning and Literature: Essays Presented to Richard William Hunt*, ed. J. J. G. Alexander and M. T. Gibson (Oxford, 1976): 115–41, esp. 137, and plates IX–XVI.

[9]Huglo, "Règlement" (n. 4 above), p. 126, includes references to some sources with black staves.

manuscripts use yellow for highlighting certain letters: I do not think it is possible to specify when highlights were added except, of course, that they were entered after the letter itself, perhaps in a separate process after the whole text was complete. Other than in the initials and capitals, the only other color is blue, mostly reserved for the paraph mark, **℃**, used less consistently than other features. It indicates the divisions (paragraphs) in long rubrics, and distinguishes various kinds of rubric. It may separate a rubric describing actions or listing items from a sentence identifying the day such as *In die . . .* or *Dominica prima in. . . .* Blue material was added after red, adding another step in the sequence above, to process 3), the addition of colored material.

b) different sizes are used for certain texts. Occasionally, rubrics are written in smaller letters. So too, in those Antiphonals that present them, may be the texts of the versicles and responses (or dialogues), of which the liturgical greeting, *Dominus vobiscum: Et cum spiritu tuo,* is the best known. The longest texts written smaller are those of the sung items (as opposed to intoned items, such as dialogues and lessons). These texts may originally have been smaller so that musical notes could be added above them. Since the latter were written after (but of course above) the text, it was the text scribe's responsibility to leave sufficient room. In early manuscripts a space of one line of text would have been enough, because the stave had not come into use.[10] Rather than leaving a blank rule, however, the scribe generally wrote on immediately consecutive rules of the page, using smaller letters. The introduction of the four-line stave by

---

[10]See pp. 175–77 below, including n. 37 (Escudier, "Les manuscrits médiévaux," n. 5 above). Books describing the details of musical notation of the Middle Ages are listed in items **124–67** of Andrew Hughes, *Medieval Music: The Sixth Liberal Art*, rev. ed. (Toronto, 1980).

the twelfth century meant that the use of smaller letters was no
longer enough: a real space of empty rules had to be left above
the text. In manuscripts with the musical stave, then, there must
have been a design decision about the spacing of lines of
continuous text relative to sections of text with stave. The size
of the text beneath the stave is no longer important since the
stave will itself identify the musical items. In manuscripts without the chant, the texts of sung items are still written smaller,
even though there was no intention or possibility of adding the
music. Tradition no doubt played a part in this decision, but a
practical result is the distinguishing of sung items by the size of
their text and, sometimes, a saving in space on these items,
which would have been performed by someone other than the
user of the non-noted book. It may be that these useful results
of traditional practices caused them to be continued.

c) identifying words or abbreviations, such as *Lectio* or *lc.* and
antiphona or *ant.* (see Plate 1), are added in red, usually for
every item in the book. I shall refer to these as IDs. As with
colored material already mentioned, a stage in the production
separate from that of black text, and perhaps separate from the
addition of other red material, would be required.

d) a hierarchy of colored initials or capital letters is used, usually
quite consistently. They identify certain points such as main
feast-days and services within the book, genres such as antiphons or prayers within the services, and structural points
such as verses within the genres.[11]

Capital letters used for these purposes are distinctly larger than
the normal script capital that begins internal sentences of a long
text such as a lesson. They normally have a highlight, sometimes
red, more often a dull yellow, which consists of a single stroke or

---

[11]See items mentioned in n. 6 above.

daub of color, depending partly on the shape of the letter. Naturally, the highlight was added later. When used in a musical item supplied with its stave, the capital normally extends upwards into the
stave or even into almost the whole width of the stave. Its size is
then similar to that of the two-line Lombard or illuminated initial.
For consecutive subsequent verses of such items as psalms, hymns,
and sequences a special capital, sometimes called a versal, is used.
Like the smaller calligraphic capital, it is larger than normal script,
but, like the initial, it is colored alternately red or blue.

The initial occupying two lines of text corresponds to an initial spanning one line of text and the stave. Larger initials appear
infrequently and denote the major feast-days or sections of the
book. They are always colored, at the left-hand margin, and often
include artwork. They must have been the last parts of the book to
be added. Some may occupy complete pages in ornate manuscripts. More often they occupy only parts of the page, and the
scribe must make the necessary textual adjustments to leave the
appropriate space. There seems to be no hierarchy of sizes within
these large initials: some consistency of size is usually maintained, but differences appear unrelated to liturgical occasion or
anything else. The artwork involved in such letters has been described and reproduced on many occasions.[12] Some medieval instructions have survived:

> Sequitur ordo scribendi hoc opus secundum artem. Ut autem
> clarius innotescat in hoc opere ordo intelligendi, talis in eo

---

[12]See, for example, Otto Pächt, *Illuminated Manuscripts in the Bodleian
Library*, 3 vols. (Oxford, 1966, 1970, 1973); and Jonathan J. G. Alexander,
"Scribes as Artists: The Arabesque Initial in Twelfth-Century English Manuscripts,"
pp. 87–116 in *Medieval Scribes, Manuscripts and Libraries: Essays Presented to N.
R. Ker*, ed. Malcolm B. Parkes and Andrew G. Watson (London, 1978). Only the
plates really make it clear that these authors are describing initials larger than two
lines of text.

scribendi servetur modus, videlicet quod majoribus litteris ru-
beis vel azureis, que sunt in ipsorum sermonum exordio, pro-
porcionaliter detur spacium sex linearum; articulorum vero in-
iciis quatuor liniarum spacium sufficiens est; capitulorum vero
principiis due linie sufficere possunt. Ex tali quidem scribendi
ordine atque modo, distinctio sermonum ab articulis et articulorum a capitulis legentibus clarius apparebit, quemadmodum,
in sequenti opere, exemplo et experientia patere potest.[13]

Although this statement does not refer explicitly to liturgical
books, the same care for distinguishing various kinds of text was
surely necessary for such volumes. For the Cistercians, of course,
litterae unius coloris fiant et non depictae.[14]

The most common initial in liturgical books, the one spanning
two lines of text or one line and the stave, has not been much investigated: Roger Mynors makes pioneer proposals.[15] Manuscript
descriptions observe that it generally alternates between blue and
red (usually with tracery of the opposite color) or, in more ornate
manuscripts, gold and red or blue with more decorative ornamentation. Since this letter occupies two consecutive lines of text, the
scribe must arrange his writing to provide space in both lines. The
letter begins the text on the upper of the two lines, although I suspect exceptions could be found: it is usually followed, as are all
larger initials, by a highlighted capital letter. Problems of layout
occur when a two-line initial is required on the top or bottom
single line of a page, or when two such initials are required for
consecutive single lines of text: such occurrences are rare and are

---

[13]BN nouv. acq. lat. 572, fol. 1ᵛ, cited in Camille Couderc, "Instructions données
à un copiste du XVᵉ siècle," *Bibliothèque de l'école des chartes* 55 (1894): 232.

[14]Alexander, "Scribes" (n. 12 above), p. 106.

[15]*Durham Cathedral Manuscripts* (Oxford, 1939), pp. 6–9.

not particularly relevant except that the scribe can try to avoid them by arranging his text suitably in ways discussed later.[16]

Capitals and initials are distinct in size and color. Capitals are calligraphic, entered by the scribe in ink as he wrote and wherever he had arrived on the page. He would avoid placing a capital letter at the right-hand margin where it could not be followed by some of the remaining letters: at the same time he would try to keep the right margin approximately justified. Initials were entered later by an illuminator in a space left by the scribe at the left margin, and normally within the writing area. The scribe had to remember to leave the appropriate space in two or more lines, or had to have an exemplar or design to remind him.

Texts: Summary

Table 1

Table 1 (see following page) correlates in a general way the main genres, sizes, colors, capitals, and initials.

column 1: genre or text
    * denotes items more important because of their position, usually at the beginning of services
column 2: subsection
column 3: red genre abbreviation (these are highly variable and here the shortest forms are given)
column 4: size of script
column 5: color of script
column 6: size of first letter, in lines
column 7: style of first letter
column 8: highlight
alt: alternating colors (usually blue and red)
ink: calligraphic letters
col: colored letters
var: variable

---

[16]See Hughes, *Medieval Manuscripts* (n. 6 above), chap. 6.

ANDREW HUGHES

1	2	3	4	5	6	7	8
ANTIPHON	(incipit)	A.	smaller	black	1+	ink	yes
*					2	col	
	ps. incipit	P.	smaller	black	1+	ink	yes
	ps. termination (EVOVAE)	-	smaller	black	1+	ink	yes
RESPONSORY	(incipit)	R.	smaller	black	1+1	ink	yes
*					2+2	col	
	repetenda	-	smaller	black	1	ink	var
	rep. cue	p	smaller	black	1+	ink	yes
	verse	V.	smaller	black	1+	ink	yes
INVITATORY		Inv	smaller	black	1+	ink	yes
*					2	col	
HYMN		Hy	smaller	black	var	var	var
	verse	-	smaller	black	var	alt	
Dialogues		v.	normal	black	1	ink	var
Rubric			normal	red	1+	red	
	identification of day or feast		normal	blue paraph sign			
	internal sentences		normal	red	1+	red	
LESSON†		lc.	normal	black	2	col	
	termination	-	normal	black	1+	ink	yes
CHAPTER†		cap.	normal	black	2	col	
PRAYER†		or.	normal	black	2	col	

† for each of these three items, the first letter will usually be a colored 1+ letter when only the incipit is given: also, many of these items have

| | internal sentences | | | normal | black | 1+ | alt | |

The scribe had little or no choice in relating genre, size, and color. Within a context of adjacent or nearby lines, an experienced scribe copying from a good exemplar would have little difficulty in managing the margins and combining runovers with initials and capitals to avoid blank spaces. Whether such copying was the normal practice for liturgical books remains an underlying question: I suspect that, even in the later Middle Ages, the process was not so much, or not entirely, that of copying one book from another, as that of conflating several books into one. Here, the choices available to the scribe and the difficulties of judging the new layout are surely increased. In any case, it is rare that one encounters a serious error of layout or balance in a good source.

An Advent Page

In the Noted Missal of St. Louis of Anjou,[17] the Advent initial for the introit *Ad te levavi* spans four staves with their texts, plus a single line of rubric preceding the chant (Fig. 1): in writing the introit, the scribe had to allow for i) the initial, taking up at the left more than half the width of the column; ii) the stave above each line of text and taking up two rules; and iii) any extra spaces between syllables that may be needed for the pitches to be added later (in this case, no extra space was needed). These are normal features of the scribe's task. Here, however, the initial also has a small one-line ascender, about an eighth of the column width, within the writing area. Normally, ascenders and descenders of initials are outside the writing area. In this instance, the ascender joins immediately onto the lower end of an five-line initial *I*, which begins the rubric at the top of the column. Such complexities must have been carefully anticipated, if not designed in advance.

---

[17]Assisi, Basilica di S. Francesco, Museo Tesoro, Missal of St. Louis of Anjou, late thirteenth century. This leaf is published as a color postcard.

Fig. 1

Making some assumptions, and before looking at other evidence, we can reconstruct the scribal procedure. I shall adopt for the moment the sequence described earlier: after the page has been ruled, all black text is written, then colored material is added. We could assume that the scribe had before him an exemplar that he then copied identically as to line-length, change of line, and size. This might have been an earlier manuscript or merely a temporary design-layout: in some cases I am convinced we shall have to posit a process involving identical copying and perhaps even measurement. Even if there is no evidence of such a procedure, in complex cases it may have been the only way accuracy, balance, and neatness could have been achieved. We should not, however, underestimate the skill and accuracy of the human eye in judging length, area, and size, especially in an experienced craftsman. Scheller refers to medieval powers of adaptation and memorization, which may have enabled the scribe to dispense with a preliminary trial, and cites the "extraordinary gift for visualizing a subject in terms of the space available for it."[18]

Let us assume, however, that the scribe had no planned layout before him, but only the texts and music. For the texts of Fig. 1, the music will not call for the syllables to be specially placed. The text represented in Fig. 1 by dashes, the rubric, is: "Incipit ordo missalis fratrum minorum secundum consuetudinem romane curie. Dominica prima de adventu stacio ad sanctam mariam maiorem." Then follows the ID *Introitus* and the text (dots in Fig. 1): "Ad te levavi animam meam deus meus in te confido non. . . ."

The scribe begins on a blank page with black text, that is, real spoken or sung text. He knows that conventionally the introit of Advent Sunday begins with a colored initial. Therefore he must begin with the *d* of *Ad te*. It will be a calligraphic capital with a highlight. Where, on the writing area already ruled, shall the *d* be placed? If the staves had already been entered as part of the ruling of the page, the problem is transferred to the scribe who ruled the staves: where does the first stave begin? The scribe must estimate how many lines of text the words down to *Ad te* will occupy in the column, and must take into account the space for the initial *I* that will begin the rubric, if the "design" calls for an initial at that point, as it normally does. I can accept, I believe, that after much experience a scribe

---

[18]Robert W. Scheller, *A Survey of Medieval Model Books* (Haarlem, 1963), p. 2.

could estimate accurately enough the area required. There are ways in which the text can be made to expand or contract by quite a considerable amount to cope with poor estimates.

But can we assume that all scribes who wrote this kind of book were so experienced? Judging by the quality of design and execution of the hundreds of sources I have seen, we must make that assumption, or we must suggest the use of a temporary exemplar in which the design has been tested, or we must question our earlier assumptions about the order in which material was entered.

The most sensible way of executing the section shown in Fig. 1 would surely be to write the red material first. The scribe will not want to change from black to red tools word by word for incidental coloring such as the brief rubric or identifier, or character by character for highlights; the length of the red material would be the deciding factor. I have seen no evidence of red text being entered before black. Because a reversal of the normal order would be likely only for large amounts of red or black text, as in Fig. 1, there is little opportunity for "intersections" where the overlay of one color onto the other would settle the matter.

Once the position of the *d* is fixed, provided the scribe knows how many lines the stave occupies and how many staves plus lines of text the initial *A* will occupy, he can write the introit text normally, in a narrow column, until the space for the initial has been passed: he would then write within the column proper. No estimate would be required here, other than that to fit a line of text suitably into the column width. If the staves had not yet been drawn, the scribe would need only to count and leave blank the rules on which they would be placed. But he must know where initials are to occur, and how large they are to be. We continue the assumption that the red text has not yet been entered: once the black text is completed, the scribe, or another whom we may call the rubricator, enters the rubric, leaving the space for the initial *I* and beginning with a large calligraphic capital *N*. Here, the rubricator has a different kind of constraint since he must now fit a prescribed text evenly and neatly into an already determined area. Later, the two initials will be executed.

Let us now examine in detail some elements illustrated by this and other examples, in the attempt to clarify which procedures are more likely, and what methods may have facilitated the task.

Ruling, Pricking, and Staves

On the subject of how the page is ruled, there is little published material and almost no medieval evidence other than that of the manuscripts themselves.[19] The rulings vary from drypoint to lead or color.[20] Drypoint scoring was done on one side of the

---

[19]For drawing my attention to the importance of the size of the writing area itself as one of the variables, and alerting me to the publications mentioned in this note, I must thank Jim Grier, who informed me about Professor Leonard Boyle's handout on the topic for his Paleography courses. Professor Boyle very kindly read this article and offered many useful suggestions. To measure the writing area had never occurred to me, and as a consequence I have no information to add to that supplied by Professor Boyle: no matter what its size, the page is treated as 5 x 4, and the writing area is calculated by a method that produces a result not too far from that achieved by the "Pythagorean method," a rectangle composed of two 5 x 4 x 3 triangles. See E. K. Rand and L. W. Jones, *The Earliest Book of Tours* (Cambridge, Mass., 1934), pp. 87–88; Jan Tschichold, "Non-arbitrary Proportions of Page and Type Area," *Calligraphy and Palaeography: Essays Presented to Alfred Fairbank*, ed. A. S. Osley (London, 1965), pp. 179–91 and figs. 45–57; and Curt F. Bühler, "The Margins in Mediaeval Books," in his *Early Books and Manuscripts: Forty Years of Research* (New York, 1973).

[20]For information on the ruling of the page see Gilissen, "Un élément" (n. 3 above), and his *Prolégomènes à la codicologie: recherches sur la construction des cahiers et la mise en page des mss médiévaux* (Ghent, 1977); van Dijk and Walker, *Origins* (n. 6 above), pp. 216 and 329–31; Sir Edward Maunde Thompson, *An Introduction to Greek and Latin Palaeography* (Oxford, 1912; repr. New York, 1964), pp. 56–59; Thomas S. Pattie, "The Ruling as a Clue to the Make-up of a

ANDREW HUGHES

leaf, firmly enough for ridges to be raised on the other[21] (an exception is described below): furthermore, few leaves were ruled directly.[22] Several sheets were prepared simultaneously, and the increasingly slighter impressions, which must have been visible during the writing process, have disappeared on lower leaves. Ruling in lead or ink is on both sides of all leaves, but is often almost invisibly faint. Ruling was done from pricks that in later medieval manuscripts were normally in the margins; those in top and bottom margins often still exist; those in outer side margins may have disappeared in trimming; pricks in gutter margins occur only if the leaf was ruled after folding, and may be hidden in tight binding.[23] The pricks were sometimes done with a special tool and often several leaves were pricked simultaneously; sometimes a single leaf has been used several times as the template.[24]

Often no special pricking was used to produce the stave-lines in manuscripts that contain the music: the staves were merely superimposed on the normal rulings in various ways.[25] This fact

---

Medieval Manuscript," *The British Library Journal* 1 (1975): 15–21; and Kathleen L. Scott, "A Mid-Fifteenth-Century English Illuminating Shop and its Customers," *Journal of the Warburg and Courtauld Institutes* 31 (1968): 170–96, esp. p. 183. See also the color plate in Jackson, *The Story of Writing* (n. 4 above), p. 79.

[21]The Noted Breviary MS. BA Borghese 5 (lat. 10505) has many examples.

[22]See Thompson, *Greek and Latin Palaeography* (n. 20 above), pp. 54–55.

[23]Terence A. M. Bishop, "The Prototype of *Liber glossarum*," pp. 69–86 in *Medieval Scribes*, ed. Parkes and Watson (n. 12 above), p. 81. Pricks in the gutter may be seen in the Bodleian MS. lat. lit. c 1.

[24]See Leslie Webber Jones, "Pricking Manuscripts: The Instruments and Their Significance," *Speculum* 21 (1946): 389–403. The Bodleian MS. Can. lit. 346 is probably a book in which a single leaf was used several times as the template.

[25]Van Dijk and Walker, *Origins* (n. 6 above), passim.

was initially somewhat of a surprise, since in the sixteenth century music of various kinds was called "pricksong," and common-sense would suggest an easy method of producing the highly visible rulings necessary for the staves. I suspect that in later manuscripts containing *only* the musical items and their texts, the staves were ruled from the pricks; such is not the case earlier, however, even with Antiphonals, which normally contain only the musical items. In fact, as a little thought reveals, the staves could not have been pricked in advance: in manuscripts where text, rubric, initial, and music were mixed, there could be no way of anticipating where staves would be needed. Moreover, the position of staves on the verso (and on subsequent pages pricked simultaneously) would be determined, incorrectly, by the pricking on the recto. Only in the case of a uniform and continuous layout of staves would this procedure be of use, and such a layout was rare, except in the simple Antiphonal.

Like the ordinary rules, staves were often drawn with a straightedge and single-pointed tool.[26] In earlier manuscripts, at least, the stave-lines were entered one at a time.[27] Although they are usually quite accurately drawn, often the lines are not exactly parallel. Sometimes the stave as a whole is not quite parallel with the page rules. Furthermore, the four lines of the stave rarely begin and end together (that is, in a neat edge at right angles to the

---

[26]That is, the tool had a single nib: that the nib was split is clear where a single line of the stave widens, drawing a pool of liquid for a short distance until the line separates briefly into two. See Jackson, *The Story of Writing* (n. 4 above), pp. 56–57. In the Bodleian MS. Can. lit. misc. 379, fol. 7, the line splits into three. See also the Bodleian MS. lat. lit. a 9 and Plate 3.

[27]In the following MSS, from about the fifteenth century, the staves are certainly or probably drawn with a four-pointed tool: BL MS. Lansdowne 463 (all stave lines curve simultaneously, with a larger gap between the top two lines, as on fol. 1); the Bodleian MSS. Bodley 948 (similar); e mus. 2; Gough lit. 1; and lat. lit. b 14.

lines); rather, beginnings and ends of
staves are ragged. Occasionally, indeed,
as on the leaf of the Missal from Assisi
already quoted, a single stave line (in
this case the top line) has (accidentally?) been drawn through a space that
should have been left empty (Fig. 2):
here it actually serves to fill out the
space, which is not completely filled by
the abbreviation *Gr.*

Fig. 2

Most Breviaries or Missals, noted or not, are laid out in two
columns. Antiphonals often use the long-line, one "column" layout, but the same principles apply. Defining the beginning and end
of each column requires
four pricks in both top
and bottom margins (see
Fig. 3). Gilissen de-
scribes what he calls *pi-
qûres maîtresses*, which
support lines other than
those for actual text, lying outside the writing
area and used to align
folio numbers or running
heads, if these are en-
tered.[28] Although a

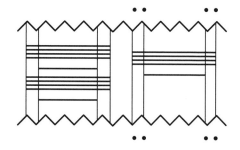

Fig. 3 (not to scale)

common-sense procedure, this tiny attention to the detail of the
layout indicates the care that was exercised. My recollection is that
such lines are less common in liturgical books. Rather, the vertical

---

[28]As in BL MS. add. 23935, the Dominican copy of Humbert's Codex, made for
the Master-General of the order. See van Dijk, *Sources* (n. 6 above), pp. 118–20.

rules that define the actual writing area extend into the margins for the same purpose.

In manuscripts with music the vertical rules are sometimes double rules separated by perhaps an eighth of an inch. The left-most rule of each column determines the position of the clef on the stave; the one next to it determines the leftmost position for the syllables and musical pitches. At the end of the stave the two rules perhaps indicate maximum and minimum lengths for the line, al-though the maximum is often exceeded, and also perhaps specify the position of the custos or direct, a musical symbol at the end of a stave that, like the clef, is not an actual note.[29] The "indenting" at beginning and end of the text with respect to the stave above is explicit in Grenoble BM MS 201, where the main horizontal ruling, for the text, extends only to the inner of the double vertical rules, while the staves extend to the outer, as in Fig. 3.

The horizontal rules sometimes extend into the margins or through the gap between the columns. A neater appearance results if they do not. Generally, however, the top and bottom rules, de-fining the limits of the writing area, are extended and are some-times doubled, like the vertical rules (for example, Carpentras BM MS 43, and Périgueux, Archives départementales, MS 166). Be-tween them, the page is ruled regularly from the marginal pricks. The number of lines on the page, one of the parameters listed in descriptions of manuscripts, is determined by the size of the script, for which a suitable pricking-wheel would be chosen.[30] Within the regular rulings the scribe must arrange texts of two different sizes, and the stave. Various methods are used, and the

---

[29]Huglo, "Règlement" (n. 4 above), passim.

[30]This is assuming the use of the pricking wheel described by Jones in "Pricking Manuscripts" (n. 24 above). The use of compasses or awls, especially for asymmetrical pricking, would be extremely laborious.

practices of individual sources must be described separately. Although there are obviously standard formats, which occur frequently, the great number of variable parameters allows many different and perhaps distinctive formats.[31] For example, in Carpentras BM MS 69, the top and bottom horizontal lines extend into the margins and between the columns, the second and penultimate horizontals extend only between the columns, and the remainder extend only to the edges of the columns. Such a ruling, consistently maintained and with other details of the layout, may be distinctive enough to identify a scriptorium. Gilissen has shown how statistics based on such minutiae can be used to arrange manuscripts in groups.[32] His methods for classifying pricks and rules could be adapted for describing the stave.

The main text may be written on alternate rules. The higher rule kept the size of the letter consistent; the space above it was for ascenders and abbreviation signs, and for descenders from the line above. In this kind of layout, if the texts of smaller size were written on alternate lines, too much blank space would occur: such text is therefore written on consecutive rules, small enough for ascenders and descenders not to interfere with adjacent lines. This arrangement can cause problems where scripts of different size meet. For example, full size text may have continued to the end of the antepenultimate rule, and then smaller text must take over: if the latter should occupy only a single rule (the penultimate), then only one rule (the last) would be available for a full-size continuation, which requires two rules. Much depends on the length of the texts, the need for abbreviation signs, and initials; each case must be

---

[31]Van Dijk and Walker, *Origins* (n. 6 above), deals only with Franciscan MSS, very briefly. His generalizations should be taken only as a starting point.

[32]Gilissen, "Un élément codicologique" (n. 3 above).

examined in context. A simple solution, ignoring other elements, can be illustrated graphically (Fig. 4). At "a," large script ends. The full line of smaller script is folded over into two half lines, "b" continuing at "c," leaving a half-line

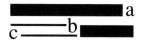

Fig. 4

of two rules for the next large script. But if that text requires an initial that must stand at the left margin, what then?

The size of staves depends on the size of the script chosen for the texts that have music.[33] Often, the script is smaller, occupying a single rule, and the stave is superimposed on two rules, occasionally three. In the latter case, the four stave lines cannot sit exactly on the three rules, which will show in the spaces of the stave: this untidy result is usually true even in the former case. Superior manuscripts, as we shall see, will avoid this problem by proper ruling of the page. Sometimes the number of rules allotted to the stave varies within a source; usually not, however, within a single page or opening where the discrepancy would be visible to the keen-eyed. The presence of a spectacular initial, however, can draw the eye away from such minor variations, allowing the scribe more flexibility: on another leaf of the Assisi Missal already mentioned, beside and immediately below the Easter initial, are fifteen rules incorporating five lines of full-size text and five staves of two rules each. Thereafter, each stave occupies three rules.[34]

When staves occupy only two rules, the text had to be written smaller. Otherwise the ascenders and descenders could have interfered with low or high notes, respectively, on the stave. Here the

---

[33]Van Dijk and Walker, *Origins* (n. 6 above).

[34]Diane Droste informs me that changing between two and three rules is not uncommon in Sarum MSS: with the introduction of the four-nibbed pen for drawing the staves, of course, the variation disappears.

scribe had no horizontal leeway, as he did with adjacent lines of text, because the pitches must sit correctly above their syllables.[35] Even with the smaller script or three-rule space for the stave, ascenders and descenders frequently touch or cross one of the stave lines or symbols on the stave. Such accidents give clues about the order in which items were added.

The stave, whose lines are usually red, was entered at a later stage, according to our initial assumptions. The scribe probably worked downward from the top stave line and, helped by the rules, judged by eye the position of the top line relative to the text or rule above, as well as the distance between each line. The distances are usually quite consistent.

In some of the Antiphonals only the rules beneath the text were drawn in, with adequate space above for the text and the stave: these rules are single lines drawn from isolated pricks. Occasionally however, as in a sixteenth-century leaf from Périgueux and leaves from Potenza, an upper rule defines the height of the letter. In such cases, both lines may have pricks (Potenza), or only the lower line, as in Avignon BM MS 191. In Grenoble BM MS 394, the double pricks remain, but no lines seem to have been drawn (the double vertical lines are faintly visible, however); I cannot explain how text was aligned accurately when no horizontal rules were drawn at all.[36] In a Breviary without music and without horizontal rules, BA MS. lat. 547, the parallel alignment

---

[35]Common sense would dictate correct underlay for books that were for use in choir, although there are a good many carelessly executed books. See Huglo, "Règlement" (n. 4 above).

[36]Some very reputable scholars have no doubt that the ruling was sometimes erased. See Harry Breslau and Hans-Walther Klewitz, *Handbuch der Urkundlehre* II, ii, 2nd ed. (Berlin, 1958; repr. of 1931 ed.), p. 505; and Hans Foerster *Abriss der lateinischen Paläographie*, 2nd ed. (Stuttgart, 1963), p. 76. This information is directly from the reader referred to in n. 2 above.

of text below the previous line would not have been impossible, although it called for great skill. Handwritten letters are produced in this way today, so the reader can easily judge the difficulty. But in manuscripts where successive lines of text may be separated by a centimeter or more, because of space left for the stave, the difficulty is considerably greater.

The pricking for a layout of consistent staves and texts may have been done with a special tool in which the spikes were widely spaced. The layout of such a manuscript does not, of course, preclude the scribe from including long rubrics or other texts without music: the problem of fitting incidental texts without staves into a layout predetermined by the music is merely the reverse of that which occurs with other books.

It may be clear already that few generalizations can be made about the pricking, ruling, and staves. Many sources seem to be unique. In a recent article, Denis Escudier refers to and prints a facsimile of a leaf using musical symbols without a stave, and thus probably from before the period I am studying: it has an unusual format, which may be compared with those discussed below.[37] To allow for the musical symbols for the office of St. Vaast in a manuscript basically without music, the scribe writes the text on alternate instead of consecutive rules. The staveless and unheighted neumes are written between the text and the blank rule above. Escudier speculates that the upper rule was left blank so that a few incidental rubrics and incipits could be added between the various items: the otherwise blank rules (and many are completely blank) were then filled out for aesthetic reasons, Escudier suggests, with the vowels of the text below (Fig. 5).

If this explanation has merit, then the scribal attempt to resolve the minor problem of what to do with incidental rubrics

---

[37]Escudier, "Les manuscrits musicaux" (n. 5 above).

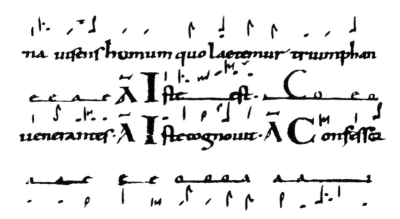

Fig. 5

has caused a major problem of format. More commonly, the
system is designed to cope with major problems while causing
only the sort of difficulty that can be resolved unobtrusively by
changing an abbreviation or the place of a runover.

Some Specific Manuscripts

i) (Fig. 6) The Antiphonal, Bodleian MS. lat. lit. c 1 (especially
fols. 172ᵛ–73 and from 221ᵛ), has a regular system of one rule for
the text, extending into the margin, above which is a gap of a
single rule, then four rules on which the stave is superimposed. The
"stave" consists only of a single red and a single yellow Guidonian
"clef"-line.[38] The red line is obviously added after the pitches but
not over them, since it stops and starts, avoiding them; the yellow
line is transparent, and probably continues over the pitches. Here,
then, the rules of the page were used as the "stave" to place the

[38]Joseph Smits van Waesberghe, "The Musical Notation of Guido of Arezzo,"
Musica Disciplina 5 (1951): 15–53, with plates and a colored table.

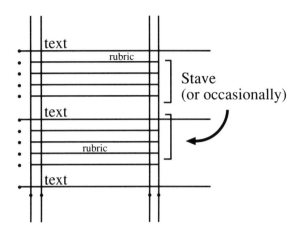

Fig. 6

pitches properly, and a subsequent true stave was not added.[39] Rubrics are written on various of the rules, in half-size letters.

ii) (Fig. 7) Fol. 86 of the guardbook Corpus Christi College, Oxford, MS. B.486 has a regular system, with rules drawn on adjacent pricks for the text, leaving the intervening unruled pricks (often two) for the staves.

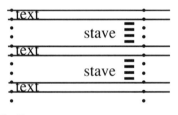

Fig. 7

The Noted Breviary, Silos Monastery Library MS 9, is similar, but all the pricks have rulings.

iii) (Fig. 8) A common arrangement is for only the pair of rulings for the text to be pricked: the intervening gap has no pricks or rules. The following manuscripts or leaves may be cited: BL MSS. Lansdowne 463, add. 23935, and add. 30072; Corpus

---

[39]The same seems to be true of the BA MS. Borghese 5, a fascinating source from which many interesting details of scribal procedure could be learned.

Christi College, Oxford, MS. B.486, fols. 25–26, 29, 78; and Bodleian MS. laud misc. 299.

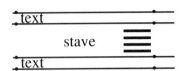

Fig. 8

iv) In the Noted Breviaries from the Bodleian Library, MSS. Can. lit. misc. 379 and lat. lit. b 14, pages of consistent music (for example, fol. 116 of MS 379) use the system of iii), gapped pricking for text lines only; but on pages where text and music are mixed, the pricks are regular and the stave is superimposed on two rules where necessary, so that a text with stave occupies three rules. In these sources, the system changes from page to page. The rubricated Antiphonal, BL MS. Lansdowne 463, is more careful, since continuous or gapped ruling, as necessary, appears not only within the page but within each column, so that staves are superimposed on visible rules only for parts of a column.

v) Even more careful is the Bodleian MS. e mus. 2, a Noted Breviary, where, to preserve clean space for the stave, rules are sometimes broken within individual lines, as on p. 732 (Fig. 9). The system of the Noted Breviary, Bodleian MS. Gough lit.1, is essentially the same, including the half-line change (fols. 86^v and 90^v).

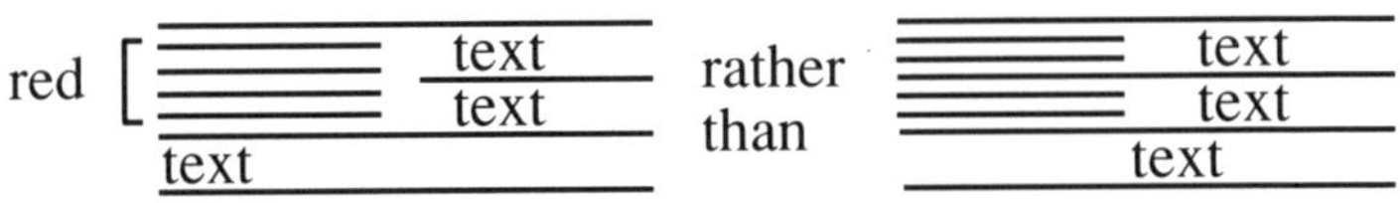

Fig. 9

Such careful layout can imply only that planning took place before the page was ruled, or that it was possible selectively to erase parts of the rule without damage to the parchment. We may perhaps generalize to this extent:

a) sources with continuous text and no music were continuously ruled;

b) sources with continuous music were normally laid out with consistently asymmetric or gapped ruling so that staves are not made untidy by visible underlying rules; and

c) sources with mixed text and chant may change the ruling as necessary from page to page, allowing some staves to stand over visible rules, or from column to column, an improvement, or even within each line.

The Writing Area: Filling the Columns and Lines

The area occupied by a text is determined by several parameters: at the beginning by the need for an initial to be at the left margin as well as by the place where the previous text ends; at the end by the requirements of the following material. Other limitations are the width of the column and the need to present evenly-spaced letters. Unlike the rubricator, the text-scribe does not have to meet these requirements within an area entirely determined by material previously written. These more severe conditions for the rubricator also apply to the scribe who adds the identifying letters, probably the rubricator himself.

Filling the Columns: Columnar layout may increase the difficulty, because of the constant necessity to add many short lines to arrive at a total area. As with the modern book, ragged feet are avoided. A discrepancy of a single line will not be too evident on facing pages, but in adjacent columns the defect will be noticeable. Bishop refers to the bottom line as a possible place for entering material accidentally omitted.[40] In manuscripts of mixed

---

[40]Bishop, "The Prototype" (n. 23 above), p. 75.

text and chant, the amount of text without chant (that is, single lines) on the page must complement the amount with chant (that is, probably three lines) to produce an equal number of lines for each column. Despite the additional difficulty imposed on the scribe by columnar layout, there are surprisingly few instances of an unequal number of lines. The right column on fol. 55^v of Avignon MS 122 is one line too long (Plate 2), apparently unavoidably. On fol. 8^v of Avignon BM MS 192, each column is one line short, the left one short at the foot, the right short at the top (Fig. 10). At first glance, this would seem to be so that the staves are all aligned, a conclusion disproved by the lower part of the page.

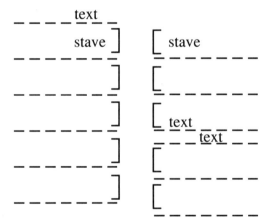

Fig. 10

On fol. 20^v of the same book, each column is one line short at the top, and it takes careful observation to note that the left-hand column is in fact two lines short in all, inserting a blank line above a two-line initial farther down the column (Plate 3): a similar method of hiding the defect was noted in the Assisi Missal. Perhaps drawn in to fill the column, the bottom stave of fol. 112^v

in Avignon BM MS 190 is quite blank (it has the ID *Responsoria*, thus, beneath it), so that the responsory can begin with a historiated four-line initial on the top of the following recto. In any book, the presence of chants makes for extra difficulty.

Filling the Lines: How does the scribe or rubricator achieve a neat text without noticeable squeezing or spacing, properly laid out within the line and on a larger scale within the page? A moment's thought will provide any medievalist with an answer. Abbreviations are, in these sources at least, a means of changing the length of the line. In liturgical books they are much less pervasive than in legal, philosophical, or literary texts and are limited mostly to universally known forms.[41] This reticence is no doubt because the texts must be read accurately the first and every time. Abbreviations are even less frequent in the texts beneath staves, allowing for an elegant spacing of the music, but perhaps because the choir could not be expected to read abbreviations fluently. In contrast, rubrics, which are instructions rather than text per se, use more abbreviations. Only a few specialized words such as genre identifications are massively contracted, and range from a single letter to a complete word. Thus, *antiphona* may be written as those nine letters, as the single letter *A*, or as *Ant.*, or in a number of other ways. The following examples, all taken from consecutive pages of a single source, Grenoble BM MS 394, indicate some of the options. Italics indicate where there is a superscript letter or other abbreviation symbol.

---

[41]Compare Escudier, "Les manuscrits musicaux" (n. 5 above), p. 40. The question about whether space was conserved because of the cost of parchment needs reconsidering. See Huglo, "Règlement" (n. 4 above), p. 126; and Michael T. Clanchy, *From Memory to Written Record: England, 1066–1307* (Cambridge, Mass., 1979), p. 95.

antiphon at Lauds	Magnificat antiphon	responsory (or anti- phon) at Vespers
In.*lb.*	ad *m* a*n*	ad *vs* R
in lau*d* a*n*t	ad .*m*.*a*	ad ves*p*as res*p*os
ad laudes an*t*	ad .*m*.ant*h*.	ad ves*ps*.a*n*.
.lau.a*n*.	ad mag ant*h*	
------------		
i l*b*.a*n*t		Benedictus antiphon
in.l*b* ant*h*		ad .*b*. antip*h*
In l*b* a*n*		.*b*. a*n*t
ad lau*d* a*n*		ad b*nd* an*t*
ad laudes a*n*		ad b*n*d*c*s antipho*n*
		.*b*.*a*

For the texts themselves, the normal abbreviations of medieval script are used and, as the reader will know, they allow a little flexibility. Some additional leeway exists, however, for all these scripts because the right margin is not justified exactly. The presence of double vertical rules in some sources may allow for a maximum and minimum length of line, but even in manuscripts with only a single vertical rule the length will usually vary up to about a half a centimeter, say two or three letters. Another technique is the deliberate horizontal expansion or contraction of the letter form itself. This technique seems to apply only to the last letter of the line and occurs rarely. Sometimes, especially in Italian manuscripts, unnecessary letters are inserted and then expunctuated. In musical circumstances, the last pitch of the chant may be similarly extended until it is a horizontal box rather than a true square: as with the letters, such expansion is rather rare.

Where chant is to be supplied, each syllable or group of syllables is written normally, but separated from the next text by blank space that is sometimes filled with ornament, usually in red. With only a single pitch for each syllable, no extra spacing is needed since individual pitches occupy less horizontal space than syllables. The pitches are invariably added after the texts so that the latter serve as a guide for spacing them. Many chants or sections of chant are in this one-pitch-to-a-syllable style. At other places, however, several pitches may need to stand above a single syllable, and all are sung to that syllable: sometimes several pitches are compressed into a single symbol, the ligature. The syllables may then need to be spaced to allow room for the musical notation. In some chants, notably responsories, many pitches may be sung to a single syllable: such phrases are called melismas, occurring in melismatic chants. When the syllables of such texts must be widely spaced, say several centimeters apart, it would appear sensible for the scribe to write the pitches first, as a guide to the spacing of the text. No evidence exists that this was ever done: rather the reverse. In the Penwortham Breviary, BL MS. add. 52359, the music for a well-known melisma at Christmas, on the word *fabrice*, has not been added on any of the three occasions it occurs, even though the chants are otherwise complete.[42] Nevertheless the word is spaced thus *fa . . . brice*, indicating that the scribe intended the melisma to appear in the chant. Presumably the music scribe did not have immediate access to the melisma be-

---

[42]Diane Droste informs me that the melisma is marked as "non-Sarum" in some Processionals. See Hughes, *Medieval Music* (n. 10 above), items **634, 677, 677.1, 677.2**, and **742**.

cause it was not in his exemplar.[43] The spacing of the text, then, must have been done without the presence of the chant. How did the text scribe judge the required spacing? We cannot assume that the text scribes knew the tunes. I do not know the answer, and we do not know either that all of the assumptions or conclusions in this case are justified. In many cases, such as the long *fabrice* melisma, I am convinced that the scribe must have measured the exemplar, if not with a tool, at least by eye. In the Penwortham Breviary the consequent implication would be that the text scribe had the melisma to measure, and the music scribe did not.

Cues: Letters and Other Marks

Cues, left by the scribe to pass information to later stages of the production, seem in liturgical books to be entered inconsistently, sparsely, and indiscriminately. Catchwords or gathering marks for the binder were often cut off in trimming after he had used them to place the fascicles in the correct order. Catchwords pointing to a page that begins with red or some other color are written in that color, implying that the rubricator had a responsibility in this respect as well as the scribe of the text. If the catchword is to a text beginning with an initial, it may anticipate exactly what will be placed on the following page. Thus, the catchword on fol. 159ᵛ of Carpentras BM MS 46 itself contains a cue for the initial: the catchword is *sce* where the *c* and *e* are in normal script and the *s* is, as usual with cues, light and small. The word on the following page is *Sce* where the *S* is a two-line initial that, presumably, also has its own cue. The BL MS. Lansdowne 463, fol. 94ᵛ, has this catchword (color in parentheses): li. (black) In *tpe* pa. (red). The

---

[43]Melismas have unusual musical characteristics and were, perhaps, added to chants in some early revision.

usual assumption is that catchwords were written by the scribe for
the binder's convenience. If this were the sole reason, would there
be a need to show, at some cost in care and time, the exact
coloring and "capitalizing" of the following words? The binder
could surely be expected to identify *sce* or *Sce* with |S|ce. Perhaps
another function was to serve as a reminder to the scribe himself,
or to another, of what should next be written, and how. With
colored initials it is usually not possible to tell whether a cue has
been written, since it will normally be covered by the opaque red
or blue paint or by the gold leaf. The blue paraph sign is also cued
in some sources: the Penwortham Breviary uses two short parallel
black lines, clearly visible in some places where the paraph has not
been added, as on fols. 300[v] and 322. In other circumstances, such
as below rubrics or below letters identifying genres, the cue will
usually remain visible. Its color is often not that of the subsequent
letter: probably the scribe used the color he was working with at
the time.[44] Black cues appear for black, red, or blue symbols, red
cues for red or blue symbols: the order of entry corresponds to the
common-sense sequence, and I have never seen a "reverse order"
such as red for a black symbol. Some sources use only black cues,
regardless of the final color: exemplary in this and other respects
is the Dominican copy of the Humbert's Codex for the Master-
General, BL MS 23935. Occasionally, a cue is not obeyed to the
letter: in the Bodleian MS. Can. lit. 346, fol. 41, the partly
trimmed cue is *ad hor*, realized in the text as *ad cursum*. In some
late manuscripts, cues are sometimes in the vernacular, pointing to
a later Latin insertion. For genre IDs, the single identifying cue-

---

[44]See Léon Gilissen, "Un élément codicologique méconnu: l'indication des
couleurs des lettrines jointe aux 'lettres d'attente'," in *Paläographie 1981:
Colloquium des Comité International de Paläographie München, 15.–18. September
1981 Referate*, ed. Gabriel Silagi (Munich, 1982), Münchener Beiträge zur
Mediävistik und Renaissance-Forschung 32 (1982), pp. 185–91.

letter is often entered, but quite inconsistently, in the sources studied. For rubrics, the cues for phrases such as *In die . . . , In laudibus . . .* are frequently entered, also inconsistently. No cues were entered (at least in the writing area) for longer rubrics. The cues for rubrics and IDs were obviously sometimes written in the margin, where traces of them occasionally remain even after trimming: nothing more can be said of these. "Trimming" suggests small-scale cutting of the sides of the page but, in fact, we do not know how many times a book may have been trimmed and can only estimate how much was cut off.[45] Even a narrow cut may have removed numerous one-letter cues, or even whole sentences if they were written vertically, as in the Silos MS 9, fol. 274ᵛ, at the feast of All Saints. If some cues were written in the margin and have disappeared in trimming, and others were entered in the writing area and remain visible within the final text, the erratic appearance of cues within the writing area would be explained. Unless such a procedure is posited, it is extremely difficult to account for the seemingly haphazard entry of reminders, which, in such complex compilations, would often have been essential.

Some scribal marks within the writing area have not been investigated in print. They are dots or short unobtrusive vertical rulings placed at disjunctions or, literally, at turning-points.[46] Like punctuation marks, they help to distinguish parts of the text according to sense. The word *distinguere* means to punctuate, a task done after the writing of the text, sometimes by a corrector; is it possible that these other marks are included in the terms *punctum,*

---

[45]Many scholars believe that the writing area and margins were related according to some simple proportions, in which case one can extrapolate from the existing gutter margin. See Tschichold, "Non-arbitrary Proportions" (n. 19 above); and Gilissen, *Prolégomènes* (n. 20 above).

[46]The special meaning of "disjunction" is explained in n. 1 above.

cola, and *commata,* which normally refer to conventional punctuation marks?[47] Trithemius adds two other terms, *nota* and *scema,* when he speaks of scribes: "in quibus fuerunt nonnulli qui scripture tam exactam adhibuere diligentiam, ut non solum recte, set etiam perite scripserint, notis, colis, et scematibus pulchra varietate volumina distinguentes, ut solo aspectu ad lectionem eorundam videaris provocari." He also refers to an assistant who "notis distinguat atque scematibus."[48]

As with letter-cues, the lines or dots may become part of a following capital or initial (as seems to be so in the Bodleian MS. lat. lit. a 9), which may partly explain why they are not often visible. They are not to be confused either with the hyphen, which may appear as a light line sloping away from the base of the letter, thus / (see Plate 4 and Fig. 16), or with the formal, neat, and full-stave "bar-line," called *pausa,* which was added at structural points of a chant as it was written.[49] The visual distinction is sometimes slight. The lines or dots appear where there is a major discontinuity, such as a change from chant to rubric or spoken material, where the stave must be broken. On fol. 1 of BL MS. Lansdowne 463 (Fig. 11), the abbreviation OR is red. The strokes and the text are black. On fols. 18ᵛ and 33 (Fig. 12) the square stands for a blue symbol over a red cue: on fol. 33 the strokes are black, on fol. 18ᵛ red.

The scribe might enter such marks if there was an adjacent multi-line runover, rubric, or initial. Here a reminder about the

---

[47]W. Wattenbach, *Das Schriftwesen im Mittelalter,* 4th ed. (1896; repr. Graz, 1958), pp. 320, 432, 655, passim. Wattenbach cites Alcuin: "Per cola distinguant proprios et commata sensus, et punctos ponant ordine quosque suo. . ." (p. 432).

[48]Trithemius, *De laude scriptorum* (n. 4 above), chaps. VIII and IX.

[49]Huglo, "Règlement" (n. 4 above), pp. 124–27. The two strokes can be seen adjacent in Plate 15 of van Dijk and Walker, *Origins* (n. 6 above).

spacing of the next lines might be useful, especially if he had to interrupt his task. Thus, in Fig. 13, the stroke written when the scribe arrived at "a" would remind him at "b" to stop. A one-line stroke would not be useful, as the scribe would already have made the decision to stop. It would serve a pur-

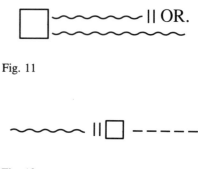

Fig. 11

Fig. 12

pose, however, where disjunctions occur between one black text and another (a runover end of the previous text); the stroke would be useful to the reader, warning of a discontinuity that might otherwise be little apparent.

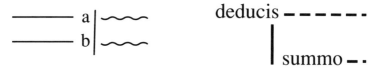

Fig. 13

Fig. 14

On the flyleaves of Bodleian MS. Douce 44 (Fig. 14), the stave has not been entered in the space above the text. The single black stroke delimits the area for a two-line initial and serves a purpose only if entered before the textual scribe started his work. After the word *Vidi* in Plate 1, the double ink-stroke at the disjunction is itself cued by a lighter double stroke. In the Douai Breviary, BM MS 166 (folio giving the Ordination of Acolytes), each of the capital letters (highlighted with yellow) in the long rubric is preceded by a black stroke, the intensity of which can hardly be distinguished from the rulings or from the oblique hair-lines over black-text *is*. The strokes are formed as in Fig. 15. Are they attempts to lay out the writing area sentence by sentence (what would be the purpose of this?), or pointers to where high-lights must be added (Plate 5)?

Fig. 15

Manuscripts are sometimes internally inconsistent. The two volumes of the St. Omer Antiphonal seem to be written and decorated throughout by the same hand and artist. Formatting cues are mostly absent (or so faint as to be invisible). On fol. 45 of vol. 1 they occur on the whole page (Plate 6), whenever the stave begins or ends in midleaf. May we speculate that formatting marks normally were erased after the completion of the necessary stages? If so, the erasure was certainly not with a scraping tool. Cennini cites the use of bread-crumbs to erase leadpoint.[50] With modern bread and pencil or ink this method can hardly be said to work well. More likely is a reference to the material normally used for pouncing (cleaning the parchment), where the "bread" is even more lethal than the modern variety: according to Daniel Thompson, "[to make the pumice used for pouncing,] powdered glass and flour and brewer's yeast were mixed and allowed to rise like bread, made into loaves, and baked in the oven.[51] Cennini also refers to saliva for erasure.[52] I find it difficult to believe that only scraping tools were used for erasure, although I can find no other evidence of an alternative.

---

[50]*A Treatise on Painting Written by Cennino Cennini (1437)*, trans. Mrs. [Mary Philadelphia] Merrifield (London, 1844), p. 7.

[51]Daniel V. Thompson, *The Materials and Techniques of Medieval Painting* (London, 1936), cited from the Dover reprint (New York, 1956), p. 29.

[52]Cennini d'Andrea, *The Craftsman's Handbook ("Il Libro dell'arte")*, trans. Daniel V. Thompson, vol. 2 (New York, 1954), p. 4.

The rubricated Antiphonal, Grenoble BM MS 867, probably a Carthusian book, uses vertical dots rather than strokes. The manuscript is not superior in quality. Frequently the stave must be ended to allow the entry of rubrics and occasionally of single-line "staves" giving reciting tones (Plate 7). Even in the latter case, the stave line may be discontinuous. Plate 7 does not show that the dots between *Amen* and *Alleluia* (top left) are red, and those after *qua* (bottom right) are black (although not, I think, as black as the script): the latter dots are five in number, including one in the bow of the *R* abbreviation. On other leaves of the book, the dots are elongated into comma-like symbols or small reversed *C*s. Although carelessly executed, these marks are deliberate.

A Complex Example

In the Avignon BM MS 122, fol. 132 (Plate 8, Fig. 16), each of the red ID letter *R*s has a cue (not shown) in exactly the same medium as the strokes 1–5. The remaining text is black; and rubrics are black, underlined in red. All the text from *R Dilexi* to *odi.* is a runover that continues the previous rubric, *Require*, with the incipit of the required responsory: the last *R* refers to *Regnum mundi*. How did the scribe enter this material? The following are possibilities for the sequence after *Require . . . passionis*:

1) a) *Dilexisti* to *odi.*, as a three-line runover, leaving space for the stave and the ID letters;
   b) *[r]egnum mun*; and
   c) the stave, in a later stage, and the *R*s.
   This order accounts for none of the strokes or cues but is otherwise quite feasible.

2) a) *[r]egnum mun*, leaving space for the stave, and for the runover in which the previous rubric will be completed. To remind himself in a later red stage not to continue the stave into the runover space, the scribe draws stroke 2; to

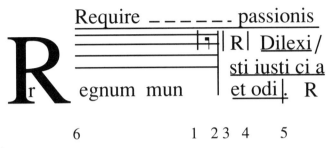

Fig. 16

remind himself of the ID for *Regnum mundi*, he draws stroke 5; and to remind himself of the need for a direct, he draws stroke 1.

b) Then, continuing with his black pen, the scribe writes *Dilexisti* to *odi.*, leaving space for the ID letters. But this renders strokes 2, 3, 4, and 5 unnecessary. The last three, in any case, seem unnecessary since the letter cue is given. The position of stroke 5 between the *i* and the dot surely implies that it was written prior to that text.

The remaining permutations can be left to the reader: in the long run a judgement rather than a proof about the entry of this passage will result. To me, it has the hallmarks of a mapping of the space for an inexperienced scribe. I can readily imagine the scribe being helped, graphically on the parchment and orally, thus: "Complete the rubric here [draws stroke 2 and points to the space at the right]; don't forget the direct [draws stroke 1]; don't forget the IDs [draws lines 3, 4, and 5 and the cue letters]." Since there is no stroke at 6, presumably the cue letter [*r*] is sufficient as a reminder about the space for the initial.

The Absence of Cues

It is relatively easy to register the presence of visible marks.

At last, I was struck by the consistent absence, in all books, of cues at certain points. Even though colored initials spanning only a single line are supplied with cues, red abbreviations identifying genres alone (that is, lacking words, such as *in laudibus*, to designate the service) rarely have them. Was the rubricator able to supply correctly these quite varied and very frequent abbreviations without assistance? To do so would require reading the black text already present to ascertain the genre. But he could equally well do the same in order to ascertain the correct colored initial. Why should the one require a cue and the other not? Might we infer that these brief red insertions were made by the textual scribe, taking up the red pen temporarily as he wrote?

Cues: Summary

Letter-cues are unquestionably for the benefit of the scribe in a later stage of his work. For whom are the other marks intended? Are they similar reminders or planning marks necessarily entered in some early stage of the work, or are they for the reader or for esthetic purposes, possibly entered very late in the process, as "finishing touches"? It is not usually possible to say whether they are like hairlines, done with the text pen as the scribe wrote, or like letter-cues, for which a change of pen was usual, perhaps implying a step separate from the writing of the text. From their appearance, then, one can learn little about when they were added. Most are slight, casual, and unobtrusive and can hardly be said to add anything esthetic. Their appearance on one leaf of a book, the St. Omer Antiphonal (Plate 6), and their absence on other leaves suggests that here esthetic purposes were better served by removing the marks and that by accident one leaf was not cleaned up. My judgement is that there is a clear distinction between what was added for esthetic reasons and these marks, which were not.

Marks that are noticeable but not obviously esthetic are probably for the reader, especially if they occur at places where confusion might arise, such as disjunctions. In Plate 1 such a mark is itself supported by a cue and raised to the status of something that must remain visible in the final copy. By far, the majority of marks are neither esthetic nor necessary for the reader. Some contribute nothing to the reader that change of color, size, or the use of a large letter, as in Figs. 11 and 12 (p. 188 above), does not convey more obviously. Some, such as those of Figs. 13 and 14 (p. 188 above), could have been added as the scribe wrote, as a reminder to himself. For both of these, however, the text the scribe actually wrote itself dictates the subsequent layout. If the runover line is already written, the scribe of the first part of the line does not need a mark to tell him he cannot go any further. If the first part of the line with a disjunction is already written, the scribe does not need a mark to remind him that he has stopped in mid-line. The scribe who comes along later to fill in a rubric or ID in the rest of the line can see where the blank space begins.

If we eliminate esthetics, and I think we often must, the mark is either a redundant emphasis for the reader, or a redundant reminder for the scribe after he has written text, or a non-redundant mark useful for the scribe before he writes text. An inference is that the marks might have preceded the text altogether. But then, how did the designer judge where on the blank or ruled page to place them? The copying from exact models, or measuring specific lengths and areas, might necessitate marking the blank leaf. So too would the process of conflation alluded to earlier. But visible signs remain in only a few manuscripts. Villard de Honnecourt (thirteenth century) is said to have done pen and ink drawings over a design in lead-point, obscuring the latter.[53] Cennini rec-

---

[53]Scheller, A Survey (n. 18 above), p. 9.

ommends the method at the end of the fourteenth century.[54] Preliminary designs were undoubtedly used in liturgical books for the initials, under which the evidence is now hidden.[55] Practice designs in lead can be seen on flyleaves in Grenoble BM MS 467, fol. 57ᵛ. But at many of the disjunctions in liturgical books, no possibility exists for hiding the design marks. An interesting suggestion about which few paleographers seem to have any information is that the design was done in silver-point.[56] This is surely expected to leave only a drypoint ruling rather than a mark. But it is said to "deteriorate": whether this means to "disappear" (perhaps as a result of aging), I do not know.[57] As for exact copying, Bishop discusses line-by-line, leaf-by-leaf, and quire-by-quire copying.[58] His suggestion that the *mise en page* was transferred from manuscript to manuscript by re-boring the pricks is clearly not applicable, since pricks have not been observed for the internal design of the writing area in liturgical books. We have seen earlier that these books, especially Breviaries and Missals, are (or were in the first stage) item-by-item conflations of several independent books. Exact copying is out of the question here.

We do not yet understand the scribal procedure thoroughly and can resolve few of the questions: apart from primary cata-

---

[54]Cennini, trans. Merrifield (n. 50 above), pp. 8–13.

[55]Jackson, *The Story of Writing* (n. 4 above), p. 82, shows color facsimiles of sketches drawn prior to initials. See also Janet Backhouse, "An Illuminator's Sketchbook," *The British Library Journal* 1 (1975): 314; and Alexander, "Scribes" (n. 12 above), pp. 87–116.

[56]Cennini refers to a silverpointed tool or silver stylus (trans. Merrifield [n. 50 above]), pp. 5–6.

[57]See Scheller, *A Survey* (n. 18 above), pp. 9–10.

[58]Bishop, "The Prototype" (n. 23 above), pp. 69–86.

loguing, adequate only for a few libraries, we must collect large amounts of additional and minute evidence. There is material for several dissertations in outlining methods and dealing with groups of sources. At the University of Toronto, Diane Droste has made an excellent start in the area of scribal habits with respect to chant notation in books of Salisbury Use.[59]

II: THE EVIDENCE OF OVERLAYS

Close examination of the sources, to discover which lines overlay earlier ones, shows that the assumptions about the order in which material was entered are accurate. Even in this process, however, there are pitfalls: in Grenoble BM MS 867 and leaf 2 from Potenza, it is clear even under a magnifying glass that the red stave lines sometimes run *over* some pitch symbols. Without question, these are exceptional instances. The absurdity of adding staves after symbols that rely on them for position is obvious (but we should remember the later addition of the Guidonian red stave-line mentioned earlier). Possibilities are:

a) that the staves were first drawn in the "disappearing" mode (for no evidence of dry or silver-point remains), and the red lines were superimposed in a subsequent "red" stage after the black material. Since the staves elsewhere in the same and similar manuscripts are invariably under the pitches, we must discard this option as a normal procedure; but

b) stave lines may have been repaired or reinforced in patches after the notation had been entered; or

c) a watery black ink for the pitches may have separated to either side of the red line because of some property of the

---

[59]Diane L. Droste, "The Musical Notation and Transmission of the Music of the Sarum Use, 1225–1500" (diss., University of Toronto, 1983).

fluids, although why this should not have occurred more frequently is unexplained.[60]

I shall now list in pairs some of the elements written on the page, with some evidence as to which element was added first. The evidence is that of overlaid lines, not often amenable to photographic reproduction. For some pairs, the evidence points clearly to the priority of one element: even here, however, there are sometimes awkward inconsistencies. For a surprising number of elements, even for such basic ones as text vis-à-vis rubrics, almost no evidence can be adduced because the likelihood of intersections is remote. Where the evidence is inconclusive, it is possible that the opposite orders of entry are equally likely. Moreover, where intersections are almost never to be found, the exceptional and therefore useless, certainly misleading, case may provide the only evidence. Sometimes two pairs taken together may be incompatible; for example, where "a" seems prior to "b," and "b" prior to "c," "c" may elsewhere appear to be prior to "a." In general the calligraphic capital letter is prior to the stave; in one manuscript (Grenoble BM MS 394) the pitches appear to be prior to the capital; the sequence logically stemming from these premises would entail the pitches prior to the stave. The dangers are obvious. For conclusions of this kind to be reliable, the evidence in both premises should come from a single, consistent source, a requirement not likely to be fulfilled frequently.

In the list below, the first element of the pair is always prior to the second (shown thus: **first** *entered before* **second**); the nature of the evidence supporting the priority is explained; and conflicting evidence is shown unless none is known. Of the musical symbols that may appear on the stave, these are relevant: pitches,

---

[60]I owe this suggestion to Prof. Robert Sellin, an expert in hydrodynamics at the University of Bristol. Diane Droste informs me that she knows of similar examples in Sarum books.

clefs, incises (calligraphically similar to bar-lines), and directs (or custodes), check-like marks at the end of staves indicating the first pitch on the next stave. To avoid confusion between "below" (or "above") meaning where lines are separated on the page, and "below" (or "above") meaning "beneath" (or "on top of"), I have adopted the phrase "prior to" (or "after") for the latter.

Black Text Stage

Black text includes capital letters done entirely in ink and obviously written by the scribe as he wrote the text itself. The evidence in Plate 9 is unmistakable. These calligraphic letters are often ligated to the next letter (for example, fol. 33 and elsewhere in the Bodleian MS. Bodley 948).

- **text** *entered before* **rubrics** or **IDs**: intersections are infrequent. Pages such as fols. 56ᵛ–57ᵛ of Grenoble BM MS 467 (Plate 9) make the priority quite explicit. A leaf from Potenza (#6) shows a capital prior to an ID. Within a lengthy rubric there are often isolated words of black text, giving the incipits of items to which the rubric refers. On fol. 128 of the Pierpont Morgan MS 682, the word *hymnus*, abbreviated and part of such a long rubric, was clearly written after the next word, *Eterne*, black for the incipit of the hymn. Elsewhere in the same book it is clear that black text within rubrics was written after the red stave lines, contradicting the generalizations below that text and rubrics are entered before staves.

- **text** *entered before* **initials** (red, blue, or colored tracery): very occasional intersections between the solid red or blue of initials and text occur, as on the recto of opening clv, Grenoble BM MS 421; between text and the tracery around the edges of initials intersections are more frequent (Plates 10 and 1).

- **text** *entered before* **staves**: intersections seem surprisingly infrequent despite the textual ascenders and descenders. In sources such as the Bodleian MS. Douce 44 (flyleaves), staves have not been entered in the spaces left above the text.
- **capitals** *entered before* **staves**: because capitals extend much higher than normal text, there are frequent intersections. In the Avignon BM MS 190, fols. 92ᵛ–93 and elsewhere, the red paint of the stave-lines has run in small pools wherever it crosses the black of the capital letter, but the black pitch-symbols are neatly added after the red lines. In the Bodleian MS. lat. lit. a 9, however, the calligraphical capital is clearly after the stave.[61]
- **text** *entered before* **musical symbols** (on the stave): intersections are rather rare. In the Avignon BM MS 122, fol. 116, the clef is after the text. In many sources otherwise complete, the staves have been left blank in certain passages, occasionally for whole sections, as though the sources from which the scribes were copying were themselves deficient.

Cues Stage

Since cues point to material to be added in spaces left blank, there are no intersections with previously written symbols. Their very location in positions unpredictable without prior texts makes this the obvious stage for their addition. Nevertheless, we should consider the possibility that a very precisely defined (and visible?) layout of the page may have enabled the scribe to enter these cues before the entry of any text, as a reminder to himself. Should we

---

[61]This is also true of fol. 12 in BL MS. Harley 978, a non-liturgical source of different character.

even consider that the cues themselves are the planning marks, entered after measurement (four lines down and two pigeon's-egg widths to the right), of which we can find little other visible evidence?[62] In this function they would be less precisely defining than the strokes and dots discussed earlier, allowing the scribe more flexibility.

-   cues *entered before* IDs, colored initials, rubrics: intersections are very frequent. Marginal examples may have been trimmed; internal examples are often covered by the final insertion. Cues for rubrics seem to be less common (Plate 1).

Red Stage

-   rubrics *entered before* initials (red, blue, or tracery): as with text and initials. In the Avignon BM MS 192, fols. 8^v and 23^v show rubrics after the tracery.
-   rubrics *entered before* blue paraph: intersections are infrequent (Avignon BM MS 122, fol. 49, and Potenza leaf #6).
-   rubrics or IDs *entered before* staves or pitches: intersections are infrequent in sources of mixed music and text. The BL MSS. add. 23935, fol. 269^v, and Lansdowne 463, fol. 94^v, have particularly clear instances. Grenoble BM MS 373, fol. xxvi, shows a rubric prior to the final incise of a stave. The Penwortham Breviary, BL MS. add. 52359, fols. 3^v, 5, and passim, has clear instances of IDs written after the stave. There are, of course, many exclusively or mostly musical sources in which the staves are continuous and were possibly drawn immediately after the ruling of

---

[62]If organ-builders can use such measurements to judge the diameter of the pipes, why not scribes for a similar purpose? See Jean Perrot, *L'Orgue de ses origines hellénistiques à la fin du XIIIe siècle* (Paris, 1965), trans. Norma Deane as *The Organ: From its Invention in the Hellenistic period to the End of the Thirteenth Century* (Oxford, 1971), p. 236.

the page, so that rubrics and IDs are always after the stave.

- **incises** *entered before* **staves** *entered before* **incises**: although most incises are after the stave, some seem to have been added prior to it (Potenza #2, Grenoble BM MS 394). The latter are generally thin and look like planning marks.

Red Musical Material

- **staves** *entered before* **pitches, clefs, directs,** and **other symbols**: despite the apparent exceptions cited earlier, the evidence for this priority is overwhelming.
- **staves** *entered before* **initials**: (red, blue, colored tracery): evidence is much the same in frequency as with text and initials.

Black Musical Material (pitches, clefs, directs, etc.)

- **all symbols** *entered before* **initials**: evidence is clear but infrequent. In Potenza #6, all symbols occur prior to the red ID letters.

Initials and Other Colored Material

No evidence suggests that this material was entered other than last in the sequence.

<h3 style="text-align:center">III: THE ORDER OF WORK</h3>

The foregoing evidence may seem to advance us little beyond what was already known or assumed, but it enables us to set up a more accurate schema for the production of liturgical books and, perhaps, the first schema for complex books involving music. As is often the case with matters of this sort, a practical attempt to write a page of a Breviary is extremely enlightening, and the opinions of a modern medieval calligrapher such as Marc Drogin might be valuable.[63] To come as close to the practical as is possible in a written description, I shall attempt to describe, in the following section, a small part of the scribe's addition of black text. The possibility that planning marks had been added to the leaf before the scribe began is ignored: the scribe in this example sees only the outline of the writing area and regular rules.

Let us begin with the decisions a scribe must make at the beginning of a line. Since special circumstances apply to the first line of a leaf or section, I consider here only subsequent lines. What the scribe does at the beginning of a line is also conditioned by decisions he has made near the end of the previous line. The point of this exercise is to demonstrate that even a short reflection about the process very quickly reveals a complex, branching network of decisions, subdecisions dependent on earlier ones, and anticipations.

AT THE BEGINNING OF THE LINE the scribe must ask certain questions. Depending on the answer he may either write the line, ask other questions, or take some other specific course. The questions include:

i) is it the penultimate line of the page?

ii) are the remaining lines sufficient for a large initial close at hand below?

i) and ii) can be subsumed under a more general question: are there sufficient lines remaining for a subsequent letter occupying

---

[63]Marc Drogin, *Medieval Calligraphy: Its History and Technique* (New Jersey and London, 1980).

more than one line? If the answer is "No," the page may already be defective, as when a two-line initial must sit on the very bottom single line of the page, extending into the margin (Fig. 17). This particular "defect" is not infrequent. If there is no problem of anticipation, the scribe must ask:

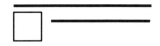

Fig. 17

iii) is there enough text to fill this line completely? This question should have been addressed before the end of the previous line, since it may already be too late to make the necessary adjustments in a satisfactory way. For example, if the layout of Fig. 18 is required, with the ID on the line preceding the next item, it may now be too late to add it. Some manuscripts clearly prefer this position for the ID, but the preference certainly should not be raised to the status of a rule. Some flexibility in matters of this kind obviously makes the scribe's job easier. The format of Fig. 19 may now be the only one possible.

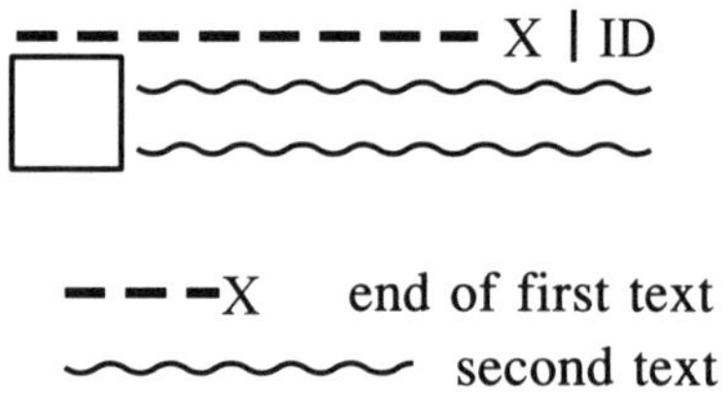

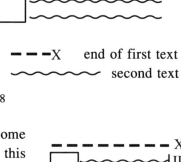

Fig. 18

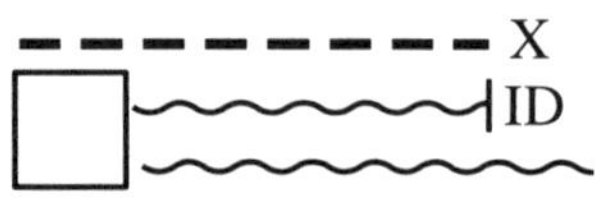

Fig. 19

NEAR THE END OF THE LINE, obviously, certain decisions must be made. The scribe must ask:

iv) is the line nearly finished? If not, he must write more and ask the question again.

v) is there enough text left to fill this and the whole of the next line? If the answer is Yes, the scribe can continue, eventually returning to the question at iv. Otherwise, he must ask:

vi) will the remaining text of this item, excluding the ID and any rubric required for the next item, fill this and the whole of the next line, but no more? If the answer is Yes, he will have to adopt the format of Fig. 19. Otherwise, whether there is too much or too little text for two lines, one of the formats shown in Figs. 20 and 21 will be used, with an extra complete line if necessary. The format of Fig. 22 is not satisfactory, although that of 23 is possible.

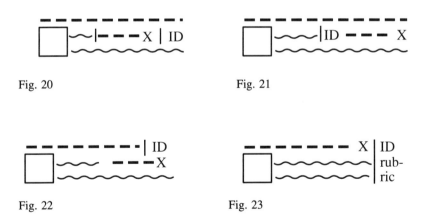

Fig. 20

Fig. 21

Fig. 22

Fig. 23

Where there is a runover, that is, an incomplete line, the scribe must judge the length of the remaining text plus the ID and rubric and must begin somewhere in the middle of the next line, leaving space at the left for the initial and the beginning of the next text. The scribe would be likely to leave less space rather than more, because text can be squeezed with abbreviation more easily than it can be extended. No doubt many other circumstances, exceptions, and problems could occur, which could be foreseen only after much practical experience. The mechanization just laid out is essentially false, of course. A skilled craftsman simultaneously and unconsciously would make more decisions than can be listed.

We can now lay out more precisely the sequence in which things were entered. I do not think it possible to say whether this sequence was completed at the end of a page or of a manuscript or, perhaps, of a fascicle: it depends partly on how many scribes were involved in the production. If a single scribe were responsible, he would not want to change tools, inkpots, and perhaps even exemplars from page to page.

The steps for the writing of complex books are as follows: (alternatives in brackets): 1) Ruling; 2) Design Marks; [Red Stave]; 3) Black Text; 4) Black Cues and Marks for the Reader; [Red Stave]; 5) Red Text; 6) Red Cues; 7) Highlights; 8) Red Stave; 9) Red Musical Symbols; 10) Black Musical Symbols; 11) Other Colors. Details of each step follow.

1) Ruling
   The writing area is outlined.
   a) Pages are pricked as required for continuous text or music, or for pages of mixed text and music. If the ruling is to be interrupted for alternating text and staves, some design of the page must be done here.
   b) The page is ruled.
   Under a), the pricking may be consistent for either format, and the difference may appear only in b), the ruling.

2) Design Marks

Was a design laid out on trial pages in a preliminary stage, as specimen pages of a modern book are roughed out? It is known that monastic authors wrote first on wax and then copied onto parchment.[64] Alexander Neckham (1157–1217) speaks of such methods: "habeat autem discipulus ejus rudis tabellam ceratam vel aeromate unctam, vel argilla oblita, ad flosculos protrahendos et depingendos variis modis, ne in offensione procedat."[65]

Nothing more can be said, since ephemeral records do not survive. I know of no surviving leaves that would qualify as full-page designs: their usefulness would be so short-lived that survival is unlikely, and recognition less so. More likely would be the use of models or specimen examples of good practice for the scribe to consult. Model-books are well-known through the Middle Ages.[66]

Whether trial pages or models were used, the blank leaf was first mapped to some extent. First the rules and vertical lines delimit the leaf. Then design marks were perhaps placed on the parchment for a) left-edge or other initials; b) rubrics or IDs; or c) staves. Items a) and b) are precisely those items for which visible letter cues do remain, or where cues can be hidden by the later material. The whole of this second stage,

---

[64]Clanchy, *From Memory to Written Record* (n. 41 above), p. 91. The citation in Jackson, *The Story of Writing* (n. 4 above), p. 72, suggests that wax tablets could hold a good deal of text.

[65]*De Utensilibus* in *Dictionnaire d'archéologie chrétienne et de liturgie*, ed. F. Cabrol and H. Leclercq, vol. 15, no. 2 (Paris, 1953), col. 1964, under "Tablettes à écrire," cited in Scheller, *A Survey* (n. 18 above), p. 2.

[66]Scheller, *A Survey* (n. 18 above), pp. 15 and 18, refers to Cassiodorus and Bede; Huglo, "Règlement" (n. 4 above), pp. 131–33, discusses exemplars.

including letter cues, may have to be put earlier, under 1a.

I have already suggested that the two-column format may have been more difficult for the scribe, lacking planning marks, to cope with. For the designer, the two-column format makes horizontal judgement easier.

[Red Stave]

In consistently musical sources, only, it is possible that the stave was added next: normally, however, the stave was added after the rubrics, at 8, below.

3) Black Text

Normal black text was added, with internal capital letters and large calligraphic capitals (up to a maximum of two lines, usually). Gathering catchwords were probably done at this stage. Many decisions and problems of layout would be avoided if the scribe changed pens and entered rubrics as he encountered them. At each switch to the red pen, he could also enter the highlights in the preceding lines.[67]

4) Black Cues and Marks for the Reader

A change of pen is normally required for cues. The scribe left small (black) cues pointing to subsequent material. Initials and rubrics are the usual candidates, but it would also be convenient to enter cues for the stave at this time. He may also have left marks at runovers or other disjunctions where it must be made clear to the user that the previous word does not continue with the next on the line. See 2, above.

---

[67]This idea stems from Diane Droste. I should like to thank her and Nancy Sacksteder for experimenting, and for suggesting useful ideas for this article. See also n. 74 below.

[Red Stave]

In consistently musical sources, the stave may have been added next: normally, however, the stave was added after the rubrics, at 8, below.

5) Red Text

The scribe adds rubrics and IDs. Rubrical material whose length would cause difficulties in judging the area to be left blank was perhaps added during the writing of black text. See 3, above.

6) Red Cues

At this point, red cues for staves or blue material may have been added.

7) Highlights

A scribe would add red highlights. Did he scan the text for all capital letters, some of which are hardly larger than normal text, to determine where highlights should be added? Perhaps this rather laborious process was combined with one of the two or three stages of proof-reading that we know took place.[68] Also, see 3, above.

8) Red Stave

The stave was drawn between limiting marks, in the spaces left.

9) Red Musical Symbols

Red incises were placed according to textual considerations, since the chant had not yet been entered.

---

[68]Huglo, "Règlement" (n. 4 above), pp. 130–31; and Trithemius, *De laude scriptorum* (n. 4 above), chaps. VIII and IX.

10) Black Musical Symbols

All other musical symbols were added on the stave, surely moving from left to right, that is, beginning with the clef and ending with the direct. Black incises and accidentals would be incorporated: frequently, other accidentals obviously have been entered by later hands. One must try to distinguish between "cue-like" but original accidentals and later casual insertions. Melismas seem sometimes to have been later insertions.

An interesting circumstance, the implications of which cannot be followed up here, occurs in the Pierpont Morgan MS 682, an Antiphonal. Folios 33–40 make up a complete quaternion. All the leaves have text, rubrics, IDs, and staves. Chant has been added only on the sides identified in Fig. 24. From this arrangement, we can certainly conclude that the chant scribe did not work sequentially through the music, and that a leaf was not finished before the next was started. It would seem that the complete outer side

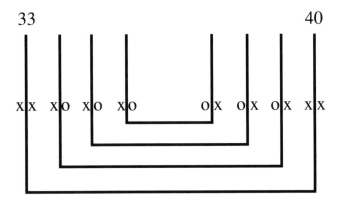

x: chant added on this page

o: chant lacking on this page

Fig. 24

of each bifolium was finished first, and then the complete inner side of each was finished. In this case the process was interrupted before the gathering was entirely filled.

11) Other Colors
This stage could include yellow highlights if they were used instead of red, and certainly included a) blue paraphs; b) initials and their tracery; and c) proof-reading.

CONCLUSIONS

Each source studied contributed evidence with respect to the matters raised above. Many elements are involved, and each source may illuminate a single instance of only one element. The collection of evidence is therefore extremely slow. A chance examination, on consecutive days, of the Bodleian MS. laud misc. 299 and the BL MS. add. 32427 allowed an adequate memory of the details of the former to remain as I looked at the latter. A sufficient number of details were similar enough to allow a tentative conclusion that both books employ the same system, perhaps one common to Noted Breviaries of Sarum Use. In general, however, the evidence presented in this study is so piecemeal, indeed sometimes contradictory, that firm conclusions hardly seem possible. A systematic examination, perhaps restricted to a single group of coherent sources, is required. Each scriptorium, each Use, each nation, and, perhaps, each individual book may have its own system.

The chancellor or precentor would proofread books in a cathedral to complete the work.[69] What official began it?[70] How

---

[69]Clanchy, *From Memory to Written Record* (n. 41 above), p. 101.

[70]Jackson, *The Story of Writing* (n. 4 above), p. 80, cites a scribe who was given precise instructions about the required size of various initials. See also the citation at n. 13 above.

many scribes were involved? Several skills were required, and the labor prior to entry of the chant and illumination can be divided in two ways: a) a careful design, ruling, and marking of the page followed by an execution of the writing within that layout; or b) a mechanical and mostly regular ruling followed by the execution of the page, which was designed, or laid out, by the scribe as he wrote. The first procedure would be best for a less experienced scribe. How many scribes were there with the necessary skills for the second? A very large number of excellently designed and executed liturgical books was produced, judging by the number of survivors.[71] Because of the increase in specialization well-documented in the late Middle Ages, only some of the people involved in the production may have been expert in the kind of judgements needed.[72] For the less skilled we may prescribe, or pre-scribe (!),

[71]Extrapolating from the number of books extant in dozens of libraries, large and small, I estimate that some ten thousand Antiphonals and Breviaries of the thirteenth, fourteenth, and fifteenth centuries still exist. For each Office book, a Mass book, raising the total to twenty thousand. If half have been lost by attrition, surely a minimal estimate, then forty thousand. Allowing twenty thousand for other similar books, Pontificals, Books of Hours, Lectionaries, Hymnals, etc., then sixty thousand. This amounts to two hundred liturgical books every year for three hundred years, to say nothing of all the other non-liturgical texts a scriptorium would produce. Statistics on the number of scriptoria in Europe, and the length of time needed to produce an average liturgical book would help to complete the estimate.

[72]Trithemius, *De laude scriptorum* (n. 4 above), refers to three scribes, and others for other tasks (chap. IX); there is evidence that the music was entered by a different scribe (see Huglo, "Règlement" [n. 4 above], pp. 122–23); the pecia system of specialization by section (rather than by script or decoration) seems occasionally to have developed (ibid., p. 131). Jackson, *The Story of Writing* (n. 4 above), p. 93, cites ten pairs of hands through which a book travelled. See also Alexander, "Scribes" (n. 12 above); and, especially, Scott, "A Mid-Fifteenth-Century English Illuminating Shop" (n. 20 above). Diane Droste informs me that in Sarum books the rubricator was certainly the same as the scribe.

a preliminary planning stage.[73] The main objection, that few visible signs of planning remain, can be answered by a) erasure, or the theory of the "deteriorating" dry- or silver-point; b) the transference from the scribal stage to the planning or prescribal stage of some cues and marks that do remain visible; or c) the careful and almost universal covering of earlier marks by the scribe. None of these theories can be adopted with great conviction: little can be known about a) if it is successful; b) runs counter to accepted knowledge; and c) would require almost all scribes to have been meticulous beyond reason.

My own tentative opinion is that there was sometimes a stage at which planning marks appeared on the page. Unless a method of clean "erasure" can be demonstrated, in good manuscripts with both text and chant, some mapping of the writing area probably took place before the ruling. Despite its challenge to standard dogma, the idea that the cues we see in all manuscripts may have been added immediately after the ruling of the page, and were to help the scribe himself as well as those who followed him, helps to solve some problems. Other difficulties are lessened if we suppose that the scribe alternated black and red pens as the need arose, at least for substantial rubrics.[74] To assert the need for a separate design stage is probably an extreme, but obviously the complexities are such that continuous sequential writing is not possible. A compromise would have the scribe anticipating many lines ahead and placing what he thinks necessary on the leaf as reminders.

A practical exercise is often worth many words. I leave the

---

[73]"Prescribo" is documented in medieval Latin from c. 1240, or approximately the date when complex, differentiated books were becoming more common, but seems not to have a specialized meaning related to this topic. See *Revised Medieval Latin Word-List*, ed. R. E. Latham (London, 1965).

[74]Plate 9 demonstrates that the scribe did not alternate between red and black in every case.

reader with the following task: without counting characters or making other measurements, write these last two sentences, neatly and evenly, in exactly seven three-inch-wide lines, with a square two-line initial at the left margin for the second sentence.[75]

SOURCES

The Media Centre of the University of Toronto, sponsored by the Centre for Medieval Studies, has produced two color videotapes, for sale or rent, which visually complement this article: *Liturgical Manuscripts of the Late Middle Ages*, Part I "The Contents," and Part II "Design and Execution" (1982).

Sources, listed by present location, follow. The two manuscripts from Assisi and Silos were examined only in photographic reproductions. This list includes only manuscripts actually cited in the study: many others were consulted. In the absence of direct evidence the dating of liturgical books, even to within a century, is exceptionally difficult because the usual criteria are less reliable.

I should like to thank the Librarians of these and other libraries for their encouragement and assistance, and for permission to publish the photographs in this article.

ASSISI, Basilica di S. Francesco, Museo Tesoro
Noted Missal of St. Louis (1260–65)

AVIGNON, BM (Musée Calvet)
MS 122 Noted Breviary, fourteenth century

---

[75]Too late to be included, Barbara Shailor's recent publication, *The Medieval Book* (Yale, 1988; repr. Toronto, 1991), with many illustrations, deals with numerous issues raised in this essay. Also useful, but dealing principally with scripts, is Michelle P. Brown's *A Guide to Western Historical Scripts from Antiquity to 1600* (Toronto, 1990).

MS 190, monastic Antiphonal, thirteenth/fourteenth century
MS 191, Antiphonal, thirteenth century
MS 192, Choir Psalter with hymns, thirteenth century

CARPENTRAS, BM

MS 43, Noted Breviary for Lyons, fourteenth century
MS 46, Breviary for the Cordeliers of Aix (?), fifteenth century
MS 69, Breviary for Autun, fifteenth century

DOUAI, BM

MS 166, Augustinian Breviary, fifteenth century

GRENOBLE, BM

MS 201, Antiphonal, thirteenth/fourteenth century
MS 373, Carthusian Gradual, (1394?)
MS 394, monastic Antiphonal (Carthusian?)
MS 421; Missal
MS 467, Handbook, containing a Tonary, music treatise, and Carthusian ordinal
MS 867, monastic Antiphonal

LONDON, BL

add. 23935, the copy of Humbert's Codex for the Master-General of the Dominican order: it is a compendium of all the liturgical books, late thirteenth century
add. 30072, Antiphonal (Dominican?), early fourteenth century
add. 32427, Noted Breviary (Sarum), early fifteenth century
add. 52359, Penwortham Noted Breviary, early fourteenth century
Lansdowne 463, Antiphonal, fifteenth century

NEW YORK, Pierpont Morgan Library
MS 682, Antiphonal, fifteenth century, Italian

OXFORD, Bodleian Library
Bodley 948, Antiphonal (Sarum, London), early fifteenth century
Can. lit. 346, monastic Noted Breviary (Benedictine), c. 1228
Can. lit. misc 379, Noted Breviary, fourteenth century
Corpus Christi College MS. B.486, a guardbook of miscellaneous leaves
Douce 44, flyleaves i and ii
e mus. 2, Noted Breviary (Sarum), fourteenth century
Gough lit. 1, Noted Breviary (York), c. 1400
lat. lit. a 9, one leaf of a secular Antiphonal
lat. lit. c 1, Antiphonal, thirteenth century
laud misc. 299, Noted Breviary (Sarum), early fifteenth century

PÉRIGUEUX, Archives départementales
MS 166, Antiphonal, late fifteenth century

POTENZA, Archivio di Stato, Biblioteca
Six fifteenth/sixteenth-century leaves from Antiphonals and Graduals under the shelf-mark Serie I, N.1–6. See *Directory of Music Research Libraries*, ed. Rita Benton (Iowa City, 1972), part III, p. 239

SILOS, Monastery Library
MS 9, monastic Noted Breviary, thirteenth century

VATICAN CITY, BA
Borghese MS 5 (lat. 10505), Noted Breviary, twelfth century

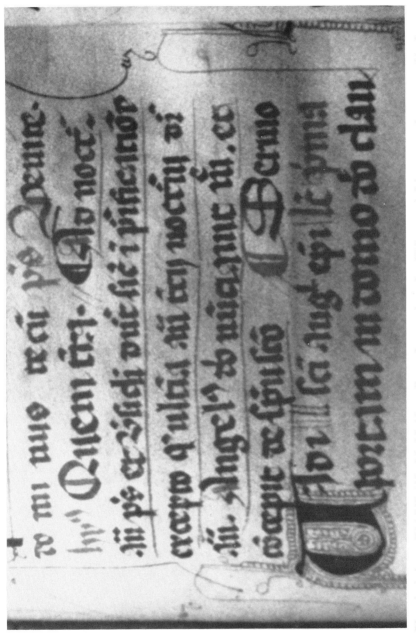

Plate 1. Avignon BM MS 122, fol. 95. Notes lines of separation after *Vidi*, preceded by cue marks, presumably from a design state; cue after *epi*; cue for *lc* is just before *prima*.

Plate 2. Avignon BM MS 122, fol. 55ᵛ. Ragged foot of column.

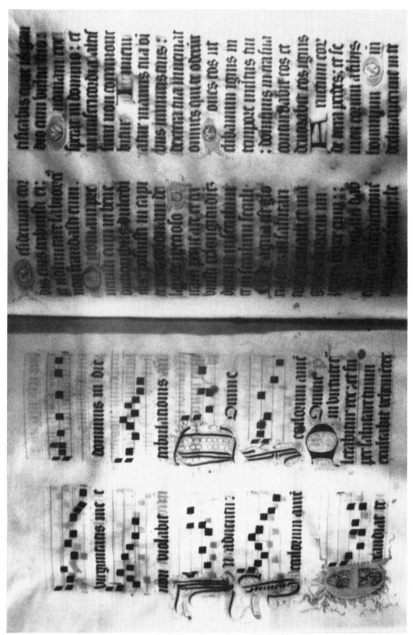

Plate 3. Avignon BM MS 192, fol. 20ᵛ. Different ways of adjusting column-length.

ANDREW HUGHES

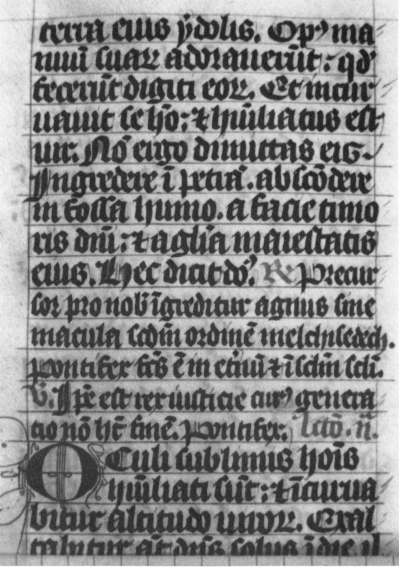

Plate 4. Clermont-Ferrand BM MS 67, fol. 52. Minimal difference in text size: double hyphen-strokes.

Plate 5. Douai BM MS 166, Ordination of Acolytes. Cues for sentences or highlights.

Plate 6. St. Omer BM MS Antiphonal, vol. 1, fol. 45. Planning frames for large letters.

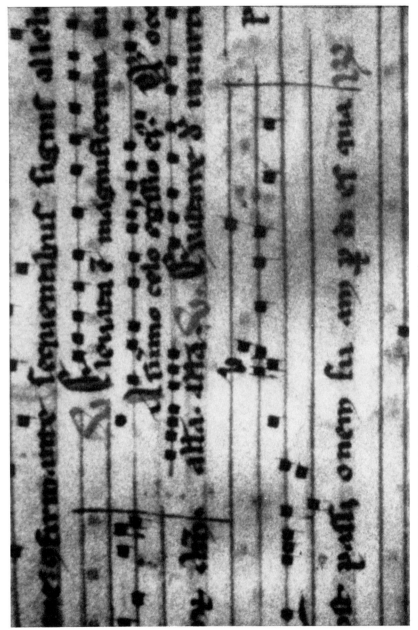

Plate 7. Grenoble BM MS 867, fol. 106. Planning dots, and split staveline.

Plate 8. Avignon BM MS 122, fol. 132. Planning marks, paraph, and cues.

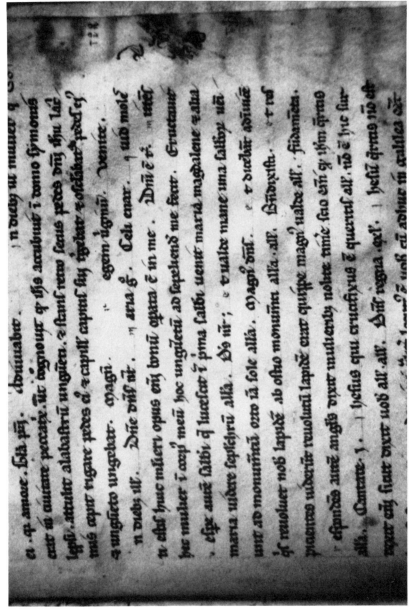

Plate 9. Grenoble BM MS 467, fol. 57. Before the addition of colored material.

ANDREW HUGHES

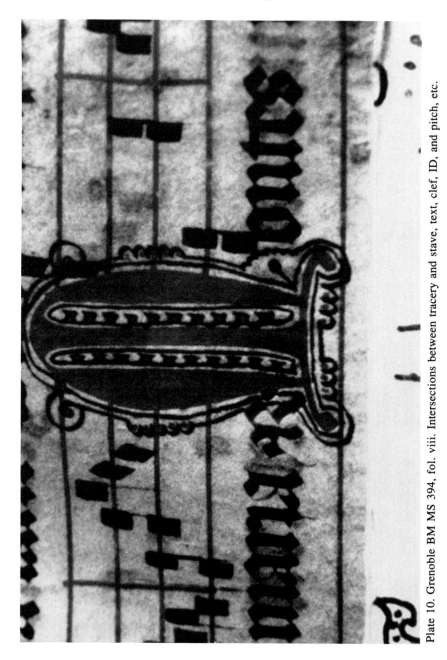

Plate 10. Grenoble BM MS 394, fol. viii. Intersections between tracery and stave, text, clef, ID, and pitch, etc.

224

The Word Made Flesh:
Augustinian Elements in the *York Cycle*

ALEXANDRA F. JOHNSTON

One of the most remarkable episodes in late medieval English Biblical drama is the episode of the Trial before Herod in the *York Cycle*.[1] For 424 gruelling lines, Christ stands silent as his tormentors shriek at him in English, French, and Latin demanding that he prophesy for them to provide sport for the king. Here the Christ figure is not only a sheep that is dumb before his shearers,[2] the willing sacrifice, the central icon in a series of devotional images; he is also the incarnate Word, the *logos*, here wordless in the act of atonement.

The effect is not accidental. Each of the long trial plays that has preceded this one has turned on the question of words—what Christ has said or taught that might impinge on the power of his judges. He has been tormented before and asked to prophesy, to use words with power, but has refused. Throughout the passion sequence, the playwrights have exploited the familiar Augustinian

---

[1] The *York Cycle* is preserved in a single manuscript (BL Add 35290) that was the city "register" or official copy of the plays. The cycle was first edited by Lucy Toulmin Smith, *York Plays* (Oxford, 1885). The most recent edition is Richard Beadle, *The York Plays* (London, 1982). All quotations from the cycle will be from the Beadle text.

[2] Isaiah 53:7; Acts 8:32.

conception of the paradox of the Incarnation:

> Verbum Patris per quod facta sunt tempora, caro factum, Natalem suum nobis fecit in tempore. . . . Ipse apud Patrem praecedit cuncta spatia saeculorum, ipse de matre in hac die cursibus se ingessit annorum. Homo factus, hominis factor: ut sugeret ubera, regens sidera; ut esuriret panis, ut sitiret fons, dormiret lux, ab itinere via fatigaretur, falsis testibus veritas accusaretur, judex vivorum et mortuorum a judice mortali judicaretur, ab injustis justitia damnaretur, flagellis disciplina caederetur, spinis botrus coronaretur, in ligno fundamentum suspenderetur, virtus infirmaretur, salus vulneraretur, vita moreretur.

> (The Word of the Father, by whom all the cycles of time were made, when He was made flesh, caused the day of His birth to take place in time. . . . With the Father he precedes all the ages of the world, by the Mother He set Himself on this day in the courses of the years. The Maker of Man was made man, that the Ruler of the stars might suck at the breast; that the Bread might be hungered; the Fountain, thirst; the Light, sleep; the Way, be wearied by the journey; the Truth, be accused by false witnesses; the Judge of the living and the dead, be judged by a mortal judge; the Chastener, be chastised with whips; the Vine, be crowned with thorns; the Foundation, be hung upon the tree; strength, be made weak; Health, be wounded; Life, die.)[3]

The *York Cycle* is a remarkable work of art that retains, despite the many hands that must have helped to shape it, a high level of theological and poetic sophistication.[4] York, in the late

---

[3]Augustine, Sermones CXCI.i.1, in J.-P. Migne et al., *Patrologia Latina*, XXXVIII, cols. 1009–10. Translation from Erich Przywara, ed., *An Augustine Synthesis* (New York, 1958), pp. 180–81.

[4]The only full-length study of the poetics of the *York Cycle* is R. J. Collier, *Poetry and Drama in the York Corpus Christi Play* (Hamden, Conn., 1977).

Middle Ages, was still the major city of the north. It was a center both of commerce and of learning, and the great civic play that was produced by the city council annually for almost two-hundred years (c. 1376–1569) served to demonstrate both aspects of the life of the city.[5] As the ecclesiastical center of northern England, the city boasted not only the Minster but monasteries, friaries, schools, hospitals, and other religious foundations. Some measure of the resources available to the playwrights can be deduced from the library list that survives from the late fourteenth century (about the time that the plays were being conceived) from the Augustinian friary.[6] The library contained 646 volumes of scripture, the Fathers, and other texts from late antiquity, including most of the works of St. Augustine and Boethius as well as the works of the scholastic theologians, the spiritual writings of such men as St. Francis and St. Bernard, and books of grammar, rhetoric, medicine, and science. That library alone contained most of the seminal writings that informed the thinking of the period, and it was only one of many in York.[7] Those who wrote the plays and those who saw them had access to a sophisticated body of material. It should not surprise us to find subtle allusions and learned interpretations in these plays.

[5]For the external evidence concerning the cycle see A. F. Johnston and Margaret Rogerson, eds., *Records of Early English Drama: York*, 2 vols. (Toronto, 1979). See also Margaret Dorrell, "Two Studies of the York Corpus Christi Play," *Leeds Studies in English*, ns 6 (1972): 63–111.

[6]The list survives in manuscript form in Trinity College, Dublin. It was edited by M. R. James in 1909 ("The Catalogue of the Library of the Augustinian Friars at York," *Fasciculum Ioannie Willis Clark Dicatus* [Cambridge, 1909]), pp. 2–96.

[7]See Jo Ann Moran, *Education and Learning in the City of York 1300–1500*, Borthwick Papers, 55 (York, 1979); and Elza Tiner, "Evidence for the Study of Rhetoric in the City of York to 1500" (unpublished licentiate report, Toronto, 1984).

Of all the English drama of this period, the *York Cycle* is the most verbal. Richard Collier, in his study of the poetics of the play, remarked that the dramatists paid "perhaps their greatest attention to the words."[8] This preoccupation of the playwrights with words and the patterns of sound that they make can be traced to two important elements of the thought of St. Augustine—his preoccupation with the paradox of the incarnate Word and his theory of language as signs.

The York playwrights, more than any other English dramatists, emphasize the paradox of the creator who was made in time. The cycle begins with the God's great statement:

Ego sum Alpha et O: vita, via, veritas, primus et nouissimus

I am gracyus and grete, God withoutyn begynnyng,
I am maker vnmade, all mighte es in me;
I am lyfe and way vnto welth-wynnyng.
I am formaste and fyrste, als I byd sall it be.　　(I, 1–4)

The scriptural statements then paraphrased by the playwright are taken from Revelation 1:8, John 14:6, and Isaiah 41:4. The citation from John is unique to this cycle. Although the other creation sequences begin with some form of Trinitarian statement, only *York* takes this particular phrase from the chapter from John that is so closely associated with orthodox Christology. By adding this attribute to the speech of Deus at the moment of creation, the figure of Deus becomes *Verbum apud Patrem, per quod facta sunt omnia* (the Word with the Father, through whom all things were made).[9] The creative power of the Word is picked up again by

[8]Collier, *Poetry and Drama*, p. 19.

[9]Augustine, *In Psalmos* CXXX.9, in *PL*, XXXVII, col. 1711, trans. Przywara, p. 283.

the angel who opens the play of the Sacrifice of Abel and remarks that the "lord of lyffe" has "wroughte þis worlde with worde" (VII, 1 and 4). Christ as creator is emphasized by Mary as she adores her newborn son as he "thurgh whos myht / All þis worlde was first begonne" (XIV, 61–62) and when he is greeted at the Entry to Jerusalem as "sege þat schoppe boþe even and morne" (XXV, 512).

In a commentary on John 14:6, Augustine wrote:

> *Ego sum via, et veritas et vita.* Veritatem et vitam omnis homo cupit: sed viam non omnis homo invenit. Deum esse quamdam vitam aeternum immutabilem, intelligibilem, intelligentem, sapientem, sapientes facientem, nonnulli etiam hujus seculi philosophi viderunt. Veritatem fixam, stabilem, indeclinabilem, ubi sunt omnes rationes rerum omnium creatarum, viderunt quidem, sed de longinquo; viderunt, sed in errore positi: et ideireo ad eam tam magnam et ineffabilem et beatificam possessionem. . . . Christus autem, quia ipse est apud Patrem veritas et vita . . . et non habebamus qua iremus ad veritatem; Filius Dei qui semper in Patre veritas et vita est, assumendo hominem factus est via. Ambula per hominem, et pervenis ad Deum. Per ipsum vadis, ad ipsum vadis. Noli quaerere qua illum venias, praeter ipsum. Si enim via esse ipse noluisset, semper erraremus. Factus ergo via est qua venias. Non tibi dico, quaere viam. Ipsa via ad te venit: surge et ambula.

("I am the way, and the truth, and the life" [John xiv, 6]. Truth and life doth every man desire, but the way is not found by every man. That God is a certain Life eternal, immutable, intelligible, intelligent, wise, and making wise, some philosophers even of this world have seen. The fixed, settled unwavering truth, wherein are all the governing principles of all created things, they saw indeed, but afar off. They saw, but amid the error in which they were placed, and hence they did not find the way to attain to that so great and ineffable

and beatific possession. . . . But Christ, in that He is with the
Father the truth and the life, . . . and we had no way by
which to go to the truth, as the Son of God, who in the
Father is ever the truth and the life, by assuming man's
nature became the way. Walk by Him the Man, and thou
comest to God. By Him thou goest, to Him thou goest. Look
not for any way except Himself by which to come to Him.
For if He had not vouchsafed to be the way, we should
always have gone astray. Therefore He became the way by
which thou shouldest come. I do not say to thee, seek the
way. The way itself is come to thee; arise and walk.)[10]

The *York* playwrights conceived their Christ much in these terms.
More than the other English collections, this cycle emphasizes the
Ministry episodes.[11] This Christ is not only a sacrifice for the
sins of the world. He is, as Augustine's gloss on John 14:6 suggests, a companion along the way. He is a teacher, a gentle presence. He is, as he constantly reminds the audience, a "mirror for
men." At the end of the Temptation, an angel rebukes him for not
destroying Satan, but he replies:

> For whan þe fende schall folke see
> And salus þam in sere degré,
> Þare myrroure may þei make of me

---

[10]*Sermones* (*de Scrpt. Nov. Test.*) CXLI.i.1 and iv.4, in *PL*, XXXVIII, cols.
776–77, trans. Przywara, p. 198.

[11]The York manuscript has seven episodes (counting the double episode of the
Woman Taken in Adultery and Lazarus as two) in the Ministry sequence. Space
was left for two further plays, one on the Marriage Feast at Cana and the other on
the scene of the repentance of Mary Magdalene, but the responsible guilds—the
Vintners and the Ironmongers—never submitted them to be registered. The
Towneley manuscript has only three and *Chester* and *N-Towne* have five each. See
A. F. Johnston, "The Christ Figure in the Four English Cycles" (Ph.D. diss.,
University of Toronto, 1964).

>   For to stande still,
>   For ouerecome schall þei noȝt be
>   Bot yf þay will.   (XXII, 193–98)

This Christ is in no way remote from those he has come to save. The episode of the Baptism, for example, ends with his companionable invitation to John the Baptist:

>   But wende we nowe
>   Wher most is nede þe folke to wisse,
>   Both I and þou.   (XXI, 166–68)

The *York* Christ is, indeed, the "Way, the Truth and the Life."

The many connotations of the "word" associated with Christ become a motif in the cycle from the episode of the Sacrifice of Isaac onward. Isaac (here made a more perfect type of Christ by being portrayed as an adult) prays for forgiveness if he has sinned "In worde, in werke, or any waye" (X, 255). In the Baptism play, John tells us that in his preaching he urges man to be "clene haly / In worde, in werke. . ." (XXI, 31–32). Later in that episode, the Word himself comes to John for Baptism saying "Fyrst schall I take, sen schall I preche" (XXI, 134). From here until the passion sequence begins, Christ is, indeed, a preacher and teacher. Unlike the other cycles, there is no other expositor to explain the action. He himself explains the Baptism to John, exhorts men to follow his example in taking baptism, and chides the angel in the Temptation for his oversimplification of sin. It is he who explains the mystery of the vision on the Mount of Transfiguration and tries to prepare his disciples for the Passion before the event. He is "the way," "the mirror," the example for all men to follow or, as he is called at the Entry, the "texte of trewþe" (XXV, 534).

The *York* playwrights, then, consciously exploited the concept of the *logos* in their portrayal of Christ. But their interest in "the

Word" went beyond Christology. Eugene Vance, in *Mervelous Signals: Poetics and Sign Theory in the Middle Ages*, writes: "Medieval linguistic theory begins at the top with speculation about the *logos*, with its presentation to the soul, and finally, with the external phonetic and textual dimensions of language which are the lowest ontological stratum of the Word."[12] The preoccupation of the *York Cycle* with the *logos* is central to the didactic purpose of the cycle. Basic to the poetics of the cycle (i.e. the "textual dimensions of language"), however, is a dramaturgical principle shared by all medieval drama that can be traced in large measure to Augustine's sign theory.

This theory, enunciated most clearly in the opening section of Book 2 of *De Doctrina Christiana*, argues for the pre-eminence of language as sign, and again and again Augustine connected this idea with Christ as the Incarnate Word. In *Sermon XXVIII*, he wrote:

> Ecce enim Verbum Dei Deus apud Deum, sapientia Dei manens incommutabiliter apud Patrem, ac procederet ad nos, carnem quasi sonum quaesivit. . . .

> (For behold, the Word of God, God with God, the Wisdom of God, abiding immutably with the Father, that He might go forth to us, sought flesh to be as it were the sound. . . .)[13]

Sound and, then, music and words take on theological significance in themselves. At the same time, silence also has significance. Because sound is associated with time ("quia verberato aere statim transeunt, nec diutius manent quam sonant"; words pass away as soon as they strike upon the air and last no longer

---

[12]Eugene Vance, *Mervelous Signals: Poetics and Sign Theory in the Middle Ages* (Lincoln, Neb., and London, 1986), p. x.

[13]*Sermones* XXVIII.v, in *PL*, XXXVIII, col. 185, trans. Przywara, p. 209.

than their sound), sound, as we know it, is of this world.[14] If man seeks truly to become one with God, then he will seek tranquility, peace, silence. As Vance has expressed it, "the very act of speaking our thought is an expenditure in time that, once apprehended, dialectically demands a movement of transcendence, through degrees of silence, to immediate union of the soul with God as timeless, indivisible immobile One."[15] The Christ in the Trial before Herod, then, is the silent Word, manifesting two characteristics of the Trinity. As the *logos*, he here refuses to be drawn into the parodic game of prophesy for entertainment, but he also stands as the "immobile One," the still silent center of the stage action that swirls around him.

That God is immutable and unchanging at the center of a harmonious universe is a common-place philosophical idea. In his early work, *De Musica*, Augustine sought to find God through harmony:

Non ergo invideamus inferioribus quam nos sumus, nosque ipsos inter illa quae infra nos sunt, et illa quae supra nos sunt, ita Deo et Domino nostro opitulante ordinemus, ut inferioribus non offendamur, solis autem superioribus delectemur. Delectatio quippe quasi pondus est animae. Delectatio ergo ordinat animam. *Ubi enim erat thesaurus tuus, ibi erit et cor tuum* (Matth. vi, 21): ubi delectatio, ibi thesaurus: ubi autem cor, ibi beatitudo aut miseria. Quae vero superiora sunt, nisi illa in quibus summa, inconcussa, incommutabilis, aeterna manet aequalitas? Ubi nullum est tempus, quia nulla mutabilitas est; et unde tempora fabricantur et ordinantur et modificandtur aeternitatem imitantia, dum coeli conversio ad idem redit, et coelestia corpora ad idem revocat, diebusque et men-

---

[14]Augustine, *DDC*, II.iv, in *PL*, XXXIV, col. 38. Translation from Philip Schaff, ed., *A Select Library of the Nicene and Post-Nicene Fathers of the Christian Church*, vol. 2 (New York, 1886), p. 536.

[15]Vance, *Mervelous Signals*, p. viii.

sibus et annis et lustris, caeterisque siderum orbibus, legibus aequalitatis et unitatis et ordinationis obtemperat. Ita coelestibus terrena subjecta, orbes temporum suorum numerosa successione quasi carmini universitatis associant.

(Let's not, then, be envious of things inferior to ourselves, and let us, our Lord and God helping, order ourselves between those below us and those above us, so we are not troubled by lower, and take delight only in higher things. For delight is a kind of weight in the soul. Therefore, delight orders the soul. "For where your treasure is, there will your heart be also" [Matt. 6:21]. Where delight, there the treasure; where the heart, there happiness or misery. But what are the higher things, if not those where the highest unchangeable undisturbed and eternal equality resides? Where there is no time because there is no change, and from where times are made and ordered and changed, imitating eternity as they do when the turn of the heavens comes back to the same state, and the heavenly bodies to the same place, and in days and months and years and centuries and other revolutions of the stars obey the laws of equality, unity and order. So terrestrial things are subject to celestial, and their time circuits join together in harmonious succession for a poem of the universe.)[16]

Here Augustine is simply adapting the common Platonic / Pythagorean notion of cosmic music. Boethius later elaborated on this theory in his *De institutione musica*.

God is the point of stability. Man is mutable, under the watchful eye of the immutable God. As Boethius put it in the *Consolation of Philosophy*, "The generation of all things, and the whole course of mutable natures and of whatever is in any way subject to change, take their causes, order, and forms from the unchang-

---

[16]*De Musica* XI.xxix, in *PL*, XXXII, col. 1179. Translation from Ludwig Schopp, ed., *Writings of St Augustine*, vol. 2, which is vol. 5 of *The Fathers of the Church* (New York, 1948), p. 355.

ing mind of God."[17] Whether, as Augustine implies in the passage from *De musica*, he is at the top of a descending scale or at the center of concentric circles, the farther away one moves from God the less stable one becomes. This is, of course, related to sin and control of the bodily appetites. By implication, therefore, good is stable, tranquil, and harmonious; evil is unstable, restless, and dissonant. Augustine expresses this notion clearly when he describes the citizens of the City of God as "tranquillus" and those of the City of Man as "turbulentus."[18]

Although Augustine rejected the idea that matter was inherently evil, arguing against the Manichees that nothing created by God is evil, by the time he came to write his commentary on the fall (*De Genesis ad litteram libri duodecim*) "the legend of Lucifer's premundane rebellion and downfall was . . . firmly established in the body of Christian doctrine."[19] In Augustine's hands the many often contradictory interpretations of the story of the fall "were welded together in a firm and systematic pattern which was to dominate the Church's thinking on the subject for the next thirteen centuries and longer."[20] The idea of good as static and evil as active seems to have become attached to the concept of "the evil one" through the Book of Job. When God asks Satan where he has come from in the prose prologue to the book, Satan replies, "From going to and fro in the earth and walking up and down in it."[21]

---

[17]Boethius, *The Consolation of Philosophy*, Book IV, Prosa 6, trans. Richard Green (Indianapolis, 1962), p. 91.

[18]*De Genesi ad litteram libri duodecim* XI.xv.20, in *PL*, XXXIV, col. 437.

[19]J. M. Evans, *Paradise Lost and the Genesis Tradition* (Oxford, 1968), p. 95.

[20]Ibid., p. 93.

[21]Job 1:7.

This passage is used in the episode of the Harrowing of Hell in the *York Cycle*. During his debate with Christ, Satan thinks he is being given leave to seek out more souls and cries that he "schall walke este and weste" (XXXVII, 333).

The depiction of frenetic activity by the wicked in contrast to the calm stillness of good is everywhere in western European art and literature in the later Middle Ages. It provided for the English playwrights an underlying theological principle around which to build their dramaturgy. When the Coventry Herod "ragis in the pagond and in the strete also" he manifests this principle as do the demons in the *Towneley Cycle* urging each other to "faste take oure rentals" as they hurry "vp watlyn strete" in response to the trumpet call of Judgement.[22] Nor is this principle confined to Biblical drama. In the *Castle of Perseverence* the Bad Angel urges *Humanum Genus* to become one with the World. *Humanum Genus* excitedly cries that he will "wyth þe Werld . . . go play," to be admonished by the Good Angel, "A, nay, man for Cristys blod, / Cum agayn, be strete and style."[23] In the *York Cycle*, the principle is manifested not only in the action but also in the complex patterns of sounds in the verse and the music.

The *York Cycle* not only teaches the story of salvation history; it also celebrates that history. The sense of celebration is conveyed by the constant use of liturgical music.[24] The playwrights

---

[22]For the Coventry Herod see Hardin Craig, ed., *Two Coventry Corpus Christi Plays*, EETS es 87 (1902), p. 27. For the demons see George England, ed., *The Towneley Plays*, EETS es 71 (1897), p. 371.

[23]Mark Eccles, ed., *The Macro Plays*, EETS es 262, (1969), pp. 14–15.

[24]Augustine, in the famous passage in the *Confessions* (X.xxxiii), recounts how the music of the church caused him to weep "in primordiis recuperate fidei meae" (at the outset of my recovered faith) and, despite his misgivings about the sensuousness of music, goes on to approve of it in church "ut per oblectamenta

knew when to use words and when to use the familiar tonalities of the church. In every other English dramatic version of the Resurrection, for example, the playwrights give the risen Christ a sermon. In contrast, the York Christ rises from the dead in silence as the familiar "Christus resurgens" is sung (XXXVIII, 186). Here the event at the heart of the Christian faith is acted out as the silent Word rises to the triumphal assurance of this hymn of praise. In each appropriate place, the familiar songs of the church are sung, punctuating the action with liturgical harmony to offset the seeming triumph of evil. The *Te deum* and the *Sanctus* are sung by the nine orders of angels at their creation (I, 24; 41 s.d.); *Cantemus Domino* at the end of the play of the Exodus (XI, 407 s.d.); *Veni Creator Spiritus* three times: at the Baptism of Christ (XXI, 154 s.d.), the Temptation (XXII, 91 s.d.), and Pentecost (XLIII, 97 s.d.); *Laus tibi cum gloria* at the Harrowing of Hell (XXXVII, 408 s.d.); and *Ascendo ad patrem meum* at the Ascension (XLII, 177 s.d.). Two settings of the three hymns sung in the play of the Assumption of the Virgin (*Surge Proxima mea, Veni de Libano*, and *Veni electa*) are provided in the manuscript.[25] At the Annunciation Gabriel sings *Ne timeas* (XII, 153 s.d.), and when she visits Elizabeth Mary sings the *Magnificat* (XII, 241 s.d.). There is a lacuna in the manuscript at the appropriate point in the Annunciation to the Shepherds, but the *Gloria* was apparently sung, as the text resumes with the shepherds attempting to imitate the harmony of the angelic choir (XV,

---

aurium infirmior animus in affectum pietatis assurgat" (that so by the delights of the ear the weaker minds may be stimulated to a devotional frame); in *PL*, XXXII, col. 800, trans. Schaff, 1:156.

[25]Beadle, *The York Plays*, pp. 465–74, prints this music in a modern version edited by John Stevens. See also JoAnna Dutka, *Music in the English Mystery Plays*. Early Drama, Art, and Music Reference Ser., 2 (Kalamazoo, 1980).

60 etc.). The cycle ends with the stage direction "Et sic facit finem, cum melodia angelorum transiens a loco ad locum" (XLVII, 381 s.d.). An appropriate ending would have been to repeat the great hymn of praise, the *Te deum*, with which the day had begun.

Similarly, the cycle is full of ritualistic poetic passages that build up a sense of a community of faith sharing in a litany of praise to the Word incarnate. Mary speaks the first lyric as she places the baby (just born in full sight of the audience) in the manger:

> Hayle my lord God, hayle prince of pees,
> Hayle my fadir, and hayle my sone;
> Hayle souereyne sege all synnes to sesse,
> Hayle God and man in erth to wonne.
> Hayle, thurgh whos myht
> All þis worlde was first begonne,
> Merknes and light. (XIV, 57–63)

Joseph, too, kneels before the child:

> Hayle my maker, hayle Crist Jesu,
> Hayle riall kyng, roote of all right,
>   Hayle saueour.
> Hayle my lorde, lemer of light,
> Hayle blessid floure. (XIV, 108–12)

Each of the three kings speaks a stanza of praise as he presents his gift (XVI, 309–44), and, although this play was registered almost a century after the rest of the cycle, Simeon in the Purification in the Temple has a similar litany of praise (XVII, 354– 73).[26] The ex-

---

[26]For the dating of the Purification episode see Beadle, *The York Plays*, pp. 434–37.

citement of the Entry into Jerusalem builds to a climax with eight stanzas of praise spoken by the eight burgesses (XXV, 489–544) before the final stage direction of "Tunc cantant" (XXV, 545).

These verbal canticles of praise spoken by the godly, however, are viciously parodied in the the Second Trial before Pilate when Christ is dressed in royal robes:

I Miles	*Aue*, riall roy and *rex judeorum*,
	Hayll, comely kyng þat no kyngdom has kende.
	Hayll vndughty duke, þi dedis ere dom,
	Hayll, man vnmyghty þe menȝé to mende.
III Miles	Hayll, lord without lande for to lende,
	Hayll kyng, hayll knave vnconand.
IV Miles	Hayll, freyke without forse þe to fende,
	Hayll strang, þat may not wele stand
	To stryve. (XXXIII, 408–16)

The calm dignity of the high style spoken in genuine praise is here brutally twisted and reinforced with plosive alliteration that descends to derisive laughter as Christ staggers under the weight of the mockery.

This verbal parody has been preceded by sixty-five lines of rapid stychomythia as the four soldiers dance around Christ with their scourges responding to Pilate's injunction to "Skelpe hym with scourges and with skathes hym scorne. / Wrayste and wrynge hym to, for wo he be wepyng" (XXXIII, 337–38). The demonic dance has been emphasized throughout the trial sequence by the reiteration of the phrase "daunce forth in þe deuyll way" (XXIX, 395; see also XXXI, 424) as the soldiers drag the passive Christ from one judge to the next as trial follows trial. Cain, the archetypal murderer, is the first to use this phrase in the cycle in his dispute with his brother Abel, the type of Christ (VII, 52). The frenetic activity of the torturers under the cover of the darkness of the night of Maundy Thursday is picked up by the more matter-of-fact crucifiers in the next episodes whose constant reference to the need to have the crucifixion over "be none" continues to place these events of eternal significance within the constraints of time.

The busyness of the henchmen of the earthly powers at the crucifixion is an extension of the exuberant haste of those sent to capture Christ in the episode of the Agony of the Garden who announce that they will "come forthe all faste" (XXVIII, 186) and "go . . . hens þan in hy and haste vs to þe halle" (XXVIII, 189). Herod's henchmen at the Slaughter of the Innocents are equally hurried (XIX), as are the doctors keen to capture the woman in the act of adultery. That episode opens with the lines:

> Steppe fourth, late vs no lenger stande,
> But smertely þat oure gere wer grayde;
> Þis felowe þat we with folye fande,
> Late haste vs fast þat she wer flayed. (XXIV, 1–4)

The *York* playwrights commanded a rich tradition in poetry. In their hands, the lines themselves are signs of the state of grace of the speaker. The two prologues to the Magi play clearly demonstrate this aspect of the poetics of the cycle.[27] The Masons' Pageant gives the prologue to Herod:

> The clowdes clapped in clerenes þat þer clematis inclosis—
> Jubiter and Jouis, Martis and Mercurij emyde—
> Raykand ouere my rialté on rawe me reioyses,
> Blonderande þer blastis to blaw when I bidde.
> Saturne my subgett, þat sotilly is hidde,
> Listes at my likyng and laies hym full lowe.
> The rakke of þe rede skye full rappely I ridde,
> Thondres full thrallye by thousandes I thrawe

---

[27]For a discussion of the history of this pageant see Beadle, *The York Plays*, pp. 429–34.

When me likis.
Venus his voice to me awe,
Þat princes to play in hym pikis.   (XVI, 1–11)

Inflated in both sentiment and style, this speech emphasizes the
folly of the king who thinks he, not God, commands the elements.
The alliteration on "cl" in line one and "bl" in line four are particularly pretentious, forcing the actor to exaggerate his delivery and
underline the ludicrous pride of the character.

The Goldsmiths' pageant, in contrast, opens with the prayers
of the three kings spoken in measured twelve-line stanzas. The
third king ends his prayer after six lines, sees the other kings, and
turns to them in greeting. The first king finishes the stanza com-
pleting the rhyme of the third king:

III Rex   Lorde God þat all goode has bygonne
        And all may ende, both goode and euyll.
        That made for man both mone and sonne,
        And stedde yone sterne to stande stone stille,
        Tille I þe cause may clerly conne,
        God wisse me with his worthy wille.
        I hope I haue her felaws fonne
        My yarnyng faþfully to fullfille.
        Sirs, God yowe saffe and see,
        And were ȝow euere fro woo.
  I Rex   Amen, so might it bee,
        And saffe yow sir, also.

These are men of God attributing to him all the movements of the
planets, including the action of the star they are following. The
contrast between them and Herod is imbedded in the lines themselves. The actors need only speak the lines as they are written,
and the prosody establishes their characters.

The sharing of stanzas and the exchange of rhymes is a device
that the playwrights frequently use to convey harmony and agree-

241

ment between characters. One of the most charming examples of this technique comes at the end of the episode of Joseph's Troubles when Joseph, reassured of Mary's virginity by the angel, returns to ask forgiveness:

Joseph	Saie Marie, wiffe, how fares þou?
Maria	Þe bettir sir, for yhou.
	Why stande yhe þare? Come nere.
Joseph	My bakke fayne wolde I bowe
	And aske forgifnesse nowe,
	Wiste I þou wolde me here.

Maria	Forgiffnesse sir? Late be, for shame,
	Slike wordis suld all gud women lakke.
Joseph	Yha, Marie, I am to blame
	For wordis lang-are I to þe spak. (XIII, 290–99)

After this tender exchange, Joseph bustles about preparing for the journey to Bethlehem, his bitterness over his asssumed betrayal forgotten.

The depth of that bitterness is also conveyed through the verse. In the earlier scenes of this play, Mary had been rapt in the wonder of her pregnancy and failed to understand Joseph's very human conviction that she has cuckolded him. To every demand to know the name of the father, she replied with a variant on "Goddis and youres" (XIII, 104). His insistence grows and as it does the lines themselves are broken and shared:

Joseph	Whose ist Marie?
Maria	Sir, Goddis and youres.
Joseph	Nay, nay,
	Now wate I wele I am begiled, (XIII, 104–05)

And again:

Joseph   But who is þe fader? Telle me his name.
Maria   None but youreselfe.
Joseph   Let be, for shame.
          I did it neuer; þou dotist dame, by bukes and belles!
          Full sakles shulde I bere þis blame aftir þou telles,
          For I wrought neuere in worde nor dede
          Thyng þat shulde marre thy maydenhede,
          To touche me till.   (XIII, 177–83)

His agitation has momentarily upset his normal pious calm, causing him to alliterate on plosives, although he recovers his balance quickly.

These metric variants have puzzled those editors of this text who are more concerned with metrical conformity than dramatic effect. Miss Toulmin Smith, commenting on this speech of Joseph's, writes, "this stanza seems to be irregular, unlike any other."[28] At a similar emotional moment in the play of Abraham and Isaac, as Abraham blesses the son he is about to sacrifice, Miss Smith leaves the irregular lines as they appear in the manuscript:

      Isaak, I take me leue for ay.
      My blissyng haue þou enterly,
                Me bus þe mys!
      And I beseke god all-myghty
                He giffe þe his.   (X, 230–34)

Richard Beadle, in contrast, amends the text and so blurs the effect:

      Isaak, I take my leue for ay—
      Me bus þe mys.

---

[28]Lucy Toulmin Smith, *York Plays*, p. 108.

My blissyng haue þou enterly,
And I beseke God allmyghty
    He giffe þe his.   (X, 230–34)

Changed relationships and understanding are also conveyed by the stanzaic pattern. In the play of the appearance of Christ to Mary Magdalene, their dialogue up to the "Noli me tangere" line ("Negh me noght, my loue, latte be"; XXXIX, 82) has shared stanzas. After this rebuke, the two exchange complete stanzas of instruction and praise. Similarly, in the next episode of the Road to Emmaus, the pilgrims speak concatenated eight-line stanzas where part of the last line of each verse is repeated in the first line of the next, conveying the heavy sense that they are locked in their despair as they re-tell the story of the crucifixion. Not even the appearance of Christ changes the verse, until he breaks the bread and vanishes. Then, after some lines of metric confusion expressing the confusion of the pilgrims at the disappearance of their companion, the stanzas change to quatrains. Although the verses are still linked, the shorter length conveys the impression not of despair but of excitement, as the speeches of the pilgrims seem to tumble over one another in their eagerness to tell the other disciples.

In this cycle, there are plays and parts of plays written in four-, eight-, eleven-, twelve-, and fourteen-line stanzas that are both syllabic and alliterative in style. There are also six-, seven-, and ten-line stanzas that are only syllabic, and nine- and thirteen-line stanzas that are only alliterative.[29] This bewildering array of verse forms has traditionally been seen to be evidence of different hands at work and of at least three "levels of composition" over the years between the inception of the cycle sometime in the last

---

[29]Beadle, *The York Plays*, pp. 475–76.

quarter of the fourteenth century and the creation of the manuscript as we have it approximately one hundred years later.[30] There is no doubt that the variations in style do reflect changes in the text. For example, we know that a major revision of the passion sequence took place in the early 1430s.[31] The working "check-list" of the pageants, the "ordo paginarum" preserved in the civic memorandum book, was compiled in 1415 but was carefully annotated during the life of the cycle to indicate changes of text and ownership.[32] This undeniable fluidity of the text has obscured the fact that the playwrights seem to have deliberately used the many verse forms available to them in the northern tradition to build characters and relationships and, above all, establish the state of grace of a character through the verse form. Augustine argued that: "Signum est . . . res, praeter speciem quam ingerit sensibus, aliud aliquid ex se faciens in cogitationem venire . . ." (a sign is a thing which, over and above the impression it makes on the senses, causes something else to come into the mind as a consequence of itself).[33] The poetry of the *York Plays* is profoundly sensuous in the richness of its language and form, but this very sensuousness, true to Augustinian doctrine, points the

---

[30]The first evidence of the cycle comes from a payment for the rental of a pageant house (a place to store the wagon stage) in 1376 (Johnston and Rogerson, *Records of Early English Drama*, 1:3). For the dating of the manuscript see Margaret Rogerson, "External Evidence for Dating the York Register," *Records of Early English Drama Newsletter*, no. 2 (1976): 4–5; and Richard Beadle and Peter Meredith, "Further External Evidence for Dating the York Register (BL Additional MS 35290)," *Leeds Studies in English*, ns 11 (1980): 51–58.

[31]Johnston and Rogerson, *Records of Early English Drama*, 1:49.

[32]Ibid., 1:16–26.

[33] *De doctrina Christiana*, II.i, in *PL*, XXXIV, col. 35, trans. Schaff, p. 535.

listener to moral significance beyond the words themselves. The language is more than just the conveyance of the meaning of the words. Its order within its prosodic structure also conveys meaning. This fact and the frequent verbal echoes backward and forward over the sequence of episodes argues, in the face of all common sense, a guiding intelligence over the course of several generations of revisions that was influenced not just by the theology of Augustine but by his theories about language. Who or what that intelligence was we have yet to discover. What is clear is that what has been preserved in the York register is not the work of clumsy versifiers but that of consciously sophisticated poets using their skill "in honour and reverence of our Lord Jesus Christ"[34]—the Word made flesh.

---

[34]Johnston and Rogerson, *Records of Early English Drama*, 2:697; see 1:11 for original Latin text.

The Topos of the Beasts of Battle in Early Welsh Poetry

DAVID N. KLAUSNER

The grouping of three beasts commonly associated with battle is a frequent motif in the literatures of Anglo-Saxon England and early Scandinavia. The motif is found generally in descriptions of battle, its anticipation, and its aftermath; and the beasts—the raven, the eagle, and the wolf—are usually seen in association with the victors, who feed them by right and for whom they serve as a kind of natural clean-up crew. The motif has received relatively little attention on its own; one of the few studies to deal with it individually is F. P. Magoun's brief article of 1956, which lists the occurrences in Old English, a total of twelve passages.[1] Magoun calls the beasts of battle a "theme," using the term specifically in its oral-formulaic sense. Since I do not wish to comment here on the possible oral-formulaic nature of early Welsh poetry, I have preferred to call it a "topos." Magoun was taken to task for the narrowness of his focus by Adrian Bonjour, who gave a thorough discussion of the topos as it appears in *Beowulf*.[2] Further discussions have generally appeared in critical commen-

---

[1]F. P. Magoun, Jr., "The Theme of the Beasts of Battle in Anglo-Saxon Poetry," *Neuphilologische Mitteilungen* 56 (1955): 81–90.

[2]Adrian Bonjour, "*Beowulf* and the Beasts of Battle," *PMLA* 72 (1957): 562–73.

tary on the individual poems in which the topos appears.[3] The beasts of battle also appear with great frequency in the skaldic poetry of early Iceland and Norway; they do not appear in their traditional grouping in continental Germanic literatures, although George Brown has shown that the topos has classical parallels.[4]

Perhaps the best-known passage describing the beasts occurs in *The Battle of Brunanburh*, following the flight from the battlefield of the survivors among the defeated, led by Anlaf and Constantinus, and the triumphant departure of the victors, Edmund and Athelstan.[5]

> Letan him behindan   hræw bryttian
> sealwigpadan,   þone sweartan hræfn
> hyrnednebban   and þane hasupadan,
> earn æftan hwit,   æses brucan
> grædigne guðhafoc   and þæt græge deor,
> wulf on wealda.   (lines 60–65a)

[They left behind them to share the corpses

---

[3]E. G. Stanley, "Old English Poetic Diction and the Interpretation of *The Wanderer, The Seafarer*, and *The Penitent's Prayer*," *Anglia* 73 (1955): 413–66, esp. 442–43; Fred C. Robinson, "Notes on the Old English *Exodus*," *Anglia* 80 (1962): 363–78, esp. 366; George H. Brown, "An Iconographic Explanation of *The Wanderer* lines 81b–82a," *Viator* 9 (1978): 31–38; and Roberta Frank, "*The Battle of Maldon* and Heroic Literature," in Donald Scragg, ed., *The Battle of Maldon: AD 991* (Oxford, 1991), pp. 196–207, esp. 201.

[4]Roberta Frank, "Did Anglo-Saxon Audiences have a Skaldic Tooth?" *Scandinavian Studies* 59 (1987): 338–55, esp. 348–51; and Brown, "Iconographic Explanation," pp. 31–38. Brown cites classical examples such as the passage in Prudentius' *Psychomachia* (lines 716–25) in which the body of Discord is rent by carrion beasts and birds.

[5]All quotations from Anglo-Saxon sources other than *Beowulf* are taken from G. P. Krapp and E. V. K. Dobbie, eds., *The Anglo-Saxon Poetic Records*, vols. 1–6 (New York, 1931–53).

the dark-coated one, the black raven
with the horned bill, and the dusky-coated one,
the white-tailed eagle, the greedy war-hawk,
to enjoy the carrion, and that grey beast,
the wolf in the forest.]

This passage contains all the elements that appear traditionally in the most fully-developed versions of the topos: the grouping of three animals, raven, eagle, and wolf; the sense that the battlefield is theirs by right (*letan him behindan*), the dividing of the spoils (*hrǽw bryttian*); the sense of enjoyment on the part of the beasts (*ǽses brucan*); and the identification of the beasts by color (*seal-wigpada, sweart, hasupada, hwit, grǽg*). Magoun identifies the motif in nine poems (*The Battle of Brunanburh, Beowulf, Elene, Exodus, The Finnsburg Fragment, Genesis A, Judith, The Battle of Maldon,* and *The Wanderer*).[6] These range from the elaborate passages of *Brunanburh* and *Judith* to a small number in which only one beast is mentioned, such as the "wanna fugol" of *Genesis A* who follows the battle over Sodom and Gomorrah waiting for carrion. In many cases, as in the *Genesis* passage, the raven and the eagle are conflated into a collective like "fugolas."

Ten of the twelve passages in Old English refer to at least two beasts; four refer to all three. Of the six passages containing two beasts, four describe the wolf along with a collective bird-word. Only one passage umambiguously refers to only one beast (the *Genesis A* passage noted above). Another possible singlet is lines 34b–35a of *The Finnsburg Fragment*:

Hræfen wandrode
sweart and sealobrun.

---

[6]To this list Stanley would add two passages from *The Fortunes of Men* (lines 10–14 and 33–42) in which the topos is used outside the context of battle as an aspect of violent death in general; see Stanley, "Old English Poetic Diction," p. 441.

[the raven circled
black and dark-gleaming.]

Line 34a makes no sense in Hickes' transcription (*Hwearflacra hrær*) and has been variously emended. One possible emendation would add a second beast to the passage: "hwearf hlacra earn" (the loud eagle circled).[7] All other suggested emendations would leave the raven as the sole beast mentioned.

The idea of food or feeding is explicit in all but three of the Old English passages, often with a noun or verb of eating, as in the *Beowulf* passage:

> ac se wonna hrefn
> fus ofer fægum [sceal] fela reordian,
> earne secgan, hu him æt æte speow,
> Þenden he wið wulf wæl reafode.   (lines 3024b–3027)

> [but the dark raven
> eager for the fated ones will talk a great deal,
> will tell the eagle how he succeeded at his meal
> while he and the wolf contended for the slain.]

Or, a verb of anticipation, enjoyment, or sharing appears:[8]

> ætes on wenan (*Exodus*, line 165b)
> hræs on wenan (*Genesis A*, line 1985a)
> earn ætes georn (*Judith*, line 210a)

---

[7]Fr. Klaeber, ed., *Beowulf and the Fight at Finnsburg*, 3rd ed. (Boston, 1950), p. 248; on the various emendations of this line, see Klaeber's notes, pp. 246 and 470. All quotations are from this edition.

[8]Robinson suggests that the beasts of battle were originally harbingers of battle rather than a part of its aftermath ("Notes on *Exodus*," p. 366). This temporal aspect of the topos is reflected in those passages which use verbs of anticipation.

earn æses georn (*The Battle of Maldon*, line 107a)
æses brucan (*The Battle of Brunanburh*, line 63b)
hræw bryttian (*The Battle of Brunanburh*, line 60b)
sumne se hara wulf
deaðe gedælde (*The Wanderer*, lines 82b–83a)

The elements of the topos as it appears in Old English are clear: more than one beast is usually cited, often all three; a verb of eating is most often present, followed in frequency by verbs of anticipation (of eating), sharing, or enjoyment. As Magoun points out, it is an ornamental rather than an essential topos, and the sense of the ornamentation is exuberant from the point of view of the victors (*The Battle of Brunanburh, Elene, Exodus, Judith*) and ominous from the point of view of the defeated (*Genesis A, The Battle of Maldon, The Wanderer*).[9]

The topos also appears in the earliest poetry of Wales, the poetry of the *cynfeirdd*, or ancient poets. The historicity of these poets cannot be established with certainty. The names of several of them are mentioned in one early source dealing with the period, though it is hardly contemporary. The genealogies and regnal lists that became a part of the *Historia Brittonum* also contain a variety of interpolations. One of these, following the note on Ida, king of Northumbria from 547 to 559, lists five contemporary Welsh poets of outstanding reputation, ". . . simul uno tempore in poemate Brittanico claruerunt."[10] Among these are two to whom a considerable body of poetry is attributed, Aneirin and Taliesin. Aneirin ("Neirin" in the *Historia Brittonum*) is identified in a colophon in the unique manuscript as the poet of *The Gododdin*, an elaborate

---

[9]Magoun, "Theme of the Beasts of Battle," p. 83.

[10]John Morris, ed., *The British History and the Welsh Annals*, History from the Sources: Arthurian Period Sources, vol. 8 (London, 1980), Cap. 62, p. 78.

series of elegies on the deaths of heroes who, after a year's feast-
ing at the court of Mynyddog Mwynfawr in the region of Edinburgh, were defeated by the Deirans and Bernicians in the vicinity
of Catterick, Yorkshire.[11] *The Book of Taliesin* (MS. Peniarth 2,
late thirteenth or early fourteenth century) contains a bewildering
variety of poetry attributed to the eponymous bard, out of which
Sir Ifor Williams identified twelve poems heroic in character addressed to princes of the late sixth century.[12] Many questions remain to be answered about the dating of the work of these two
poets, traditionally called *hengerdd* (old poetry). The events and
persons with which it is concerned are dateable to the late sixth
century, but the poetry itself survives only in manuscripts of the
thirteenth century and later. Questions of how the texts could have
been preserved, transmitted, and repeatedly modernized over the
course of seven centuries during a period of great change in the
language have not yet been fully answered, though the discussion
is not essential to my primarily descriptive study of the topos of
the beasts of battle.[13]

[11]Sir Ifor Williams, *Canu Aneirin* (Cardiff, 1938). All quotations will be taken
from this edition. All translations are my own.

[12]Sir Ifor Williams, ed., *The Poems of Taliesin*, English version by J. E.
Caerwyn Williams, Dublin Institute for Advanced Studies, Medieval and Modern
Welsh Series III (Dublin, 1968). All quotations will be taken from this edition. All
translations are my own.

[13]A great deal of research is being done on this subject. Among the most
important recent works are the following: T. Charles-Edwards, "The Authenticity of
the *Gododdin*: An Historian's View," in Rachel Bromwich and R. Brinley Jones,
eds., *Astudiaethau ar yr Hengerdd: Studies in Old Welsh Poetry* (Cardiff, 1978),
pp. 44–71; and a volume of important studies deriving from an international
colloquium sponsored by the University of Wales Centre for Advanced Welsh and
Celtic Studies and the National Library of Wales, Aberystwyth in 1984: Brynley F.
Roberts, ed., *Early Welsh Poetry: Studies in the Book of Aneirin* (Aberysthwyth,
1988). A new edition and extensive study of the *Gododdin* is being prepared by

In early Welsh poetry, references to the raven (*bran*, pl. *brein*), eagle (*eryr*, pl. *eryron*), and wolf (*bleidd*, pl. *bleiddyeu*; also *cnut* "wolf-pack" and *gwydgwn* "wolves," "wild dogs") occur not only in the context of the topos of the beasts of battle but also in what I will call warrior similes, in which the beast is used either as a simile or a metaphor for the war-like and praiseworthy characteristics of the hero.[14] In most cases these two contexts are easily distinguished, though there are a few ambiguous cases. The warrior similes can occur either with or (more often) without the preposition *mal* (like), and their usage is not restricted to the traditional three beasts of battle; comparisons of heroes to lions, hounds, boars, bulls, or serpents are also common, as are similes referring to inanimate objects—rocks, pillars, anchors, shields. Warrior similes are usually easily identified. These examples include direct comparison, using *mal* as the preposition:

Pan gryssyei garadawc y gat;
mal baed coet trychwn trychyat.　　(*Gododdin*, lines 343–44)
[When Caradog attacked in battle
like a wild boar, slayer of three hounds.]

Owein ae cospes yn drut
　mal cnut [y]n dylut deueit.　　(Taliesin X, lines 17–18)
[Owein punished them fiercely,
　like a pack of wolves pursuing sheep.]

More commonly, the comparison is implicit, with simple juxtaposition replacing the prepositional phrase:

Eve Sweetser, Kathryn Klar, and the late Brendan o Hehir of the University of California, Berkeley.

[14]The use of simile and metaphor in Old English poetry is discussed by Stanley, "Old English Poetic Diction."

Kaeawc kynnivyat kywlat e rwyt.
ruthyr eryr en *ebyr*[15] pan llithywyt.   (*Gododdin*, lines 31–32)
[Brooch-adorned, a warrior, an ensnarer of the enemy,
the rush of an eagle in the estuaries when it is fed.]

Kaeawc kynhorawc bleid e maran   (*Gododdin*, line 39)
[Brooch-adorned, in the vanguard, a wolf in fury.]

y am wyr eryr gwydyen.   (*Gododdin*, line 462)
[for his men, Gwyddien was an eagle.]

laguen udat
stadal vleidiat bleid ciman   (*Gododdin*, lines 766–67)
[he was happy
defending his post, the wolf of the host]

Common to all uses of the warrior simile is the idea that the hero being described exhibits appropriate qualities of the beast: speed, fierceness, ruthlessness, protectiveness.

Examples of the beasts of battle topos are clearly different from these. No comparison is involved, either implicit or explicit, and the principal element is the feeding of the beasts by right. In the following passage from Taliesin's poem on the battle of Argoet Llwyfein, the ravens' feast is used as a metonym for the battle itself:

1.   A rac [gweith] argoet llwyfein
     bu llawer kelein.
     Rudei vrein rac ryfel gwyr.   (Taliesin VI, lines 20–22)

---

[15]This phrase is also found in saga poetry associated with the story of Llywarch Hen, where it describes Llywarch's son Gwen: "*ruthyr* eryr yn ebyr oedut" (he was the rush of an eagle in the estuary), quoted from Jenny Rowland, *Early Welsh Saga Poetry: A Study and Edition of the Englynion* (Cambridge, 1990), *Canu Llywarch*, st. 19b.

[And before (the battle of) Argoet Llwyfein
there were many corpses.
   Ravens grew red on warriors.][16]

Here we can see the principal difference between the topos as it
appears in early Welsh poetry and in Old English; the Welsh examples entirely lack the three-animal grouping. All three beasts
appear in the corpus, but almost always individually. The raven
passages stress the bird's nature as a carrion feeder, with frequent
references to corpses and dead flesh.

2.   ym pen coet cledyfein.
     Atuyd kalaned gwein.
     A brein ar disperawt.   (Taliesin XI, lines 38–40)

     [In Pen Coet are daggers,
     there'll be rotten corpses
     and scattered ravens.]

3.   kynt y waet e lawr
     nogyt y neithyawr.
     kynt y vwyt y vrein
     noc y argyurein.   (Gododdin, lines 13–16)

     [Sooner to the field of blood
     than to his wedding;
     sooner to the raven's feast
     than to his burial.]

In this well-known description of a youthful warrior from the
Gododdin, the topos is used metonymically to express the young

---

[16]Williams, *Poems of Taliesin*, p. 77, suggests that, since line 20 is too long by
a syllable, the word "gweith" (battle) may very well have been inserted from the
title of the poem, when in fact only the place name should follow the preposition.

man's preference for battle over a normal life. "Burial" here is likely to imply a natural death and, perhaps, the rites of the Church.

4. kynt y gic e vleid nogyt e neithyawr.
    kynt e vud e vran nogyt e allawr.   (*Gododdin*, lines 52–53)

    [Sooner food for wolves than to his wedding,
    Sooner a benefit to ravens than to the altar.]

This variant of passage 3 gives a rare association of more than one beast.

5. bu bwyt brein bu bud e vran   (*Gododdin*, line 281)

    [He was food for ravens, a profit to the raven.]

The second phrase in this line may simply be an individualization of the first. "Bud" (profit, benefit) is frequently used in the *hengerdd* poetry with the sense of sustenance, food.

6. gochore brein du ar uur
    caer ceni bei ef arthur   (*Gododdin*, lines 1241–42)

    [He fed black ravens on the wall
    of the fortress, although he was not Arthur.]

This is probably the most famous example of the topos in early Welsh poetry, incorporating as it does what is possibly the earliest surviving reference to Arthur. The name is used in an allusive fashion that implies the audience's familiarity with Arthur as paragon of warriors.[17] Here again, the use of the topos conveys

---

[17]A. O. H. Jarman, "The Arthurian Allusions in the Book of Aneirin," *Studia Celtica* 24–25 (1989–90): 15–25, esp. 17–20.

that the feeding of the ravens is one of the defining characteristics
of the heroic warrior.

7.   mawr meint e vehyr
    ygkyuaruot gwyr.
        bwyt e eryr erysmygei.   (*Gododdin*, lines 203–05)

    [Many were his spears
    in the attack of men,
        he made food for eagles.]

Similar to passage 6, feeding the eagles is here used as a metaphor (perhaps euphemistically) for the killing of adversaries.

8.   dimcones lovlen benn eryron.
    llwyt; ef gorev vwyt y ysgylvyon.   (*Gododdin*, lines 802–03)

    [He fed the grasp of the beaks of grey eagles,
    he fed the birds of prey.]

The collective noun (*ysgylvyon*) is unusual; more commonly in the
Welsh poetry only one beast is mentioned in either singular or
plural form.

9.   Pan gryssyei garadawc y gat;
    mal baed coet trychwn trychyat.
    tarw bedin en trin gomynyat;
    ef llithyei wydgwn oe anghat.   (*Gododdin*, lines 343–46)

    [When Caradog attacked in battle
    like a wild boar, slayer of three hounds,
    bull of the army, a slayer in fighting,
    he fed the wolves with his hand.]

In this passage a pair of warrior similes (one quoted above) are followed by a reference to the wolf as beast of battle. Feeding the wolves "with his hand" certainly refers to the killing of enemy warriors but may also include a more domestic image of the hand-feeding of a pet, perhaps as *litotes*. This possibility is enhanced by a passage in *Judith*, in which a similar tone more clearly uses the feeding of the beasts of battle as *litotes* in the form of pet-feeding:

> sweardum geheawen,
> wulfum to willan   and eac wæl-gifrum
> fugolum to frofre.   (*Judith*, lines 294b–96a)

> [they (the Assyrians) cut down with swords
> to satisfy the wolves, also as a treat
> for the gore-greedy birds.]

In a few cases it is difficult to tell whether we are dealing with an example of the beasts of battle topos or not. In this passage from the *Gwarchan Kynfelyn*, one of four longer poems appended to the *Gododdin*, the wolf reference is more likely to be a simple metaphor for warriors:

> Pan vyrywyt arveu
> tros benn cat vleidyeu
>   buan deu en dyd reit.   (*Gododdin*, lines 1398–1400)

> [When weapons were thrown
> over the heads of the wolves of battle,
>   the two were swift in the day of battle.]

Similarly, the various references to fighting with a wolf are demonstrations of the extraordinary bravery and prowess of the hero, rather than examples of the topos:

a dalwy mwng bleid heb prenn. ene law;
  gnawt gwychnawt eny lenn.   (*Gododdin*, lines 482–83)

[He who grasps a wolf's pelt in his hand without a spear
usually has a brave spirit under his mantle.]

The topos is also found, though in rather different form, in Welsh poetry more nearly contemporaneous with the Old English poems that preserve it. The two groups of saga poetry associated with the story of Llywarch Hen and his sons, and with Heledd and her brother Cynddylan contain limited use of the topos, and in the latter case an expansion of it as the central theme of two poems.[18] The use of the eagle in a warrior simile in the Llywarch Hen poems has already been noted above (n. 10), and a small number of further instances also occur in which the eagle is used as description of both Urien Rheged (in the Llywarch Hen poems) and Cynddylan (in the Heledd poems). Remains of the topos are clearly present (in its "defeat" mode) in the poem placed in the voice of Llywarch as he carries the head of his dead lord, Urien, from the battlefield:

Penn a borthaf ar vyn tu.
penn uryen llary llywei llu.
ac ar y vronn wenn vran du.

Penn a borthaf mywn vyg crys.
penn vryen llary llywyei llys.
ac ar y vronn wen vrein ae hys.   (*Canu Urien*, st. 8–9)

[The head which I carry at my side,
the head of the generous Urien, he ruled a host;
and on his white breast a black raven.

---

[18]Rowland, *Early Welsh Saga Poetry*. All quotations are from this edition.

The head which I carry in my bag,
the head of the generous Urien, he ruled a court;
and on his white breast, ravens gnaw at him.]

These two *englynion* show the extensive stanza-linking frequently found in the Llywarch Hen poetry; here the nouns at the end of lines one and two are changed ornamentally, leading to a substantive change at the end of line three, in which the static image of the first stanza, where the major interest is the starkness of the color contrast, is changed to a frighteningly active image drawn from the "feeding" element of the beasts of battle topos.

Of even more interest are two poems in the Heledd group, perhaps best described as invocations spoken by Heledd to the birds who feast on the dead bodies of her brother, Cynddylan, and his army.

ERYR ELI

Eryr eli ban y lef [heno]
llewssei gwy[a]r llynn.
creu callon kyndylan wynn.

Eryr eli gorelwi heno
ygwaet gwyr gwynn novi.
ef ygoet *trwm* hoet ymi.

Eryr eli a glywaf heno.
creulyt yw nys beidyaf.
ef ygoet *trwm* hoet arnaf.

Eryr eli gorthrymet heno.
diffrynt meissir [myget]
dir brochuael hir ry godet.

Eryr eli echeidw myr.
ny threid pyscawt yn ebyr.
gelwit gwelit o waet gwyr.

Eryr eli gorymda coet. [heno]
kyuor e kinyawa.
ae llawch llwydit y draha.   (*Canu Heledd*, st. 34–39)

[Eagle of Eli, loud its cry tonight;
it was drinking a pool of blood,
the heart-blood of Cynddylan Wyn.

Eagle of Eli, it was shouting tonight,
it was swimming in the blood of men;
it's in the trees, there is heavy sorrow with me.

Eagle of Eli which I hear tonight,
it is bloodstained, I do not dare it;
it's in the trees, there is heavy sorrow on me.

Eagle of Eli, how oppressive tonight
the fine valley of Meissir;
long has the land of Brochfael offended it.

Eagle of Eli watches the seas,
it no longer fishes in the estuary.
It calls the blood of men a feast.

Eagle of Eli walks in the wood tonight,
its meal is complete.
Who pampers it, his oppression will prosper.][19]

ERYR PENNGWERN

Eryr penngwern penngarn llwyt. [heno]
aruchel y *atleis*.
eidic am gic. [a gereis].

---

[19]Rowland, *Early Welsh Saga Poetry*, n. on p. 590, suggests that in this line
"the eagle is chillingly pictured as the pet of the victorious English."

Eryr penngwern penngarn llwyt. [heno]
aruchel y euan.
eidic am gic kynndylan.

Eryr penngwern pengarn llwyt. [heno]
aruchel y adaf
eidic am gic a garaf.

Eryr penngwern pell galwawt heno.
ar waet gwyr *gwylawt*
ry gelwir trenn tref difawt.

Eryr penngwern pell gelwit heno.
ar waet gwyr gwelit.
ry gelwir trenn tref lethrit.   (*Canu Heledd*, st. 40–44)

[The grey-crested eagle of Pengwern, tonight
his cry is loud,
greedy for the flesh I loved.

The grey-crested eagle of Pengwern, tonight
his yell is loud,
greedy for Cynddylan's flesh.

The grey-crested eagle of Pengwern, tonight
his claw is raised high,
greedy for the flesh I love.

The eagle of Pengwern cries long tonight;
he will feast on the blood of men.
Tren is called an unlucky town.

The eagle of Pengwern cries long tonight;
he feasts on the blood of men.
Tren is called a famous town.]

These two poems clearly derive from the topos of the beasts of battle in their use of the image of the eagle controlling the battlefield following combat and in their insistent use of verbs of eating (and drinking). The topos here is no longer ornamental, however, but is the core of the poems. The elaborate repetition of whole and partial lines now ornaments the central image of the bloody and well-fed eagle, pampered companion of the victorious English. The topos has been extended to produce a post-combat image far more frightening than the battle itself. These two poems provide an extraordinary glimpse of the effects a fine poet could produce by utilizing a traditional topos in an unusual manner.

There is, I think, no question that these early Welsh poems dealing with combat and warfare utilize a topos very similar, though not identical, to that found in the later poetry of Anglo-Saxon England. The animals that constitute the basis of the topos are identical; their grouping in two or three is rare in Welsh, though common in Old English. The central concept of feeding is common to both literatures, as is the frequent implication that this feeding is the right of the beasts and the duty of the warrior. The anticipatory element found in some Old English poems, in which the beasts are harbingers of battle, is not found in any clear form in the Welsh examples, where the beasts are generally a part of the battle's aftermath.

If the *hengerdd* poetry does in fact date from the sixth century, it antedates the earliest surviving Old English battle poetry by perhaps two centuries or more. There is insufficient information to postulate any kind of direct connection between the two literatures, but the existence of the beasts of battle topos in early Welsh poetry may well suggest that it was a normal ornament to the heroic literatures of northwestern Europe, and thus was readily available to the Old English poets in the form of an existing tradition.

Chaucer's Wheel of False Religion: Theology and Obscenity in The Summoner's Tale[1]

V. A. KOLVE

Iconographic criticism is a discipline still in its first youth, in quest of self-knowledge, essential rules, preferred procedures. For a number of years now, in the company of colleagues like John Leyerle and Patricia Eberle, I have been investigating the relation of Chaucer's *Canterbury Tales* to the visual arts of his time, paying particular attention to the iconographic traditions that inform the making and meaning of those fictions. In publishing those researches,[2] I have found it convenient to use pictures from

---

[1]A brief account of this research was presented at the International Congress of the New Chaucer Society held at the University of York in England in 1984. It is a pleasure to revive, test, and further extend this argument in honor of my friend and colleague, John Leyerle, for he himself—in a witty and eloquent essay, "Chaucer's Windy Eagle," *University of Toronto Quarterly* 40 (1971)—dared to write seriously about matters closely allied, matters our scholarly grandfathers (perhaps correctly) thought too indecent to be spoken of at all. Helen Cooper, with my permission, published a brief summary of the York version of this argument in her *Oxford Guides to Chaucer: The Canterbury Tales* (Oxford, 1989), pp. 177–78.

[2]See my *Chaucer and the Imagery of Narrative: The First Five Canterbury Tales* (Stanford, 1984), and these further essays: "From Cleopatra to Alceste: An Iconographic Study of *The Legend of Good Women*," in *Signs and Symbols in Chaucer's Poetry*, ed. John P. Hermann and John Burke, Jr. (University, Ala., 1981), pp. 130–78; "Chaucer's *Second Nun's Tale* and the Iconography of St.

illuminated manuscripts more often than any other sort of visual evidence—not only because such pictures bear a special relationship to written texts, but because they survive in greater number and often in better condition than any other art form of the age. Equally important to the theory behind my practice, however, is the fact that the images I choose to study are almost never restricted to the pages of books alone. They can be found in stained glass and wall paintings, in tapestries and ivory carvings, on roof bosses and misericords, as well as in other texts that, like Chaucer's own, invite the reader/listener to imagine with "the eye of the mind." It is *because* these images occur in many places and in many artistic media that one may argue their relevance for a reading of Chaucer's tales. Traditions restricted to a single text and its pictorial program are rarer by far, and their usefulness in the critical enterprise more problematic.

Such traditions do exist, however, and require of the critic both a special candor and a special discipline. Above all, we must keep in mind their more limited relevance, for only those who had actual access to a copy of that text, or had heard it read, described, or quoted, would have possessed the knowledge necessary to make the interpretative connection. Such persons were not necessarily few. Noblemen, churchmen, secular clerks, prosperous bourgeois, and women of corresponding station might (in any given instance) have been privileged in this way. But such meanings were not accessible to everyone, and we must be careful not to speak as though they were.

Cecilia," in *New Perspectives in Chaucer Criticism*, ed. Donald M. Rose (Norman, Okla., 1981), pp. 137–74; "'Man in the Middle': Art and Religion in Chaucer's *Friar's Tale*," *Studies in the Age of Chaucer* 12 (1990); and "Rocky Shores and Pleasure Gardens: Poetry vs. Magic in Chaucer's *Franklin's Tale*," in *Poetics: Theory and Practice in Medieval English Literature*, ed. Piero Boitani and Anna Torti (Woodbridge, Suffolk, 1991) pp. 165–95.

Mindful of such limits, I nevertheless wish to propose a tantalizing possibility of this kind. Though it might have been known, at best, to only a few among Chaucer's first audiences, I think it may have furnished him the source—an iconographic source—for his ending to The Summoner's Tale: Jankyn's witty solution to a friar's dilemma, how to share equally with his brethren the legacy of an angry parishioner's fart. Jankyn's proposal calls for a reprise of the gift—this time above a wheel with twelve spokes, with a friar on his knees at the end of each, and Friar John kneeling directly beneath its hub. Its every detail is savorous: [III. 2253–77].

> "My lord," quod he, "whan that the weder is fair,
> Withouten wynd or perturbynge of air,
> Lat brynge a cartwheel heere into this halle;
> But looke that it have his spokes alle—
> Twelve spokes hath a cartwheel comunly.
> And bryng me thanne twelve freres. Woot ye why?
> For thrittene is a covent, as I gesse.
> Youre confessour heere, for his worthynesse,
> Shal parfourne up the nombre of his covent.
> Thanne shal they knele doun, by oon assent,
> And to every spokes ende, in this manere,
> Ful sadly leye his nose shal a frere.
> Youre noble confessour—there God hym save!—
> Shal holde his nose upright under the nave.
> Thanne shal this cherl, with bely stif and toght
> As any tabour, hyder been ybroght;
> And sette hym on the wheel right of this cart,
> Upon the nave, and make hym lete a fart.
> And ye shul seen, up peril of my lyf,
> By preeve which that is demonstratif,
> That equally the soun of it wol wende,
> And eke the stynk, unto the spokes ende,
> Save that this worthy man, youre confessour,
> By cause he is a man of greet honour,
> Shal have the firste fruyt, as resoun is."

At this late date in the history of Chaucer criticism, I trust there are few who believe that the scatology of the tale serves to characterize its teller and no more. The Summoner is indeed a coarse and vicious man, enraged at the pilgrim Friar; and the movement of his tale toward a fart and its division, like his Prologue vision of friars inhabiting the devil's arsehole in hell, sits comfortably within the stipulated range of his temperament, his inner "condicioun." Chaucer means us to delight in this obscenity in its own terms—and I have no wish to sanitize it or explain it away. But Chaucer characteristically gives us something *through* such obscenity as well, which scholarship may help us recover. In the second part of this paper, I shall propose a new answer to this question: Where does the cartwheel come from that makes so comic—and so memorable—the fart-division at the end of The Summoner's Tale? But first, using evidence from manuscript illustrations alone, let me sketch in the logic of angry Thomas's original legacy, the fart into Friar John's greedy and groping hand.

The frontispiece to Queen Mary's Psalter, for instance—an English manuscript dating from about 1310–20—would have taught those who viewed it to locate obscenity within a metaphysical framework authorized by God himself. That opening page (Figure 1) uses two wildly divergent visual languages to depict the realms of heaven and hell, reverence and rebellion, order and chaos.[3] It shows Lucifer enthroned in hell, squatting above Hell Mouth in a posture unmistakably suggestive of farting or defecation—an anal orientation familiar to Chaucer's early audiences from the cycle plays as well, where devils frequently made their exits farting, sometimes propelled by firecrackers exploding

[3]Figure 1: London, BL MS. Royal 2 B. vii, fol. 1ᵛ. There is a facsimile ed. by Sir George Warner, *Queen Mary's Psalter* (London, 1912).

268

Figure 1. God in Heaven, Satan in Hell. Queen Mary's Psalter (London: BL MS. Royal 2 B. vii, fol. 1ᵛ, English c. 1310–20). By permission of the British Library.

in their breeches.[4] In the picture before us, attendant devils tug at Satan in a chaos of will and cross-purposes, in strong contrast to the decorum and grace with which the angels adore God above. The deity is there enthroned within a sacred geometry of inter- twining circles, holding the compass that identifies him as creator of the world. The full range of medieval pictorial language—from the most lyrical and graceful to the most violent and gro- tesque—is here seamlessly/theologically deployed. Medieval men and women were reminded by such pictures that the proper role of art was not to simplify or evade, but instead to call things by their proper names and to indicate their place within an inclusive, tran- scendental whole. There were specific words, and signs, and styles for all things—rooted in their moral and metaphysical natures. In The Summoner's Tale, we might say, the mellifluous grace of the friar's speech and the dignity of the apostolic ideals by which he claims to live are juxtaposed to the fraudulence of his life and to the comic obscenity of his punishment, in a manner thematically similar to that of the psalter frontispiece.

A medieval apologist moving closer to Chaucer's text might have argued yet another kind of decorum for the fart—one that is specifically contextual. In the Luttrell Psalter, for instance—an

---

[4]As in the devil's exit near the end of the N-Town "Fall of Man" play: "I falle down here a fowle freke; / For þis falle I gynne to qweke. / With a fart my brech I breke! / My sorwe comyth ful sone." The motif is repeated at the end of the "Temptation of Christ," when the devil concludes: "Whethyr god or man what þat he be / I kannot telle in no degré. / For sorwe I lete a crakke," flatulent noise immediately followed by angel song—"Hic uenient Angeli cantantes et ministrantes ei. 'Gloria tibi domine'"—a musical juxtaposition thematically akin to the two worlds of the psalter frontispiece reproduced above. I quote from Stephen Spector, ed., *The N-Town Play: Cotton MS Vespasian D.8*, 2 vols., EETS ss 11 (Oxford, 1991), I.32.219; see aslo p. 24. The play dates from the thrid quarter of the fifteenth century. The devil can also be farted *at*, to drive him off in a time of temptation; on this tradition see Karl P. Wentersdorf, "The Motif of Exorcism in The Summoner's Tale," *Studies in Short Fiction* 17 (1980): 249–54.

English manuscript to be dated c. 1320–40—Psalm 104 is decorated at bottom page with one of the vividly imagined grotesques
that give that psalter its very special character. Unlike most of the
monsters that adorn its margins, however, this one may claim a
discursive significance, if one thinks about it in relation to the
picture just above. In that initial "C," beginning the Psalm *Confitemini domino* (Figure 2), we see a man kneeling before Christ,
who listens in the posture of a priestly confessor.[5] Since Christ is
shown listening with patience and compassion, we may confidently infer the kind of speech the picture represents: a true confes-
sion of sin and a contrite plea for forgiveness, as the sacrament of
penance requires. The picture brings together Christ as redeemer
(the forgiving Word) and man as supplicant (the penitent word) in
a relation sufficient to undo man's disobedience and fall. This picture occupies a privileged position on the page: painted within an
initial, it shares space with—is indeed part of—the sacred text itself. And thus it offers a vantage point from which to view the
grotesque monster in the margin just below, an elegant if somewhat sinister creature who makes noise at each end of its body:
his bagpipe symbolically an instrument of "the old song," the
music of the flesh; and his arse trumpet (familiar from many another medieval manuscript's borders) a traditional way of suggest-

---

[5]Figure 2: London, BL MS. Add. 42130, fol. 185ᵛ; for a facsimile edition see
E. G. Millar, *The Luttrell Psalter* (London, 1932), and for a recent, generously
illustrated introduction to the MS see Janet Backhouse, *Illuminated Manuscripts in
the British Library: The Luttrell Psalter* (New York, 1989). Backhouse dates the
MS and discusses its provenance on pp. 48–49. The historiated initial deftly
Christianizes the Old Testament text. In the Douay/Rheims translation the opening
verse is appropriately rendered "Give glory to the Lord, and call upon his name:
declare his deeds among the Gentiles" taking the opening verb, *confitemini*, to
mean "acknowledge" or "avow." The Luttrell artist, or his director, gives the psalm
a specifically Christian coloring by construing the word to mean "confess,"
"admit," "reveal."

Figure 2. A penitent confesses to Christ (initial "C"), with a parody grotesque in margin. The Luttrell Psalter (London: BL MS. Add. 42130, fol. 185ᵛ, English 1320–40). By permission of the British Library.

ing visually the noise and stench of a fart.[6] This margin-painter, however, by transforming the arse into a second human head and mouth, has extended the trumpet's usual meaning. Here its music may be thought to symbolize words used frivolously or hypocritically, speech whose only meaning is the sound it makes. And since sound (as Chaucer puts it in *The House of Fame*) is nothing more than "eyr ybroken," such speech, to medieval physics and ethics alike, is indistinguishable from a fart.[7] For Chaucer in The Summoner's Tale, as for the director of the two painters who decorated this manuscript page, there is no moral difference.

Chaucer's angry Thomas is, of course, no scholar, and we should not attribute much *intentional* subtlety to his choice of gift.[8] It comes as naturally to him as does the coarse rebuke that Harry Bailly delivers to the pilgrim Chaucer, abruptly ending his Tale of Sir Thopas: "Thy drasty rymyng is nat worth a toord!" [VII. 930]. But Jankyn's proposal for the fart division, intended to amuse the lord's household, represents a very different level of

---

[6]On symbolic bagpipes see my *Chaucer and the Imagery of Narrative*, pp. 75–77, 402–03, and the further references there. For depictions in margins see, e.g., Lilian M. C. Randall, *Images in the Margins of Gothic Manuscripts* (Berkeley and Los Angeles, 1966), fig. 543; and Karl P. Wentersdorf, "The Symbolic Significance of *Figurae Scatologicae* in Gothic Manuscripts," pp. 1–19 and figs. 1–27, in Clifford Davidson, ed., *Word, Picture, and Spectacle*, Early Drama, Art, and Music Monograph Series, 5 (Kalamazoo, Mich., 1984).

[7]*HF* 765; on this connection see John Leyerle, "Chaucer's Windy Eagle," esp. pp. 254–55.

[8]In a learned and often illuminating essay, Ian Lancashire, "Moses, Elijah and the Back Parts of God: Satiric Scatology in Chaucer's *Summoner's Tale*," *Mosaic* 14 (1981): 17–30, credits Thomas with purposing "a rude scatological distortion of certain Biblical events that prefigured Pentecost" (p. 18). I think the Biblical parallels Lancashire adduces point to the poet, not the parishioner—another example of what Donald Howard terms "unimpersonated artistry."

273

sophistication. Though he offers it as a solution to the friar's dilemma, his hidden purpose is to prove the original gift most excellently suitable and decorous. Mindful of the sermon they have *all* heard from the friar that morning, Jankyn declares Thomas's gift worth giving again, this time (by implication) on behalf of the company at large:

> "certeinly he hath it weel disserved.
> He hath to-day taught us so muche good
> With prechyng in the pulpit ther he stood,
> That I may vouche sauf, I sey for me,
> He hadde the firste smel of fartes thre." (III. 2280–84)

For thus uncovering the witty likeness between a hypocritical sermon and the insulting gift of a fart, Jankyn triumphantly wins a new gown. But he also offers, from within the fiction, Chaucer's own defense of the decorum of the fart, proving it no *random* obscenity, just as the attention paid by the company to its division represents something more than solemn-faced merrymaking for the sake of bawdry alone. As on the page from the Luttrell Psalter, context redeems content, transforming the broadest obscenity into finely pointed satiric art.

The evidence brought forward so far serves simply to illustrate (to make pictorial) certain explanations for Chaucer's use of obscenity, explanations that can be made on textual grounds alone. I offer it without apology, in the belief that the discovery of parallel themes in the visual arts can lend both confidence and cultural richness to our reading of The Summoner's Tale. But I turn now to a pictorial image that may, in fact, be *necessary* to a full understanding of Chaucer's text—an image whose currency was restricted to manuscript illumination alone.

The picture I refer to is part of a treatise on the monastic life,

De rota verae et falsae religionis, written by a Frenchman, Hugh of Fouilloy (in Latin, Hugo de Folieto), in the third quarter of the twelfth century. Its title alone—*Concerning the Wheel of True and of False Religion*—should be enough to pique the curiosity of anyone who has delighted in the conclusion to The Summoner's Tale.[9] And the text it introduces does not disappoint, for it was written to explain the full-page pictures that open each of its two parts and epitomize their meaning. These pictures, be it noted, are more than mere illustrations: they *generate* the text, which is dedicated to explaining them. Because Hugh wrote this work to teach members of religious orders (monastic and other) how to better govern their lives, he sought to make it as memorable as possible, *conceiving it* in terms of parallel images easily drawn and readily accessible to the "eye of the mind"—an enterprise (I have argued elsewhere) that is central to Chaucer's mature art as well.[10] If what follows proves convincing, we are once again dealing with a narrative image—Jankyn's fantastic proposal for the fart-division—that holds at its core, for those able to recognize it, a non-fictional image meant to guide and enrich their response.

Hugh of Fouilloy was born in the first decade of the twelfth century and died in 1173/74. A Canon Regular of St. Augustine, he wrote several treatises based upon the apostolic ideals that

---

[9]On Hugh's life and work see Henri Peltier, "Hugues de Fouilloy: Chanoine Régulier, Prieur de Saint-Laurent-au-Bois," *Revue du Moyen Age Latin* 2 (1946): 25–44. The text is edited by Carlo de Clercq, "Le 'Liber de Rota Verae Religionis' d'Hugues de Fouilloi," in two parts, *Bulletin du Cange (Archivum Latinitatis Medii Aevi)* 29 (1959): 219–28, and 30 (1960): 15–37; I shall cite it by page number alone. See also de Clercq's study of the illustrations, "Hugues de Fouilloy, Imagier de ses Propres Oeuvres?" *Revue du Nord* 45 (1963): 31–43; he signs this study as Charles de Clercq. Some manuscripts title its two parts *De rota praelationis* and *De rota simulationis*, with the second title richly worked into the text itself.

[10]See my *Chaucer and the Imagery of Narrative*, esp. chaps. 1 and 2.

inspired the astonishing growth of his order, a movement meant to reform the laxity and luxury of much twelfth-century monastic life.[11] The *De rota* is part of that program, addressing itself especially to abbots and priors. Though its text is mostly a patchwork of quotations from the Bible and from Gregory the Great, particularly his *Pastoral Care* and the *Moralia* on Job, its pictures—and the explanations Hugh wrote to explain them—are substantially original.[12] (It seems likely that Hugh illustrated the first copies of his writings with his own hand.[13]) Despite Hugh's relative obscurity as an author—on which more later—manuscript provenance makes it clear that in the medieval centuries the work was prized in Benedictine, Cistercian, and Carthusian monasteries, as well as in the abbeys and small houses of the "Austin Canons," Hugh's own order.[14]

---

[11]On this order see J. C. Dickinson, *The Origins of the Austin Canons and their Introduction into England* (London, 1950). See John V. Fleming, "Chaucer's Ascetical Images," *Christianity and literature* 28 (1979): 19–26, for evidence of Chaucer's frequent (if paradoxical) use of texts "monastic in aspiration" and "unworldly in doctrine," part of a widespread "appropriation of essentially monastic patterns of thought adapted to the purposes of an increasingly self-confident secular society" (p. 19).

[12]De Clercq, ". . . Imagier," p. 40, charts the sources.

[13]De Clercq, ". . . Imagier," p. 42. Hugh writes in the Prologue to *De rota*, "Ut igitur ante oculos claustralium quasi speculum quoddam ponam, rotam praelationis in capite presentis opusculi pingam" (Therefore, so as to place a kind of mirror before the eyes of those in monastic orders, let me paint the prelate's wheel at the head of this small work; p. 221).

[14]De Clercq, ". . . Imagier," p. 37, lists thirteen extant MSS and what is known of their provenance, though his list needs correction and supplemention. His Oxford MS. Digby 72 should read Digby 172, for example, and he himself refers elsewhere to another thirteenth-century MS, now in Paris (BN MS 2494B; see "Le 'Liber de Rota'," p. 220 n. 3), bringing the number to fourteen. My own researches had uncovered another six copies: a late twelfth-century leaf illustrating the Wheel

The image I reproduce as Figure 3 begins the treatise and represents the Wheel of True Religion.[15] Its indebtedness to another wheel that haunted the medieval imagination, the Wheel of Fortune, is immediately obvious, for though it lacks a blindfolded goddess turning the wheel, the four men traditionally shown in motion upon it are all represented, here as members of a monastic order. "The form of the religious life," Hugh writes,

> can indeed be compared with the motion of a wheel. . . . For
> at one time the monk is subject to a master, and at another he

---

of False Religion, in the University of Indiana, Bloomington, Lilly Library MS. Poole 102 (Jeanne Krochalis told me of this); a late twelfth-/early thirteenth-century copy, Cremona, Bibl. Gov. MS 199; a thirteenth-century copy, Vatican, Reg. Lat. MS 246; a late thirteenth-century copy, Cambridge, Corpus Christi College MS 164, part II; a fourteenth-century copy, Oxford, Bodley MS. Laud. Misc. 345; and a copy made in 1437, Chantilly, Musée Condé MS 1401, apparently misattributed in the MS to Jean de Stavelot. As I was making final revisions to this essay, a conversation with Willene B. Clark, who had then at press an edition, translation, and study of Hugh's *Aviarium—The Medieval Book of Birds*, Medieval and Renaissance Texts and Studies, vol. 80 (SUNY, Binghamton)—added four more: a late twelfth-century copy, Bruges, Grootseminarie MS 89/54; from c. 1200, Zwettl Abbey, Stiftsbibl. MS 253; an early thirteenth-century copy, London, Lambeth Palace MS 107; and Bamberg, Staatsbibl. Misc. Theol. MS 233 (Q.v.26), dated 1469. This brings the number of known copies to twenty-four. Detailed information on the many manuscripts that also contain the *De avibus* is now (1992) available with the publication of Professor Clark's book. I thank her for sharing her knowledge with me and for lending me the photo from Oxford, Bodley MS. Digby 172 which I reproduce as Figure 5. Clark's earlier publications on Hugh, "The Illustrated Medieval Aviary and the Lay-Brotherhood," *Gesta* 21 (1982): pp. 63–74, and "Three Manuscripts for Clairmarais; A Cistercian Contribution to Early Gothic Figure Style," *Studies in Cistercian Art and Architecture* 3 (1987): 97–110, have also been useful to me.

[15]Figure 3: Oxford, Bodley MS. Lyell 71, fol. 29ᵛ; from the beginning of the thirteenth century, probably made for a Cistercian house in upper Italy. On this MS see Carlo de Clercq, "Le Rôle de l'image dans un manuscrit médiéval (Bodleian, Lyell 71)," *Gutenberg Jahrbuch* (1962): 23–30.

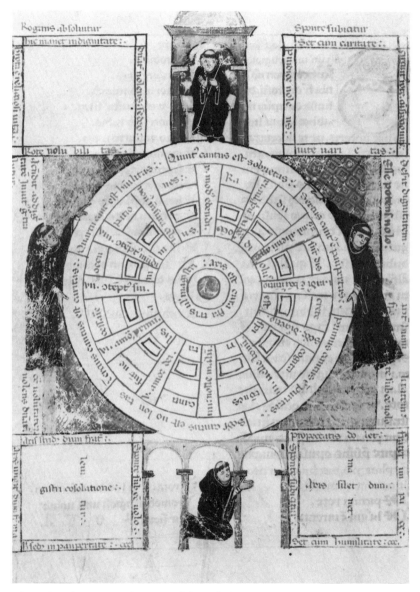

Figure 3. The Wheel of True Religion. Oxford: Bodley MS. Lyell 71, fol. 29ᵛ, Italian, early thirteenth century. By permission of the Bodleian Library.

is elected to the office of prelate and is raised on high. This
wheel, that is, the life of the monk, has an axle and hub,
spokes and a perimeter.[16]

And then his preliminary explanation of the diagram begins, with
tituli inscribed upon the wheel itself. The nave (or hub) of the
wheel, Hugh tells us, is the spirit of the master (*magistri animus*),
elected to highest office in the monastery; his care for those in his
charge (*cura fratris*) *encloses* the life of a brother in the monastery as a hub encloses the axle of a wheel. The twelve spokes,
representing prudent thoughts (*discretae cogitationes*), connect the
hub to the perimeter of the wheel, divided into six segments
representing the necessary conditions or occupations of a true
religious life. The segments of the outer wheel are moralized, as
are the two spokes that attach each to the hub, in this fashion:
Purity is attached by good intention and prudence; Good Will by
benevolence and repudiation of evil; Charity by love of God and
love of neighbor; Humility by contempt of self and contempt of
the world; Sobriety by moderate portions of food and a disci-
plined manner of eating; Poverty by having no personal possessions, and not coveting the possessions of others.[17] Such a
wheel, writes Hugh, gives motion to a true religious life—and one
notices that, apart from the value it places upon living under a

---

[16]"Forma nim[i]rum religiosae vitae assimilari potest volubilita[ti] materialis
rotae. . . . Quandoque enim vir religiosus magistro subiicitur, quandoque vero per
electionem ad honorem praelationis sublimatur. Haec rota, id est viri religiosi vita,
habet axem et modiolum, radios et cantos" (p. 221).

[17]In Hugh's Latin, the six outer segments of the wheel are named *puritas*,
voluntas, *caritas*, *humilitas*, *sobrietas*, *paupertas*, and the twelve spokes that join
them to the axle are *bona intentio in animo*, *discretio*, *velle bonum*, *nolle malum*,
amor dei, *amor proximi*, *contemptus sui*, *contemptus mundi*, *mensura cibi*, *modus
edendi*, *nil proprium habere*, *nil alienum appetere* (pp. 221–22).

279

rule and eschewing personal possessions, it represents the kind of life Christianity enjoins upon all its members, clerical or illiterate, religious or lay. "The roundness of the wheel," writes Hugh, represents "a thoughtful [circumspect] contemplation of life, and its turning motion, the variety of life."[18] The four members of the community displayed about its rim (evoking the Wheel of Fortune) are praised for enduring the wheel's motion virtuously, whatever their place upon it. Indeed, they rise and fall with dignity, as though they were turning the wheel rather than being turned by it. The inscriptions in the rectangular frame and corners describe the brother who rises to highest office as rising *against* his will; the abbot who rules, as not wishing to rule; the abbot who relinquishes office, as doing so in humility; the abbot who is no longer in office as cheerful in tranquility, thinking longingly of his heavenly home.[19]

If this first section comprised the entire treatise, it could on its own provide an image against which Chaucer's Friar John might appropriately be measured. But Hugh furnishes a corresponding Wheel of Religious Hypocrisy—a *rota simulationis* (Figure 4)—ready, as it were, for Chaucer's direct appropriation in the section that follows.[20] "Haec rota est ypocritae vita" (this wheel is the life of the hypocrite), he declares, focusing first on the wicked abbot (at the top of the wheel, with a glutton's bowl in his hand) who rules over brothers seeking worldly things. Such an abbot, Hugh explains, ascends to that position through money,

---

[18]"Rotunditas rotae circumspectio vitae, volubilitas est vitae varietas" (p. 222).

[19]"Hic ascendit ad dignitatem sed contra propriam voluntatem"; "Nolens dominatur"; "Invitus trahitur"; "Hic manet in dignitate sed cum caritate"; "Sedeo pro iudice nolens"; "Non ascendo volens"; etc. (p. 223).

[20]Figure 4: Oxford, Bodley MS. Lyell 71, fol. 34[v].

Figure 4. The Wheel of False Religion. Oxford: Bodley MS. Lyell 71, fol. 34ᵛ, Italian, early thirteenth century. By permission of the Bodleian Library.

remains there through pride, descends through neglect, and is finally cast into poverty and despair, ashamed that he possesses nothing.[21] (The monks who ascend and descend on *this* wheel are at its mercy, desperately hanging on to its rim, or falling from it gracelessly.[22]) Here the axle of the wheel represents the wickedness of the brother and its hub the carnal spirit of the abbot, tolerant of the vices of those in his charge.[23] The rim of this wheel is made of six segments standing for worldly deeds (*actus*

---

[21]"Haec rota tociens super terram volvitur quotiens fratribus terrena querentibus perversus magister dominatur. Hic ascendit ad locum praelationis per pecuniam, stat in loco regiminis per superbiam, descendit ab eodem loco per negligentiam, iacet per inopiam. Hic est labor acquirantis, honor possidentis, dolor amittentis, pudor nil habentis" (p. 222).

[22]For illustrations of these wheels from other MSS see Adolf Katzenellenbogen, *Allegories of the Virtues and Vices in Mediaeval Art from Early Christian Times to the Thirteenth Century* (1939; repr. New York, 1964, figs. 70, 71, reproducing Heiligenkreuz, Stiftsbibl. MS 226, fols. 146, 149^v, Lower Austrian, late twelfth century; de Clercq "Le 'Liber de Rota'," reproducing Brussels, Bibl. Royale MS. II. 1076, fols. 82, 87, early thirteenth century, from the Cistercian Abbey of Sainte-Marie d'Aulne (the basis of his diplomatic text); Otto Pächt and J. J. G. Alexander, *Illuminated Manuscripts in the Bodleian Library, Oxford*, vol. 3 (Oxford, 1973), pl. XXXV (423), reproducing Bodley MS 188, fol. 120^v, from the library of Haughmond Monastery in Shropshire, mid-thirteenth century [here the Wheel of Fortune dominates, with inscribed frames but no inscriptions on the wheel and its spokes]; de Clercq, "Le Role de l'Image," fig. 5, reproducing Saint-Omer, Bibl. publ. MS 94 (wrongly identified as MS 74), c. 1200–10, made for the Cistercian abbey of Clairmarais; Clark, "Three Manuscripts," fig. 4 (for the same); de Clercq, ". . . Imagier," figs. 2 and 3, reproducing Charleville, Bibl. Mun. MS 89, dated 1346, from the Carthusian house of Mont-Dieu; and Dom Peter Batselier, *Saint Benedict: Father of Western Civilization* (New York, 1981), figs. 391, 392, reproducing (in color) Chantilly, Musée Condé MS 1401, dated 1437 and wrongly attributed to Jean de Stavelot.

[23]"Axis est perversitas fratris, modiolus carnalis animus id est perversus frater et carnalis magister. Axis tenetur in modiolo dum perversus frater toleratur a carnali magistro" (p. 222).

terreni), in contrast to the virtuous deeds and conditions that comprise the other. And the spokes that join this rim to the axle represent the carnal affections of the mind (*carnales affectus . . . procedunt ab animo*), as distinguished from the other wheel's wise and inward thoughts (*discretae cogitationes*). The first segment of this Wheel of Simulated Religion is Guile, attached to the hub by two spokes, skill in acquiring goods and diligence in keeping them. There follow in turn: Avarice, attached by rapacity and tenacity; Pride, by contempt of others and disobedience; Negligence, by carelessness and confusion; Sloth, by inactivity and unsuitable diet; and Indigence or Lack, by rejection and despondency.[24]

The rim and spokes of this Wheel of False Religion epitomize in a most comprehensive fashion the character traits out of which Chaucer invents Friar John—a portrait that later will be casually enlarged to include all the friars of his house. And intrinsic to this picture is an idea of punishment and humiliation as strict and inevitable as fabliau justice itself. In its terms, Chaucer's friar John might be said to ride the wheel from top to bottom, from the height of the pulpit in which he preached a morning sermon before the village lord and his household to his concluding position (in Jankyn's fantastic proposal) beneath the arse of a flatulent churl.

That, of course, would be in a manner of speaking only. Since there is no reference to a Wheel of Fortune in Chaucer's text, we have no authorial cue to think in its terms. But even in Hugh's treatise, the Wheel of Fortune—an emblem of the temptation and transience of earthly power—is finally only *a small part* of the

---

[24]The segments of the wheel are named *astutia, avaricia, superbia, negligentia, desidia,* and *inopia*; the spokes are described as *intelligentia acquirendi, diligentia custodiendi, rapacitas, tenacitas, contemptus, inobedientia, oblivio sui, confusio animi, otium, alienus cibus, eiectio,* and *abiectio* (pp. 222–23).

text, its explication far less detailed than that given to the moralized Wheels of the Religious Life which its rising and falling
figures surround. And the Wheel of Fortune, as an iconographic
motif, disappears completely as we are told that one of those
wheels moves through the world circumspectly, truly practicing
devotion, whereas the other is moved by worldly curiosity, its
devotion mere pretence. This use of the image triumphantly
concludes the work, giving it a generality not limited to the
careers of abbots and priors alone, and altering its implicit
reference from the Boethian Wheel of Fortune to an ordinary cart-
or wagon-wheel. Like such a wheel, Hugh tells us, the false
religious takes too much interest in worldly affairs, forever
moving about, seeking out news and spreading gossip.[25] And just
as the rim of such a wheel is worn away by contact with the
earth, so such a monk is reduced to nothing because earthly desires consume his mind. As a wheel is made dirty by the mud
through which it rolls, so a false monk is sprinkled (asperged)
with dust as he boasts of worldly things. And in a set of final
distinctions, such a wheel may be thought of as moving across

---

[25]Cf. John V. Fleming's suggestion that the clue to Jankyn's cartwheel may be
the common antifraternal complaint that friars were *gyrovagi* (roamers, vagabonds,
wanderers): "The similarity between a *gyrus* and a *rota* did not escape comment,"
Fleming writes ("The Antifraternalism of the *Summoner's Tale*," *Journal of English
and Germanic Philology* 65 [1966]: 688–700, esp. 699–700), citing Friar John
Pecham, Archbishop of Canterbury, who defended the friars as being more
accurately the chariot wheels of the Lord (Daniel 7:9): *non sunt girovagi ap-
pellandi sed rote Domini. . . .* Other major studies of the antifraternal backgrounds
to the tale include: Alan Levitan, "The Parody of Pentecost in the *Summoner's
Tale*," *University of Toronto Quarterly* 40 (1971): 236–46, on which, see n. 31
below; Penn R. Szittya, "The Friar as False Apostle: Anti-Fraternal Exegesis and
the *Summoner's Tale*," *Studies in Philology* 71 (1974): 19–46, developing Levitan's
argument further, and anticipating his own book-length study, *The Antifraternal
Tradition in Medieval Literature* (Princeton, 1986), esp. chap. 6; and Paul A.
Olson, *The* Canterbury Tales *and the Good Society* (Princeton, 1986), esp. chap. 8.

rocky ground, when the master is in charge of harsh and bitter brothers in the monastery; as moving across soft and slippery ground when the master willingly associates with brothers who are in a state of sin; and as moving in darkness or shadow, when the mind is blinded by carnal pleasures.[26]

The Wheel of Fortune has nothing to do with any of this final use of the image, a fact fortuitously confirmed by the omission of monks rising and falling alongside the wheel in six of the surviving manuscripts of this work—six furnished *with wheel-diagrams only*. Some of these (I have not seen them all) may represent an incomplete program of illustration, as in the case of an English manuscript—Bodley MS. Digby 172—from the second half of the thirteenth century that I reproduce as Figure 5, where spaces have been left for monks to be painted in their accustomed places, and the inscriptions in the rectangular frames assume their presence.[27] But even such manuscripts are of interest, for they make clear the wheel diagram's coherence and self-sufficiency without them. These six include several of the oldest manuscripts of the

---

[26]"Circuitus rotae est curiositas perversae vitae. . . . Rotae circulus undique terram tangit, quia curiosus animus non tantum de terrenis loquitur sed etiam terrena concupiscit. . . . Rotae circulus exterius a terra roditur, ita videlicet ut canti eius ad nichilum redigantur, quia terrena desideria mentem consumunt. Rota per lutum volvitur, dum vita carnalium immundis desideriis delectatur. Aspergitur pulvere, dum gloriatur rerum secularium vanitate. Super petrosam terram rota trahitur, dum duris et asperis fratribus magister dominatur. . . . Super mollem et lubricam terram rota volvitur, cum fratribus in lapsu positis magister consentiens sociatur. . . . In tenebris ambulat, cuius mentem delectatio carnalis obscurat. . ." (Part II, chap. XV; p. 37).

[27]Figure 5: Oxford, Bodley MS. Digby 172, fol. 74, English, thirteenth century, once owned by William Marshall, fellow of Merton College, Oxford, who died in 1583. On his bequest of books, see N. R. Ker, *Books, Collectors and Libraries: Studies in the Medieval Heritage*, ed. Andrew G. Watson (London, 1985), pp. 425–26.

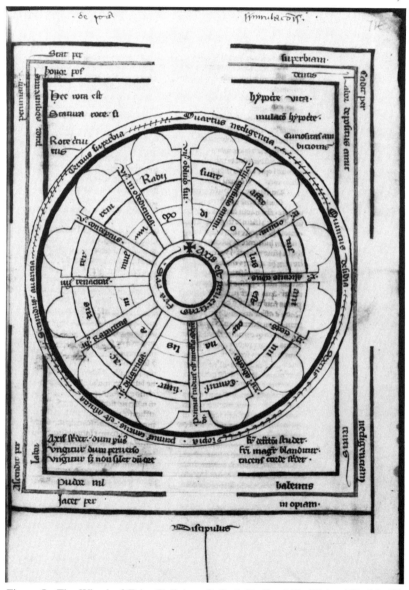

Figure 5. The Wheel of False Religion. Oxford: Bodley MS. Digby 172, fol. 74, English, thirteenth century. By permission of the Bodleian Library.

work, and they led Hugh's editor, Charles de Clercq, to conclude that in his original manuscript Hugh illustrated the wheels only.[28] True or not, regarding The Summoner's Tale it is important that the image offered by these six manuscripts could have been readily transformed into the cartwheel of a fabliau fiction, without iconographic "surplus" unrelated to the case.

So the fit with Chaucer's tale is seductively good—and for any text of the very distant past, "fit" is one of the primary tests of relevance. But a harder test remains. What is the likelihood that Chaucer and/or some members of his first audiences might have been familiar with this work? The question needs to be asked, even if it cannot be definitively answered. Let me summarize such evidence as exists.

It is worth noting, first of all, that the popularity in England of Hugh's order, the Austin Canons, was very great—more than two hundred English houses had been founded by the end of the

---

[28]The other manuscripts having wheel diagrams only are: from the twelfth century, Paris, BN MS. lat. 17468 (from the Benedictine Abbey of Saint-Martin-des-Champs in Paris), and Cambrai, Bibl. Mun. 211 (possibly from the Cistercian Abbey of Ourscamp); from the late twelfth or early thirteenth century, London, BL MS. Arundel 25 (provenance unknown); from the fourteenth century, Bodley MS. Laud Misc. 345 (Durham Cathedral); from the fifteenth century, Troyes, Bibl. Mun. 908 (from the Cistercian Abbey of Clairvaux). See de Clercq, ". . . Imagier," p. 37 for all but MS. Laud Misc. 345. See de Clercq, ". . . Imagier," p. 42: "Hugues dit lui-meme qu'il a peint . . . les deux roues monastiques. . . . En ce qui concerne les personnages et les cadres extérieurs ajoutés aux roues monastiques, les plus anciens manuscrits ne les ont pas, il faut cependant signaler que celles des expressions des cadres, qui se trouvent autour de la roue de la deuxième section du *De Rota*, figurent précisément dans le prologue de cette section immédiatement avant le passage ou Hugues dit qu'il peindra la roue, mais cela n'est pas une preuve suffisante pour dire que de tels cadres figuraient dans son manuscrit." Since three of these manuscripts date from the twelfth or early thirteenth centuries, one may doubt Katzenellenbogen's conclusion that wheels-without-monks represent a later, diminished tradition, one born of "the usual shrinking-process, such as may be frequently observed" (*Allegories*, p. 72). The wheels-alone tradition has its own long history.

thirteenth century—and the libraries of the greatest of them, together with the prestige the order enjoyed, contribute to the
possibility that Chaucer and some part of his first readers and
listeners might have had access to the work.[29] (So too the fact,
already mentioned, that several copies survive from Benedictine,
Cistercian, and Carthusian houses: the popularity of the *Rota* was
not confined to the Austin Canons alone.)

We should note as well that the work was known and read
throughout much of medieval Europe. A large number of copies
(twenty-four) survive, representing every century from the twelfth
through the fifteenth, with geographical origins correspondingly
diverse. Six of these manuscripts are today deposited in English
libraries, three of them English in origin—manuscripts associated
with Haughmond Monastery (in Shropshire), Durham Cathedral,
and (Figure 5) Merton College, Oxford, a manuscript that may
have been long associated with Oxford University, though it did
not enter the Merton library until 1583. Two of the three manuscripts made in England, interestingly enough, present wheel diagrams only, without human figures rising and falling on their
rims.[30]

Finally, it is worth noting that, until the pioneering researches
of the Maurist scholar Jean Mabillon, in the seventeenth century,
the *De rota* was uniformly attributed (where not anonymous) to a
greater Hugh—Hugh of St. Victor—another Austin Canon, whose
name gave this treatise on the Wheels of True and Hypocritical

---

[29]According to J. C. Dickinson, in his brief article on "Canons Regular of St.
Augustine," *New Catholic Encyclopedia*, vol. 3 (New York, 1967), pp. 62–64, 206
houses had been founded by the late thirteenth century (p. 63); see his *Origins of
the Austin Canons* for further details, esp. p. 153 and Appendix V.

[30]The other is Bodley MS. Laud Misc. 345 (Durham Cathedral, second half of
the fourteenth century).

Religion an authority well beyond anything one imagines the modest Hugh of Fouilloy ever claiming for himself. That innocent error in attribution no doubt served the work well, expanding its currency and influence.

But for all that, I cannot prove that Chaucer knew the work, or its diagrams, or even its title (to put the question of relevance at its absolute minimum). Nor can I prove (to cast a wider, though still relevant, net) that some members of his first audiences might have been reminded of it, in suggestive ways, while reading or listening to his The Summoner's Tale. Both situations are possible, since the fit is so good; and the first is certainly attractive, since no wholly convincing source has yet been proposed for Jankyn's twelve-spoke, fart-dividing wheel.[31] In the only ana-

---

[31]Levitan, "The Parody of Pentecost," brilliantly connects the fart with the great wind at Pentecost described in Acts 2:1–4: "And when the days of the Pentecost were accomplished, they were all together in one place: And suddenly there came a sound from heaven, as of a mighty wind coming, and it filled the whole house where they were sitting. And there appeared to them parted tongues as it were of fire, and it sat upon every one of them: And they were all filled with the Holy Ghost, and they began to speak with divers tongues, according as the Holy Ghost gave them to speak." Because friars saw themselves as the new apostles, spreading God's word throughout the world, this text was foundational to the mendicant orders. And Levitan usefully connects Jankyn's wheel with "the exalted wheels" of light Dante sees in *Paradiso* 10–12, with certain great friars at their rim. But Levitan's other major thesis, relating Jankyn's wheel to representations in medieval visual art of the Pentecostal gift of tongues, leaves me unconvinced. Those pictures depict tongues of flame, not the great wind; the text they illustrate (quoted above) has nothing to say of wheels or rotundity; and the standard iconography of the Pentecost, among the most familiar images in all of Christian art, presents the apostles frontally (or only slightly turned toward each other), with Mary at their center, in a straight row, a semi-circle, or an inverted "U"; flames *descend* from the Holy Ghost above, either as flames or in abstract lines more reminiscent of a tent than of a wheel; see Levitan's own figs. 3a, 3b. The other examples he reproduces are (for obvious reasons) likewise devoid of wheels, though three of them arrange the apostles more-or-less in a circle and another three paint lines, or rays, or torches (emanating from a center to the apostles) that could be said to *resemble*

logue earlier than Chaucer's tale, a dying priest (corresponding to Chaucer's angry Thomas) bequeaths "a precious jewel" (his bladder) to certain Jacobin friars, telling them they can make of it a leather pouch to store their peppercorns, a favored seasoning in their shamefully luxurious, "non-apostolic" meals.[32]   What can be said finally goes no further than this. *If Chaucer knew* Hugh's treatise, then its wheel of false religion may well constitute the hidden logic (the ultimate propriety) of Jankyn's solution to the

---

spokes. But these latter (which alone could make the case) are very rare: one a Byzantine dome (Venice, twelfth century), one an early twelfth-century German manuscript illumination, one a late fourteenth-century German altar-wing. Attractive though they are, they represent a marginal tradition, completely overshadowed by the more standard iconography. For confirmation of that fact one need only examine the seventy-six examples reproduced by Gertrud Schiller, *Ikonographie der Christlichen Kunst*, vol. 4 (1) (Gütersloh, 1976), pp. 11–32 (text) and 202–30 (pictures); I have tested this against hundreds more.

[32]Jacques de Baisieux, "Tale of the Priest's Bladder," from the first quarter of the fourteenth century. It may be read in *The Literary Context of Chaucer's Fabliaux: Texts and Translations*, ed. Larry D. Benson and Theodore M. Andersson (Indianapolis, 1971), pp. 344–59. Richard Firth Green, "A Possible Source for Chaucer's Summoner's Tale," *English Language Notes* 24 (4) (1987), 24–27, finds a precise analogue in a courtly collection of riddles and verbal games written in northern France c. 1470: "Question: How can one divide a fart into twelve parts? Answer: Make the fart in the middle of a wheel, with twelve people, each with his nose between the twelve spokes (lit., in the twelve holes), so that each shall thus get his share." Green translates from *Amorous Games: A Critical Edition of 'Les Adevineaux amoureux,'* ed. James W. Hassell (Austin, 1974), p. 166, and is properly cautious in his claims, since the French work was written some eighty years after Chaucer's tale, and Chaucer's work circulated in France in the fifteenth century. At first glance, Green acknowledges, it seems more probably "a crude echo, at several removes, of Chaucer's work itself" than an independent analogue. But since Chaucer presents the friar's dilemma as a punning riddle ("What is a ferthyng worth parted in twelve?") Green speculates that some similarly simple riddle, possibly in the oral tradition, may have been known to Chaucer. Even if this speculation could be proved, Green allows that "Chaucer might have exploited [the wheel's] potential for more recondite parody," p. 27.

friar's dilemma. *And if Chaucer knew* the treatise, this essay points as well to something exceedingly rare in his art, a central narrative image drawn from a text always and necessarily illustrated, but whose iconographic tradition seems to have been limited to manuscript transmission alone.[33] *If Chaucer did not know* the treatise—and we are unlikely ever to prove it one way or the other—it has, of course, no status as either source or influence. But even in that most negative circumstance, this essay may hope to be relevant in two distinct ways.

At the very least—for anyone seeking to think about medieval

---

[33]I cannot otherwise trace its influence, *unless* it underlies an extraordinarily cryptic passage in the C-text of *Piers Plowman*, XV: 158–62, where Patience preaches on the theme *Pacientes vincunt* (the patient conquer):

> "For, by hym þat me made, myhte neuere pouerte,
> Meseyse ne meschief, ne man with his tonge
> Tene þe eny tyme and þou take pacience
> And bere hit in thy bosom aboute wher þou wendest
> In þe corner of a cart-whel, with a crow croune."

As we have seen, the turning cartwheel as an image for human life figures significantly in Hugh's treatise; and patience, he tells us, allows it to turn silently ("Silet quando patienter adversa sustinet") without the noise of complaint and lamentation (p. 222). This is expanded in Chapter VII, "Quod axis perunctus silet," p. 18, to mean not showing anger and living in peace with all men. Might the mysterious "corner of a cartwheel" (Skeat noted its impossibility) be a confused memorial reference to the rectangular frame of Hugh's diagram, at the bottom of which the virtuous former abbot lives patiently? ("Hic absolutus abbas sedet. Librum apertum tenet. Legendo discat quid faciat. De quiete sua gaudet. Pro celesti patria suspirat. Non vult aliis praesse sed magis subesse.") He does not desire to rule over others, but rather to be under them. And might the "crow croune" (crow's crown) be an allusion to the black monastic hood shown in many of the MSS diagrams? It is not difficult to imagine that Langland might have known Hugh's work, or that he would have found it sympathetic, or that he might have thought its diagramatic counsel applicable beyond the cloister. But the verses in question are so tersely written no confident reading is possible. For other attempts, including reference to a simple "wheel of the virtues," see *Piers Plowman by William Langland: An Edition of the C-text*, ed. Derek Pearsall (Berkeley and Los Angeles, 1979), p. 253 n. 162, whose passus numbering I follow above.

literature in the light of medieval visual art—it can emphasize the importance of focusing upon images fully and demonstrably in the public domain: images to be found in a variety of literary texts and visual media; images in glass, stone, wood, textiles, as well as in manuscript painting; images of the kind I normally (and more confidently) choose to study.

But guesses are sometimes worth making, even if they cannot be proved; and somewhere between the two possibilities outlined above—between relevance and non-relevance—in a realm of critical explication less historically rigorous, this essay may claim, at the least, to have thrown medieval light upon a medieval text, in a way that gives priority to what seems on many grounds most comic and most powerful in the tale. For the hypocrite friars in The Summoner's Tale, there can be no posture more suitable—compare the poor fellow in Figure 6, ready to sniff real buttocks on a misericord from northern France—than to kneel around and beneath the arse of an angry churl: a satiric tableau in which flatulence answers to hypocrisy, broken wind to broken wind, with a cartwheel guaranteeing to every friar his equal portion of a bequest richly deserved.[34] That Hugh's grandly schematic Wheel of False Religion might appear in this fiction as an ordinary cartwheel will not surprise students of Chaucer's mature art. A preference for disguised symbolism is everywhere characteristic of it, including the Summoner's own Prologue, with its eschatological vision of friars in hell, flying in and out of the devil's arsehole, as he raises and lowers his great tail. This audacious insult, John Fleming has taught us, parodies a claim made by Caesarius of Heisterbach in the thirteenth century that the

---

[34]Figure 6: from Saumur, the Church of St.-Pierre (fifteenth century); photo by Pascal Corbierre, first published by Dorothy and Henry Kraus, *The Hidden World of Misericords* (London, 1976), p. 112 (fig. 89).

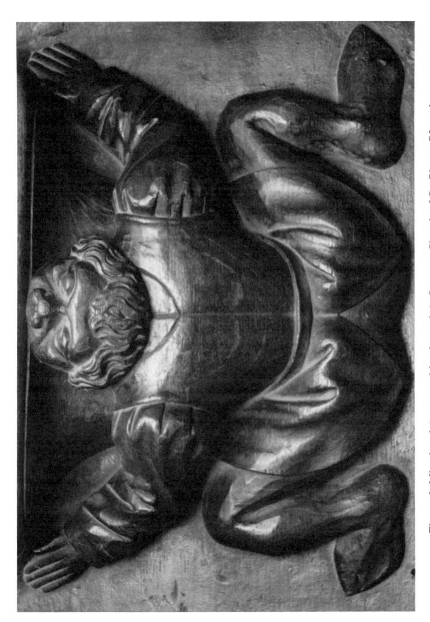

Figure 6. Misericord (nose awaiting buttocks). Saumur, Church of St.-Pierre, fifteenth century. Photo: Pascal Corbierre (courtesy of Dorothy and Henry Kraus).

Figure 7. The Madonna of Mercy. New York, Pierpont Morgan Library MS 196, fol. 162ᵛ, Besançon or Savoy, c. 1470. By permission of the Pierpont Morgan Library.

Cistercian dead dwell in Paradise under the cloak of the Virgin—an iconographic theme later appropriated by lay confraternities associated with the Dominicans and Franciscans as well, and soon popular in the visual arts as the Madonna of Mercy (Figure 7).[35] In the Summoner's vision, the devil's tail (broad as the sail of a large ship) shelters the damned friars just as the Virgin's cloak encloses and protects the souls of those who reverence her. Iconographic likeness carries the meaning, its symbolism (in Panofsky's phrase) "disguised." But if one misses it, one has missed much of the prologue's brilliance; only the scatalogy remains.

As in the tale's prologue, so at the tale's end: a transparent overlayering of images—one fictional and obscene, the other symbolic and ethical—is used to destroy (wittily, triumphantly)

---

[35]Figure 7: New York, Pierpont Morgan Library MS 196, fol. 162ᵛ, a Book of Hours from Besançon or Savoy, c. 1470; on this MS see John Plummer, *The Last Flowering: French Painting in Manuscripts 1420–1530* (New York, 1982), p. 56 (#73). See also the Morgan Library's MS 829, fol. 88, a Martyrology and Rule of St. Benedict, from northern Italy, end of the fourteenth century, which shows St. Benedict with with six nuns in white habits (presumably Cistercians) kneeling beneath his robe, held open by two angels. John V. Fleming, developing a brief remark by J. S. P. Tatlock, traces the mendicant appropriation of the theme in "The Summoner's Prologue: An Iconographic Adjustment," *Chaucer Review* 2 (1967): 95–107; see also his "Antifraternalism," p. 689 n. 4. Louis Réau, *Iconographie de l'art chrétien*, 6 parts in 3 vols. (Paris, 1955–59), part 2, 2:112–20, observes that the tradition of a "sheltering cloak" long predates Caesarius, and surveys its medieval variations. The *Speculum humanae salvationis*, chap. 38, combining pictures and text, gave further currency to this tradition; it dates from 1324. For a fifteenth-century English translation (and a German woodcut image) see *The Mirour of Mans Saluacioun*, ed. Avril Henry (Philadelphia, 1987), pp. 190–94. A magnificent painting of the Last Judgment usually attributed to one of the van Eycks (New York, The Metropolitan Museum) offers an interesting parallel, with Christ and the blessed souls above, some of them sheltered by the mantle of the Virgin, and with Satan below, an enormous skeletal figure of death, who seems to defecate newly arrived souls into hell, and whose huge, shadowy wings cover them all. It can be seen in Giorgio T. Faggin, *The Complete Paintings of the Van Eycks* (New York, 1968), color pl. LXIII, discussed p. 88.

the hypocritical pretensions of a friar and his order. Angry
Thomas is allowed a churl's revenge: a rude bequest of fart,
hugely to be savored. He is allowed his day, his way. But the poet
who created him can imagine something wittier by far. It is to the
scholar Jankyn that Chaucer finally awards the prize—a prize his
own learned and witty poetry often claimed from duke or
king—the gift of a new gown.

Medieval to Renaissance: Plays and the London Drapers' Company to 1558

ANNE LANCASHIRE

Of all the London craft guilds, or livery companies (for in London the two terms are almost synonymous), the Drapers' Company is the most rewarding to examine today for those interested, whether from a theatrical, social, or political perspective, in the continuing London craft-guild sponsorship of drama, music, and pageantry from medieval times through to the early Renaissance. One of the so-called twelve Great Companies of London—the twelve companies foremost in prestige, power, and wealth among all the London livery companies—the Drapers' Company, existing well before its 1438 charter of incorporation and continuing into the present,[1] has extant today, in its London Hall, large numbers of major manuscripts (detailed account books, minute books, books of ordinances, etc.) going back in part to the early fifteenth century. And, unlike the early records of some of the other London Great Companies (some of which go back further), the Drapers' records contain numerous entries on, and sometimes much detail of, the Company's use of music, pageant-

---

[1]See, e.g., Arthur H. Johnson, *History of the Worshipful Company of the Drapers of London*, 5 vols. (Oxford, 1914–22), and Tom Girtin, *The Triple Crowns: A Narrative History of The Drapers' Company, 1364–1964* (London, 1964), passim.

ry, and plays. We have, in short, with the Drapers' Company, a major company both with a significant number of early MSS and with records, relating to drama, music, and pageantry, that are both chronologically extensive and often also extensive in terms of information provided. The Drapers' records are a unique resource for study and analysis.[2]

The London guilds in general, and especially the twelve Great Companies, were involved in drama, music, and/or pageantry, from the medieval period to the early Renaissance, both on external, public occasions and on internal, private or semi-private occasions, for reasons political, religious, and social. Music, drama, and spectacle enhanced the prestige and authority of a guild, could make political points, sometimes involved religious observance, and always entertained. Occasions for guild-sponsored music, pageantry, and drama in London included, for example, the oath-taking days of newly-elected sheriffs and mayors of London (in September and in October annually), royal entries, the Midsummer Watch held annually in late June, and internal company celebrations such as a company's own annual (or sometimes biennial or triennial) election feast/dinner, at which former company officers and senior members were honored and new officers were elected and/or inducted into office. The Drapers' Company sponsored music, pageantry, and/or drama on all these kinds of occasions. Drama, as opposed to pageantry, was most likely to be featured at a London company's election feasts (and the feast-time itself could spread over more than one day), both as entertainment and as a demonstration, both to company members themselves and to invited guests, of a company's wealth, status, and taste. And the extant Drapers' MSS indicate that from the early fifteenth

---

[2] I am most grateful to the Drapers' Company, and especially to its Education Officer, Mr. R. T. Brown, for generous provision of access to the Drapers' MSS.

century to the mid sixteenth century, that is, over a span of just over one hundred years, medieval to Renaissance, the Company regularly hired actors to perform, perhaps normally *two* plays (at least from 1516), at its annual election feast-time, c. 15 August, the Feast of the Assumption of Our Lady. Many, though not all, of the records involved have been previously printed, but they have not all been grouped together, and some have been misinterpreted and misdated. Nor has the full run of the records been dealt with as a whole.

References to plays/players in the records of the Drapers' Company may begin (depending on the dates of the individual items involved) with the earliest Drapers' manuscript ordinance book, in the early fifteenth century.[3] A Company ordinance near the beginning of the so-called "Book of Ordinances 1405"—a MS volume containing Company bylaws ranging in date from 1405 to the latter half of the sixteenth century—indirectly specifies players as a required component of the regular entertainment provided at the Company's annual election feast, or dinner, which was given by the Company wardens for the whole brotherhood c. 15 August each year. That the feast concerned is the Company's annual August election feast is clear from the MS context in which the ordinance occurs. The date of the ordinance could be any time between c. 1418 and, at the latest, 1462.[4]

---

[3]Drapers' MS +795. All Drapers' MSS cited are at Drapers' Hall, London.

[4]The ordinance (MS +795, p. 29) comes from a group headed 1418 but including ordinances originating before 1418 (see MS heading p. 26) and after 1418, with revisions of various dates. At least the final part of the ordinance immediately preceding this one is internally dated 7 August 33 Henry VI (i.e., 1455—or perhaps 1454 if the start of the new regnal year on 1 September is being anticipated); but the c. 1418+ ordinances are apparently not set down in chronological order. The first group of ordinances in the MS (pp. 19–21), from 1405, was copied down on 19 February 1 Edward IV, according to their MS heading on p. 19; and the date 1460/1 has been

299

For The ffeeste What Eu*er*y Brother shal Paye[5]

Also that eu*er*y Brothir Whet‸ ⌐h⌐ er[6] that he be In Towne
or noon shall Paye hys aferant for the Dynn*er* or feeste that ys
to seye that ʒer þ*at* they haue Clothyng ij s. And that ʒer no
Clothyng ys iij s. And eu*er*y Brother shall Paye for his
Quart*er*age xij d a ʒer [And þouʒ he be Wedyd he schall Paye
for him and for hys Wyfe but xij d /[7] And also the Wardeyns
as for þe ʒer beyng shal haue to þ*er* alouans As for Rysches
Mynst*r*als Pleyers and oþ*er* Pety Costys xx s. And no more
Also yf yt so be y*at* ther be a Mayr at þe Dynn*er* And he be
of the seyd felyschypp the Wardens to be alouyd for his Mes
xl s. And yf yt lyke the Wardens to haue at the Dynner ‸ ⌐a
meir⌐ of anoþ*er* Crafte w*ithoute*n the assent of þe felyshypp
þa*n* they to haue noon Alowans As for the Meyrs Messe][8]

The wardens of the Drapers thus received, by ordinance, from
some time in the first part of the fifteenth century, an allowance
from Company funds to cover the costs of rushes, minstrels, *players*, and "other petty costs" of the annual Company election din-

---

entered in the margin, i.e., 1461 by our modern calendar. 19 February 1 Edward IV is,
however, 1462. Probably the marginal date is a later error. The c. 1418+ ordinances
were probably copied down at about the same time as the 1405 ordinances they
follow, as the same copying format and red and blue coloring are involved.

[5]In this and following quotations from the MS records, the lineation of the
original has not been preserved, and no marginal markings are recorded since none
changes the meaning of the text itself.

[6]Later correction: letter inserted above.

[7]Later mark.

[8]The whole section I have placed within square brackets has been cancelled at
a later date. (For subsequent changes in feast funding arrangements, see below.)
This ordinance has been printed in Johnson, 1:266–67.

ner, which the wardens arranged and paid for; and in years when a Draper was mayor, or when a mayor of another company was invited by general assent to the dinner, the allowance included additional funds for the "mayor's mess": that is, for the mayor and his party dining together.[9] The specifying of players as part of the regular costs of the feast, met by a standing Company allowance, shows that players were a regular, expected part of the proceedings. And that these players were indeed actors, and not musicians, is indicated by the specifying of minstrels and players as two different groups and by an ordinance slightly later in the MS, to be dated between 1436 and 1462, which refers specifically to plays as ordained for the feast time.[10]

> The ordinans Made to Exchewe pres off Menis Men
> In þe Halle þe day off þe ffeeste.

> Also Ordeynd ys By All The hooll ffelischipp off This ffrater-
> nite that for As moche as here to fore This tyme At The ffeste
> or Dynner off This forseyd fraternite hath ben Greet pres And
> Multitud of ȝonge Men In Greet Dyshonour of All the Breth-
> eryn And Prynspally to the Mayster And Wardens for the tyme
> Beynge for They myȝht have no Rome nor space to serve nor
> to do her Besynes In savyng of þer Worshipp And of alle the
> Bretheryn And Prynspaly That þe statys ne þe Brethryn myȝht
> not se ne be holde Pleyes & oþer dyuers sportys ffor that
> Tyme Ordeynd Ther fore ordeynd ys be the Avyce of all the
> Brethryn That Noman of þe ffraternyte Except Aldermen And

---

[9]See *OED*, *s.v.* Mess, *sb.*, II.4.

[10]The ordinance must be dated no earlier than 1436–39 because it refers to Company masters past and present, and we first hear of a master in the early wardens' accounts (1413–14 [?] to 1440–41, incomplete: Drapers' MS +140) in 1439, with the accounts being missing for 1435–36 to 1438–39. It also comes second-to-last in the group of ordinances, not all chronologically ordered, to be dated, overall, c. 1418–62 (see n. 4 above).

they That haue borne states In the Cyttee schal brynge noman
Wyth hy*m* ne Chyld to þe feeste or Dynn*er* Wheþir yt be saffe
only They that hau*e* ben Mayster or Wardens to fore . . .[11]

The two above ordinances together indicate that plays were
regularly performed, by bylaw, at the Drapers' annual election
feasts, from some date in the first sixty-two years of the fifteenth
century. And the first extant set of Drapers' wardens' accounts
(Drapers' MS +140), which begins more or less in the early 1420s
(with one complete and one partial earlier account year) and runs,
though with numerous gaps, to 1440–41, records regular payments
to players (along with minstrels) at the Drapers' election-time
feasts from 1430 on.[12] There are no payments to players before
1430 (though the MS is incomplete); but from 1430 to 1441,
feast-time players are paid in all years for which accounts are extant.[13] Tom Girtin, in *The Triple Crowns*, has suggested (p. 52)
that the Drapers, who built a new Hall for themselves in the late
1420s, first occupied this Hall in 1430. If so, perhaps the Company began more elaborate feast-time practices, including the
regular appearance of players, in that year.

The first set of extant Drapers' wardens' accounts (Drapers'
MS +140) ends in 1440–41; the next set (Drapers' MS +403) does
not begin until 1475–76. That feast-time players continued to be a
norm for the Drapers' Company through the mid fifteenth century,
however, is indicated by another ordinance from the Drapers'
early Book of Ordinances, this one specifically dated in August

---

[11]MS +795, p. 39. Also printed in Johnson, 1:273–74.

[12]These wardens' accounts (Drapers' MS +140) have been transcribed by
Johnson, vol. 1, and are also published in *Drapers' Company: Transcripts of the
Earliest Records in the possession of the Company* (London, 1910).

[13]See fols. F3ʳ, G3ʳ, H3ᵛ, I4ʳ, and K2ᵛ.

1474. The ordinance concerns a change in (presumably ongoing) funding arrangements for the annual feast; that is, it implies a continuation to August 1474 of the conditions it is now changing.

> Also by the said assent aggrement and consent It is ordeyned the day & yere aforsaid that the wardeyns of the said ffraternite for the tyme beyng shall haue none allowaunce vpon the dyner for the Meyres Messe though*e* he be there Nor for none of those Straungers Which by my maisters the Aldremen and by the Wardeyns for the tyme beyng With the Counseill of the Craft shall be appoynted and boden to the dyner for garnysshyng of the high Table nor for rysshes mynstrell*es* nor players[14]

Again, players are cited as a normal part of the annual election dinner costs—though within the context now of withdrawal of the Company's standing allowance covering them. The Company was probably not, however, financially mistreating its wardens, in this ordinance, in withdrawing the whole Company funding allowance for these specified dinner costs and leaving all these expenses to be paid by the wardens themselves, out of their own pockets. In August 1473, one year earlier, another bylaw had been passed, providing the wardens with other sources of income (fines and apprentice-enrollment fees) from which dinner expenses in general could be met; and these sources were further augmented in August 1474.[15] But that the Company itself, or the wardens, were going through financial changes and/or problems is suggest-

---

[14]MS +795, p. 45. Johnson calendars, 1:278, and misdates as 1476.

[15]For 1473 see MS +795, p. 44 and Johnson's calendaring, 1:277 (misdated 1475). See also the ordinance passed on 17 Dec. 1466 (MS +795, p. 42; Johnson, 1:276), which gives the wardens some Assumption-time fines for funding of their (unspecified) costs and charges. For 1474 see MS +795, p. 45.

ed by the fact that the second MS volume of extant wardens' accounts (Drapers' MS +403), which begins in 1475–76, does not
record any feast-time payments for players, minstrels, etc. until
1481 (fol. 20ʳ), after another bylaw had been passed in August
1478 restoring the above Company funding allowance to the
wardens for the annual feast. This bylaw again mentions players
as a part of the expected feast expenses.

> . . . that the wardeins that shall be frohensforth shall haue for
> theire Allowaunce yerely for the Meyres messe and for suche
> as shall be Appointed by my maisters the Aldermen and by
> the Wardeins for þe tyme being for þe Garnisshing of the
> high table Also for players mynstrell*es* and Russhis the
> somme of vj li xiij s iiij d s*terling* . . .[16]

(The ordinance continues, naming other income sources also for
the wardens.)

Once this new funding bylaw of 1478 had been passed, the
extant wardens' accounts running 1475–76 to 1508–09 indicate
players performing at the Drapers' annual election feast every
year but three, from 1481 to 1507. The accounting formula used,
however, unfortunately provides no details of who is performing,
of what is being performed, or of what the specific performance
costs are. The usual formula runs:

> It*em* for the Meyrys Messe mynstrell*es* pleyers and Russhis vj
> li xiij s iiij d.[17]

In the three years between 1481 and 1507 in which players are not
mentioned in the formula, the formula once (in 1488) omits the

---

[16]MS +795, p. 46; see also Johnson's calendaring, 1:278 (dated 1477–78).

[17]MS +403, fol. 20ʳ. This specific example is from 1481.

players only, once (in 1489) cites only the mayor's mess, and once (in 1493) refers only to the mayor's mess and rushes.[18] The total allowance claimed by the wardens is always, however, the full £6. 13s. 4d. set in the Company's 1478 ordinance quoted above. It is impossible to tell whether the words are being varied deliberately, to provide an accurate record of what usual expenses were and were not involved in those three years, or are simply being arbitrarily abbreviated by the scribe since the amount of allowance to be paid by the Company to the wardens is the same in each year. Players thus may or may not have performed in the three years in question; and the same is true for the years 1479 and 1480, immediately after the passing of the 1478 ordinance, when the full allowance is also claimed (at once) by the wardens in the account payment records but only the mayor's mess is mentioned.[19]

The two latest feast years, however, covered by this second extant volume of wardens' accounts, that is, the years 1508 and 1509, also contain no record of players at the annual feast, and no formula or allowance otherwise. And the next set of wardens' accounts (Drapers' MS +143), running on to 1546–47, similarly contains no players expenses, no allowance, no mayor's mess, until 1512, when the players, minstrels, rushes, and mayor's mess formula occurs once again (fol. 22ᵛ) and then not for the next three years, though for 1515 the formula is found once more in its abbreviated form (fol. 45ᵛ), citing only the mayor's mess. (Significantly, in both August 1512 and August 1515 a Draper Lord Mayor was in office.[20]) As in the 1470s, the fact that few feast-

---

[18]See MS +403, fols. 41ᵛ, 45ᵛ, and 56ʳ.

[19]MS +403, fols. 15ᵛ and 17ᵛ.

[20]See John Stow, *Survey of London*, ed. C. L. Kingsford, 2 vols. (Oxford, 1908), 2:180.

time players records—or mayor's mess records—are to be found over this eight-year period may be associated with financial re-arrangements or problems, in that the period coincides with a time when, as seen in the early Book of Ordinances, the Company seems to have been making a number of (limiting) changes in the kinds and terms of Company income available to the wardens for payment of their recurring expenses of office. In 1505, for ex-ample, the Company further regulated the wardens' income from apprenticeship fees; in 1512 it made a major reduction in the wardens' income overall; and in 1515 it limited the years in which the feast-time funding formula would be paid, though this 1515 act was then annulled 4 August 1519.[21] (Also the Company's Court minutes record, for 8 August 1519, some new funding arrangements for the wardens.[22]) And, after 1515, no record of payment to players, and very few references to the mayor's mess, occur again in the wardens' accounts, to 1558.

This does not mean, however, that players ceased performing at the Drapers' annual election feast; for the Drapers' regular Court minutes are extant from 1515–16.[23] And the Court min-utes, which include some accounting records, show that, from 1516 to 1541, players were paid by the wardens to perform plays at the annual August feast-time—normally one play on each of two separate days during the celebrations—for all years in which Draper feast dinners were held and records are extant: though the

[21]For 1505 see MS +795, p. 48; Johnson calendars, 1:279. For 1512 see MS +795, p. 48; Johnson calendars, 1:279. For 1515 and 1519 see MS +795, p. 28; Johnson, 1:265.

[22]Drapers' MS +130/1, p. 116.

[23]From 1515–16 to 1558 see esp. Drapers' MSS +130/1-3 (1515–16 to 1552–53), and also MSS +128, +253, +254, +255, +140a, and +252.

performance in 1519, the year of the annulment in August of the 1515 funding bylaw, was minimal—simply one performer (status unknown) at a supper held by the junior members of the Company.[24] And, much of the time, the Court minutes provide detail about payment amounts (usually 6s. 8d. per play, 13s. 4d. for two plays, and often dinner for the actors) and—unlike the earlier wardens' accounts—about the playing companies involved, which seem usually to have been professional companies with royal or aristocratic patronage. There are performances by the King's Players in at least seven years from 1517 to 1541.[25] Individual King's players named include John English, [William] Rutter, and [Robert] Hinstock.[26] A (John) Sly and his company perform in at least four years from 1516 to 1530, probably the same John Sly who was player to Queen Jane Seymour before her death in 1537, and/or the same John Sly who was interluder to Henry VIII.[27] In 1521 payment is made, for two performances, to English, Sly, and their fellows.[28] Were they performing together, in one company, or in two separate companies (perhaps the King's and the Queen's, performing one each day for two days)? By 1529 other

---

[24]MS +130/1, p. 101. There were no regular feast-time dinners 1522–26 (inclusive) and 1536.

[25]1517, 1527, 1528, 1532, 1534, 1535, and 1541.

[26]For English's acting company see, e.g., Ian Lancashire, *Dramatic Texts and Records of Britain: A Chronological Topography to 1558* (Toronto, 1984), #1.267, 1 (where Rutter and Hinstock are also listed). In these Drapers' records, Rutter's company membership follows from English's; and Hinstock's is specified.

[27]Sly and his company perform for the Drapers in 1516, 1518, 1520, and 1530. For John Sly, player to the Queen and John Sly, interluder to Henry VIII, see, e.g., *Dramatic Texts and Records*, #285, #1.267,1, and #1.275.

[28]MS +130/1, p. 157.

companies are being employed, in different years, as well: the Prince's Players (1529, 1540), the Duke of Norfolk's Players (1529), the Duke of Suffolk's Players (1531, 1532). The Queen's Players are specifically recorded in 1539. In 1540 we also find the only seemingly amateur play performance recorded over this period: a performance by "our paryshe clerck and his compeny pleyers."[29] Finally, after 1541, feast-time play performance records cease. And in the Company's revised 1543 ordinances (MS +795, from p. 55) no ordinances involving feast-time plays / players are to be found.

The Drapers' specific play performance records, from 1485 on, have in large part, but not entirely, been published by the Malone Society in *Collections III*, a part-edition, part-calendar of MS records of plays and civic pageants sponsored by the twelve Great Companies of London, 1485–1640.[30] The continuity and significance of the Drapers' records, however, as part of an election feast-time pattern existing from medieval times to the early Renaissance, is not apparent in *Collections III* for three reasons. First, *Collections III* deliberately begins only in 1485, and so includes none of the Drapers' fifteenth-century ordinances referring to plays/players (and no pre-1485 player records). Second, because the editors of *Collections III* thus apparently did not look at the fifteenth-century ordinances (and also missed a 1516 "mayor's mess" and players entry in Drapers' MS +130/1, p. 5), they misinterpreted and misdated the post-1484 performance records they found, through a misunderstanding of the term "mayor's mess."

---

[29]MS +130/2, p. 607.

[30]*Collections*, vol. III ("A Calendar of Dramatic Records in the Books of the Livery Companies of London 1485–1640"), ed. J. Robertson and D. J. Gordon (Malone Society, 1954). The Drapers' play records are printed in part in the main body of collected records (under "III. Miscellaneous") and in part as Addenda (pp. 183–84).

The term is used clearly in the early ordinances to refer to the mayor and his party dining together at the Drapers' annual election feast in August. Thinking the term (as they found it from 1485) to refer, however, to a dinner held on Lord Mayor's Day each year, in late October, after the Westminster oath-taking of the new London mayor, the editors of *Collections III* dated all Drapers' play performance records, 1485–1511, as belonging to Lord Mayor's Day, and the post-1511 play performance records they found, because no longer using the term "mayor's mess" and clearly involving the election feast, as belonging to the Drapers' own August feast time.[31] Third, because the Drapers' accounting and minuting year at this time runs from mid-August to mid-August, and includes for each year the Lord Mayor's Day expenses (in late October) of the accounts' and minutes' opening year and the Company's feast expenses (in mid August) of the accounts' and minutes' closing year, a *Collections III* Lord Mayor's Day dating, rather than a Company election feast dating, of performance records in any one Drapers' annual accounts or set of minutes puts the records' date out by one year. And even after 1511, when *Collections III* correctly assigns play performances to the Drapers' own feast time, it incorrectly assumes they are for each accounts'—and set of minutes'—opening, not closing, year. In *Collections III*, in short, the real continuity and pattern of the records, from the medieval period through to the early Renaissance, cannot be discerned.[32]

---

[31]The volume further confuses the matter by conflating, in notes (pp. 132 and 136) to the Drapers' play performance records first from 1485 and then from 1515, the mayor's election day, 13 October at this time, with his Westminster oath-taking day, 29 October.

[32]The contributions of *Collections III* in general to our knowledge of London livery company (including Drapers') pageantry and drama have been, however, very great. Some misinterpretations are inevitable when dealing with extensive and

A new look at the MS records, then, shows that the London Drapers' Company included play performances as a regular, expected part of its annual election feast celebrations over a period of about 112 years, from at least 1430 to 1541. Occasional interruptions or gaps in the regular pattern of recorded performances— in the 1470s and in the early sixteenth century, in the extant records—are perhaps to be associated with funding rearrangements between the Company itself and its wardens; or, given the silence in the wardens' accounts on payments to players after 1516, when we know from the Court minutes that performances were indeed taking place, it is also possible that it was the records, and not the performances themselves, that temporarily stopped. The fifteenth-century records unfortunately do not tell us what kinds of actors are involved; but from 1516 the details provided in the Court minutes show that the players at that time, at least, are almost invariably well-known professionals with court / aristocratic patronage, and at least sometimes (perhaps usually?) numbering about four, since part of their payment sometimes is specified to involve a dinner "mess."[33] Finally, two plays per feast time, at c. 6s. 8d. per play, seems to have been the norm from at least 1516 until 1540. The comparatively large sum at least sometimes paid to players before 1442, as recorded in the earliest wardens' accounts—8s., for example, for the feast time in 1430, at a time when the London Cutlers' Company and Blacksmiths' Company

---

sometimes highly complex records materials.

[33]See *OED*, *s.v.* Mess, *sb.* 4 (a mess usually involved four people); also Drapers' MS +252, fol. 11ʳ (ten messes as involving forty-two people). The London Cutlers' Company from 1486–87 to 1497–98 also regularly in part paid its feast-time players with apparently four dinners; see Anne Lancashire, "Players for the London Cutlers' company," *REED Newsletter* (1981), 2:10–11. The Brewers also sometimes, in the 1430s, fed their players (specified to be four); see Guildhall Library (London) MS 5440, fols. 220ᵛ, 229ᵛ, and 249ʳ.

were paying players 3*s.* 4*d.* for feast-time performance—might suggest more than one play per feast-time in at least the first part of the fifteenth century as well.[34] But fees in general to players at this time can vary; the Brewers, for example, in 1421 paid 7*s.* for a single play, and in 1432, 3*s.* 4*d.*[35] Perhaps the Drapers' early players simply were more generally expensive than the players regularly employed by the Cutlers at first and by the Blacksmiths overall. Did the Drapers, for example, consistently use troops with royal or aristocratic patrons while the Blacksmiths did not? In 1525 the Blacksmiths employed the King's Players—and paid out the unusually large sum, for the Blacksmiths, of 6*s.* 8*d.* Blacksmiths' payments to (unidentified) players had never before exceeded 5*s.* 4*d.* (in 1523).[36] The Brewers' 1421 7*s.* play, however, was performed by clerks. The situation is unclear; and the early fifteenth-century Drapers' records so far remain unexplained in terms of play numbers involved and types of players employed. And from 1481 to 1507, the Drapers' records give us only the overall funding formula, so we have no specific information on costs on the basis of which even to begin to speculate.

Was the London Drapers' Company unusual, or was it a typical London livery company, in its regular use of players at its major annual feast time in the fifteenth to sixteenth centuries, and in at least the sixteenth-century identity of those players as largely

---

[34]For the 1430 payment see MS +140, fol. F3ʳ. For the Cutters and the Blacksmiths see Anne Lancashire, "London Cutlers' company," p. 10 (though the payment to players increases to 7*s.* by 1449), and "Plays for the London Blacksmiths' company," *REED Newsletter* (1981), 1:12 (the payment increases to c. 5*s.* in the sixteenth century).

[35]G.L. MS 5440, fols. 58ᵛ and 194ʳ.

[36]See Anne Lancashire, "London Blacksmiths' company," p. 13. In 1525 the Grocers paid the King's Players 10*s.* 4*d.* (G.L. MS 11571/4, fol. 153ʳ).

court interluders? The Drapers' Company is the only Great Company to show in its extant records a regular, ordained involvement with feast-time players over this medieval-to-Renaissance period (to 1558). But for three other Great Companies (Fishmongers, Haberdashers, Salters), there are no surviving major records for this period; and, where other Great Companies' major records *have* in part survived, the vagaries of what has survived, and the varying accounting and minuting practices of London companies in general, do not permit us to infer from MS silence that feast-time plays either were or were not performed. (Even the Drapers' own wardens' accounts after 1515 show that, from MS silence, play non-existence cannot safely be inferred.)

It *is* notable, however, that no regular plays/players are ordered or recorded in the extensive early, extant MSS of the Goldsmiths, Mercers, or Merchant Taylors (all Great Companies).[37] But the non-Great companies, far more numerous than the Great, do include some with some surviving records of regular (I do not here include occasional) feast-time play performance, though usually the actors involved are not identified. The Blacksmiths both legislated and recorded regular fifteenth- to sixteenth-century feast-time plays; the Cutlers recorded regular feast-time players in the fifteenth century, as did the Brewers (G.L. MS 5440) and, in the early sixteenth century, the Carpenters (G.L. MS 4326/1) and the yeomanry of the Tallow Chandlers (G.L. MS 6155/1).[38] These performance records, however, are far less in-

---

[37]The Grocers, a Great Company also with extensive surviving records, are seen to have had regular feast-time entertainments (minstrels, tumblers, etc.), from the mid fifteenth to mid sixteenth centuries (G.L. MS 11571/1–5), but only occasionally are players or a play specified.

[38]For the Blacksmiths see Anne Lancashire, "London Blacksmiths' company," pp. 12–14; for the Cutlers see Anne Lancashire, "London Cutlers' company," pp. 10–11. The Carpenters also had some players in the late fifteenth century, but not

formative than the Drapers', and, except for the Blacksmiths', less extensive over time. Seldom are the recorded players identified: once in 1525 as the King's Players, by the Blacksmiths (see above), several times in the fifteenth century as clerks, by the Brewers, but not otherwise.[39]

From the Drapers' records, however, taken together with those of the non-Great companies named, it would seem legitimate to suggest that regular feast-time plays, by bylaw or not, perhaps were not uncommon for London livery companies in the fifteenth to early sixteenth centuries. Furthermore, the Drapers' sixteenth-century use of players with royal and aristocratic patrons—especially given the Great Company status of the Drapers in civic London—points to London livery company drama as perhaps an area in which interesting cross-connections may have existed between City and court. Did other livery companies too, especially in the sixteenth century, regularly employ acting groups such as the King's and the Queen's Players?

The medieval-to-Renaissance regular play performances for the Drapers' Company are significant from a theatre history perspective, but also from a sociopolitical perspective. In considering City-court relationships and maneuverings in general, we should also not now leave out of our speculations, especially on the early sixteenth century, the possible significance(s) of play performances at the feasts of the London livery companies.

---

regularly. A Pewterers' order of 1559 (G.L. MS 7094, fol. 65^r) refers to plays as though they were a tradition at the Pewterers' yeomanry dinner—but no such plays are recorded in the extant Pewterers' yeomanry accounts from 1496.

[39] Very occasionally a player (as yet) unknown to us is named.

Chaucer's Repetends from The General Prologue of *The Canterbury Tales*

IAN LANCASHIRE

The scale of Chaucer's habits of phrasal self-repetition—nearly 640 repeating exact phrases within the General Prologue alone, and over 460 linking it with the rest of the tales—exceeds by twenty-fold the tags, stock formulas, or proverbs previously recognized. Repetends appear, on average, once every line-and-a-half in its 858 lines. Computer analysis brings to light so many phrasal repetends that current explanations hardly account for them. Some do not survive beyond The General Prologue; most are repeated in later tales. Repetends appear to form semantic clusters, some of which convey aspects of Chaucer's world-view. They focus on meaningful topics (such as saying, telling, and speaking) and include proverbs and merisms, but seldom do clusters realize narrative elements of particular tales. In phrasal repetends that do survive, we may see fragments of what was successfully implanted by Chaucer's short-term, working memory in a declarative or procedural semantic memory, that is, phrases (not words), bound together by the context they share. The distribution of such repetends across Chaucer's works may help to date them because, as a system, repetends differ from one time in his life to another. (The General Prologue, for example, shares many more repetends than expected with The Manciple's Prologue and Tale and The Merchant's Prologue and Tale, so that they seem to have been written at about the same period.) As a system, phrasal repetends may be a "fingerprint" of authorship.[1]

CRITICAL ATTITUDES TO PHRASAL REPETITION IN CHAUCER

Ralph W. V. Elliott, like Derek Brewer, Norman Davis, and others, attributes "stock phrases, clichés, tags," etc., to Chaucer, but many fewer than to medieval romances or Corpus Christi plays. Elliott notes about twenty instances, and Davis mentions just seven formulas, most inherited from anonymous bards. Brewer says that "Chaucer makes progressively less use of this traditional formulaic style as he develops his art."[2] No one since B. J. Whiting has tried to detect Chaucer's stock phrases.

While Larry Benson does not single out repeating phrases for

---

[1]I wish to acknowledge gratefully the generous support of the Social Sciences and Humanities Research Council of Canada in this research, and the warm encouragement and friendship of Professors Jan Svartvik and Magnus Ljung and my other friends at Lund and Stockholm universities during my visits in February 1991. I want especially to thank my Toronto colleagues Patricia Eberle and Fergus Craik for their helpful comments and warm encouragement.

[2]Ralph W. V. Elliott, *Chaucer's English* (London, 1974), p. 191. Elliott begins with *ParlF* usage ("I dar nat seyn," "I can na moore," "as I yow tolde," "as I shal telle," "as shortly as I can it trete" and "I wol yow seyn"; p. 192) and cites examples from various works afterwards: "also mot I the" (*Mars* 267; p. 192), "thurgh thikke and thurgh thenne" (RvT 4066) and "by stokkes and by stones" (*Tr* III.589; p. 193) and "And by that lord that clepid is Seint Yve" (ShipT 227 and SumT 1943; pp. 276–77). Elliott does not give references for the following tags: "for Goddes love" and "God help me so" (p. 266), "so God me save," "so God me wisse," "so God me speede" and "so God yow blesse" (p. 267), and "for Goddes bones" and "for cokkes bones" (p. 271). See Brewer's "Chaucer's poetic style," in *The Cambridge Chaucer Companion*, ed. Piero Boitani and Jill Mann (Cambridge, 1986), pp. 229–30. Norman Davis identifies "joye and blis," "joye and solas," "cares colde," "stille as ston," "bright in bour" and "over stile and stoon" ("Chaucer and Fourteenth-century English," in *Geoffrey Chaucer*, ed. Derek Brewer [London, 1974], pp. 76–77; 83–84).

comment in the introduction to *The Riverside Chaucer*, twenty of his notes to the General Prologue to *The Canterbury Tales* helpfully identify half a dozen kinds of repetition. Chaucer's "worthy" and "wys," for example, is termed a "common collocation."[3] Current language usage, or idiom, explains others, such as the Monk's "pulled hen": negative comparisons of this sort "are common in Chaucer and throughout Middle English."[4] The same explains "for the nones" (an intensive phrase, if not a "line-filler"), "out of alle charitee" ("merely idiomatic"), "good felawe" and "to shorte with."[5] "Merisms" or yoked contraries in Middle English, such as "thogh him gamed or smerte," is the third type.[6] The fourth derives from B. J. Whiting's ground-breaking study of Chaucer's proverbs.[7] Proverbs account for the comparisons "broun as a berye," "His *purchas* was wel bettre than his *rente*," and "He made

---

[3]*The Riverside Chaucer*, Larry D. Benson, Gen. ed., 3rd ed. (Boston, 1987), p. 801, n. to line 68 (cf. *Tr* 2.180). Another instance appears at *LGW* 171–73, cited for "Whan Zephirus eek with his sweete breeth / Inspired hath in every holt and heeth": a collocation of "Zephirus" and "swoote breth" (*Riverside*, p. 799, n. to lines 5–6). Charles Fries and John Halliday popularized, especially in systemic linguistics, the study of collocations, both as distinctive, frequent yokings of two or more words in a sense different from their senses when they appear separately (e.g., "home runs"), or simply as frequently paired words without an abrupt change in their meanings (e.g., "nice" and "day," or "nice" and "fix").

[4]*Riverside*, p. 807, n. to line 177, which refers to WBT III.1112, "nat worth an hen," citations of Robert Whiting's work on proverbs, and an article by Hein in *Anglia* in 1893.

[5]*Riverside*, pp. 814 (n. to line 379), 820 (n. to line 545), 818 (n. to line 452; cf. KnT I.1623), 815 (n. to line 395; cf. GP I.650, I.648, and FrT III.1385), and 826 (n. to line 791; cf. I.3119, VI.345, VII.273).

[6]Lawrence L. Besserman, "Merisms in Middle English Poetry," *Annuale Mediaevale* 17 (1976): 58–65; and *Riverside*, p. 820, n. to line 534.

[7]Bartlett Jere Whiting, *Chaucer's Use of Proverbs* (Cambridge, Mass., 1934).

the person and the peple his *apes.*"[8] The *Riverside* editors identify
two more "proverbs": "sette hir aller cappe," despite its appearance
only in *The Canterbury Tales,* and "If even-song and morwe-song
accorde."[9] The terms "tag" and "rhetorical formula," the fifth type
of generic repetition, apply to "clad in blak or reed," "shortly for
to tellen" and "what nedeth wordes mo."[10] Finally, both "fees and
robes" and "In heigh and lough" reflect separate linguistic registers, Latin financial and legal formulas, although no other English
example in Chaucer can be found.[11]

Such attempts to explain repeating phrases abruptly fail before
two basic problems. First, no one knows which phrases actually repeat. Second, no one has classified repeated phrases coherently.
Scholars often assume that a phrase repeats itself, without checking
to be sure that it does. For example, all merisms and "proverbs" do
not necessarily recur. Unique examples, used once and abandoned,
must occur. Potential merisms may never appear at all (for example, about people who are bald and who have full heads of hair).
Are phrases such as "sette hir aller cappe" proverbial if we can
only find them in one author, Chaucer? Whiting identified Chaucer's phrases as proverbs, not because authors used them repeatedly
(often he cited no evidence of repetition, inside or outside Chaucer's works), but because they compared two things or were senten-

[8]*Riverside,* pp. 807 (n. to line 207; cf. CkT I.4368 and NPT VII.2843–44), 808
(n. to line 256; cf. RR 11566 and Rom 6838) and 825 (n. to line 706; cf. MilT
I.3389, ShipT VII.440, and CYT VIII.1313).

[9]*Riverside,* pp. 821 (n. to line 586; cf. MilP I.3143 and RvP I.3911) and 826 (n.
to line 830).

[10]*Riverside,* pp. 811 (n. to line 294, "Perhaps a tag"; cf. *HF* 1074–78), 826 (n.
to line 843; cf. KnT I.875–88n), and 826 (n. to line 849; cf. KnT I.1029, 1715).

[11]*Riverside,* pp. 812 (n. to line 317) and 826 (n. to line 817).

tious. Until scholars know that something is repeated, they ought to refrain from saying that it is. The best tools to find repeating phrases, concordances and computer textbases accessed by retrieval systems, are not yet widely used in Chaucer studies, as they are in Biblical or Classical studies.[12] I propose to use them here.

Grouping phrases by features such as collocation, legal formula, and merism is like sorting people by male gender, a southern Ontario home address, and pastoral daydreams. Some people are female, many live on boats, and those who daydream of making money are not unknown. Each feature, then, is one possible instantiation of a more general characteristic. With phrases, these characteristics are verbal form, source, and semantic content. Verbal form may have two sub-forms—collocation (that is, a repeated phrase with shifting word order) or fixed sequence (that is, one with the same words in the same order). These sub-forms may be further subclassified by internal acoustic similarity (none, or some alliteration, rhyme, assonance, etc.), by ratio of function and content words, by inflectional or morphological variation, etc., but collocation cannot be mentioned without its alternative, the fixed phrase. Each repeated phrase may also be globally classified by its source: is it the speaker (that is, Chaucer) or someone else, either the general population, a subset of that (a linguistic register), or another person? In other words, who created the phrase, and who reused it? Idioms, poetic tags or formulas, and financial and legal phrases explain phrases by source. It is possible, however, that Chaucer invented a legal phrase, and that some poetic tags came from his wool customs office. Theory cannot predict source. Chaucer's works must be compared with other English texts that

---

[12]Tatlock and Kennedy's old published concordance of Chaucer's works, for instance, is not listed by *The Riverside Chaucer* among "Dictionaries and Other Reference Works" (pp. 781–82), although works on proverbs by Skeat, Tilley, and Whiting find a place.

survive from the fourteenth century (and of course that evidence is fragmentary). Finally, a third global classification appeals to semantics, aspects of meaning. Merisms and proverbs fall into this category, but many other semantic relations exist in repetends.

In this article I will suggest that constraints of our working memory help explain the verbal form of repeated phrases but that only the semantics of long-term memory, rather than form or source, can account for the phenomenon. Besserman's work on merisms, then, points research in the right direction, although only after a full study of repeating phrases in the period will we be in a position to tell which semantic phrases belong to Chaucer and which to his sources.

CHAUCER'S PHRASAL REPETITIONS IN THE GENERAL PROLOGUE

Computer analysis of The General Prologue reveals that Chaucer reuses language at a high rate. There are 639 exact "maximal" phrasal repetitions within it.[13] Three in four lines, then, contain several words repeated elsewhere in this poem alone. If we looked for language from The General Prologue that occurred in the rest of Chaucer's works and allowed for variation in word order (that is, collocations) as well as in inflection, the number of repeating phrases would be higher.

Much of this repetition comes with English itself. Chaucer could not help but repeat function words such as determiners, prepositions, conjunctions, verbal auxiliaries, and pro-forms. Most

---

[13]That is, substrings of repetends are not included in this number unless their frequency is greater than the longer repeated phrase of which they form a part. For example, "a draughte of" (with a frequency of 2) makes unnecessary the inclusion of "a draughte" (same frequency) in this list, but since the substring "a good" occurs more often than the longer string "a good felawe," both are included in the count of 639.

common nouns occur after a determiner; it follows, then, that if Chaucer used a noun twice, he may have repeated a phrase. Dozens of function-word sequences also crop up: "after the," "al hir," "and a," "as dooth," "been at," "but he was," etc. For this reason I distinguish between unavoidable repetitions occasioned by using closed-class "grammatical" words and repetitions open to choice. Writers can select content or "open-class" nouns, verbs, and adjectives. A more accurate measure of Chaucer's degree of self-repetition, then, will be how often he re-used phrases or collocations with more than one content word.[14]

What should we expect to find? Of the 1,850 different words in The General Prologue—the poem's word types, or its vocabulary—Chaucer employs 67.3% once, 14.1% twice, 5.7% three times, and 3.6% four times *in that poem by itself.* That is, low-frequency words (of between one and four occurrences each) make up 90.7% of the poem. In modern English 50% of the vocabulary appears once only, and 80% one to four times. Chaucer clearly repeats single words to a much lesser degree than we do today.[15] One of Zipf's predictions of vocabulary distribution is that the product of multiplying the rank of a word in a descending word-frequency list, and the number of times the word occurs at that rank, should remain constant for all ranks. Chaucer's high-frequency words in ranks 1–3 are a third to a half of what they should be. Zipf also predicts that *"the number of different words in the sample* must equal *the number of occurrences of the most*

---

[14]Content analysis is described in *The Humanities Computing Yearbook 1989–1990: A Comprehensive Guide to Software and other Resources,* ed. Ian Lancashire (Oxford, 1991), pp. 489–97.

[15]Only 10% of Chaucer's vocabulary occurs more than four times, as against 20% in modern English. Gerard Salton, *Automatic Text Processing: The Transformation, Analysis, and Retrieval of Information by Computer* (Addison-Wesley, 1989), pp. 105–08.

frequently used word."[16] The most frequent word in The General Prologue, "and," occurs 348 times, far short of the predicted 1,850, the total word types. Since 120,000-word samples are regarded as best for Zipf's predictions—"for smaller samples one finds too many words that occur only once"—we might expect *The Canterbury Tales* as a whole, about 182,000 words, to be a better test of Zipf's prediction.[17] Yet its most frequent word, again "and," occurs only 8,426 times, well below the total vocabulary of 12,164 different words.[18]

From the "behavior" of Chaucer's vocabulary (individual words), then, we should not expect unusual phrasal repetition.[19] The figures, however, are startling. After eliminating repetitions in which function words dominate, I found 464 different phrases and collocations from The General Prologue that appear throughout *The Canterbury Tales.*[20] A different repeating phrase occurs, on average, every second line in The General Prologue. Each one comprises either at least four consecutive words, or at least two co-occurring content or "open class" words, or a prepositional

---

[16]John R. Pierce, *An Introduction to Information Theory: Symbols, Signals and Noise*, 2nd ed. (New York, 1980), p. 244.

[17]Ibid., p. 245. Pierce notes that the "law" works as predicted on a 340-word passage by James Joyce.

[18]Spelling variants and the increased inflection of Chaucer's vocabulary may partly explain this effect. So may the genre, verse.

[19]I do not know of any estimate of the frequency of phrasal repetition in the language, although work has been done on individual authors. The total possible phrases in a poem 1850 words long (two-word, three-word, etc.) is 1849 + 1848 + 1847 . . . 2, or about 1.7 million, but this assumes that phrases as long as 1849 words are possible.

[20]I have not tried to identify phrases from The General Prologue that are repeated in Chaucer's writings outside *The Canterbury Tales.*

phrase.[21] Otherwise, I usually exclude sequences with only one content word and one or two function words, such as "quod he." With them, the number would have swelled to as many as there are lines in The General Prologue. Phrasal repetitions, unlike word repetitions, dominate Chaucer's poetic: he had remarkable skill in constructing, varying, and using word-sequences and collocations.

TECHNICAL MATTERS

How does one collect all repetitions in The General Prologue? Resorting to concordances is not the answer. Reading through Tatlock's concordance, entry by entry, will catch exact repetitions, but verbatim repeated phrases make up a small percentage of the total, in part because Middle English morphology dictates that nouns, verbs, and adjectives have different inflectional forms; and these appear in different concordance entries. There is some spelling variation as well. Second, collocations are hard to recover from a keyword-in-context (KWIC) concordance. Often a regular "collocate" to a given "node" word—the "node" is the anchor word in a collocation, and the collocate, which occurs before or after, is its "floating" partner—will appear outside the brief line that makes up the context for Tatlock's typical concordance entry.[22] Third, some complex patterns of repetition are elusive because they combine inflectionally-diverse words and collocations. For this reason I use an interactive text-retrieval and analysis program on an electronic text of Chaucer's tales.

I first had John Fisher's edition of *The Canterbury Tales* con-

---

[21]"Open-class" words include nouns, verbs, and adjectives, not function words such as articles, auxiliary verbs, and conjunctions.

[22]This is a matter of perspective. Every node is, of course, collocate to its own collocates if the latter are viewed as nodes.

verted into a computer file with a Kurzweil 4000 optical scan-
ner.[23] I subdivided the text into fifty-five sections, corresponding
to the prologues, introductions, tales, epilogues, and other linking
passages (for example, the Host's three interpolations); and these
and other features were identified by means of tags or COCOA
markers. A typical tag consists of opening and closing diamond
brackets (these ensure that we do not confuse the tags with the
text), a variable name (for the kind of thing the tag concerns) and
a value (for the actual instance of the variable).[24] Afterwards I
compared the Fisher edition of The General Prologue to the text
employed by *The Riverside Chaucer*. The changes introduced only
one new phrasal repetition ("as ye may heere," line 858).[25]

Then I used *TACT*, a text-retrieval and analysis program for
MS/PC-DOS, to turn the tales into a textbase, which allowed me
interactively—on the computer screen—to create indexes, concordances, and collocate tables (lists of all words occurring near a
search word, ordered according to their strength of association)
for any word, word pattern, or combination of these in the text.[26]

---

[23]Unfortunately I do not have the publisher's permission to distribute this text.
However, Oxford University Press plans to publish the electronic *Riverside* text.

[24]For instance, *<SHORTPOEMTITLE GP>* was added to the start of The
General Prologue and tagged each word following—up to the next such tag
(*<SHORTPOEMTITLE KnT>*)—as belonging to The General Prologue.

[25]Some repetitions in later tales may have been missed owing to differences
between the Fisher and Riverside editions of the rest of the tales, but the proper
way to handle these variants would be to go back to the original manuscripts. That
was beyond the scope of my study.

[26]*TACT*, written by John Bradley and Lidio Presutti, with help from Michael
Stairs, is available with a manual by writing the Centre for Computing in the
Humanities, Robarts Library, University of Toronto, 130 St. George St., Toronto,
Ont. M5S 1A5, Canada. *TACT* may also be obtained by FTP over the network.
After accessing the Toronto server, "epas.utoronto.ca," and signing on as "anony-

TACT's ancillary program, *COLLGEN*, permitted me to list every exact repeated phrase (from two to eight words long) throughout the 182,000-word poem.[27] When run on The General Prologue, *COLLGEN* produces 1695 entries for 639 exact repetends of between two and eight words long, although because the program indexes repetends alphabetically *under each word in it* and records all substrings of a repetend, for convenience of reference, the list has much redundancy.[28] I began identifying from this file all exact repetitions of any phrases in the total poem. Surprisingly, Chaucer repeated whole and near-whole lines. The *Riverside* edition notices nine of them, but at least another twenty-five exist.[29]

Using *TACT*, I manually searched the tales for each content word in The General Prologue, looking for collocations with other nearby words as well as searching each word's concordance for patterns of repetition. Because TACT allowed searching for "regular expressions" (word patterns with "wildcards"), I was able to collect all inflectional forms of a given word. In this way, query-by-query, the repetitions grew. After the first pass through The General Prologue, I roughly classified repeating patterns, sifted out strings of function words, and added prepositional phrases. While resembling single content words, prepositional phrases are idiomatic units.

---

mous" with one's own computer name and address as the password, change directory to "/pub/cch/tact" and select the files for transferring.

[27]This program took four to five hours and 60 Mb of hard disk space to produce the list of repeated phrases in a file exceeding 4 Mb in size. An 86-386 MS/PC-DOS microcomputer was used.

[28]The phrase "he was a verray parfit," for instance, has six substrings around the key word "verray": *word* + "verray," "verray" + *word*, *word* + *word* + "verray," etc. This repetend will also be exhaustively indexed under "he," "was," "a" and "parfit."

[29]See Appendix. Asterisked repetends do not appear to be noticed in *Riverside*.

To record repetitions fully and precisely, I represented each by a special notation that included metacharacters employed in *TACT* search requests. These derive ultimately from UNIX regular expressions and, like "wildcards" in computer file management, retrieve different realizations of the same repeated pattern at once. Consider the first three repetitions in the list (Table I).[30]

Table I: First Three Repetitions

Ref. No.	Repetend	Locations	DB No.
1	(the I yonge I sonne I hath , that) I in I the I ram) & y*ronne	GP 7–8; SqT 385–86	1
2	shoures & droghte	GP 1–2; MilT 3196; SqT 118	2
3	corages* & pilgr[iy]mages*	GP 11–12, 21–22; KnT 2213–14	3

This annotation preserves eight variants of the three phrases. An asterisk indicates that the preceding letter (e.g., "y" in "yronne") may be present zero, one, or many times. The square brackets surround characters, only one of which may appear at this point (for instance, "[iy]" for "pilgrimages" or "pilgrymages"). A bar ("I") means that the two words or phrases it links follow one another in that order. An ampersand ("&") represents a collocation: that is, the two words or phrases it connects may appear together in any order (generally within ten words of one another). Finally, parentheses group words or phrases. This grouping has two aspects. The first and last parentheses in the first rule specify that the seven-slot sequence, not just the word "ram," col-

[30]My main data files are available for FTP access from the host epas.utoronto.ca (subdirectory /pub/cch/chaucer).

locates with "y*ronne."[31] Second, parentheses group alternative words. For instance, the seven-word sequence described in the first "rule" varies in the fourth slot: "the yonge sonne" and "in the ram" are connected *either* by "hath" *or* by "that."

Because *TACT* cannot do calculations on the 464 repetitions, I recast them as interrelated tables and imported them into *Quattro Pro 3.0*, a spreadsheet program, and into *Paradox 3.5*, a database management system. *Quattro Pro* does statistical calculations and displays them in graphs. *Paradox 3.5* shares files with *Quattro Pro* and produces subsets of the data tables.[32]

I have described these procedures to show that no program could automatically generate these results. Critical judgement accompanied every step of data collection. Decisions whether to conflate several patterns into one were not always obvious.[33] The graphs and any conclusions drawn from them thus follow from the "rules" on which they are based. Space prevents listing all the repetends here. For that reason I am making the tables available in ASCII delimited form for others to evaluate.[34]

---

[31]If the final parenthesis had been omitted, "y*ronne" would collocate with just the word "ram."

[32]*Quattro Pro* 3.0 (1991) and *Paradox* 3.5 (1990) are sold by Borland International, 1800 Green Hills Road, P.O. Box 660001, Scotts Valley, CA 95067-0001, USA. I selected them because they work together simply.

[33]For example, is the rule "(wel I (ye , I) I woot) , (wel & (ye , I) I woot) , (wel & woot I (ye , I))" one pattern (as I believe) or two? Or would everyone agree that "(the I ho*ly I blisful I martir) , (the I blisful I martir) , (the I ho*ly I blisful I faire*)" exemplify a single phrasal pattern?

[34]They may be obtained by writing the Centre for Computing in the Humanities, Robarts Library, 14th Floor, University of Toronto, 130 St. George St., Toronto, Ont. M5S 1A5, Canada. They are also available for downloading by FTP from the Toronto server (see n. 26 above).

Single words

Lucy B. Palache in *The Princeton Encyclopedia of Poetry and Poetics* defines "repetend" as "A recurring word, phrase, or line . . . usually . . . a repetition occurring irregularly rather than regularly within a poem, or to a partial rather than a complete repetition."[35] She did not coin this word. The *OED* traces it to the neuter gerundive of Latin *repetere* and identifies two English senses: the "recurring figure or figures in an interminate decimal fraction" (from 1714) and a "recurring note, word, or phrase; a refrain" (evidently a late nineteenth-century literary term). Because "repetition" suggests intention—like "formula," "proverb," and "tag"—I use "repetend," which indicates recurrence without implying a prior explanation for it.

Palache regards all words appearing more than once in a text as repetends. Of the 1850 word-types in The General Prologue (different word forms), about 600 appear more than once. Table II gives the forty-one most common lemmatized open-class words in this section of the poem, comprising frequencies 6–38.

Literary behaviorists normally use low-frequency open-class words to describe a work's content and attend less to high-frequency words, since "the value of a word as an indicator of text content is taken to be an inverse function of its frequency of occurrence."[36] Yet high-frequency content words, like high-frequency function words, hold *the writer's general assumptions* ab-

---

[35]*Princeton Encyclopedia of Poetry and Poetics*, ed. Alex. Preminger, Frank J. Warnke, and O. B. Hardison, Jr. (Princeton, 1974), p. 699.

[36]Salton, *Automatic Text Processing*, p. 111. A word occurring a hundred times has a value of 1/10, but one occurring twice has one of 1/2.

out society, human nature, and time because they permeate everything he describes.[37] As Derek Brewer says, stock phrases rest
on "static" concepts.[38] They depend on stable beliefs, accepted
from society or nurtured from within the writer himself.

Table II: High-Frequency Content Words in The General Prologue

38 m[ae]n (man, men)	9 beste*
21 ma*[dk]e*n* (make, made, etc.)	9 y*c[ao]me*t*h* (cam, cometh, etc.)
21 s[ae][iy]de , se[iy]e*n*t*h*	9 go*n , wente
(seyde, seyn, seith, etc.)	9 weye*
20 r[ioy]*de*n* (riden, etc.)	8 horse
18 goode*	8 lovede*
17 tel*e*t*h*n* (telle, etc.)	8 reed
15 faire*r*	8 thynge*s*
15 greet	8 tymes*
14 sp[ae]ke*n* (speke, spak, etc.)	8 wyn
13 worde*s*	7 berd
12 ba*re*n*t*h* (bar, bereth, etc.)	7 gold
12 b*i*g[ay]n*e* (bigan, gan, etc.)	7 knyght
12 right	7 povre
12 tales*	6 bet*r*e*
12 worthy	6 day
11 heed	6 eyen
11 lorde*s*	6 longe*
11 y[aei][fv]e*n* (yaf, yeven, etc.)	6 newe
10 do*n*t*h* (dooth, doon, etc.)	6 wiste
10 y*kn[eo]we*n* (knew, etc.)	6 wys

---

[37]William McColly, "*The Book of Cupid* as an Imitation of Chaucer: A Stylo-
Statistical View," *The Chaucer Review* 18 (3) (1983–84): 239–49.

[38]"Chaucer's Poetic Style," p. 230.

For instance, men dominate women among the pilgrims; the most frequent open-class word is "man" or "men." Story-telling also pervades the poem: see words like "say," "tell," "speak," "words," and "tales" in the list. Means of travel appears in "ride," "way," and "horse." Complimentary adjectives—"good," "fair," "greet," and "worthy"—hint at Chaucer's diplomacy. It is impossible to be sure that *single* words such as "tell" and "tales," or "ride" and "way," of course, are any more closely related than "horse" and "good."

By looking for words that co-occur more often than expected in a random distribution, we see larger, more meaningful structures. Figure 1 graphs the associations among nineteen of the thirty-two open-class words among the ninety-five top high-frequency words, repeating from 9 to 238 times, in The General Prologue. Before searching for collocates I lemmatized the text, ensuring that all word-forms of the same root would be treated as the same thing.[39] This reduced the vocabulary from 1850 to 1401 words. Squares (nodes) on the graph represent the high-frequency words; circles represent the collocates they "attract." Arrowed arcs represent the direction of attraction. For example, three of the four occurrences of the word "curse" (in its various forms) appear within five words on either side of the word "man" (which occurs forty times). In order to compare words of differing frequencies, a z-score procedure ranked the collocates of any given high-frequency node word by descending strength of association.[40]

---

[39]Lemmatization reduced all nouns to their nominative singular, all verbs to the infinitive, and comparative and superlative adjectives to their uninflected form. In addition, words having more than one noun, verb, adverb, or adjective form (e.g., "worthy," "worthiness," and "worth," or "wise" and "wisdom") were conflated into one form.

[40]In 1973 Godelieve L. M. Berry-Rogghe published this method to order a word's collocates by strength of mutual association ("The Computation of Collocations and their Relevance in Lexical Studies," in *The Computer and Literary*

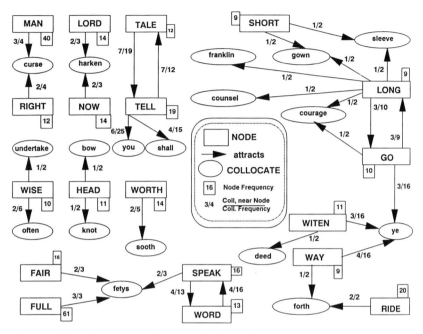

Figure 1. High-frequency Collocating Words in The General Prologue

Every pair of nodes joined by an arc represents repeated collocating terms in The General Prologue. Some structures, including
"tale" and "tell," "speak" and "word," "harken" and "lord," and
"ride" and "way" (the last mediated by a common collocate), are

Studies, ed. A. J. Aitken, R. W. Bailey, and N. Hamilton-Smith [Edinburgh, 1973],
pp. 103–12). This calculates the "expected" number of occurrences of a collocate
within a given span around the node by assuming the occurrences are randomly
(evenly) distributed through the text. Then the expected and actual number of occurrences are compared. A z-score test arranges the collocates in descending order
of associativity. Only collocates with a z-score of 5.3 or higher appear on the
graph. *TACT* includes this collocate table at my request. For a recent application of
this method see Mark Olsen, "The Language of Enlightened Politics: The *Société
de 1789* in the French Revolution," *Computers and the Humanities* 23 (4–5)
(1989): 357–64.

semantic ones. Others are latent phrases, headed by nouns ("short" and "sleeve"), verbs ("witen" and "deed"), or modifiers ("fair" and "fetys"). "Short" and "long" make up a merism; the "man"-"curse"-"right" association speaks volumes in little about Chaucer's Christian beliefs. These arcs, then, indicate semantic fields even if they do not represent them (e.g., why are "tell" and "speak" in different networks and why are "courage" and "long" linked?).

Phrases

By examining all open-class words (not just high-frequency ones), by looking for phrases, and by focusing on repetends from The General Prologue that occur in the tales as a whole, we see semantic clusters. Chaucer's 464 repetends evidently belong to a group of "constituent structures" of his memory when he wrote The General Prologue. Chaucer would have added to these constantly during his life. Each repetend would have had a "birth date." Its availability afterwards would not necessarily have depended on conscious recall. Memory of it might be procedural rather than declarative.[41] Experiments in cognitive psychology show that frequency of use (a "refreshing"), context (including association with other much- or little-used phrases), and "acoustic similarity" affect conscious recall.[42] The situation for unconscious procedural memory is not clear. As Chaucer wrote, he drew previously-stored phrases from memory clusters or made new

---

[41]Larry R. Squire describes how declarative (long-term episodic and "semantic") and procedural memories differ (*Memory and Brain* [New York and Oxford, 1987], pp. 151–74). Global amnesia loses only the first. Memories of words are both. We can consciously recall them and declare their meaning, as well as access them unconsciously as a procedural skill during speaking.

[42]Alan Baddeley, "Working Memory," *Science* 255 (31 Jan. 1992): 556–59.

phrases, each of which in turn joined his memory. A few of these new phrasal repetends survived into later poems, just as earlier ones came to be used in The General Prologue. Open-class repetends, then, reveal part of Chaucer's poetic, his semantic clusters.

Table III gives some facts about some twenty-four repetends with twenty-six repeating structures found in The General Prologue but not in the rest of the tales. Table IV gives the repetends themselves. Chaucer only used one of these repetends elsewhere,[43] and so their attributes may teach us something about why repetends fail to survive in memory. Although the majority, twenty, are two or three words long, six repetends extend to four words, with single instances of five and six words in length. Total function words exceed total content words slightly (forty-three to thirty-eight), albeit five repetends (nos. 11, 17, 24, 26, and 27) consist entirely of content words (and no repetend is made up exclusively of function words). Where function words occur, they tend to run in a string (nos. 5, 13, 19, 21, 23, and 25). Links by sequence or (word) order overwhelm links by collocation or co-occurrence independent of word order: forty-eight to seven. The average repetend, then, has three words (somewhat over half of which are function words), linked by word order six of seven times.

Chaucer repeated at least three (nos. 20, 25, 27) within four lines of one another, possibly for rhetorical effect or for cohesion. Still others, including some prepositional phrases, may arise because Chaucer returned to the subject of the only content word found in the repetend (for example, nos. 4, 6–7, 19, 21–22). Three more repetends (nos. 9, 17, 18) may belong with these. Should we dismiss the rest as accidents? Some readers will believe—and there seems to be no way to decide the question—that Chaucer did not

---

[43]No. 26 also occurs in TC 3.607–08 as a variant according to Tatlock's concordance.

Table III: Formal Characteristics of Chaucer's Repetends

	Units	No. C-S	C-S Size	&-Links	l-Links	Rhyme	FW	CW
Total	81	26		7	48	1	43	38
Average	3.38	1.08	3.12	0.29	2		1.79	1.58
Maximum	7	2	6	1	5	1	5	4
Minimum	2	1	2	0	0	0	0	1

Table IV: Repetends Not Found in the Rest of the Tales

Ref. No.	Repetend	Locations	DB No.
4	in I southwerk	GP 20, 718	253
5	as I ny I as I evere* I he I kan	GP 588, 732	136
6	of & port	GP 69, 138	343
7	in & cote	GP 103, 328	389
8	(cote I and I hood) , ((cote I and) & hood)	GP 103, 564, 612	32
9	arm I s*he I ba*r	GP 111, 158	38
10	faire* I and I fetisly	GP 124, 273	43
11	eyen I step.*	GP 201, 753	85
12	(as I a) & forneys	GP 202, 559	366
13	certeinly I he I was I a	GP 204, 395	22
14	(was I he) & (in I his I contree)	GP 215–16, 339–40	92
15	swich I a I worthy	GP 243, 360	75
16	wel I lovede* I he	GP 334, 634	217
17	faire*r* I burgeys	GP 369, 754	125
18	he I rood I u*p*on I a	GP 390, 541	23
19	but I of I his I craft	GP 401, 692	140
20	of I physik	GP 411, 413	308
21	in I all*e* I the I parisshe , in I his I parisshe	GP 449, 494	411
22	a I po[uv]re I persou*n	GP 478, 702	166
23	he I was I with I eyen	GP 625, 753	26
24	stronge* & wyn	GP 635, 750	218
25	thanne I wolde I he I speken*	GP 636, 638	27
26	sett*e* & soper	GP 748, 815	256
27	now I drawth I cut	GP 835, 838	287

write anything unintentionally, but common sense suggests other-wise. Instances of striking phrases are "cote and hood" (no. 8, which occurs three times), "faire and fetisly" (no. 10), "eyen step.*" (no. 11), "as a . . . forneys" (no. 12), "faire*r* burgeys" (no. 17), and "a po[uv]re parsou*n" (no. 22). These all describe a pilgrim's face, clothing, or social position, Chaucer's professed aim in writing the prologue (see GP 37–41). Seven alliterate or assonate (nos. 8–12, 22, and 26). Another (no. 14) forms a strong rhyming couplet: ". . . was he / . . . in his contree." A small group of repetends do not have a clear explanation: "as ny as evere* he kan" (no. 3), "certeinly he was a" (no. 13), "swich a worthy" (no. 15), "but of his craft" (no. 19), and "he was with eyen" (no. 23). They are longer than the average repetend (at four to six words) and have strings of function words (two to four, consecutively). None, as far as I know, recurs elsewhere in Chaucer's writing.

Why did only no. 26 survive into or from his other poems? If Chaucer's phrases came from memory, this question asks for the "key" to his "remembrance." Scholars have thought that factors external to Chaucer—rhetoric, metrics, and proverbs—might be such a key. These twenty-four lost phrases then pose a problem. Why did "faire and fetisly" and "cote and hood" vanish? Both are "memorable" to readers. The first occurs earlier in *The Romance of the Rose*.[44] A library of "poetic phrases" might store both in long-term memory. Instead, evidence suggests that Chaucer's memory follows general cognitive "rules."

The concept of "working memory," arrived at experimentally by cognitive psychologists and neuroscientists to explain how people commit things to memory, has three parts in its model: a "central executive" brain function and "two slave systems," a

---

[44]See John S. P. Tatlock and Arthur G. Kennedy, *A Concordance to the Complete Works of Chaucer* (1927; repr. Gloucester, Mass., 1963), p. 307.

"visuospatial sketch pad, which manipulates visual images," and a "phonological loop, which stores and rehearses speech-based information and is necessary for the acquisition of both native and second-language vocabulary."[45] Experiments on which this model is based may be relevant to an understanding of Chaucer's poetic memory. One series of tests shows that a working human memory can only "hold"—for memorization—the number of words that the person can utter in one-to-two seconds.[46] Another series demonstrate the "acoustic similarity effect." This shows that "hearing and repeating [phonologically, not semantically] dissimilar words such as 'pit, day, cow, pen, rig' is easier than a phonologically similar sequence such as 'man, cap, can, map, mad.'"[47]

Chaucer must have already "known" these phrasal repetends or they could not have been repeated so soon after they appeared, but he also must have been subject to the same memory constraints people face today. Although all these "lost" repetends can be spoken in or in just under two seconds—their length, then, corresponds to what we have found can be stored in the "phonological loop"—six of the twenty-four are "acoustically similar" (nos. 5, 9, 10–11, 22, 26) and so might be retained less easily. Six have 75% function words (nos. 5, 13–14, 18, 21, 25) and so lack in distinctiveness. The loss of twelve of twenty-four, then, makes

---

[45]Baddeley, "Working Memory," p. 556. See also his *Human Memory: Theory and Practice* (Hove and London, 1990), pp. 67–141.

[46]Alan D. Baddeley, Neil Thomson, and Mary Buchanan, "Word Length and the Structure of Short-Term Memory," *Journal of Verbal Learning and Verbal Behavior* 14 (6) (Dec. 1975): 575–89. For digits, the maximum memory span has been shown to be about eight (Bryan Kolb and Ian Q. Whishaw, *Fundamentals of Human Neuropsychology*, 3rd ed. [New York, 1990], pp. 527–28).

[47]Baddeley, "Working Memory," p. 558. See also his *Human Memory*, pp. 54–57, 72.

sense within the current model of working memory. This may suggest that phrasal repetends, however, are part of declarative rather than procedural memory.

All 464 repetends differ from the subset used only within The General Prologue in ways consistent with this model. Table V shows that the survivors are shorter: their length drops from 3.12 to 2.45 words. An apparent increase in size, from 3.38 to 3.68 words, arises not from length but rather from flexibility: most repetends here have multiple variant forms. Only 8 and 21 among the 24 repetends limited to The General Prologue had variant forms, so that the ratio of all repeating forms (variant and simple) to repetends there was 26:24 (1.08:1). The total repetend population has a 798:464 (1.7:1) ratio. Chaucer, then, appears not to have re-used verbatim tags as well as he did flexible patterns in which sequences could have optional words at various points, or where word order did not matter. The increased collocations reflect this.

Table V: Formal Characteristics of all Repetends

	Units	No. C-S	C-S Size	&-Links	l-Links	Rhyme	FW	CW
Total	1709	798		210	727	10	848	863
Average	3.68	1.72	2.45	0.45	1.57		1.83	1.86
Maximum	17	21	9	3	12	1	15	8
Minimum	2	1	1	0	0	0	0	0

The repetends limited to The General Prologue (ones Chaucer did not use again in the tales) heavily prefer word order to collocation—the ratio of &-links to l-links being about 1:7 (Table III) but the overall ratio is 2:7 (Table V). Word-order sequence still defines the average repetend, but almost a third of them link collocates. Rhyme pairs fixed in a collocation appear once among the 24, but there are just nine instances in the remaining 440, half as many as we might expect. Finally, the ratio of function words to content words has dropped, from 43:38 to 848:863. These results are consistent with the working memory model. Short phrases are easier to recall than long ones. Phrases with "acoustic similarity" diminish, shown here in decreased rhymes. Undistinctive function words play a reduced role in the repetends.

WHAT ACCOUNTS FOR PHRASAL REPETENDS AS A WHOLE?

Traditional Explanations

It is not obvious at first how to classify the repetends as a whole. B. J. Whiting identifies fifteen of them as proverbial and two as a proverb ("And yet he hadde a thombe of gold, pardee," line 563) and as one of seven sententious remarks (Plato's "The wordes moote be cosyn to the dede," line 742).[48] See Table VI for repetends identified by Whiting.[49] He includes some thirty-three comparisons and seven miscellaneous passages among pro-verbial phrases in The General Prologue.[50]

---

[48]GP 162, 256, 438, 500–04, 642–43, 741–42, and 830.

[49]Whiting's proverb, sententious remark, comparisons, and "proverbial phrase" are marked below as *P*, *S*, *C*, and *PP*.

[50]Comparisons are found at GP 69 (p. 167), 89 (p. 168), 92 (p. 167), 113 (p. 173), 152 (p. 162), 179 (p. 161), 190 (p. 161), 198 (p. 163), 205 (p. 163), 207 (p. 157), 238 (p. 161), 257 (p. 177), 267 (p. 174), 287 (p. 170), 332 (p. 160), 357 (p. 168), 470 (2) (pp. 157, 176), 552 (2) (pp. 162, 173), 553 (p. 173), 555 (p. 173), 559 (p. 161), 591 (p. 173), 616 (p. 169), 624 (p. 162), 626 (p. 173), 635 (p. 157), 675 (p. 177), 676 (p. 175), 684 (p. 164), 688 (p. 163), and 774 (pp. 174–75). These entries are ordered alphabetically by the key word of the comparison. On p. 8 Whiting notes that he has thirty-one comparisons, but thirty-three are listed on pp. 155–77, and he has conflated the double similes at lines 470 and 552. Miscellan-eous passages are GP 177 (p. 190), 182 (p. 189), 399 (p. 186), 476 (p. 189), 586

Table VI: Repetends in Whiting's *Proverbs*

Ref. No.	Repetend	Locations	DB No.
28/C	((as | fres*he* | as | is) & May) , ((fres*he* | as & May) , ((as | fres*he* | as) & May))	GP 92*; MerT 1895–96; SqT 281; MkT 2120	25
29/C	eyen	greye	as	GP 152*; MilT 3317; RvT 3974*	80
12/C	(as | a) & forneys	GP 202, 559*	366
29a/PP	sett*e* & cappe	GP 586; MilT 3143	206
30/C	(bro[uw]n.* | as) & (a | ber*y.*)	GP 207*; CkT 4368*	89
31/C	(round.* | as) & (a | belle)	GP 263; PardT 331	103
32/C	(all*e* | of | silk) & (wh[iy]te* | as | morne | milk)	GP 357*; MilT 3235–36*	123
33/C	brood & bokeler	GP 471*; MilT 3266	159
33a/P	thombe & gold	GP 563; SqT 83	198
34/C	that	was	al	pomely	gre*ys*	GP 616*; CYP 559	211
35/C	narwe & (as | a | sparwe)	GP 626*; SumT 1803–04	215
36/C	as	an*	hare	GP 684*, FrT 1327*	451
37/C	ho*te* & (as & (a | goot))	GP 687*; CYT 886–87	235
37a/S	worde*s* & ((cosyn	to) , (ac*ord.*	with) , ((as , bothe , eek)	in)) & de*de*	GP 7441–42; KnT 1775; PhyT 108; MancT 208; ParsT 579, 795	255
38/C	as & sto*ne*s*	GP 774*; MilT 3472*; MLT 670*; ClT 121*; MerT 1818*, 1990*, 2156; SqT 171*	71

Only eleven of these thirty-three comparisons are repetends within the tales.[51] Just one of the seven "other proverbial phrases" repeats itself

---

(p. 190), 652 (p. 189), and 706 (p. 178). Whiting has chosen one of the nouns in each phrase as a basis for alphabetizing the list.

[51]An asterisk in Table VI marks the repetends Whiting found. He also found 11 of 13 in GP and 10 of 19 in the rest of the tales but missed one comparison that repeated itself (no. 103) later in the tales.

later in the tales: "sett*e* & cappe" (no. 206, GP 586; MilT 3143).[52]

Just as there is no one-to-one equivalence between proverbs and repetends, so other classifications fail to account for the diversity we see. Lawrence L. Besserman retrieves the term "merism" from Biblical scholarship to describe "a synechdoche [sic] in which a totality is expressed by two contrasting parts" (e.g., "heven and earth," "old and young")[53] and finds seven in Dame Sirith (450 lines), twenty-three in *The Owl and the Nightingale* (about 1200 lines) and ninety-three in *Havelock the Dane* (2821 lines). There are only five among the General Prologue repetends (see Table VII). Chaucer must have employed dozens more, but clearly he did not use most of them more than once. Merisms are only semantic subsets of phrasal repetends.

Table VII: Merisms Among the Repetends

Ref. No.	Repetend	Locations	DB No.
2/M	shoures & droghte	GP 1–2; MilT 3196; SqT 118	2
39/M	ho*te & co*lde*	GP 420; KnT 1811; MilT 3754; CkT 4348; SqT 520; CYT 252	144
40/M	thou*ghte* & werke*s*	GP 479; ClT 363; CYT 1303; MancT 148	421
41/M	muche*1* & litel*	GP 494; Mel 1215, 1627–28; NPP 2769–70; MancT 350	177
42/M	(heighe* , hye*) & lou*g*w*h*e*	GP 522, 817; MLT 993, 1142; FranT 1035; MancT 361	185

Metrical factors, collocating rhyming pairs, and the alliterative formulas and tags so common in Old English poetry and poems such as *Sir Gawain and the Green Knight* and *Piers Plowman* are no different. Of thirty-four repetends in Table VIII, about 7.5% (eight phrases) cement rhymes (prefixed by "R") and twenty-six

[52]Whiting, *Chaucer's Use of Proverbs*, p. 190.

[53]"Merisms in Middle English Poetry," *Annuale Mediaevale* 17 (1976): 59.

(prefixed by "A") involve strong alliteration, often by collocating terms. Metrics might explain more repetends than proverbs, comparisons, or merisms but does not account for the phenomenon.

Table VIII: Metrical Repetends

Ref. No.	Repetend	Locations	DB No.
1/R	the I yonge I sonne I (hath , that) I in I the I ram) & y*ronne	GP 7–8; SqT 385–86	1
3/R	corages* & pilgr[iy]m-ages*	GP 11–12, 21–22; KnT 2213–14	3
42a/R	gypoun & hau*berge-ou*n	GP 75–76; KnT 2119–20	19
43/R	(atte I beste*) & (to I reste)	GP 29–30; RvT 4147–48	7
44/A	worthy & w[iy]se*	GP 68; MLT 579; FranT 787	15
45/A	me*ke* & mayden*	GP 69; MilT 3202; SNP 57	16
46/R	(litel* I space) & grace	GP 87; MLT 207–08; MerT 1687–88; PhyT 239–40; PrT 603–04; ParsP 71–72	65
47/A	((ful I of) & floures) , (of I floures)	GP 90; FranT 908, 913; MkT 2373; SNT 279	349
48/A	the I monthe I of I May	GP 92; FranT 216	350
49/A	ful I faire*	GP 124, 376, 539, 573, 606; KnT 1523, 2291, 2697; MilT 3322; RvT 3951; MLT 731; MkP 1932; SNT 132, 536	131
50/A	dr[aioy]nken*t*h* & draughte	GP 135; WBP 459; PardP 360, 363, 456	46
51/R	cheere & (of I manere*)	GP 140; SqT 545–46	48
52/A	hardn*e*s*s*e* & herted*	GP 229; MerT 1990; Mel 1317, 1695; ParsT 485	95
53/A	many I a I man*e*s*	GP 229; KnT 2101; Host1 50; WBP 146; ClT 248; MerT 1443, 2408; Mel 995, 1035; MkT 2604, 2629; NPT 2934, 2938, 2975; CYT 985; MancT 326; ParsT 370, 460	69
54/A	so*re I smert.*	GP 230; SumT 2092; MkT 2713; CYT 871	96

55/A	sooth I to I s[ae][iy][en]	GP 284; MilT 3337; MLT 443; MerT 2082; SqT 590; NPT 3021; CYT 1285	60
56/A	tel*e*n*t*h* & tales*	GP 330, 731, 735, 792, 831, 847; KtT 890; MilP 3116; CkP 4360–61; Host1 34; MLT 1167, 1185; WBP 186, 193, 413, 842, 846, 851, 853; FrP 1289, 1300; FrT 1335, 1425; SumP 1671; SumT 1763; ClP 9, 26; MerT 2440; SqI 6; FranW 697–98, 702; PardP 341, 455, 460; PardT 660; Host3 449–50; ThopP 706; ThopT 846; ThopEp 966; Mel 1200; MkP 1925, 1968; NPT 2824, 3149; CYP 597; CYT 1020; MancP 13, 59, 68, 103; MancT, 135; ParsP 21, 46, 53–54, 66; ParsT 1023	251
32/R	(all*e* I of I silk) & (wh[iy]te* I as I morne I milk)	GP 357–58; MilT 3235–36	123
57/A	caus.* & y*kn[eo]w.*	GP 419, 423; WBP 122–23; MerT 1975; SqT 466; FranT 887, 1176	145
58/A	faire* & face	GP 458; WBP 295–96; ShipT 28; ThopT 702	155
59/A	(so*the*r*s* , so*thly , so*thnesse, so*thfastnesse) & (s[ae][iy]d*e*n* , se[iy]s*th*o*[uw]*)	GP 468; KnT 1521, 1625, 2447; MilT 3670; RvT 4319; CkP 4355, 4356, 4357; WBP 195, 450, 601, 666; WBT 941; ClT 855; MerP 1230; MerT 2082, 2125; SqT 536; FranT 770; PardT 686; Mel 1112, 1175, 1342, 1532; MkP 1964; NPP 2781; NPT 3328, 3425; SNT 214, 260–61, 334–35; CYP 662; MancT 143; ParsP 23; ParsT 613, 671, 702, 895	158
33/A	brood & bokeler	GP 471; MilT 3266	159
60/A	spores* & sharpe	GP 473; KnT 2603	161
61/R	.*sel[fv].* & del[fv].*	GP 535–36; SqT 637–38	191
62/A	b[iy]g & (of I bones)	GP 546; KnT 1424	196
63/A	brawn.* & (of I bones)	GP 546; MkP 1941	197

64/A	(wel l (ye , I) l woot), (wel & (ye , I) l woot), (wel & woot l (ye, I))	GP 659, 740, 771; KnT 1140, 1324, 2398, 2400; MilT 3296, 3771; RvT 4255; WBP 27, 30, 55, 63, 79, 200, 849; WBT 1059; SumT 2199; ClT 309, 477; MerP 1217; MerT 1498, 2277, 2343; FranW 708; FranT 885, 972, 1001, 1041, 1323, 1327, 1338; PardI 312; PardT 786; ShipT 173; Mel 988, 1258, 1760; MkP 1917; NPP 2803; CYT 904, 931, 954, 1001, 1206; MancP 32; ParsT 188, 346, 764, 872, 932	59
65/A	y*kn[eo]w.* & conseil	GP 665; MkT 2028	225
66/A	ba*r & (h[iy]m l a) & burdou*n	GP 673; RvT 4165	230
67/A	ho*lde* l up l (his , youre) l h[ao]nde*s*	GP 783; PardT 697	275
68/A	withouten l wordes l mo	GP 808; MilT 3408, 3650, 3819; FranW 702; PardT 678; CYT 1255	278
69/A	shortly l for l to l (tellen* , speken* , s[ea]yn*e*)	GP 843; KnT 985, 1000, 1341; RvT 4197; MLT 428, 564; MerT 1472; PardT 502; ShipT 305; MkT 2355; CYT 1111, 1217	54
70/A	what l nedes*t*h* l wor-des l mo	GP 849; KnT 1029, 1715	297
71/A	whan & (saugh l that l it l was)	GP 850; CYT 1242	299

Grammatical structure gives a clue to repetend function. Fifteen percent are clausal (sentences, complete clauses, and near-sentences); 17% are verb phrases; 25% are noun phrases; and 42% are prepositional phrases. Because the last take noun phrases as their head, the noun—modified by adjectives, introduced by a preposition—dominates two-thirds of all repetends. This distribution corresponds to normal sentence structure.[54] The repetend, then, seems to belong to writing generally.

---

[54]SVO (subject, verb, object), in which two of the three normally take nouns as their heads.

343

Semantic Memory

The working memory model, which explains short-term memory, indicates *why* some repetends might be better retained than others. Paradoxically, repetition itself does not explain *how* repetends are retained. *Association in long-term memory explains their organization and thus our ability to reuse them.*[55] They accumulate in semantically-related clusters of phrases; when these clusters overlap, networks emerge.[56] The "semantic network" model of long-term memory relies on experiments showing that people store not single words or concepts but, rather, words in a phrasal context.[57] The semantic network model explains how Chaucer's repetends (which individually seem chaotic) hold together. For the purposes of textual study, a network is a set of all phrasal repetends that share a minimum of one content word with at least one other phrasal repetend in the group. For example, the first phrasal repetend, "(the | yonge | sonne (hath, that) | in | the

---

[55]Experimental cognitive psychology has shown that repeating a phrase does not aid in recalling it; only context does, the extent of the network of associations that a word or idea or experience has. Instead, "Repetition affects the process of integrating the representation of an event; it establishes its familiarity independent of its context or its relations to other mental contents" ([George Mandler], "Remembering," *The Oxford Companion to the Mind*, ed. Richard L. Gregory [Oxford, 1987], p. 680).

[56]For a recent discussion of long-term memory see Baddeley, *Human Memory*, pp. 328–55, and Squire, *Memory and Brain*, pp. 151–74. Note that "semantic" declarative memory in this field refers to events, facts, propositions, etc., that may be consciously recalled and "declared." People do not, however, consciously recollect semantic networks. Accessing them resembles a procedural skill.

[57]"For example, the word *PIANO* might be presented in either *The man tuned the PIANO* or *The man lifted the PIANO*. Recall was subsequently cued with a phrase such as *something melodious* or *something heavy*" (Baddeley, *Human Memory*, p. 285).

| ram) & y*ronne" (Table I), consists of four content words that do not occur elsewhere in the body of phrasal repetends. It is, then, an out-lier, one that does not associate with any other phrase (in the part of Chaucer's writings discussed here): a network of one. The second repetend, "shoures & droghte," is also an out-lier, but the third, "corages* & pilgr[iy]mages*," forms part of a five-phrase network including "in hire* corages*" (no. 323), "with & corages" (no. 328), "(in, on) & pilgr[iy]mages*" (no. 324), and "of & pilgr[iy]mages*" (no. 459). Thus a network results when two different phrases share a content word at which they may be said to "cross" or "intersect."

The 464 repetends fall into 177 networks of different sizes (15 repetends lack content words and so cannot fall into any network). See Table IX for a breakdown by frequency. Two-thirds of all repetends (67.9%) belong in one multiple-phrase semantic network. Clearly a principle of association operates here. Proverbs, merisms, comparisons, maxims, and metrical patterns account for only a small number of repetends, in comparison. It is not clear how anyone could have produced coherent verse by stringing together phrases from an immense unorganized list. Although people alphabetize *written* words and phrases to make finding them easy, human memory does not store words by their alphabetical order but rather by their context or associations, and Chaucer presumably was like us. These networks might be called "semantic fields," although that phrase describes the range of meanings a word has, not the range of associations any one person gives a word. One of the smaller networks coheres around the content words "black," "flesh," "milk," "red," "silk," and "white." Two different representations of this network will show how an abstract associational cluster—comparable to how concepts might be stored in long-term memory—can be derived from a concordance-like list of phrasal repetends.

Table IX: Phrasal Repetend Networks

No. of Networks	No. of Phrases in Network	Total Phrases
1	153	153
1	20	20
1	16	16
1	13	13
2	6	12
3	5	15
3	4	12
12	3	36
19	2	38
134	1	134
0	15	15
Total: 177		464

I call both representations "phrasal repetend graphs." The first, Figure 2, shows both how various phrasal repetends share the same node word—for example, nos. 74, 154, and 328 all end with the word "red"—and how the non-node words in these repetends belong to still other repetends, which attach to one another in an associational chain. Although the node word "red" does not occur with the word "beard," one of the collocates of "red"—"black"— does. In turn, "black" appears in a phrasal repetend with "silk," and "silk" in another that has "white" and "milk." Another link between the node words "red" and "silk" occurs through the word "white," which belongs both to repetends 74 and 123. The second graph of this cluster (Figure 3) reduces the phrasal repetends to nodes (the shared words, capitalized with boxes), out-lying words (uncapitalized), and arcs (lines with arrows that indicate the direction of the association) labelled with phrasal repetend numbers. Word-forms are lemmatized, and an individual repetend has to be reconstructed by following the arcs labelled with its number, but the structure of the network is clarified. In particular, we can see

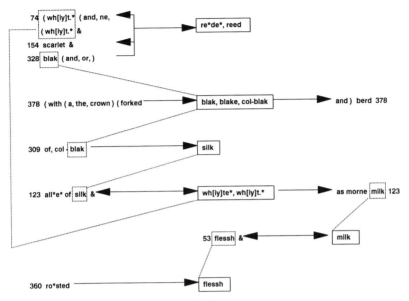

Figure 2. The "White-Red" Repetend Graph

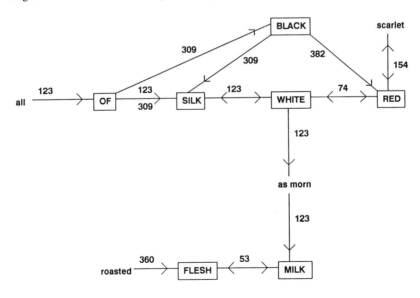

Figure 3. The "White-Red" Network

around which keywords the associational cluster coalesces and is perhaps strongest. Clusters like these draw attention to how Chaucer thought about commonplace things.

The phrasal repetend graph of nodes and arcs has obvious resemblances to a neural network, in which dendrites (arcs) from any one neuron (node) connect with other neuron axons across synapses.[58] The concept of "spreading activation," where stimulating one neuron produces a corresponding if diminished stimulus in all other linked neurons, seems generally consistent with the organization of the phrasal repetends into clusters.[59]

The massive network of 153 phrases breaks down into semantic middle-size clusters linked to one another somewhat weakly by means of single, non-obvious repetends. The largest clusters in this mass center on the words "great" (11 phrases), "man/men" and "woman/women" (21), and "speak," "say," and "tell" (20). Lesser clusters focus on "wine," "ale," and "drink" (8 phrases), "best" (5), "love" (6), "worthy" and "wise" (6), and "way" and "ride" (5). This massive network, that is, comprises clusters of a size like the smaller independent networks, which have between five and twenty repetends each. Clearly the smaller, isolated networks could be easily absorbed into this mass, with the addition of only a few connecting phrases. An analysis of phrasal repetends from Chaucer's works as a whole, however, might not change this distribution, just enlarge its constituent parts.

The speak-tell-say cluster (twenty repetends; see Figure 4) be-

---

[58]Kolb and Whishaw, *Fundamentals of Human Neuropsychology*, pp. 528–32 (note that this is a college textbook).

[59]Baddeley observes that total spreading activation fails to account for various recorded deficits in long-term memory and, following experimental work, suggests that semantic memory falls into "domains," where "different parts of the brain" relate to different kinds of memory (e.g., animate, inanimate, self, etc.; *Human Memory*, pp. 350–54).

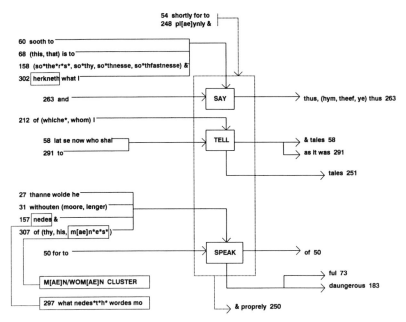

Figure 4. The "Say-Tell-Speak" Repetend Graph

longs to the 153-phrase network, like the *man-woman* and *love* clusters. It distinguishes between speaking (words), telling tales, and saying truths or sooths. Words arise from "need" and belong to the working world: they may be "daungerous" (i.e., disdainful). Truths, in contrast, are said. Soothsayers belong to the contemplative, not active, life. The third utterance, tales, are told, not spoken or said. Chaucer's repetend network both privileges and undermines his tales by dissociating them from work and truth. Is it too far a reach to say this network implies that Chaucer's retraction is based on a scepticism about fictions? He may have had reservations about tale-telling even as he undertook his great, unfinished epic. Last, Chaucer has only three terms that apply to all three utterances: "short," "plain," and "proper." Few readers would disagree that his poetry ranks as the most spare, unflamboyant, unmetaphorical of all major English poets.

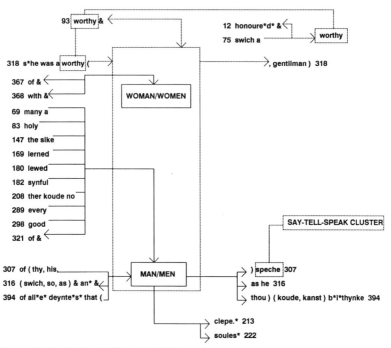

Figure 5. The "M[ae]n/Wom[ae]n" Network

When he speaks of men and women together (twenty-one repetends; see Figure 5), Chaucer calls them worthy, i.e., honorable and wise. In describing men alone, however, the terms "sick," "sinful," "lewed," "learned," "good," and "holy" appear. Chaucer "protected" his women characters from responsibility for moral decisions. While allotting women the same God-given virtues as men, his religious beliefs place them apart from man in the hierarchy of God's creatures. (Dorigen, Criseyde, the Prioress, and the Wife of Bath, for example, tend to escape judgement, at least by Chaucer.) The *love* cluster (nine repetends; see Figure 6) appears morally bi-polar. It is Christian charity (loving one's neighbor as one's self), a remedy and an aspect of chivalry, as well as venery or something "hot" (which may turn goat-like or

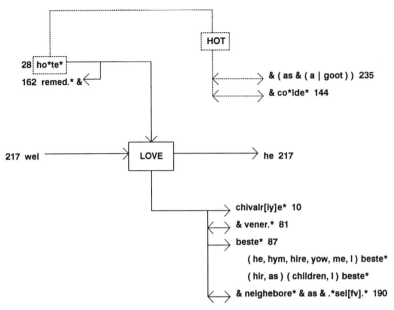

Figure 6. The "Love" Repetend Graph

cold). The cluster also splits along lines of gender. Men are the instigators (the subject of the verb), and women the recipients.

The last two clusters (Figures 7 and 8), *sundry-land* and *merry*, unify fewer repetends (only nine each) but are both separate networks. The first associates people and countries through a common adjective, "sundry," and the latter by collocation to income and livestock. Note that the idioms "now draw cut" and "draw folk to" link this cluster to another focusing on fortune. This kind of (non-semantic?) linkage suggests that the 153-repetend network is a group of smaller semantic clusters. The second cluster behaves similarly. Being merry associates with singing, playing, and being in company (not, interestingly, with milk, silk, and roasts). The phrase "of manere," likewise, attaches merriment to another cluster on poverty and learning, which at first appears separate but may perhaps be connected. Riches and happiness belong together in the Franklin, of all the pilgrims.

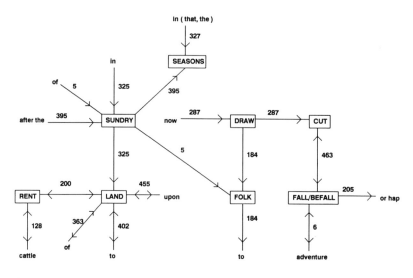

Figure 7. The "Sundry-Land" Repetend Graph

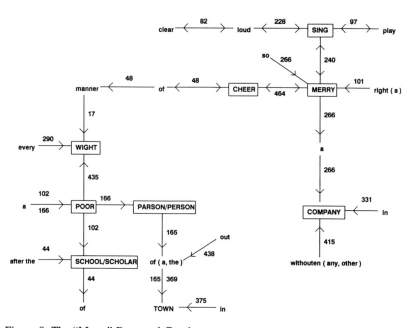

Figure 8. The "Merry" Repetend Graph

These networks give new perspectives on deceptively familiar aspects of Chaucer's writing but they are only fragments and they raise more issues than they settle. First, did Chaucer recall repetend networks consciously from declarative memory or access them unconsciously as a procedural skill with words? Evidence from their form and survivability suggests that they proceeded through working memory, but as a whole they do not look like formulas that could be memorized. They appear part of Chaucer's poetic skill (notice how few of them survive into Chaucer's prose works), but does "semantic style" belong to procedural memory? If it does, then Chaucer could not declare what that skill was, even while he knew it to be an "art." It remained a mystery, to him as to early bards termed "oral formulaic." Second, how does this procedural knowledge, if it is that, relate to musical skill, which operates separably from linguistic skill? More than one memory system is active at once. Finally, although The General Prologue describes all orders of medieval English society, only a few of repetend networks surface *obviously*, that is, repeatedly. By exploring repetends throughout his works, we may see a fuller map. If our own minds are a guide, Chaucer's repetend networks changed over time. They did not form a stable system. Repetend networks in *The House of Fame* (another poem in which Chaucer depicts the whole world in which he lived) are probably not the same as those in The General Prologue.

Besides perhaps revealing something about Chaucer's mind, a map of his repetend networks may help us, when compared with like maps for Gower, the *Gawain* and *Piers Plowman* poets, and still others, to refine an understanding of Middle English. It may suit scholars to define language as single words, but "Experience, though noon auctoritee / Were in this world, is right ynogh for me" to believe that we think in phrases.

REPETEND DISTRIBUTION

Within The General Prologue

If repetends reflect stable aspects of Chaucer's memory, their density from one passage to another should vary according to the degree of conventional subject matter present. To measure this tendency in The General Prologue, I graphed, for each of its thirty-two sections, the actual frequency of repetends against the "expected" frequency (see Figure 9). The expected frequency is the number of times repetends should occur, assuming an even spread of repetends throughout the entire poem. There are about 550 repetend occurrences in 858 lines, but of course the number expected in each section will vary according to its length.

Heavy concentrations of repetends—between a third and twice as many as expected—occur in the descriptions of the Tabard Inn (lines 19–34), the Squire (lines 79–100), the Yeoman (lines 101–17), the Wife of Bath (lines 445–76), the Plowman (lines 529–41), the Manciple (lines 567–86), and the Host (lines 747–57), and in the conclusion (lines 842–58). Some passages, particularly the last, do little more than gracefully knit a fabric of repetends. Consider Chaucer's ends in the poem's final seventeen lines. Words belonging to repetends appear in bold face followed by their numbers in superscript. Underlining distinguishes collocations from fixed-order phrases. Forty-nine percent of the words belong to one or more repetends in this section:

> Anon to drawen **every**[290] **wigh**[290] bigan,
> And **shortly**[54] **for**[54] **to**[54] **tellen**[54] **as**[292] **it**[292] **was**[292],
> Were it **by**[160] <u>**aventure**</u>[160,293], or sort, or <u>**cas**</u>[293],
> The **sothe**[294] **is**[294] **this**[294]: the <u>**cut**[463] **fil**[463] **to**[268]</u> the **Knyght**[268],
> Of which ful **blithe**[295] and **glad**[295] was **every**[290] **wyght**[290],
> And **telle**[251] he moste his **tale**[251], as was resoun,

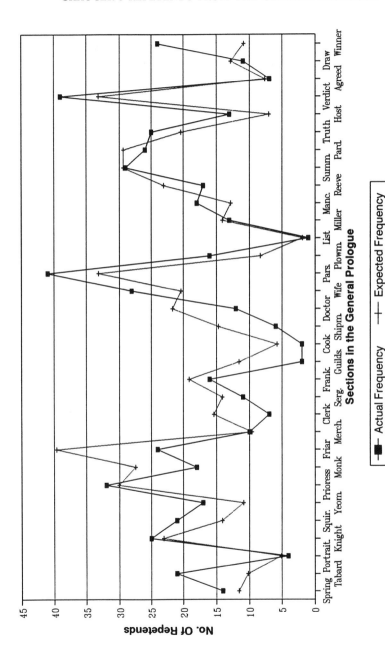

Figure 9. Repetend Distribution in The General Prologue

By[296] foreward and **by**[296] **composicioun**[296],
As[55] ye[55] han[55] herd[55]; what[297] nedeth[297] wordes[297] mo[297]?
And **whan**[299] this goode[298] man[298] **saugh**[299] that[299] it[299] was[299] so[299],
As he that wys was and obedient
To kepe his foreward by his **free**[300] assent[300],
He seyde, "Syn I shal bigynne the game,
What, welcome be the cut, a[301] Goddes[301] name[301]!
Now lat us ryde, and **herkneth**[302] what[302] I[302] seye[302]."
And[56] with[56] that[56] word[56] we ryden[57] forth[57] oure[57] weye[57],
And he bigan with **right**[101] a[101] **myrie**[101,464] cheere[464]
His tale anon, and seyde as[303] ye[303] may[303] heere[303].

In contrast, light concentrations of repetends—between a third and half of what is expected—occur in the portraits of the Monk, the Friar, the Clerk, the Craftsmen, the Cook, the Shipman, and the Doctor of Physic. In phraseology, these passages stand out as unconventional; for example, they contain lists of authorities (the Doctor of Physic) and of place names (Shipman). Despite the liveliness of their portraits, the Prioress, the Miller, the Reeve, the Summoner, and the Pardoner use an average number of repetends.

Throughout *The Canterbury Tales*

Variation in repetend distribution also occurs throughout the complete *Canterbury Tales*. Figure 10 shows how many repetends are expected in each section (assuming they are distributed randomly) in contrast to how many actually appear there. Fragments I–III, V, and VI show approximately the same distribution as a random model predicts, but Fragments IV and IX well exceed expectations, with more General Prologue repetends than expected, and Fragments VII, VIII, and X fall well below the same expectations. The increase appears mainly in The Merchant's Tale and The Manciple's Tale, and the drop just in The Tale of Melibee, The Second Nun's Tale, and The Parson's Tale.

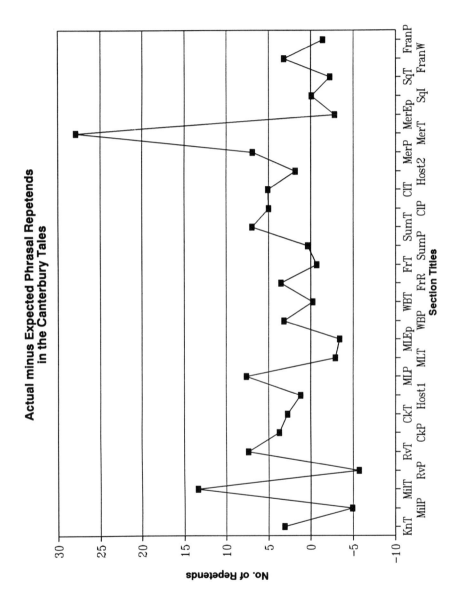

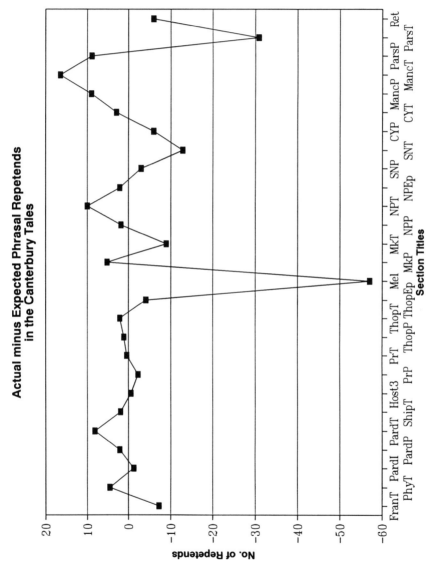

Figure 10. Repetend Distribution by Section in the *Tales*

What explains this variation? The drop in Fragments VII and X might have occurred because Chaucer translated them (and so they contain idioms foreign to his own). Yet The Clerk's Tale, also translated (from Petrarch), has more repetends than predicted. The change from verse to prose in both fragments looks to be a factor. Chaucer's repetend networks may well differ by genre.

The drop in Fragment VIII occurs in The Second Nun's Tale, a poem. Conventionality of expression may be a factor, as The Man of Law's Tale and The Prioress' Tale have marginally fewer repetends than average. "Unconventional," however, is not the term most readers would use to describe The Second Nun's Tale. I think analysis will show that it operates with a significantly different group of repetends than occur in the rest of the tales. Chaucer evidently wrote it before The General Prologue, on the basis of rhyme scheme and the tale-teller's reference to himself as an "unworthy sone of Eve" (line 62). Most editors independently date this tale early in Chaucer's career, about 1373 or 1372–80, well before The General Prologue (c. 1388–92).[60] Chronology, then, may explain the anomaly.

The Merchant's Tale, of all the tales, has by far the most General Prologue repetends. Because it refers often to Jerome's *Epistola adversus Jovinianum*, which Chaucer acknowledged in the revised Prologue to *The Legend of Good Women* (c. 1395–96) but not in the original Prologue (c. 1386–88),[61] The Merchant's Tale has been assigned to 1386–94. These limits center on the five-year period independently suggested for The General Prologue. Again, chronology seems to be a factor.

Next closest are Fragment IX, The Manciple's Tale, buttressed

---

[60]See *Riverside*, pp. xxix, 942.

[61]See *Riverside*, pp. 864, 1060.

by its own prologue and, in Fragment X, The Parson's Prologue. Since the last mentions The Manciple's Tale, the three sections clearly belong together. Dating Fragment IX has proved difficult for lack of evidence. If composed about the same time as the tales in Fragment I, the Host's and Manciple's mocking of the Cook as too drunken to tell a tale would jar with the fragmentary Cook's Tale. Larry Benson says: "Perhaps Chaucer intended to cancel the Cook's Prologue and the fragmentary Cook's Tale."[62] If so, the writing of Fragment IX followed that of the close of Fragment I. Does the repetend distribution, then, imply that Fragment IX and The General Prologue were composed about the same time, after the rest of Fragment I? Or are both The General Prologue and Fragment IX unusually "conventional"?

Table X lists the repetends common to The General Prologue and The Manciple's Tale. Repetends occur at forty-nine places in the tale, about once every five lines.

Table X: Common MancT-GP Repetends

MancT	Repetend	GP	DB No.
107	lusty I bach[ie]ler	80	20
108	in I all*e* I th.* I worlde	412	142
110	u*p*on I a I da[iy]e*	19, 703	238
113–14	s[aioy]nge*n*t*h*s* & pleye*n*	236	97
124	honoure*d* & worthynesse	50	12
129	in I (his , thyn , hire* , hethen , myne* , ootheres , straunge , youre* , the) I h[ao]nde*s*	108, 495	285
130	in I (his , that , the , every , this , myn , thyn , Cristes , noon , hire) I hous	252, 345, 578	202
134	of & m[ae]n*e*s*	575	321
134	every I man*e*s*	841	289
135	tel*e*n*t*h* & tales*	330, 731, 735, 792, 831, 847	251

---

[62]*Riverside*, p. 952.

136	in I all*e* I th.* I worlde*	412	142
138	s[aioy]nge*n*t*h*s* & m[uy]rie*r*l*y*	714	240
139	in I (his , that , the , every , this , myn , thyn , Cristes , noon , hire) I hous	252, 345, 578	202
143	(so*the*r*s* , so*thly , so*thnesse, so*thfastnesse) & (s[ae][iy]d*e*n* , se[iy]s*th*o*[uw]*)	468	158
146	every I w[iy]ght	842, 846	290
146	in & degre*	744	461
148	thou*ghte* & werke*s*	479	421
148	goode* I w[iy]f.*	445	150
165	(mete I (and , his , or) I dr[aioy]nke*) , (mete I and I dr[aioy]nke* I of I all*e* I deynte*s*)	345	119
166	of I all*e* I deynte*s* I that I (m[ae]n , thou) I (koude , kanst) I b*i*thynke	346	394
168	of I gold	160, 196, 563	304
175–76	flessh & milk	147	53
176	(of I s[iy]lk) , (of I col-blak I s[iy]lk)	329, 357	309
177	(saugh , seen) I a I mous	144	52
178	flessh & milk	147	53
179	in I (his , that , the , every , this , myn , thyn , Cristes , noon , hire) I hous	252	202
208	worde*s* & ((cosyn I to) , (ac*ord.* I with) , ((as , bothe , eek) I in)) & de*-de*	742	255
209	(speken* , tellen* , ryme) & proprely	729	250
213	of I (what , his , heighe* , hye*, smale* , ech , no , lou*g*w*h*e*) I degre*	40, 55	334
232	so I gre*te* I an*	318, 674	130
232	(gre*te* I harme*s*) , (gre*te* I an I harme*s*)	385	133
234	m[ae]n I clepe.*	620	213
245	s[aioy]nge*n*t*h*s* & m[uy]rie*r*l*y*	714	240
249	for I his I worthynesse , for I all*e* I thy I worthynesse	50	338
261	with & (eye , eyen)	10, 625, 753	322
263	h[iy]m I thou*ghte*	682	232
276	(of I hewe) , (of I hire* I hewe) , (of I a I leden I hewe)	458	414
283	every I man*e*s*	841	289

297	(all*e* I (his , hir , thy , my , oure) I l[iy][fv].*) , (in I all*e* I (his , my , thy , hir) I l[iy][fv]. *)	71, 459	72
309	by & ensample	520	430
310	t[oa]*k.* & ke*pe*	398, 503	139
318	a I goddes I name	854	301
326	many I a I man*e*s*	229	69
330	at I all*e* I tymes*	534	189
331	of I God	573	440
331	(in I (honours*, honourable)) , (in I greet I honour) , (in I ful I greet I honour)	582	444
346	with & heed	551	436
350	muche*l* & litel*	494	177
361	(heighe* , hye*) & lou*g*w*h*e*	522	185

The longest gap is twenty-eight lines (180–207); the greatest con-
centration, thirteen repetends, occurs at lines 129–48. Other than
repetend no. 251 ("tel*e*n*t*h* & tales"), at line 135, none applies especially to the Manciple's story. Most repetends focus on
very common nouns ("hand," "house," "man," "world," "merry,"
"sooth," "wight," "degree," "thought," "work," and "wife") or
verbs ("tell," "say," and "play"). All belong centrally to Chaucer's
general worldview. Repetends no. 394 and 255 (at lines 166 and
208), however, stand out for length and specificity. The first, "of
I all*e* I deynte*s* I that I (m[ae]n , thou) I koude , kanst) I
b*i*thynke," has three content words, a prepositional phrase, and
a complete subordinate clause. Whiting calls the second a senten-
tial phrase or maxim: "worde*s & ((cosyn I to) , (ac*ord.* I
with) , (as , bothe , eek) I in)) & de*de*." It also has three
content words. Finally, at least three merisms, also specific, occur
(lines 148, 350, 361; cf. 165, 175–76, 178).

Two factors in the unexpectedly numerous common repetends
point to the conventionality of The Manciple's Tale as an explanation: the pervasiveness of common nouns and verbs, and the
spread of repetends throughout the tale. The merisms and the two

very specific repetends suggest that Chaucer echoed himself because he wrote the two works in the same period. Lacking other guidance, we should take both factors seriously.[63]

CONCLUSION

In this essay I discuss phrasal repetends from The General Prologue that occur only in *The Canterbury Tales*. The organization of these repetends reflects Chaucer's mind and suggests that the key to his remembrance may lie in understanding human memory itself rather than rhetorical or literary traditions. Repetends, falling into semantic clusters, may be part of Chaucer's unique "signature." Changing with time, like most people's handwriting, such clusters appear useful in mundane tasks such as assigning a chronology to Chaucer's poems and, once fully collected and analyzed, may enhance knowledge of how Chaucer's usage differed from that of his contemporaries.

---

[63]My analysis of the distribution of all the Manciple's repeated phrases through the tales confirms the distribution found here ("Phrasal Repetends and 'The Manciple's Tale'," in *Computer-based Chaucer Studies*, ed. Ian Lancashire [Toronto, forthcoming 1993]).

IAN LANCASHIRE

APPENDIX:
Single-line Repetends in *The Canterbury Tales*

1. Housbondes at chirche dore she hadde fyve (GP 460, WBP 6 ["dore I have had . . ."]; *Riverside*, p. 865)
2. * . . . wynne; / And ther I lefte I wol ayeyn bigynne (KnT 891–92, SqT 669–70)
3. For in this world he loved no man so (KnT 1196, SNT 236; *Riverside*, p. 831)
4. * In swich a gyse as I you tellen shal (KnT 1208, SqT 332 [". . . I shal to yow seyn"], 540 [". . . I have seyd above"])
5. * But seen his lady shal he nevere mo (KnT 1352, 1357 ["For seen . . ."])
6. * That is, or shal, whil that the world may dure (KnT 1360, MLT 1078 ["Hath seyn or shal . . ."])
7. * Is riden into the feeldes hym to pleye (KnT 1503, Melibee 968)
8. For pitee renneth soone in gentil herte (KnT 1761, MerT 1986 ["Lo, pitee . . ."], SqT 479 ["That pitee . . ."]; *Riverside*, p. 834)
9. * A bowe he bar and arwes brighte and kene (KnT 1966, FrT 1381)
10. * This is th'effect; ther is namoore to seye (KnT 2366, MancT 266)
11. * In al the world to seken up and doun (KnT 2587, MilT 3252)
12. Allone, withouten any compaignye (KnT 2779, MilT 3204; *Riverside*, p. 840)
13. * a wyf, / Which that he lovede moore than his lyf (MilT 3221–22, MancT 139–40)
14. With empty hand men na haukes tulle (RvT 4134, WBP 415; *Riverside*, pp. 851, 869; Whiting H89)
15. * The day is come, I may no lenger byde (RvT 4237, MerchT 1856 ["Now day . . . lenger wake"])
16. * For by that lord that called is Seint Jame (RvT 4264, WBP 312 ["Now by . . ."])
17. And lordynges, by youre leve, that am nat I (WBP 112, MerchT 1456 ["But sires, by . . ."], Mel 1085 ["And sire, by . . ."]; *Riverside* p. 866)
18. * Now, sire, now wol I telle forth my tale (WBP 193, PardT 660 ["But, sires, now . . ."])
19. * And he up stirte as dooth a wood leoun (WBP 794, SumT 2152 ["The frere up . . ."])
20. * Whan that she saugh hir tyme, upon a day (WBT 901, MerchT 2001 ["And whan she .."])

364

21. * "Nay, thanne," quod she, "I shrewe us bothe two!" (WBT 1062, NPT 3426 ["quod he . . ."])
22. * And it shal been amended, if I may (WBT 1097, SumT 2175)
23. * And by that lord that clepid is Seint Yve (SumT 1943, ShipT 227; *Riverside*, p. 878)
24. * And forth he gooth, with a ful angry cheere (SumT 2158, ClT 366 ["Ful sobre . . ."])
25. * And in his herte he rolled up and doun (SumT 2217, PardT 838 ["Ful ofte in . . . rolleth . . ."])
26. Thanne was she oon the faireste under sonne (ClT 212, FrankT 734; cf. *Riverside*, pp. 881, 896)
27. "'This is ynogh, Grisilde myn,'" quod he (ClT 365, 1051; *Riverside*, p. 882)
28. * That day that maked was oure mariage (ClT 497, 854 ["The day . . ."])
29. That is bitwixe an housbonde and his wyf (MerchT 1260, FrankT 805; *Riverside*, p. 885)
30. * And after that he sang ful loude and cleere (MerchT 1845, Topas 771 ["She sang . . ."])
31. * That is or was sith that the world bigan (FrankT 930, MancT 120)
32. * By thilke God that yaf me soule and lyf (FrankT 984, ShipT 115 ["For, by that God . . ."])
33. * And toold hym al as ye han herd bifore (FrankT 1465, 1593 ["And tolde . . ."])
34. * And forth he gooth, no lenger wolde he tarie (PardT 851, NPT 3034 ["wolde he lette"], ShipT 250 ["And doun . . ."])

How to See Through Women:
Medieval Blazons and the Male Gaze

JAMES MILLER

According to Geoffrey of Vinsauf, a good way to begin a sententious work is with an amusingly salacious *exemplum*. That is how I am going to begin this case study of medieval gynophany—the imaginary unveiling of women's bodies by and for the dominating male gaze—though I suspect my modern example of this age-old sexist fantasy would probably have been censured (though not censored) as a vulgar *digressio* by Chaucer's "deere maister soverayn."[1]

The male gaze has never been more cunningly exposed or chivalrously excused than in a romantic scene between Lois Lane and the Man of Steel in the 1978 Hollywood hit *Superman* (absurdly subtitled *The Movie* in case one mistook its celluloid theophany for the Real Thing). When Superman drops by—he literally drops from the heavens onto a penthouse deck—for an exclusive interview soon after his début in Metropolis, Lois finds herself playing two incompatible roles. At one moment she is a tough investigative journalist, aggressively questioning her elusive guest

---

[1] Like Chauntecleer hailing Geoffrey of Vinsauf (The Nun's Priest's Tale), I shall take this opportunity to hail my "deere maister soverayn," John Leyerle, who has never been one to crow over his own "sentence" and "loore." All quotations from Chaucer in this essay have been taken from *The Riverside Chaucer*, Gen. ed. Larry D. Benson (Boston, 1987).

in order to win acclaim at the *Daily Planet* and possibly even a
Pulitzer Prize. At another she is a vulnerable heroine, a Single Girl
in the Big City coyly flirting with the man of her dreams as if they
were on a blind date. A "blind" date it hardly can be, however, for
the normally shy Superman is soon directing his x-ray vision at
Lois amid the dense foliage of her rooftop garden. Their dialogue
is "dangerous" in the old courtly love sense, alternating between
teasingly reticent courtesies and boldly erotic confessions:

> Lois: Is it true you can see through anything?
> Superman: Ah yes, I can . . . pretty much.
> Lois: What color underwear am I wearing?
> Superman: Hmmmmmm. . . .
> Lois: Oh, I'm sorry. I've embarrassed you.
> Superman: Oh no, Miss Lane, that planter you're standing
>   behind . . . it must be made of lead.
> Lois: I see. Do you have a first name?
> [She moves away from the planter and stands before him.]
> Superman: You mean like Ralph, or something? Yes . . .
>   pink!
> Lois: Pink?
> Superman: Pink underwear. . . , you're wearing pink under-
>   wear.
> Lois [shyly]: Do you like pink?[2]

Of course he does, though he is too much of a good old boy to
admit passionate fondness for so feminine a hue. The ethical conclusion one could draw from this revealing scene is that it is hard
to have x-ray vision and remain unembarrassed as a gentleman:
you'd have to be a real superman to see your way out of it—or
through it—without causing embarrassment to the lady.

---

[2]*Superman: The Movie* (Warner Brothers, 1978), screenplay by Mario Puzo,
David Newman, Leslie Newman, and Robert Benton.

What first struck me about this rather courtly scene was its success as a visual allegorization or external projection (in a literal cinematic sense) of a common male fantasy. While some men might dream of flying like the Man of Steel, many more have imaginatively endowed themselves with his voyeuristic ability to penetrate a woman's outer defenses, her clothes, without alerting or alarming her. The woman whose imagined figure is thus exposed is charmed by her visionary voyeur: she has no power (and more importantly no desire) either to hide her charms or to cover her deficiencies. Her will has been temporarily suspended, perhaps even absorbed into that of her male beholder. She may even (like poor Lois) invite the erotic inspector to display his magical powers of visual penetration.

When ordinary unheroic men indulge in this gynophanic fantasy, it is commonly called "mental stripping." Though the fantasy may be played out in dreams, most bouts of it seem to occur during periods when a woman is stationed before the (straight) male eye. I suspect that it is almost always a covert activity, a secret engagement of the male imagination, and therefore should not be confused with "lust of the eyes" or its modern counterpart, "bedroom eyes," which are supposed to be noticed and reciprocated by the person inspected. Should we assume that this imaginative act is an exclusively male fantasy? Certainly not. According to a female oracle I consulted on this question, women can easily play the game of mental stripping but rarely do. They are much more likely to be mental dressers.

Suddenly I feel exposed. I really am not qualified to speak on the female version of this fantasy (if it exists) either in a contemporary social or psychological context or in the medieval rhetorical and philosophical contexts in which I am going to talk about its male realizations. Since mental stripping is a Pygmalionesque act, a creative process of posing and composing in order to vest and divest, its products on the culturally dominant male side have necessarily been countless images of women—Lois in her pink underwear being but the latest in a long line of Galatheas. The medieval images of the feminine I shall be considering are all of this sort. They are not only descriptive and figurative but also erotic in their selection and arrangement of details, sculptural in their impression of surfaces and inner depths, and, most important, x-rayable, that is to say, set up for male intrusion and investigation.

Back to Metropolis for a moment. I couldn't help thinking as I watched Superman's classically platonic eyes zapping their ocular rays into Lois's billowing chiffon evening dress that here was the debased modern equivalent of what medieval Latin rhetors were trying to do in their *descriptiones puellarum*. These highly stylized verbal portraits of women were known in the late Renaissance as "blazons" and are still called that in modern discussions of courtly literature. The Old French noun "blason" originally denoted a painted heraldic shield, but by assimilation with the English verb "blaze" in Shakespeare's day it came to mean an elaborate advertisement for a lady's radiant beauty.

I have long been inclined to dismiss blazons as boring eulogistic set-pieces. Like heraldic paintings they seemed artificially bright, rigidly formal, and not long on psychological interest. My eye, I confess, has always tended to leap over the interminable blazon of Blanche in Chaucer's *The Book of the Duchess*:

> But swich a fairnesse of a nekke
> Had that swete that boon nor brekke
> Nas ther non sene that myssat.
> Hyt was whit, smothe, streght, and pure flat,
> Wythouten hole or canel-boon,
> As be semynge had she noon.
> Hyr throte, as I have now memoyre,
> Semed a round tour of yvoyre,
> Of good gretnesse, and noght to gret.

> And goode faire White she het;
> That was my lady name ryght.
> She was bothe fair and bryght;
> She hadde not hir name wrong.
> Ryght faire shuldres and body long
> She had, and armes, every lyth
> Fattyssh, flesshy, not gret therwith;
> Ryght white handes, and nayles rede;
> Rounde brestes; and of good brede
> Hyr hippes were; a streight flat bak.
> I knew on hir noon other lak
> That al hir lymmes nere pure sewynge
> In as fer as I had knowynge.   (lines 939–60)

And that was pretty far, of course, once he had married her. Now I am inclined to argue that in this portrait there is more going on than meets the eye—than normally meets the eye, that is—for if you examine most blazons (even the most innocent-looking ones) from the supermanly perspective of the medieval rhetor they begin to look like ecphrastic realizations of the fantasy of mental stripping.

What *is* the Black Knight doing in this passage? He is not just praising his lady's physical charms in the beauty-queen idiom of Machaut, whose elaborate blazon of a snow-white damsel in *Le Jugement dou Roy de Behaingne* has long been recognized as Chaucer's immediate source for the description of Blanche:

> White as snow, smooth, pleasantly plump
> Was her throat, and without any wrinkle or bone;
> Her neck was beautiful, which I prize and praise.
>   It's also fitting
> That I speak of her arms, long and straight,
> Which were in every way well-fashioned;
> But her hands were white and her fingers long.
>   As far as I could tell
> Her bosom was white, firm, and high-seated,

371

Her breasts pointed, round, and small enough,
Suiting her body, gracious and agreeable. . . . (lines 361–71)[3]

In contrast to Machaut, Chaucer exposes these idealized features to the imaginary male gaze of an erotic naïf, the I-narrator, who gets in his dream what he has not been able to get in his moribund life: a healthy eyeful of white female flesh. The narrator may or may not have guessed at this point in the poem that the Lady White is in fact dead, her pallor now being that of a corpse. But Chaucer the poet knew it, and John of Gaunt (I assume) knew it, and even the most naïve reader can guess it from the funereal weeds of the Knight and the past tense in which his blazon is delivered.

When the forlorn "chevaliers" in Machaut's *Jugement* praised his lady from head to toe, he used the past tense because she had passed out of his life into the arms of a rival. But she certainly had not passed away. Her living beauty, in fact, was what agonized him and won him his case at the Court of Love. In Chaucer's elegy there is no Court of Love, or question d'amour, or rival—unless Death is considered the Black Knight's rival. Why then does the Black Knight insistently commend his lady's fleshly limbs and round breasts and broad hips and other parts "in so fer as he had knowynge"?

Professor Kittredge (whose eternal rest I am no doubt disturbing by these psychosexual investigations) long ago taught us to regard the blazon of Blanche as perfectly and pleasantly conventional—as if that explains what the Black Knight is doing in his unsettling inventory of the lady's "flesshy" white parts. Was Kittredge a medievalizing romantic at heart? Though he pours scorn on medieval poets for itemizing female beauty and dismiss-

---

[3]Guillaume de Mauchaut, *The Judgement of the King of Bohemia (Le Jugement dou Roy de Behaingne)*, ed. and trans. R. Barton Palmer (New York, 1984). The translation is Palmer's.

es Machaut's blazon for its "total effect of absurd formality," his critical male gaze is nevertheless captivated by the "charm" of the itemized lady. If conventionality can be so charming, think what true poetic originality can do for a woman's sex appeal—even if she happens to be dead. To protect Chaucer from the charge of mere conventionality "in the very place where his indebtedness is most conspicuous," Kittredge makes the absurd claim that certain details in the Chaucerian blazon (he cites the lady's downcast "lokyng" as an obvious example, though it comes straight from Machaut) were undoubtedly "true to life in the case of the Duchess Blanche."[4] Obviously, Kittredge's male gaze—an academic variation of the supervisory eye of Orthodox Victorian Manhood—did not like to risk contact with the leering eyes of brazen hussies or to face the dagger glances of upstart advocates for women's rights. How much truer "to the life" it was, to the romantic life of Black Knights and their patriarchal heirs, for ladies to keep their sharp looks to themselves and their modest eyes on the ground!

You do not have to be a radical feminist reader of Chaucer to blanche (as it were) at the presentation of the lady's body as an object of desire for sensitive connoisseurs, a "fattyssh" but of course not flabby spectacle for male admiration. You do not have to be a rigorous Christian to wonder what could have possessed Chaucer to spread Blanche out before us in this seductive, quasi-necrophiliac manner. Has grief robbed the Black Knight of all sense of propriety? Has "sorwful ymagynacioun" blinded Chaucer to the conventional decorum of the elegy?

Talbot Donaldson (another great Chaucerian susceptible to the

---

[4]On the originality and conventionality of Chaucer as a blazon-writer see George Lyman Kittredge, *Chaucer and his Poetry* (Cambridge, Mass., 1915), pp. 64–66.

charms of downcast female eyes) would have us regard Chaucer as the most tactful of poets.[5] Yet how can we explain away the apparent tactlessness of the poet behind the personas in *The Book of the Duchess*, the idiot savant who praises the pudenda of his boss's late-lamented wife, without resorting to the lame excuse that he was a young poet at the time? I can think of no other dignified, courtly, philosophically serious elegy in our literature that commends a dead woman's virtues by exposing her breasts and extolling her hips. Since my faith in Chaucer's poetic tact is stronger than any Victorian prudery lurking in my soul, I am compelled to wonder whether my conventional (i.e., male) understanding of the rhetorical function of the blazon has not blinded me to the medieval reasons why Blanche's erotic image is graven in the heart of this poem.

Praising a woman's beauty may have been the ostensible social function of the blazon, but beneath its blaze of rhetorical colors it served to expose the bare nature of the feminine before the critical eye of the male rhetor and his male readers. This exposure was persistently erotic, but it could also be satiric or even mystical. Let me expose the blazon for what it is by examining three examples of it from Latin works familiar to Chaucer: first, Geoffrey of Vinsauf's prototypic description of womanly beauty from the *Poetria nova*; next, Joseph of Exeter's anatomical examination of Helen of Troy from the *Yliados*; and, finally, Alan of Lille's luminous exhibition of Lady Nature from the *De planctu Naturae*. When we have learned how to see through women from

---

[5]See, for instance, his reading of the poem as a foreshadowing of modern grief therapy in *Chaucer's Poetry*, ed. E. T. Donaldson (New York, 1959), pp. 952–53: "Chaucer was, of course, far too tactful to point up a lesson in textbook style," Donaldson assures us, thinking, no doubt, of rhetoric manuals rather than anatomy textbooks, "but the knight's speeches progressively demonstrate the fact, if not the knight's realization of it, that despite his loss he has much to rejoice for."

these unelegiac viewpoints, we will come back to Chaucer's elegy for another look at the mental stripping of Blanche.

Geoffrey of Vinsauf offers us two versions of the same female figure—one stripped, the other clothed—much as Goya paints a twin picture of Maja both "nuda" and "vestida." Since the medieval rhetorical term *descriptio* originally denoted a drawing or painting, it is not surprising that Geoffrey's paradigmatic description should read like a series of instructions to an artist. What is surprising about this, however, is that the artist he instructs turns out to be Lady Nature! The rhetor assumes a godlike or supermanlike status superior to the humble craftsmanlike role of Natura; he endows himself with the mythical power to order up from Natura's workshop a female figure entirely in accord with his aesthetic specifications, one that he can examine naked or clothed whenever he pleases without fear of social entanglement or religious censure. She literally comes together before the eye of his mind, part by alluring part, starting with her head and proceeding in an orderly fashion to her toes:

> Let Nature's compass describe first a circle for her head. Let the color of gold be gilt in her hair; let lilies spring in the eminence of her forehead; let the appearance of her eyebrows be like dark blueberries; let a milk-white path divide those twin arches. Let strict rule govern the shape of the nose, and neither stop on this side of perfection nor transgress what is fitting. Let the lookouts of her brows, both her eyes, shine with the lights of gems or stars. Let her face rival the dawn, neither red nor bright, but at once both and neither color. Let her mouth gleam in a small semicircle. . . .

She is nothing if not geometrical, this lady:

> Let her lips, as if pregnant, rise in a swell, and let them be moderately red and warm with a gentle heat. Let order

compose her snowy teeth, all of one proportion; let the fragrance of her mouth and that of incense be of like scent. And let Natura, more potent than art, polish her chin more highly than polished marble.

She gains sculptural solidity the lower down you go:

Let a milk-white column be with its precious color a handmaiden to the head, a column which bears up the mirror of the face on high. From her crystal throat let a kind of radiance go forth which can strike the eyes of the beholder and madden his heart.

If her *throat* can drive Geoffrey mad with desire, think what effect the subglottal regions will have on him! But hold on, a bit of restraint is called for:

Let her shoulders adjust together with a certain discipline, and neither fall away as if sloping downward, nor stand, as it were, upraised, but rather rest in place correctly; and let her arms be pleasing, as slender in their form as delightful in their length. Let substance soft and lean join together in her slender fingers, and appearance smooth and milk-white, lines long and straight: the beauty of the hands lies in these qualities.

So far the public parts of the lady have been shaped, colored, polished, and dressed up by a series of highly concrete and decorative metaphors. The metaphoric production continues for a spell into the semi-private region of the bosom: "Let her breast, a picture of snow, bring forth either bosom as if they were in effect uncut jewels side by side." Thank heavens they are uncut! But now, at last, we are entering the forbidden zone. Suddenly the metaphors cease; the rhetorical veils fall away; and the rest is silence: "Let the circumference of her waist be narrowly confined, circumscribable by the small reach of a hand. I am silent about the parts just below: more fittingly does the imagination speak of these things than the tongue."[6] The rhetorical build-up climaxes in a moment of silence, an interval for the male reader's inflamed imagination to engage in a private inspection of the *belle chose* before Geoffrey takes us on a tour of his lady's legs.

The same pattern of wordy adorning and wordless stripping recurs in his description of how this ideal woman should be clothed. He catalogues the various parts of her wardrobe—golden headband, starry necklace, burnished mantle with a white linen hem, sparkling girdle for tiny waist—as he drapes or fastens them one by one onto her fashionably attenuated figure. This display of "bright attire" culminates in a long rhetorical question in which the male reader (who has barely had time to recover from his last vision of her) is invited to imagine himself as Jove tearing off or burning away every shred of fabric on the bodies of his various Ovidian mistresses before penetrating them in his uniquely Jovial ways. Unlike our scrupulously modest Superman, Jove did not hesitate to employ his superhuman power for erotic ends.

Joseph of Exeter's blazon of Helen of Troy compels the male reader to take an even more penetrating look at the bare nature of the feminine than Geoffrey of Vinsauf's now-you-see-it, now-you don't *descriptio*. Joseph is not what I would call a witty author, but in the following verses from his B-movie rewrite of the Trojan War he comes close to displaying a crackling sort of misogynist humor. His blazon starts off in a Vinsaufian manner with an erotic inventory of Helen's corporeal charms:

> The renowned Spartan woman resembles her Laconian

---

[6]Geoffroi de Vinsauf, *Poetria nova*, lines 564–95 (subject nude) and 601–21 (subject clothed), in *Les arts poétiques de XIIe et du XIIIe siècle* (Paris, 1958), pp. 214–16. I cite the translation of Vinsauf by James Jerome Murphy, *Three Medieval Rhetorical Arts* (Berkeley, 1971), pp. 54–55.

brothers and sisters in face, hair, eyes. Her beautiful face bears a strong family resemblance to theirs. But Leda's daughter drank in more of the starry Jove, and through all her limbs flowed the milky whiteness of the Swan that deceived her mother.

With a bird for a papa, Helen could easily have turned out plain; but the avian genes showed through in all the right ways (at least on the surface), so that her Laconian beauty was enhanced by a divine whiteness. Like Herman Melville, whom he otherwise does not resemble in the least, Joseph is fascinated by the alluring but ultimately evil radiance of his white subject:

Her forehead shines with the whiteness of pure ivory. Her blonde hair is evenly arranged on her head. Her white cheek is like fine linen, her hands like snow, her teeth like lilies, and her neck like the white privet plant. Her ears, which are curved like a blank scroll; her eyes, which act like vigilant guards; her nose, which pursues fleeting odours—each feature strives for the highest honour and claims victory.

Merely to observe Helen is to be drawn into an imaginary Trojan War (including the inevitable divestment scene) going on all around her body. The rhetor's erotic temperature inevitably arises as he lowers his gaze over the rest of Helen's Monroesque physique:

Her slightly protruding chin begins to glow with a white heat, and her lips rise together slightly and swell to form a rosy pout so that kisses, when pressed upon them, might alight there more gently. She is tall with broad spreading shoulders. A tight bodice presses together and conceals her paps. Her flanks are light and slender, her arms long. Her feet are small, and with a lazy gait she lightly skims the ground as she moves on her lascivious way. Her graceful legs lend a decorous poise to her body. Splashed like a drop between her eyebrows is a single mole, which audaciously separates their delicate arches.

Ah, the flaw that makes the gem. Here, if Geoffrey of Vinsauf had been painting the portrait, we would be asked to imagine Paris stripping off Helen's tight bodice and beholding the superficial glories of her pudenda. But Joseph was evidently not content with implicit mental stripping. An explicit dissection was more to his taste. With surprising audacity he endows himself with x-ray vision in order to get under Helen's skin *literaliter*. Through his rhetorical radioscopy we are invited to observe Helen's *interior natura*. At first he encourages us to conclude that her beauty is more than skin deep:

> In like manner her inner nature has secretly adorned the glorious world of her private parts, inhabiting her generative chambers and governing the city of her viscera. Her heart is the prime mover and chief governor of the inner works. Her loquacious lung refines the modulations of her tongue. Her spleen dispenses laughter through a little opening. Her comely little gall-bladder is set afire by quick anger.

Everything seems in pretty good shape. But, alas, there is an inner flaw that proves tragic: "An itching in her tender liver gently titillates her even when she is calm, and overwhelms the remarkable qualities for which she is deservedly famous, and defiles the natural glory of her sexuality." Like a patient etherized upon a table Helen has been penetrated by her male physician in the interests of setting the medical and military record straight. If she had only taken something for her liver condition, there never would have been a Trojan War! No king or hero or any other male figure could possibly have brought on the disaster. And if you doubt that the Trojan War was caused by a woman's ticklish innards, Joseph has this to say to you:

> Her monstrous flaw no ravenous bird, no sliding rock, no spinning wheel, no deceptive wave might overcome. No

sooner has her libido died down after being smashed, cooled, or smothered, than the old fires flare up again when the lobes of the liver are full. Thus a single part defiles Helen as a whole, causing conflict between kingdoms and bringing the whole world to disaster.[7]

Here was an itch that could not be scratched, a woman that could not be satisfied, a world that could not be saved. Where was Prometheus's ravenous bird when the world really needed it?

Joseph was clearly not in the vanguard of the medieval women's movement, and we may condemn him for his ideological short-sightedness. Still, I cannot help admiring his rhetorical cunning, the clever way he manipulated for his satiric ends the erotic function of the blazon as a stimulus for mental stripping. His anatomical blazon turns into a fiery blast against the weakness inherent in the nature of the feminine. In the *Yliados* mental stripping becomes mental flaying.

To complete my triptych of blazons, I shall now turn to the opening sentences of the first prosa of Alan of Lille's *De planctu Naturae*. It sounds very much like a Vinsaufian blazon, at first, but this time Lady Nature is both the female subject of the portrait and the artist who creates and exhibits it to the male eye:

... a woman glided down from the inner palace of the unchangeable world and seemed in haste to approach me. Her hair glittered with a light that was her own—it was not borrowed—for it exhibited a portrait of rays which surpassed mere imitation since it transcended nature from its inborn brilliance and formed in an artistic fashion the image of a woman's head upon a starry body. Without deserting the

---

[7]Joseph of Exeter, *Frigii Daretis Yliados*, liber IV, lines 172–207, in *Joseph of Exeter: Werke und Briefe*, ed. Ludwig Gompf (Leiden and Cologne, 1970), pp. 146–47.

> heavens her hair fell in two unclasped tresses which did not
> scorn to touch the earth laughingly with a kiss. The space of
> a lily white path, divided crosswise under a slanting band,
> parted the strife of her hair. But that slant, I say, did not spoil
> her appearance. It was the outstanding feature of her beauty.
> A golden comb gathered together the gold of her hair into the
> dance of lawful order, and was amazed to discover the simi-
> lar orderliness of her face. Indeed the fantastic appearance of
> the colour, so like gold, caused the eye to draw one false
> conclusion and then another . . .

namely, that the color was merely an optical illusion and that the
hair was actually gold in substance. Her wide and even forehead
(in true Vinsaufian style)

> was truly milk-white like a lily and seemed to vie with the
> lily in colour. Her eyebrows were starry in their golden radi-
> ance. Since they neither spread aimlessly into a forest of
> hairs nor diminished into excessive sparseness, they truly pre-
> served a mean between both extremes. The serene calm of
> her eyes, alluring with their amiable light, displayed the fresh
> beauty of twin stars. Her nose, fragrant with honey-sweet
> odour, was neither too low nor unduly prominent on her face,
> and had about it a certain mark of distinction. The nard of
> her mouth offered her nostrils delicate banquets of fragrance.
> Her lips, rising with a gentle roundness, invited the young re-
> cruits of Venus to kiss her.[8]

So florid, so blazing, so heavily scented with literary allusions is
the language of the *De planctu* that a modern reader may well
wonder how such a luxuriant growth could ever have sprung from
the gritty compost of Late Antique philology and Chartrian

---

[8]Nikolaus M. Häring, "Alan of Lille, 'De planctu naturae'," *Studi Medievali*
Series 3, vol. 19 (1978): 797–879; this is from section ii (prosa 1), lines 1–20, pp.
808–09.

Platonism. The plot of the allegory, by contrast, is almost austere in its simplicity, being little more than a series of entrances and encounters and embraces enacted by a small cast of characters in the tempo of a melancholy adagio. The first character to enter (a moment or two before Natura's descent) is a mournful poet who rails in solitude at the sexual vices of mankind, especially sodomy, and concludes that contemporary lovers are far more sinful than their ancient counterparts.

His elegiac verses are suddenly interrupted by the entrance of the beautiful virgin Natura, who descends from the Primum Mobile and causes the poet's wintry world to blossom with spring flowers. The poet swoons on first seeing the majestic damsel, but she embraces him and with soothing words brings him back to his senses. He observes that she is weeping and politely asks her the cause of her sorrow. This request initiates a long conversation in which Natura consoles the poet with a vision of God's harmonious kingdom, laments the discord caused by human intemperance, and decides to rally her forces against the idolatrous worshippers of Venus, Cupid, and Bacchus. Her divine allies—Hymen, Chastity, Temperance, Humility, and Generosity—enter in the final two prose passages and are embraced by Natura in the joyful expectation that their presence on earth will revive the long-lost Golden Age. Finally, at Natura's summons, a weird wizard-like priest named Genius makes an appearance in order to read a solemn writ of excommunication against the sodomites and all others who break Natura's holy laws. With this anathema the allegory abruptly ends.

The philosophical significance of the poet's description of Natura is rooted in the Latin *Timaeus* and the scholastic commentary appended to it in the fourth-century A.D. by the Middle Platonist Calcidius. Like all Platonic cosmologists, Alan of Lille is eager to describe the visible beauty of the natural world as the original and abiding stimulus for man's philosophical yearning to understand the Divine Plan. And like Calcidius, who had bewailed the "excessively feeble nature of the human race," Alan also laments the corrupted nature of his contemporaries and is wary of the latent incapacity of the human eye to appreciate fully, without distortions or blindspots, the dazzling spectacle of order set before it.[9] Through mournful eyes that are prone to misinterpret the fantastic appearance of the cosmos, he observes a "portrait of rays" representing the light streaming down from the stars and planets. His fascination with the disorderly order of Natura's light is the predictable response of a Platonic cosmologist to the harmonious union of contraries throughout nature, especially to the linking of the ecliptic to the celestial equator. Predictable also is his perception of the luminous design as a single concordant "chorea" recalling the "spectacle of the celestial dance" glimpsed by Calcidius through the dingy curtains of the earth's atmosphere.[10]

Over this Calcidian vision Alan unexpectedly superimposes a second unifying image—a figure springing (one might suppose) purely from poetic fancy. The stars and planets and the incalculable diversity of natural phenomena under their influence are gathered together into the female form of Natura, whom the celestial rays are said to create before the enraptured eyes of the poet. The magically creative light and the form it creates merge in the poet's visual imagination so that he cannot tell the dancer with her flowing hair from the dance that releases and governs its flow. Rays of starlight are transformed by his fantasy into golden

---

[9]See *Timaeus a Calcidio translatus commentarioque instructus*, ed. Jan Hendrik Waszink, 2nd ed. (London and Leiden, 1975), p. cxxxii.

[10]Ibid.pp. cxxiii–iv. On the Calcidian and Chartrian vision of the cosmic "chorea" see James Miller, *Measures of Wisdom: The Cosmic Dance in Classical and Christian Antiquity* (Toronto and Buffalo, 1986), pp. 233–46.

tresses, the beams of the sun into a lady's golden comb, the celestial equator into a sparkling diadem, and the zodiac into a string of beads encircling the diadem at an arrestingly beautiful angle. He also observes how the slanted circuit cuts across "the space of a lily-white path"—the Milky Way. The platonic vision of the concordant cosmos, which in Calcidius could no longer correspond to astronomical observation but had largely become an imaginary construct of nature, has in Alan's allegory become wholly, unreservedly imaginary. Like the dancing light, the poet has assumed the power not only to define but also to synthesize the visual form of the cosmos.

The splendor of Natura's presence the poet declares to be neither a rhetorical fiction nor an artistic imitation at some remove from its model: rather, it is an intense reality that transcends man's ordinary perceptions of the cosmos and paradoxically converts the sublimely arcane into the sublimely commonplace. The rarefied intellectual desire of a platonist to lay bare the eternal design of the cosmos—to strip it mentally of its distracting phenomena in order to perceive its archetypal form—is here translated and subsumed into the common passion of a heterosexual male to feast his eyes on a beautiful woman's body.

By focusing on Natura's physical beauty, Alan seems at first to defeat the moral purpose of his satire. He does not add his voice to the droning chorus of medieval misogynists who denounced the sin of sexual incontinence by insisting that all women (especially women who danced) were vile temptresses ever eager to rob Adam's sons of their eternal reward. If he had actually painted the portrait he describes, and if he had exhibited it apart from its allegorical context, the seductive beauty of the maiden would no doubt have inclined most male beholders (though not as many as Alan might have wished) to engage in the unphilosophical kind of mental stripping—lust of the x-ray eyes.

For their intellectual edification he could have portrayed Natura as a second Lady Philosophy, a heavily draped sombre figure, dignified, mature, nun-like. Natura does indeed retain the majestic stature and star-like eyes of her Boethian ancestress, but there the physical resemblance ends. Sweetly perfumed and glowingly beautiful, Natura first reveals herself to the poet as a graceful nude. Her gently rounded lips call out to be kissed with Ovidian passion by the young recruits in Venus's army, and her small rounded breasts are described with Catullan fondness as "little apples."[11]

Unembarrassed by her nudity, the poet lowers his penetrating gaze to her pudenda, and like Joseph of Exeter, though for mystical rather than satiric purposes, he secretly casts his eye-beams into her "inner room" or "bridal chamber" that is concealed from all other eyes by her unruptured maidenhead. "Within her body," this most intellectual of mental strippers avows, "was hidden a more blessed form than the loveliness shown in her face, which was but its prelude."[12]

The Chartrian platonists might have recognized in this "more blessed form" the symmetrical structure of the platonic World-Soul with its invisible circles representing the rational thought processes of the living cosmos. This geometrical design, glimpsed only by the inward eye of a platonic sage during ecstasy, was foreshadowed in all the externally beautiful aspects of nature and particularly in the symmetry of the astral chorus. Perhaps this mysterious form, since

---

[11]*De planctu Naturae*, ed. Häring, section ii (prosa 1), pp. 27–28: "Mamillarum uero pomula graciose iuuentutis maturitatem spondebant."

[12]Ibid., pp. 31–34: "Cetera uero que thalamus secretior absentabat meliora fides esse loquatur. In corpora etenim, uultus latebat beatior, cuius facies ostendabat preludium." On the image of the cosmic "thalamus" see Miller, *Measure of Wisdom*, pp. 320–33.

it was specifically located within Natura's womb, would have suggested to a medieval platonist the eternal Model from which each thing born in time received its share of visible beauty. It may also have signified the fertile sources of all the models for temporal species, the unchanging life-forms that determined the potential shape of every newly-conceived creature and preserved the characteristics of its family from generation to generation.

These philosophical concepts, strange to say, do not obscure the poet's frankly erotic object of meditation. They remain latent in the gynophanic allegory, unstated and unobtrusive, much as the abiding sources of freshness and beauty in nature lie hidden beneath the surfaces of the visual field. For Alan, the male instinct to gaze upon and penetrate a maiden's womb was more than a mere analogue of the platonists' desire to pierce the barrier of sensory experience and participate in eternity. It was, in its own way, a natural stimulus for participation in the Divine Order.

By responding to Natura's physical graces, glimpsed in the bodies of individual damsels, the young recruits of Venus would be encouraged to procreate new images of the ideal beauty hidden in the universal womb and thus help to perpetuate the moving image of eternity. For modesty's sake the poet draws over Natura's lily-white figure the gossamer veil of air and the translucent mantle of the seas and the gown of the living earth, queenly garments embroidered with the shapes of plants, insects, fishes, birds, and furry creatures; yet as any Venereal recruit will tell you, sumptuous clothing only serves to enhance the allure of the blazon-lady by increasing the desire of those who wish to see her *au naturel*.

We can return to Blanche now with some understanding of why female figures were mentally stripped by medieval rhetors. Geoffrey of Vinsauf was out to prove his superiority to Lady Nature as a poetic craftsman, his Pygmalionesque virtuosity. Joseph of Exeter was out to prove the inherent physical inferiority of women and their moral responsibility for all that is calamitous to the world of men: Helen in her ultimate nakedness, divested of her skin, became the Eve of classical history. And Alan of Lille was out to prove the natural erotic power of the male intellect to transcend all material obstacles in its quest for mystical vision. What does Chaucer (or the Black Knight) prove by showing us how to see through Blanche's robes and beyond her winding sheet?

It cannot have been to demonstrate his supernatural poetic potency: unlike Geoffrey of Vinsauf the Black Knight spins his "new poetry" out of the old philosophical feeling of humanity's desperate powerlessness against the seemingly combined forces of Love, Time, Fortune, and Death. He is a Boethius without a Lady Philosophy to drape in the garments of practical and theoretical wisdom, a Stoic manqué who can only unveil the physical loveliness of the woman he has loved too well and lost. And unlike Joseph of Exeter he cannot be called a mental stripper of the misogynist school. His loving reverie remains just that. It never becomes a contemptuous satiric dissection.

Might Chaucer's not-so-naïf narrator have encouraged the Black Knight to unveil his intimate memories of Blanche's body to him, and to us, for therapeutic reasons connected with the platonic eroticism of Alan of Lille? If so, then Chaucer's boldness in displaying Blanche might not be tactless after all: it might have a subtle intellectual justification not immediately apparent to voyeuristic modern readers.

Set side by side, the blazons of Natura and Blanche blaze with a remarkably similar light. The white radiance of Blanche's peerless skin might be seen as a temporal reflection of the eternal rays that fashion the portrait of Natura before the philosopher-poet's eyes. Both blazons present the female figure in a socially dynamic light before zeroing in on the socially concealed regions of her physique. Just as Natura performs her alluring "chorea" in the heavens, so Blanche is seen to

> . . . daunce so comlily,
> Carole and synge so swetely,
> Laughe and pleye so womanly,
> And loke so debonairly,   (lines 848–51)

here on earth that every male beholder is eager to see more of her. Both blazons emphasize the perfect proportions and measured motions of the female paragon. The Black Knight even acknowledges Natura as the *archē* and archetype of Blanche's beauty in his description of her comely glances:

> Hyt nas no countrefeted thyng;
> Hyt was hir owne pure lokyng,
> That the goddesse, dame Nature,
> Had mad hem opene by mesure
> And close; for were she never so glad,
> Hyr lokynge was not foly sprad,
> Ne wildely, thogh that she pleyde. . . .   (lines 869–75)

Through remembrance, of which such poetry is the key, the Black Knight (and any male spectator aroused by his vision of womanhood) might learn, like the platonist undergoing intensive anamnesis, to see through the love-objects of this world to a higher world where Fortune and Death in their violent attacks on the body cannot strip Blanche of her abiding beauty and virtue. The Black Knight does not glimpse eternity in the poem. He is not Dante. But perhaps, like Alan's complaining poet, he manages to stop complaining by changing his point of view and indeed his way of seeing. We catch him in the process of translating the prurient voyeurism of the Vinsaufian love-poet into the "pure lokyng" of the Chaucerian dreamer.

The Legend of Hugh Capet:
The English Tradition

A. G. RIGG

As I began to write this article, I had just returned from an entertaining lecture on Edward I and Philip the Fair.[1] I noticed that the speaker, when discussing Philip's motivation, did not mention the inferiority complex that might have resulted from his being a butcher by trade, who was rescued from his shop by a French heiress because of his great beauty. The omission is not surprising, as this little-known detail of Philip's biography comes from the fertile imagination of a late fourteenth-century Augustinian friar, John Ergom (who was trying to explain some obscure lines in the verse prophecy by John of Bridlington). Since Philip IV, whatever his faults from an English perspective, is usually credited with an orthodox pedigree and descent from his father Philip III, where did Ergom get this extraordinary idea? The search for an answer takes us through Italian, French, and Anglo-Latin literature, and is, thus, a suitable offering for a scholar of such multidisciplinary interests as John Leyerle. The Italian and French material is already known to scholars in those fields (though it will do no harm to draw it together briefly); the Latin material from England, however, has never been noticed, although

---

[1] Elizabeth A. R. Brown, "Philip the Fair, Nemesis of Edward I," Bertie Wilkinson Memorial Lecture, Toronto, 1 February 1991.

it has been in print for more than a century.

Ergom, in fact, had got his legendary history wrong. The current gossip about the butcher connections of the French royal line was not about Philip IV but about his ancestor, Hugh Capet, founder of the Capetian line in 987. The story has direct bearing on the political history of the time and, in part, testifies to the use of scurrilous tales as part of war propaganda. It was a period when, for example, King David of Scotland was said to have soiled the font at his baptism. This type of underground pseudo-information will be familiar to a veteran of World War II, who will recall the song about Hitler, Himmler, and Goebbels (who had no balls at all). Briefly, the political-historical background is as follows:

1) The ancestry of Hugh Capet, who succeeded the Emperor Louis, last of the Carolingians, was generally unknown to chroniclers.

2) When Philip IV (the Fair) died in 1314, he left three sons and a daughter. The eldest son, Louis X, died in 1316, and his posthumous son shortly after; Louis was succeeded by his brother, Philip V (d. 1322), and youngest brother, Charles IV (d. 1328). Louis X also had a daughter, Joan of Navarre, but she was excluded from succession by the invocation of Salic Law in 1312 to ensure that succession should not pass *to* a woman. As Philip V and Charles IV had daughters only, in 1328 the natural succession would have been through Philip IV's daughter Isabella (wife of Edward II) to her son, Edward III. The French parliament, however, in 1328 extended Salic Law to prevent succession *through* a woman, thus disbarring Edward III. Thus, Philip of Valois, Philip IV's brother's son, succeeded as Philip VI in 1328. (See Figure 1.)

3) Edward III argued that French rules of succession were con-

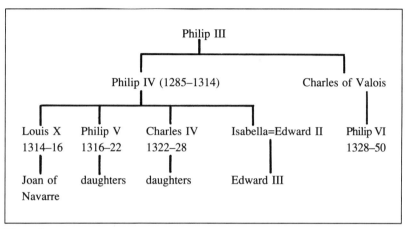

Figure 1.

trary to divine law; perhaps not surprisingly, his appeals to the Pope on this went unanswered.[2] In 1339 he withdrew the homage he had pledged to Philip VI in 1329 as Duke of Guienne, and in 1346 he began a land and sea invasion of France.

Both the French and Anglo-Latin versions of the origins of Hugh Capet associate him with the introduction of Salic Law. It is possible that the "butcher" story arose about 1312, when the future of the French royal line first came into doubt, in time for Dante's use of it.

---

[2]On 5 March 1340 Benedict XII wrote deploring Edward's claim to France and his quartering of his own arms with the fleur-de-lys, arguing that such a descent was contrary to French custom; see *Benoit XII. Lettres closes, patentes et curiales se rapportant à la France*, ed. Georges Daumet (Paris, 1899–1920), No. 699, cols. 427–29. Also in 1340, perhaps in reply, Edward wrote to Benedict explaining the details of his claim to the French throne, namely that he was in the second line of descent from Philip IV, whereas Philip VI was only in the third; he explained also that his act of homage had been made when he was a minor; see *Benoit XII. Lettres closes et patentes intéressant les pays autres que la France*, ed. José M. Vidal (Paris, 1913), No. 2982, cols. 125–30.

The first mention of the story is in Dante, *Purgatorio*, 20:52, completed in 1315.[3] Among the souls in Purgatory Dante encounters Hugh Capet:

> Chiamato fui di là Ugo Ciapetta;
> di me son nati i Filippi e i Luigi
> per cui novellamente è Francia retta.
> Figliuol fu' io d'un beccaio di Parigi.　　　　　(XX.49–52)

> (Then I was called Hugh Capet; from me were born the Philips and the Louis by whom France has recently been ruled. I was the son of a butcher of Paris.)

Hugh goes on to lament the actions of his line down to Philip the Fair (under whom the Whites in Florence had suffered). It was once thought that Dante might have picked up the story on his visit to Paris in 1308–09, but Bossuat (below) rightly points out that such an inherently anti-Capetian story probably arose outside France.

Two fourteenth-century commentators on Dante had further information, though it may not derive from the French or English versions: the elaborations may be their own. Buti says that Hugh was the son of a butcher in Paris but was so virtuous that he became seneschal and privy adviser to the king and so married the king's daughter.[4] In his commentary on the *Purgatorio* made about 1360, Benevenuti de Rambaldis de Imola reported that dur-

---

[3]See, for example, Dante Alighieri, *The Divine Comedy*, trans. with commentary by Charles S. Singleton, *Purgatorio: 2 Commentary* (Princeton, 1973), pp. 476–77, with many references. I would like to thank Joseph Goering for pointing out the Dante reference to me some years ago.

[4]Cited in Dante Alighieri, *La Divina Commedia*, ed. Natalino Sapegno (Milan, 1957), p. 622.

ing his stay in Paris Dante discovered that Hugh was "filius carnificis"; he was named Capet because he used to steal the head-
coverings (*caputia*) of other boys while playing; he refused the
French crown for himself because of a prophecy that his sons
would rule for seven generations.[5]

FRANCE

The fourteenth-century romance *Hugues Capet* turns Hugh's
lowly origins (what Benevenuti called the "vilitatem originis") to
his advantage.[6] The romance was once dated about 1312, but it
may allude to the extension of Salic Law in 1328, and Bossuat argues strongly for 1356–58.[7] It relates that Hugh was the son of a
chevalier who had married the daughter of a Parisian butcher
(making Hugh the grandson of a butcher, not the son). After his
parents' death, Hugh wasted his inheritance and was taken in by
his maternal uncle Simon, who had inherited the butcher's busi-
ness. Hugh was discontented with the butcher's trade, and em-
barked on a career first of debauchery—fathering bastards all over
Northern France, Holland, and Germany—and later of heroism.

---

[5]Benevenuti de Rambaldis de Imola, *Comentum super Dantis Allighereij
Comediam* (c. 1360), ed. James P. Lacaita, vol. 3 (Florence, 1887), pp. 524–27. I
owe this reference to Dr. Giulio Silano.

[6]*Hughes Capet*, ed. Le marquis de la Grange (Paris, 1864).

[7]Robert Bossuat, "La chanson de *Hugues Capet*," *Romania* 71 (1950): 450–81,
and articles by Bossuat in *Dictionnaire des lettres françaises: Le moyen âge* (Paris,
1964), pp. 382–83, and in *Manuel bibliographique de la littérature française du
Moyen âge* (Melun, 1951), pp. 382–83, and second supplement for 1954–60 (Paris,
1961), No. 6770. The legend is discussed by Ferdinand Lot, *Les derniers carolingi-
ens*, Bibliothèque de l'École des hautes études (Paris, 1891; repr. Geneva, 1975),
Appendix 11, pp. 382–83.

The emperor Louis was poisoned by his rival, Savary of Champagne, who then sought to marry Louis' daughter Marie. Hugh championed Marie and her mother Blanchefleur and killed Savary, but Savary's brother Fédry besieged Paris. Hugh successfully aroused the bourgeois of Paris and, with the aid of his many sons, defeated Fédry, married Marie, and was crowned king of France. The French parliament, anxious to prevent a similar civil war between rivals for the heiress of the French throne, passed a law that in future the succession could not pass to a woman:

> Pour çou que la couronne en fu sy convoitie,
> Fu adont acordé par euvre fianchie
> Que, s'en Franche avoit roy qui ne laissast en vie
> Hoir malle aprez se mort, la cose fu jugie,
> La fille n'y aroit une pomme pourie
> For ceulle la douaire où seroit adrechie,
> Anchois prenderoit on en la quinte lignie
> Ung prinche de ce sanc de la roial partie;
> Au jugement des pers de Franche le garnie,
> En feroient ung roy tenant la signourie,
> Que mais famme en tenist derée ne demye,
> Ne qu'elle fust en France con roine servie[8]

(Because her crown had been so coveted, it was then agreed by sworn covenant that if a king in France did not leave a male heir alive after his death—so it was judged—the daughter would not get a rotten apple, except the dowry to which she was entitled. Instead, they would take a prince of the royal blood up to the fifth line. By the judgement of the peers of powerful France they would make him king, holding authority, in such a way that never would a woman get a penny or crumb of it, nor would she be served as queen in France.)

---

[8]Lines 4183–94, ed. La Grange, pp. 175–76. I am indebted to Robert Taylor for the translation.

In addition to providing a stirring tale, the romance celebrates the solidarity of chevalerie and bourgeoisie and produces a politically sound reason for the introduction of Salic Law, clearly intended to be one of the foundation stones of the French monarchy.

There is a brief allusion to the story in Villon, but this could have been taken as easily from Dante as from the romance: "Se feusse des hoirs Hue Cappel / Qui fut estrait de boucherie."[9]

The story of Hugh's origin was not widely known in England. It is not mentioned by chroniclers such as Matthew Paris, Ralph Higden, Henry Knighton, or Ralph de Diceto (who was very anti-Capetian). In fact Thomas Walsingham, an ardent supporter of English claims to the French throne, specifically states that Hugh Capet was the son of Hugh the Great. There are, however, three hitherto unnoticed allusions to Hugh's humble origins.

The Anonymous of Calais

The poem entitled *An Invective against France* consists, in Wright's composite text, of 391 lines.[10] Its author, whom I have

---

[9]*Poésies diverses*, No. 16, 9–10, in François Villon, *Ouevres*, ed. A. Longnon, 4th ed. by L. Foulet (Paris, 1967), p. 98.

[10]*Political Poems and Songs*, ed. Thomas Wright, 2 vols., Rolls Series (London, 1859), 1:26–40, "Francia feminea." There are three manuscripts, of which two are closely related: London, British Library, Cotton Titus A. xx, and Oxford, Bodleian Library, Rawlinson B. 214: see A. G. Rigg, "Medieval Latin Poetic Anthologies (I)," *Mediaeval Studies* 39 (1977): 281–330. The third is considerably shorter, Oxford, Bodleian Library, Bodley 851: see Rigg, "Medieval Latin Poetic Anthologies (II)," *Mediaeval Studies* 40 (1978): 387–407. Wright's text is very inaccurate, so for the lines I have quoted I have retranscribed the texts, using the following sigla (in the order given above): Tx, Rb, Bd.

named the "Anonymous of Calais," wrote other satires against the French and the Scots; he writes in an exuberant meter of variously rhymed hexameters and elegiac couplets, employing Leonines, single-sound couplets, collaterals, cruciferi, and three-part rhymes.[11] There is a great deal of onomastic punning and word play, in Latin, French, English, and even Cornish. This kind of polemic, in which the sound often seems to take precedence over the syntax, has parallels in other Anglo-Latin literature of the thirteenth and fourteenth centuries.[12]

The poem begins with general abuse of the French and of Philip de Valois. France seeks an heir, but it is not Philip but Edward:[13]

> Heredem queris, Philip non est tuus heres. . .
> Tercius Edwardus, aper Anglicus et leopardus,[14]
> Rex tuus est verus, veniens tibi dente seuerus.

> (You seek an heir, but Philip is not your heir. Edward the Third, the English boar and leopard, is your true king, and comes on you savage in tooth.)

Edward says that his act of homage in 1329 was invalid, because he was a minor, and he now revokes it:[15]

---

[11]His other poems are on the battle of Neville's Cross and the siege of Calais; see Wright, *Political Poems*, 1:42–51, 53–58.

[12]For example, the thirteenth-century Michael of Cornwall, the fourteenth-century Robert Baston (who wrote on Bannockburn), and the Scots poet Thomas Varoye (who wrote on the battle of Otterburn).

[13]Wright, *Political Poems*, 1:27 (Wright gives no line numbers).

[14]et: vt Rb.

[15]Wright, *Political Poems*, 1:31.

Quondam seductus iuuenis rex trans mare ductus,[16]
Fraudibus adductus, Christi virtute reductus,
Philippo feci feodum sub lege minorum;
Maior id infeci cum magna laude meorum.

(Once, when I was a young king, I was led astray and taken
overseas, misled by tricks, but called back by Christ's power;
I paid homage to Philip when still a minor. Now I am older I
have invalidated my act, to the great acclaim of my people.)

Philip is unfit to be king: he cannot cure the King's Evil
("morbum non sanas regalem") and the proper oil was lacking for
his anointing ("Deficiens oleum te monstrat non fore regem").[17]
The poet goes into detail on the subject of Salic Law and its institution by the butcher Hugh Capet:[18]

Francorum lege mulieri regna negantur;
A summo rege contraria iura dabantur.
Sub duce carnifice Capoth lex illa dabatur;[19]
Ergo magnifice modo talis rex reprobatur.
Capoth carnificis Hugonis lex fuit illa;[20]
Hec lex ancilla merito priuatur amicis.

(By French law rule is denied to a woman; opposite laws
were given by the highest king.[21] This law was given by the

---

[16]Quondam: Quodam Tx. iuuenis rex trans mare: vltra mare rex male Bd.

[17]Wright, *Political Poems*, 1:32. fore: esse Tx.

[18]Ibid., 1:33.

[19]Capoth: capech Bd; circa anno domini 987 Bd (margin).

[20]Capoth: Caphoth Rb, capech Bd.

[21]See below, p. 400.

butcher Capet, so such a king is now spendidly rejected. This
was the law of the butcher Hugh Capet; this servile law is
rightly deprived of supporters.)

The poet now adds a detail, found nowhere else, that Hugh adopted the name Pippin, presumably to establish a link with the Carolingians: "Nomen mutauit: dictus fuit ipse Pipinus;[22] / Cautus,
vulpinus, legem domini reprobauit"[23] (He changed his name: he
was called Pippin; cunning, foxy, he rejected God's law).[24] Hugh
married the royal heiress of France, but in his pride agreed to a
law that no woman should succeed to the throne:[25]

Heres Francorum regalis nupta Pipino[26]
Munere diuino vixit regina suorum.
Vir suus elatus, per eam nimium veneratus,
Stultus et ingratus, oblitus et insimulatus,[27]
Consentit legi quod femina nulla futura
Succedat regi vel ei sit regia cura.[28]

(The royal heiress of the French, married to Pippin, by God's
grace lived as queen of her people. Her proud husband, too
revered by her, foolish, ungrateful, forgetful and false, agreed

---

[22]Nomen: Nomine TxRb.

[23]domini: domine Tx.

[24]Wright, *Political Poems*, 1:34.

[25]Ibid., 1:34.

[26]regalis: regales Tx.

[27]insimulatus: immoderatus Bd.

[28]succedat: succedit TxRb.

to a law that in future no woman would succeed to the kingship nor have any royal concern.)

This, says the poet, is a law for butchers, not kingdoms:[29] "Carni-
fices pecorum componant iura suorum:[30] / Leges regnorum vertex
non tangit eorum"[31] (Let butchers frame laws for their cattle; the
summit of kingdoms does not touch their laws). He goes on to
show that the "butcher's law" is contrary to divine law:[32]

> Carnifices plane lex est contraria sane[33]
> Voci diuine; donabitur ergo ruine.
> Vox est diuina quod Salphays filia quina[34]
> Juri confesse patris heres vindicat esse;[35]
> Postulant rem iustam, rectam, racione venustam,[36]
> Rem ratam, gratam, diuina voce probatam.
> Summo rege datur lex quod, cum quis moriatur,[37]

---

[29]Wright, *Political Poems*, 1:34.

[30]suorum: duorum Bd.

[31]Leges MSS: Reges Wright.

[32]Wright, *Political Poems*, 1:34.

[33]plane: pane Bd.

[34]Salphays: salphad Bd.

[35]Juri: Ad ius Bd; vindicat: vendicat Bd.

[36]This and the next line omitted by Bd. Postulant: Postulat Rb; rectam: rem Rb.
The faulty meter of "Postulant rem iustam" is explained by the fact that it is a
quotation (see below, p. 400).

[37]This and the next three lines follow "Francorum cor hebet" (below, p. 400) in
Bd. Lex a rege datur domino cum quis moriatur Bd.

Si tenuit bene ius, est heres filius eius;[38]
Si mas defuerit, succedet filia patri;[39]
Filia si deerit, dabitur possessio fratri.
Lex non distinguit; ergo distinguere noli:
    Fraus non extinguit debita iura poli.[40]

(The law of the butcher is quite clearly contrary to God's word, so it will be handed over to ruin. The word of God says that the five daughters of Salphaad (Zelophehad), appealing to the law, claim to be their father's heir. Their claim is just, righteous, pleasing in its reason, valid, welcome, and approved by the voice of God. The law is given by the highest king that, when someone dies, his son is heir if he has kept the law. If a male heir is lacking, the daughter succeeds the father. If there is no daughter, ownership will be granted to the brother. The law makes no distinction, so do not distinguish! Fraud does not extinguish the proper laws of heaven.)

The allusion is to Numbers 27:1–11; the five daughters of Zelophehad appealed to Moses, who asked God's advice; God replied "Iustam rem postulant filiae Salphaad" and laid out the law as the poet has described it. The poet now proceeds to set out Edward III's claim in detail:[41]

Ergo duces, reges, omnes lex tangere debet.[42]
    Francorum cor hebet; deficit ampla seges.

---

[38]bene ius: ius erit Bd; est: erit Rb.

[39]succedet: succedit que TxRb.

[40]Fraus: Fraux Bd; iura: iure TxRb.

[41]Wright, *Political Poems*, 1:34–35.

[42]omnes: plebem TxRb.

Mater Ysabella nostri regis generosa,
Prudens, formosa, virtutum lucida stella,
Regis Francorum Philippi filia cara
Nupserat Anglorum regi, pacis via clara.
Eius tres fratres sine semine morte ruerunt;[43]
Lex, Deus, et patres sibi regni iura dederunt.[44]
Quicquid iuris habet mater proli pia donat;
Proles non tabet sed matris dona coronat.

(So the law ought to apply to all dukes and kings. The heart
of the French is feeble; an ample crop fails. Isabella, noble
mother of our king, wise, beautiful, shining star of virtues,
dear daughter of Philip [IV], king of France, had married the
king of England, a renowned pathway of peace. Her three
brothers fell in death, lacking issue. Law, God and the fathers
gave her the rights of the kingdom. Whatever legal right she
possesses, the pious mother passes to her son; the offspring is
not feeble, but crowns the mother's gifts.)

The lavish praise of Isabella shows just how short human memory
can be. Further, Edward's claim to France is supported by that of
Christ to Judea:[45] "Est Judeorum Christus rex sanguine matris;[46] / Ergo Francorum rex fiet aper vice matris"[47] (Christ is
king of the Jews through his mother's bloodline. Therefore, the
boar will be king of France in right of his mother). Edward is
Duke of Normandy by succession and king of the Scots by con-

---

[43]Eius: Eo Tx; ruerunt: fuerunt TxRb.

[44]et patres: ac pueris TxRb.

[45]Wright, *Political Poems*, 1:35.

[46]sanguine: sub vice TxRb.

[47]fiet: fiat Tx.

quest. The poet now alludes to a story, perhaps echoed by John of Bridlington (below), that the Emperor Charles (which one is not clear) was instructed in a vision that Louis' daughter would succeed him as king:[48]

Karolus imperator, rex patricius, dominator,
Celitus instructus, subito de corpore ductus
Audiuit dici per responsum Lodowyci[49]
Quod rex regnaret sua filia quam generaret.[50]
Nomine materno rexit quasi iure paterno;
Ergo magnifico credamus in hoc Lodowyco.[51]

(The Emperor Charles, noble king and ruler, instructed from heaven, suddenly removed from his body, heard it said in Louis' reply that the daughter whom he (Louis) would bear would rule as king. She ruled in her mother's name but by her father's right. Therefore let us trust in this magnificent Louis.)

The remainder of the poem reports the English victories, taunts the French, and advises Edward to avoid truces.

Even if we discount Bossuat's proposed date of 1356–58 for *Hugues Capet*, it is unlikely that the "Anonymous of Calais" (writing probably 1347–49) knew the romance; if he had done so, he would hardly have passed up the opportunity to write about Hugh Capet's youth of debauchery.

---

[48]Wright, *Political Poems*, 1:35.

[49]Audiuit: Audiui Tx Rb; Lodowyci: lodewici Tx.

[50]rex: om. Tx.

[51]in hoc: nos Bd; Lodowyco: lodowico Rb, lodewico Tx.

John of Bridlington's *Prophecy*

The political prophecy ascribed to John of Bridlington was, in my opinion, written in about 1349–50.[52] It is written in the future tense, and employs several types of cryptogram. It purports to be prophetic, but up to Book III, poem 8, it is fairly clearly a cryptic account of the events from the reign of Edward II to the siege of Calais in 1348–49. From III.9 to the end its allusions are vaguer and less verifiable, but the general message is the ultimate defeat of the French. The passage that concerns us here is III.10: the poet begins by "foretelling" that the Black Death (which began in 1348) will last two and a half years; the Scottish king ("Cancer") will break a treaty, and John (the heir to Philip of Valois) will "refuse the good crown to prosper." After this allusion to French intransigence, the poet continues with a clear reference to the butcher story and Salic Law:[53]

> Nunquam Gallorum cessabit fraus patruorum:
> Carnificum nati patrui de stirpe creati
> Iura paterna pati renuent, quia magnificati,
> Predecessoris proprii quia non meminere[54]
> Iura per uxoris qui regnum cepit habere.
> Dedecus artificem fit propria facta negare,
> Necnon carnificem decreta patris reprobare.

---

[52]See A. G. Rigg, "John of Bridlington's *Prophecy*: A New Look," *Speculum* 63 (1988): 596–613, where previous scholarship on the work is reviewed; some of the material on the Hugh Capet legend was outlined in that article.

[53]I quote from the edition by Michael J. Curley, *"Versus propheciales, Prophecia Johannis Bridlingtoniensis*: an edition" (Ph.D. diss., University of Chicago, 1973); the earlier edition was in *Political Poems*, ed. Wright, 1:123–215 (this passage on p. 206).

[54]On the reading *predecessoris* (*praedecessores* Wright), see Rigg, "John of Bridlington's *Prophecy*," p. 598, n. 8.

(Never will the treachery of the Gauls who descend from the father cease. The descendant sons, born from the stock of butchers, will refuse to endure their ancestral laws, since they are puffed up, because they do not remember their own predecessor, who began to rule through the rights of his wife. It is a shame for a workman to deny his own deeds, and for a butcher to reject the decrees of the father.)

John Ergom's interpretation (below) is wide of the mark, but he is probably right to take *patruorum* in the first line quoted as "descendentium a patre." I have taken *patrui* in the second line similarly; it could conceivably mean (taking *patruus* in its more usual sense) "the sons of butchers, created from the uncle's stock." In the latter interpretation, the "uncle" would be Hugh's uncle Simon, mentioned in the romance; this seems less likely, however, as the Capetians were not descended from Simon. The final line seems to allude to the story mentioned above, that King Louis said that his daughter would reign as "king" after him, an order that Hugh Capet rejected when he allowed Salic Law to be passed.

Could John of Bridlington (whoever he may be) and the "Anonymous of Calais" be the same poet?[55] I am not inclined to think so: although both poets use the rhymed hexameter, their styles are very different; also, whereas the "Anonymous" praised Edward III's mother Isabella fulsomely, John of Bridlington (I.7) refers disparagingly to Roger Mortimer, Isabella's love, and his "illicitis scortis."

John Ergom

We turn now to the writer with whom I began this essay. In

---

[55]For some speculation about the identity of John of Bridlington, see ibid., p. 613.

1362–64 John Ergom, a learned Augustininan friar of York and a collector of texts of prophecies, wrote a detailed commentary on John of Bridlington's *Prophecy*.[56] He explicates the riddling style and explains how the cryptograms work, but, in my view, his interpretations are often wrong. In explanation of the passage from the *Prophecy* cited above (III.10), he writes:[57]

> lex fuit in Francia quod mulieres deberent portare hereditatem usque ad tempus Philippi le Bewes, quem una de heredibus Francie tulit sibi in coniugem de macello propter eius pulchritudinem, et tunc ordinatum fuit quod mulieres non gauderent hereditate propter despectum persone, quod carnifex factus fuit rex; unde omnes reges Francie ab illo tempore de genere fuerunt carnificum.

> (It was the law in France that women should carry the inheritance until the time of Philip the Fair. One of the heiresses of France took him as her husband from a butcher's shop because of his beauty; then it was ordained that women would not enjoy inheritance, because of the disrespect for the person, that a butcher became king. Consequently, from that time all kings of France have come from a race of butchers.)

Ergom is thus a third English witness to the butcher story and its link with Salic Law. Although he gets the story wrong, he knows more than the bare text of John of Bridlington would have revealed: he knows that the story concerns the Capetian kings, and that one of them had been a butcher. The inference that Philip

---

[56]For bibliography on Ergom, see ibid., passim, where I argue that Ergom could not have been the author of John of Bridlington's *Prophecy*, as sometimes supposed; one of the pieces of evidence is his misunderstanding of the "butcher" passage.

[57]I quote from Wright, *Political Poems,* 1:207, removing his classical spellings.

IV had something to do with the tale could easily have been made from his nickname "the Fair" ("le Bews"), but he must have had some other source—possibly oral—that told him that a butcher had been king of France. He also knows that this butcher-king was somehow responsible for a law that blocked inheritance by a woman, thus excluding Edward III from the crown of France. All he, or his informant, has done is to bring the story forward by nearly three hundred and fifty years, detaching it from the first Capetian king and applying it to the last undisputed and stable monarch of the Capetian line.

Thus, these three English writers, the "Anonymous of Calais," John of Bridlington, and John Ergom, offer independent testimony that the disparaging legend of Hugh Capet's origin did circulate in England and that it formed part of the chauvinist propaganda of the early part of the Hundred Years War.

Another Eighteenth-Century Transcription of *Maldon*?

FRED C. ROBINSON

In the volume *Illustrations of Anglo-Saxon Poetry* by John Josias Conybeare (London, 1826), the author's brother, William Daniel Conybeare, the editor of this posthumous volume, included a prose translation of all but the first thirty lines of *The Battle of Maldon*.[1] This translation is as literal as Conybeare's somewhat imperfect command of Old English could make it. One would think, therefore, that the only interest this translation of 165 years ago could have for a modern audience would be its indication of the tastes and accuracy of scholars at this early period in the history of Anglo-Saxon studies.

But in the introduction to his translation Conybeare made an arresting allusion to a "Mr. Price (to whose kindness he is indebted for the transcript whence the following version is made)."[2] The man referred to is Richard Price, the philologist and antiquary who was born in 1790 and died in 1833, just seven years after *Illustrations of Anglo-Saxon Poetry* was published. In 1824 Price had published an edition of Warton's *History of English Poetry*, and in that volume he made reference several times to the poem

---

[1] Conybeare, *Illustrations*, pp. xc–xcvi.

[2] Ibid., p. lxxxvii.

that we call *The Battle of Maldon* and that he repeatedly called "The Fragment of Brithnoth [sic]."[3] Conybeare (p. lxxxvi) said that Price intended to publish *Maldon* "critically in the work on Saxon Poetry which he has announced" and gave this expected edition by Price as the reason why he did not reproduce the Old English text along with his prose translation. Price did not live to complete his edition.

Now what is the "transcript" that Richard Price lent to Conybeare and from which Conybeare made his prose translation? It can hardly be that eighteenth-century transcription of British Museum MS. Cotton Otho A.xii on which our modern editions are based—that which we long thought was made by John Elphinstone but which we now know was made by David Casley.[4] That transcript, from which Thomas Hearne published the *editio principes* of *The Battle of Maldon* in 1726, was lost among Hearne's papers in the Bodleian Library, where, in the words of E. V. Gordon, "[It] has remained ever since [1755], unnoticed by editors and students of the poem, until it was recently identified by Mr. N. R. Ker."[5] Price's transcript can hardly have been made from the published edition by Thomas Hearne, from which it de-

---

[3] *The History of English Poetry, from the Close of the Eleventh to the Commencement of the Eighteenth Century*, by Thomas Warton, ed. Richard Price, 4 vols. (London, 1824).

[4] H. L. Rogers, "*The Battle of Maldon*: David Casley's Transcript," *Notes and Queries* (1985): 147–55. The Casley transcript can now be consulted in *Old English Verse Texts from Many Sources: A Comprehensive Collection*, ed. Fred C. Robinson and E. G. Stanley, Early English Manuscripts in Facsimile, vol. 23 (Copenhagen, 1991), plates 15.1–15.12, and (reduced) in *The Battle of Maldon A.D. 991*, ed. Donald Scragg (Oxford, 1991), pp. 3–14.

[5] E. V. Gordon, ed., *The Battle of Maldon* (London, 1937; corr. repr. 1957), p. 34. For the transcript see Thomas Hearne, *Johannis Confratris et Monachi Chronica sive Historia de Rebus Glastoniensibus*, vol. 2 (Oxford, 1726), pp. 570–77.

parts (as we shall see) in spelling, word division, punctuation, and in other particulars. Also, it is difficult to imagine that Conybeare would seek out and use a transcript of a published book that he could consult in a library or might even own himself.[6]

Since Conybeare published only his prose translation of Price's transcript and not the Old English text itself, we might think that the question as to the nature of Price's transcript must remain forever a mystery. We know that it was a transcript of the same Anglo-Saxon manuscript that Casley transcribed, because in Price's edition of Warton's *History of English Poetry* it is stated that Cotton Otho A.xii was the source of the poem. Moreover, Conybeare's prose translation breaks off at precisely the same verse where the Otho manuscript breaks off. The question before us, then, is whether Price's transcript and Casley's transcript could be two separate witnesses to the Anglo-Saxon manuscript that was lost in the Ashburnham House fire. Does anything survive from Price's transcription on which we might base an exploration of this question?

Several passages from Price's transcript are, in fact, available for comparison with the Casley transcript. Some of these passages are quoted in footnotes to Conybeare's prose translation, when he comments on a problematic reading. Others are quoted in Price's edition of *The Battle of Brunanburh* published as an addendum to

---

[6]The only other way I can account for Conybeare's reference to Price's "transcript" is to assume that this is a rather inexact way of referring to Price's manuscript edition of the poem, which he intended to publish in his projected "work on Saxon poetry" (in which case Price's "transcript" would have interest only as the first attempt to prepare an edition from the diplomatic transcript printed by Hearne). Readers may judge for themselves which of the two explanations best fits the evidence presented here. Although my concern in what follows is to emphasize the value Price's "transcript" would have if it is an independent witness to the text of the poem in Cotton Otho A.xii, I call the reader's attention to the question mark in my title.

Warton's *History* in 1824 (assuming Price would have been referring to his own transcript and not to the Casley-Hearne text, from which he consistently differed in details).[7] Following are collations of Casley's transcript, first with the Old English passages in the footnotes to Conybeare's translation and, second, with the Old English passages from *The Battle of Maldon* quoted in Price's edition of *The Battle of Brunanburh*.[8]

	Price's Transcript	Casley's Transcript
85	ðat hi ðær bricge-weandas bitene fundon	ꝥ hi þær bricg weardas bitere fundon
103	ða wæs fohte neh . tir æt getohte	þa wæs fohte nehtir æt ge tohte
121	ðam burðene ða he byre hæfde	þā burþene þa he byre hæfde
134	Suðerne gar	suþerne gar
189	he geleop ðone eoh . ðe ahte his hlaford . on ðam gerædum	he ge hleop þone eoh þe ahte his hlaford on þā ge rædū
194	Hyra feore burgon . and manna maðon . hit ænig mæð were . gif hi ða gearnunga . ealle gemund-	7 hyra feoreburgon 7 manna ma þoñ hit ænig mæð wære gyf hi þa ge earnunga ealle ge mundon þe he him

---

[7]"Note on the Saxon Ode on the Victory of Athelstan," in *History of English Poetry*, 1:lxxxvii–cii.

[8]Conybeare's errata following p. 286 of *Illustrations* correct *bricge-weandas bitene* to *Bricge-weardas bitere* (line 85) and *maðon* to *ma ðon* (line 194). Also, in his edition of Warton's *History* Price consistently renders ð and þ as *th* in all his quotations from Old English. From the bits that Conybeare quotes it would appear that in Price's transcription the sound is always represented with ð. Price always renders the character *wen* as *w*, as I have done everywhere. In Casley's transcript the Old English character is used.

on . ðe he him to dugoðe . ged- on hæfde	duguþe gedon hæfde
265 Him se gysel ongan . gromlice fylstan	him se gysel ongan geornlice fylstan
285 And seo byrne sang . gryre leoða sum	7 seo byrne sang gryre leoða sū

Warton's *History of English Poetry*	from Casley's Transcript
40 We willath mid tham sceattum, us to scype gangan, on-flot feran, and eow frithes healdan.	we willaþ mid þam sceattū us to scype gangan. on flot feran. 7 eow friþes healdan;
72 Se flod ut-gewat, thá flotan stodon gearowe, wicinga fela, wiges georne.	Se flod ut ge wat þa flotan stodon gearowe wicinga fela wiges georne
168 Tha gyt that word gecwæth, hár hilderinc.	þa gyt ꝥ word ge cwæð harhilderinc
216 Ic will minc athelo, eallum gecythan, that ic wæs on Myrcon, miccles cynnes.	ic wylle mine æþelo eallū ge cyþan ꝥ ic wæs on myrcon miccles cynnes
244 Leofsunu gemælde, and his lind ahof, bord to gebeorge	leof sunu ge mælde 7 his linde a hof bord to ge beorge.

Price's and Casley's transcripts are sufficiently close that there is
no doubt that Cotton Otho A.xii lies behind both of them, and yet
there are enough divergences to suggest that they might have been
independent transcriptions of the same manuscript rather than one
being a rather inaccurate copy of the other. None of the deviations
from Casley in Price's transcript, we should note, is suggested by
readings in Hearne's printed text, which follows Casley slavishly
and mechanically, and so there is no strong evidence that Price

copied from the printed book. Price's word division is generally more rational than Casley's and Hearne's, and his punctuation seems independent of theirs. Among a number of minor differences between the transcripts, the most startling discrepancy is in the next-to-last passage in the first list of collations, where Price has *gromlice* and Casley *geornlice*. Both of these adverbs make sense in the context. Future editors will have to decide which of the transcripts to follow in this instance.[9]

It would seem, then, that we may have two independent witnesses to the poem in Cotton Otho A.xii and that one of these (Casley's) has come down to us complete while the other (made sometime before 1731 and eventually acquired by Richard Price) survives only in bits of the Old English transcript and as the text used by Conybeare in his translation of the poem.

Of what interest, if any, is this to students of *The Battle of Maldon*? If there are two independent transcripts in question, this might be of interest at several points. Up to now, whenever editors or other scholars have discussed textual problems in *The Battle of Maldon*, they have always had to acknowledge that presumed transcriptional corruptions may result from an error either by the original scribe of the Anglo-Saxon manuscript or by Casley in his eighteenth-century transcription. If we now have a second witness to the original Anglo-Saxon manuscript, then we can in some instances determine that a copying error is not an error by the later transcriber (if both transcripts agree) and so must have been in the original Old English manuscript. For example, there are several places in the poem where the narrative flow is broken, and scholars have therefore surmised that there must have been a lacuna either in the eighteenth-century transcription or else in the original manuscript. By comparing Conybeare's translation of the

---

[9]In doing so they should bear in mind that in *The Battle of Maldon* palatal *g* does not alliterate with velar *g*, a fact which tells in favor of *geornlice*.

Price transcript with Casley's transcript we can now establish that if there were lacunae they must have existed in the original Anglo-Saxon manuscript and are not the fault of the eighteenth-century transcribers, since they agree on the amount of text that they copy. It has been noticed repeatedly that *The Battle of Maldon* has several instances of unexpressed pronoun subjects, and one person has suggested that these may be part of the poet's artistry—a way of suggesting the breathless haste of the speeches that the characters make in the heat of battle.[10] Others have thought that since there were two stages of copying during which short words such as pronouns might have been overlooked by scribe or transcriber we should hesitate to see these omitted pronouns as deliberate effects. A reexamination of these passages in the translation by Conybeare may in some cases help us to tell whether the transcribers disagree about omissions. Conybeare's translation, if it is based upon a transcript different from Casley's, would also provide confirmation that unusual proper names in the poem are not the result of errors by transcribers but were apparently the forms that the Anglo-Saxon scribe wrote. In particular we might note that several scholars have suggested that the name *Wigelines* in line 300 may be a miswriting of *Wigelmes* (a presumed form of the Old English name *Wighelm*), the eighteenth-century transcriber having been confused by the minims in the Anglo-Saxon manuscript. But if Conybeare was working from a transcript independent of Casley, then *Wigelines* is confirmed as the original reading in Cotton Otho A. xii.[11]

---

[10]Fred C. Robinson, "Some Aspects of the *Maldon* Poet's Artistry," *JEGP* 75 (1976): 37.

[11]In "A Metronymic in *The Battle of Maldon*?" I have suggested some reasons for accepting the reading *Wigelines*; see *Essays in Honor of Edward B. King* ed. Robert G. Benson and Eric W. Naylor (Sewanee, Tenn., 1991), pp. 239–43.

There are other bits of information to be found in the Old English words and phrases that we have been able to salvage from the Price transcript as it is reflected in the collations presented here. The second quotation in the first set of collations (line 103 of the poem) has two spellings—*fohte* for *feohte* and *neh* for *neah* —that some editors have thought needed emending and that others have suggested are valuable evidence of date and dialect. If two independent transcripts give witness that the Old English scribe wrote *fohte* and *neh* (which is the reading of both Price and Casley), then this would give more weight to the arguments of those who would retain these spellings. The first quotation in the second set of collations would seem to confirm that the genitive *friþes* and not the expected dative *friþe* is the reading of the original manuscript, and if so this may lend support to the argument that this is a deliberately deviant construction used to suggest the grammar of a foreigner speaking Old English.[12]

Needless to say, if we had the entire transcript that Price lent to Conybeare, we would be able to assess its probable origin more confidently than we can from fragments and a translation. I had hoped that there might be an archive of Price's papers preserved in some library in England, but in a reply to my inquiry as to the possible whereabouts of a Casley archive David L. Prior, Curatorial Officer of the Royal Commission on Historical Manuscripts in Chancery Lane, says (in a letter dated 7 August 1990), "I regret that the indexes to the National Register of Archives have no reference to the papers of Richard Price." If Price's papers should turn up somewhere outside of the British Isles, it would be worth the while of an Old English scholar to search for a full transcription of *The Battle of Maldon*, from which it would be possible to determine more certainly whether it represents an independent

---

[12]Robinson, "Some Aspects of the *Maldon* Poet's Artistry," pp. 27–28.

witness to the contents of Cotton Otho A.xii and, if the answer is affirmative, to address other textual problems in the poem.[13]

---

[13]This essay may well seem to some to be too modest in scope and aim to serve as a tribute to so accomplished a scholar as John Leyerle, but by closing with a call for future work by other scholars I believe I may appropriately echo in a small way Professor Leyerle's role throughout his career as an implementer of scholarship. His major role in realizing some of the most important medieval projects of this century, supreme among them *The Dictionary of Old English*, is one which I would want to celebrate on this occasion.

Chrétien de Troyes and His Narrator/s[1]

DAVID STAINES

In his influential late nineteenth-century study, *Epic and Romance: Essays on Medieval Literature*, W. P. Ker offered many insights into the two major literary genres of the Middle Ages. He all but ignored, however, the figure of the narrator. His only explicit comments occurred in his opening chapter:

> Romance by itself is a kind of literature that does not allow the full exercise of dramatic imagination; a limited and abstract form, as compared with the fulness and variety of Epic; though episodes of romance, and romantic moods and digressions, may have their place, along with all other human things, in the epic scheme.
>
> The difference between the greater and the lesser kinds of narrative literature is vital and essential, whatever names may be assigned to them. In the one kind, of which Aristotle knew no other examples than the *Iliad* and the *Odyssey*, the personages are made individual through their dramatic conduct and their speeches in varying circumstances; in the other kind, in place of the moods and sentiments of a multitude of different people entering into the story and working it out, there is the sentiment of the author in his own person; there is one voice, the voice of the story-teller, and his theory of

---

[1]Early versions of this paper were presented at the Medieval Institute, Western Michigan University; the Center for Medieval and Early Renaissance Studies, State University of New York (Binghamton); and the Center for Medieval and Renaissance Studies, The Ohio State University. I am grateful to Alfred David, F. T. Flahiff, and Norris J. Lacy for their careful readings of a later version of this essay.

the characters is made to do duty for the characters themselves. There may be every poetic grace, except that of
dramatic variety; and wherever, in narrative, the independence of the characters is merged in the sequence of adventures, or in the beauty of the landscape, or in the effusion of
poetic sentiment, the narrative falls below the highest order,
though the art be the art of Ovid or Spenser.[2]

For Aristotle, it is the mediating presence of a narrative voice that
distinguishes epic with its authorial presence from drama, the
highest form of poetry, where no such voice is present. Ker virtually ignored Aristotle's distinction between drama and epic and
accorded epic the same high status Aristotle reserved for drama.
Then, like Aristotle, he drew his distinction between genres, in his
case between epic and romance, on the basis of the presence of a
narrative voice.

On the four subsequent occasions when he refers to a narrator,
Ker always revealed his prejudice against this literary figure.
About the *Lament of Oddrun*, he observed:

This form of indirect narration, by giving so great a dramatic
value to the person of the narrator, before the beginning of
her story, of course tends to depreciate or to exclude the
vivid dramatic scenes that are common everywhere else in
the Northern poems.[3]

He praised the Icelandic Sagas because the narrator is not a
presence: "The reserve of the narrator in the most exciting passages of the Sagas is not dulness or want of sensibility; it is a

---

[2]W. P. Ker, *Epic and Romance: Essays on Medieval Literature*, 2nd rev. ed.
(New York, 1957), p. 33.

[3]Ibid., pp. 107–08.

consistent mode of procedure, to allow things to make their own impression."[4] And he singled out the thirteenth-century Saga writer Sturla Þorðarson, the nephew of Snorri Sturluson for special praise:

> he is obliged by the Icelandic custom to keep himself out of the story, except when he is necessary; and then he only appears in the third person on the same terms as the other actors, . . . To let the story take care of itself is the first rule of the Icelandic authors.[5]

Sturla's French contemporary, the historian Jean de Joinville, stands in contrast because of his narrative intrusion:

> Joinville, for all his exceptional genius in narrative, is yet like all the host of medieval authors except the Icelandic school, in his readiness to give his opinion, to improve the occasion, and to add to his plain story something like the intonation of the preacher.[6]

It is evident that Ker, and the many critics who followed him, assumed that epic is a higher order of poetry than romance.[7] The

---

[4]Ibid., pp. 236–37.

[5]Ibid., pp. 270–71.

[6]Ibid., p. 274.

[7]No study of medieval epic or romance written in the first six decades of the century fails to acknowledge indebtedness to W. P. Ker and his writings. For example, the final chapter of R. W. Southern, *The Making of the Middle Ages* (New Haven, 1953) is titled "From Epic to Romance," and Southern notes that "the title of this chapter was suggested by the work of W. P. Ker, *Epic and Romance*, which appeared in 1896 and still retains all its freshness and value" (265). And Eugène Vinaver's *The Rise of Romance* (New York, 1971) uses the Ker volume as

reason for the assumption is simple. Ker's chapter on epic and romance begins with a discussion of Aristotle's *Poetics*, and Ker accepted Aristotle's principles, namely that the truth and validity of poetry lie in its imitation of actions. For Aristotle, Homer was the greatest non-dramatic poet because he, more than any other poet, represented actions and their characters without the mediating presence of a narrator. Homer, Aristotle claimed,

> admirable as he is in many other respects, is particularly so in the fact that he alone among epic poets is not unaware of the poet's own function. The poet should say very little *in propria persona*, for he is no imitator when doing that.[8]

Accordingly, for Aristotle, drama is superior to epic because it attains more effectively the end of imitation, for the narrator disappears completely.

Ker, therefore, had to favor epic over romance because his primary focus is imitation, the basis of Aristotle's approach to poetry. The narrator of romance runs the risk of interfering with the story, of making the story less real, of distancing art from the actions it imitates.

Nearly six decades after Ker's study appeared, Erich Auerbach in *Mimesis* devoted a whole chapter to Chrétien de Troyes, yet he never mentioned Chrétien's narrator.[9] Again the reason is evident. The subtitle to Auerbach's book, "The Representation of Reality in Western Literature," places his position not far from

---

a point of departure for its analysis of romance.

[8]Aristotle, *Poetics*, trans. John Warrington (London, 1963), p. 45.

[9]Erich Auerbach, *Mimesis: The Representation of Reality in Western Literature*, trans. Willard R. Trask (Princeton, 1953), chap. 6, "The Knight Sets Forth."

Ker's: for both critics, realism is the highest goal of literary imitation, drama, letting events speak for themselves, the highest literary form. The tacit assumption is that the less the audience or the reader is reminded of a narrator in the narrative, the truer the seemingly unmediated narrative is to reality.

Early criticism of Chrétien de Troyes was concerned with philology. Then studies focused on sources and analogues: Chrétien became the subject of investigations of the possible Celtic origins of his romances, of the relationship between the Bible and his romances, and of the influence of such Latin sources as Virgil and Ovid. Only in the last two decades has critical attention looked at Chrétien's narrator. And this new direction parallels, to some degree, the advent of postmodernism, structuralism, other developments in criticism, and especially recent reflections on narrative and narratology, which tend to see narrative as an overarching principle that breaks down traditional distinctions between novel and poetry. John L. Grigsby's "Narrative Voices in Chrétien de Troyes: A Prolegomenon to Dissection," for example, identifies Chrétien's narrator through a table of eight voices first applied to Proust's *A la recherche du temps perdu*.[10] Such approaches, however, borrow critical terminology from modern literature and literary studies that may not always be appropriate to medieval literature. The author's relationship to his audience in the twelfth century is different from that of a modern novelist's relationship to his audience, primarily because of the direct connection the twelfth-century narrator has with his audience, the people before him in space and then after him in time. I intend to examine Chrétien's narrator through that narrator's own words to see if we cannot reach some conclusions

---

[10]John L. Grigsby, "Narrative Voices in Chrétien de Troyes: A Prolegomenon to Dissection," *Romance Philology* 32 (1979): 261–73.

DAVID STAINES

about the narrator's function and place, for Chrétien's poetry
occupies a crucial position, both generically and historically,
between epic and romance.

Chrétien's first extant poem, *Erec and Enide*, begins:

> Li vilains dit an son respit
> que tel chose a l'an an despit
> qui molt valt mialz que l'an ne cuide;
> por ce fet bien qui son estuide
> atorne a bien quel que il l'ait;
> car qui son estuide antrelait,
> tost i puet tel chose teisir
> qui molt vandroit puis a pleisir.
> Por ce dist Crestïens de Troies
> que reisons est que totevoies
> doit chascuns panser et antandre
> a bien dire et a bien aprandre;
> et tret d'un conte d'avanture
> une molt bele conjointure
> par qu'an puet prover et savoir
> que cil ne fet mie savoir
> qui s'escïence n'abandone
> tant con Dex la grasce l'an done:
> d'Erec, le fil Lac, est li contes
> que devant rois et devant contes
> depecier et corronpre suelent
> cil qui de conter vivre vuelent.
> Des or comancerai l'estoire
> qui toz jorz mes iert an mimoire
> tant con durra crestïantez;
> de ce s'est Crestïens vantez.[11]

---

[11]Chrétien de Troyes, *Erec et Enide*, ed. Mario Roques (Paris, 1952), lines
1–26. All quotations from Chrétien's romances are taken from the editions based
on Bibliothèque Nationale manuscript 794 in the Classiques Français du Moyen
Age series. The other romances are *Cliges*, ed. Alexandre Micha (Paris, 1957); *Le*

(The Peasant has a proverb: "What you scorn may be worth much more than you think." For the man does well who turns to good use whatever talents he has, while the man who neglects his talents could well be being silent about something which otherwise might bring much delight. That is why Christian of Troyes maintains it is right that all always aspire and endeavor to speak eloquently and to teach well. And he elicits a most pleasing pattern from a tale of adventure, in order to demonstrate and to prove that the man does not act wisely who fails to make full use of his knowledge so long as God grants him the grace to do so.

This is the tale of Erec, the son of Lac, which those who wish to make their living by storytelling in the presence of counts and kings usually mutilate and spoil. Now I am going to begin the story that henceforth will be remembered as long as Christianity endures. This is Christian's boast.)

In this announcement, Chrétien is setting himself up in opposition to storytellers, *conteurs*, who earn their living through their tales. He himself is eliciting from a tale of adventure a most pleasing pattern, his own composition. In his writings he uses the noun *conte*, meaning tale or story, twenty-seven times. Most often it means a simple story, either the tale Chrétien received from his source, or a story recounted in his own poem, such as Calogrenant's tale of his adventure in *The Knight with the Lion. Conte* is a story, a sequence of actions or events that is not carefully designed. Sometimes there is even a pejorative connotation:

Lors li conta et reconut
comant Erec vint a Laluth,

Chevalier de la charette, ed. Mario Roques (Paris, 1958); *Le Chevalier au lion*, ed. Mario Roques (Paris, 1960); *Le Conte du graal*, ed. Félix Lecoy (Paris, 1973–75). All translations are from *The Complete Romances of Chrétien de Troyes*, trans. David Staines (Bloomington, 1990).

car ele n'ot del celer cure;
bien li reconta l'avanture
tot mot a mot sanz antrelais;
mes a reconter vos an lais,
por ce que d'enui croist son conte
qui deus foiz une chose conte.   (lines 6267–74)

(Then she talked to her, telling her how Erec had come to
Laluth, for she did not care about keeping anything from her.
Omitting no details, she carefully recounted the adventure to
her word for word. But I am not going to tell it to you again
because the man who recounts the same thing twice lengthens
his tale in a tiresome way.)

Thus when Chrétien is noting how to create, elaborate, or design,
the word he uses for the original material is *conte*, and this word
often describes Chrétien's own work, though it is always his
materials or his creation *before* his design has been imposed.
Chrétien's literary world, as we shall see, is the new realm of the
romance.

The prologue to *Erec and Enide*, as Donald Maddox observes,

> provides evidence that Chrétien was consciously writing not
> only for the delight but also for the enlightenment of his con-
> temporaries and that he envisioned for his first major work a
> mode of existence based on collective recognition of both
> esthetic and instructive features.[12]

"Collective recognition" is an important concept, for it hearkens
back to the world of the epic, which also finds its origin and
power in another kind of collective recognition. In the Homeric
epic, there is no first-person narrator. Since the epic presents a

---

[12]Donald L. Maddox, *Structure and Sacring: The Systematic Kingdom in Chrétien's Erec et Enide* (Lexington, Ky., 1978), p. 15.

narrative of its audience's own heritage, the narrating voice will bear no traces of a single person, personality, or sensibility. Instead, the epic poet functions

> as a spokesman for values generally acknowledged as significant for communal stability and social well-being. Within the fiction of the poem, the dominant, locatable source of narration will not be a particular individual (the poet), but rather the voice of the community's heritage "telling itself."[13]

The epic poet is the wordsmith of his society, the person capable of recording society's history. Between the artist and his audience there must always be some formal engagement, a need, so to speak, to be validated. What right has the author or artist to be a spokesperson? In an epic, the voice speaks for the community, the society, the tribe; the voice is the voice of the tribe and takes its artistic authority from the public expression of communal truths and heritages. The audience of the epic is, in a sense, both the audience and the voice of the poet.

The movement from epic to romance is the movement to a first-person narrator. No longer a part of the epic world where the implied author or official scribe, to borrow Wayne Booth's phrase, has authority as the voice of the tribe, Chrétien's narrator must locate his own position in this new literary world.[14] The prologue to *Erec and Enide* underlines the movement from third-person to first-person narrator. Chrétien's narrator uses the third-person to refer to the author of the poem, and by doing so makes himself a figure distinct from the author, for he himself names the author; in

---

[13]Michael André Bernstein, *The Tale of the Tribe: Ezra Pound and the Modern Verse Epic* (Princeton, 1980), p. 14.

[14]Wayne C. Booth, *The Rhetoric of Fiction* (Chicago, 1961) pp. 70ff.

the first-person voice he asserts narrative control. Only once in this prologue does he use the first-person, "Now I am going to begin the story."

The prologue to Chrétien's second poem, *Cliges*, is longer, more emphatic, and more complex than the prologue to *Erec and Enide*:

Cil qui fist d'Erec et d'Enide,
Et les comandemanz d'Ovide
Et l'art d'amors an romans mist,
Et le mors de l'espaule fist,
Del roi Marc et d'Ysalt la blonde,
Et de la hupe et de l'aronde
Et del rossignol la muance,
Un novel conte rancomance
D'un vaslet qui an Grece fu
Del linage le roi Artu.
Mes ainz que de lui rien vos die,
Orroiz de son pere la vie,
Dom il fu, et de quel linage.
Tant fu preuz et de fier corage
Que por pris et por los conquerre
Ala de Grece an Engleterre,
Qui lors estoit Bretaigne dite.
Ceste estoire *trovons* escrite,
Que conter vos vuel et retraire,
En un des livres de l'aumaire
Mon seignor saint Pere a Biauvez;
De la fu li contes estrez
Qui tesmoingne l'estoire a voire:
Por ce fet ele mialz a croire.
Par les livres que *nos avons*
Les fez des ancïens *savons*
Et del siegle qui fu jadis.
Ce *nos* ont *nostre* livre apris
Qu'an Grece ot de chevalerie
Le premier los et de clergie.

Puis vint chevalerie a Rome
Et de la clergie la some,
Qui or est an France venue.
Dex doint qu'ele i soit maintenue
Et que li leus li abelisse
Tant que ja mes de France n'isse
L'enors qui s'i est arestee.
Dex l'avoit as altres prestee:
Car des Grezois ne des Romains
Ne dit an mes ne plus ne mains,
D'ax est la parole remese
Et estainte la vive brese.
Crestïens comance son conte,
Si con li livres *nos* reconte,
Qui trez fu d'un empereor
Puissant de richesce et d'enor
Qui tint Grece et Constantinoble.   (lines 1–47)

(The man who wrote of Erec and Enide, translated Ovid's *Commandments* and his *Art of Love*, composed *The Shoulder Bite*, and wrote of King Mark and the blonde Iseult, and about the metamorphoses of the hoopoe, the swallow, and the nightingale, takes up a new tale about a Greek youth of the line of King Arthur. But before I tell you about him, you will hear of his father's life, of his family and where he was from. He was so brave and stouthearted that, to win honor and renown, he travelled from Greece to England, which in those days was called Britain. The story I wish to recount to you, *we* find written down in one of the books in the library of Saint Peter's Cathedral in Beauvais. The fact that the tale was taken from there is evidence of the truth of the account. Hence its greater credibility.

From the books in *our* possession *we* know of the deeds of the ancients and of the world as it was in olden days. These books of *ours* have taught *us* that Greece once stood preeminent in both chivalry and learning. Then chivalry proceeded to Rome in company with the highest learning. Now they have come into France. God grant that they be sustained

427

here and their stay be so pleasing that the honor that has
stopped here in France never depart. God had lent them to
the others, for no one ever speaks now of the Greeks or the
Romans. Talk of them is over; their burning coals are spent.

Christian begins his tale, as the book recounts to *us*, with
an emperor of great wealth and honor, who governed Greece
and Constantinople. (my italics)

This prologue opens with a portrait of Chrétien's career as an
author. His listing of his writings establishes his authority. The
third-person pronoun acknowledges and affirms authorial status
and reputation.

The third-person pronoun gives way in the prologue, more
quickly than it did in the prologue to *Erec and Enide*, to the first-
person pronoun. And unlike the earlier prologue, this opening passage invokes the first-person plural pronoun, which Chrétien employs six times (italicized words in lines 18, 25, 26, 28, 44).[15]
The plural pronoun emphasizes the bond Chrétien would establish
between himself as narrator and his audience. Sylvia Huot describes scribal employment of the first-person plural:

> Such language recalls the language of literary forms known
> to have been part of the oral repertory of the *jongleurs*, such
> as saints' lives and chanson de geste. The scribe assumes a
> role analogous to the performer: he is an intermediary be-
> tween the audience and the story, and the book is the space
> in which his written "performance" takes place.[16]

---

[15]Chrétien continues this employment of the first-person plural again a few
lines later: "La parole a tant lesseron; / D'Alixandre vos conteron" (For the
moment we shall say nothing . . . We shall tell you of Alexander; lines 61–62).

[16]Sylvia Huot, *From Song to Book: The Poetics of Writing in Old French Lyric
and Lyrical Narrative Poetry* (Ithaca, 1987), p. 26.

Chrétien, of course, is not a scribe; his use of the third-person establishes his status as author, his use of the first-person plural his bond with his audience.

In these two prologues, Chrétien is defining the relationship between himself as author and his source *and* between himself as narrator and his audience. In the world of the epic, there is no need to establish such a relationship: the poet's position as spokesperson privileges the poet with a natural shared identity with his tribe. In the world of the romance, as Chrétien is suggesting, there is a need to define and assert the narrator's role for the audience since there is no longer a wholly shared identity. For Chrétien, the authority of the author is defined first by his list of works and then by his expressed mode of treatment of his source materials. The role of the narrator is more complex, for the first-person singular, unlike the first-person plural, separates the narrator from the audience and requires the establishment of a defined relationship between them.

There are, then, three self-referential pronouns used by the narrator: the third-person refers to the author of the poem, and its employment emphasizes the distinction between author and narrator; the first-person plural acknowledges the relationship between the narrator and his audience; and the first-person singular underlines the bond the narrator establishes and observes between himself and his literary materials.

Chrétien's first-person narrator is an oral reciter, not a creator, and constantly seeks to assure his audience of the credibility of his story. The epic poet, both an oral reciter and a creator, offers a record of events that his listeners accept as true; since he and his audience have a shared communal identity, there is no need for his audience to question or doubt the truth of his narrative. By moving into the first-person singular, Chrétien's narrator rejects the bond that unites the epic poet with his society. He is now aware of possibilities of interpretation and misreading, possibilities that never confront the epic poet. He becomes, accordingly, the audience's guide; convinced of the credibility of his material, he seeks to convince his audience: "The fact that the tale was taken from there is evidence of the truth of the account. Hence its greater credibility."

The prologue to *Cliges* introduces irony, which will become a familiar feature of the narrator's presentation of his material. "No one," he tells his audience, "ever speaks now of the Greeks or the Romans." Then, in the next few lines, he turns to Constantinople, where his romance begins and ends. If there is irony here, and I believe there is, then the romance's ending confirms the ironic possibilities in Chrétien's narrator. *Cliges* concludes with happiness, joy, and the marriage celebrations of Cliges and Fenice. But the final lines turn the traditional love-story ending into an explanation for the existence of the eunuchs of Constantinople, as the narrator again indulges in irony, winking at his audience, an audience that probably included some men recently returned from the crusades who would have heard tales about the eunuchs of Constantinople.

It is the opening of *The Knight with the Lion*, which Peter Haidu correctly calls a "non-prologial prologue,"[17] that reveals an assured voice in Chrétien's narrator. No longer in need of establishing or confirming the bond between himself and his audience but certain and conscious of his role, the narrator begins his story immediately:

> Artus, li boens rois de Bretaingne
> la cui proesce nos enseigne

---

[17]Peter Haidu, "Romance: Idealistic Genre or Historical Text?" in *The Craft of Fiction: Essays in Medieval Poetics*, ed. Leigh A. Arrathoon (Rochester, Mich., 1984), p. 20.

que nos soiens preu et cortois,
tint cort si riche come rois
a cele feste qui tant coste,
qu'an doit clamer la Pantecoste.   (lines 1–6)

(Arthur, the good king of Britain, whose valor teaches us that
we too should be courteous and brave, was holding court with
all kinglike splendor at Carlisle in Wales on the feast so
worth its cost one has to call it Pentecost.)

The first-person plural of the second line returns briefly: "Mes or
parlons de cez qui furent, / si leissons cez qui ancor durent" (But
now let us speak of those who once were and leave aside those
who still are; lines 29–30), then gives way at once to the confidence of the first-person singular:

car molt valt mialz, ce m'est a vis,
uns cortois morz c'uns vilains vis.
Por ce me plest a reconter
chose qui face a escouter
del roi qui fu de tel tesmoing
qu'an en parole et pres et loing;
si m'acort de tant as Bretons
que toz jorz durra li renons   (lines 31–38)

(for a courteous man, though dead, is worth a great deal
more, in my opinion, than a living churl. So it is my pleasure
to relate a story worth listening to about the king whose fame
spreads near and far. And I do agree with the belief of so
many Bretons that his renown will last forever.)

From its opening, *The Knight with the Lion* indulges in the
same ironic juxtaposition that opens *Cliges*. After the pun of "tant
coste . . . Pantecoste," the romance juxtaposes the narrator's vision of the famous King Arthur and his forever renowned knights
with the first glimpse of Arthurian society: the king retires early,

forgets himself, and falls asleep, thereby missing an entire story, and returns so late—and only after a dispute among his knights— that his wife has to retell the tale so that he can know what has happened. The narrator's irony does not undercut the idealism of the Arthurian world. Erec and Yvain, for example, are taught chivalric idealism in the course of their adventures, and the court aspires to the ideal. But all is not perfect: Chrétien's Arthurian world is far from being prelapsarian. It is, on the contrary, a humanized world that tries to be what it should be, but often remains more successful in the reaching than in the grasping. And this tension becomes evident through the narrator's placement of his materials: it is he who sets the pre-eminence of Greece beside the eunuchs of Constantinople and contrasts the idealism of Camelot with its sleeping king.

The confident opening of *The Knight with the Lion* leads to Calogrenant's tale, the only extended tale-within-a-tale in Chrétien's romances, which serves as a reflexive commentary on the art of narration and on Chrétien's own narrative voice. Deeply concerned about his audience and troubled that the queen should hear his tale, Calogrenant employs the first-person singular, never the first-person plural, as he attempts to relate himself as narrator to his audience. For Peter Dembowski, Calogrenant's narratorial presence is indistinguishable from Chrétien's own narrative voice: "Calogrenant's story is told in the first person. But apart from this syntactic peculiarity, it could very well have been told by Chrétien himself. . . . an extended narration becomes indistinguishable from the voice of the author-narrator himself."[18] Calogrenant, however, is less a voice of Chrétien's narrator than a commentary on him. His "prologue" to his tale "so completely evokes the *métier* of the

---

[18]Peter Dembowski, "Monologue, Author's Monologue and Related Problems in the Romances of Chrétien de Troyes," *Yale French Studies* 51 (1974): 105.

romancer that Calogrenant unmistakably adopts the role of courtly narrator," although his language—he tells his queen that he would prefer to have one of his teeth pulled out than tell his story—reveals his poor understanding of linguistic propriety.[19] Furthermore, as Hunt notes, audience reception is "an integral narrative problem" in *The Knight with the Lion*, yet this "problem" has always been a concern of Chrétien's narrator, who, in *Erec and Enide* and *Cliges*, examined the bond that must be established between the narrator and his audience.[20] It is the assured voice of Chrétien's own narrator in this romance that allows him to introduce Calogrenant, a narrator with no understanding of irony, who suddenly confronts the nature of audience reception and other narrative questions that Chrétien himself has already explored.

Like *Cliges*, *The Knight with the Lion* closes with a brief return to the third-person author. Now, however, that third-person reference gives way at once to a first-person assertion based on the bond between narrator and audience, and the separation between narrator and author:

> Del *Chevalier au lyeon* fine
> Crestïens son romans ensi;
> n'onques plus conter n'en oï
> ne ja plus n'en orroiz conter
> s'an n'i vialt mançonge ajoster   (lines 6804–08)

(And so Christian brings to a close his romance about the *Knight with the Lion*. I have never heard tell more about him, and you will never hear more told unless someone wants to add lies.)

---

[19]Tony Hunt, "Beginnings, Middles, and Ends: Some Interpretative Problems in Chrétien's *Yvain* and Its Medieval Adaptations," in *The Craft of Fiction*, ed. Arrathoon, p. 85.

[20]Ibid.

Chrétien's other two romances, *The Knight of the Cart* and *The Story of the Grail*, open with eulogies to his two patrons. In the former, his tribute to Marie, Countess of Champagne, who presented the author with his story, reflects and honors two relationships: his professional devotion to her and her command, and his authorial dependence on his source, here provided by the Countess herself. The movement from third-person to first-person, which characterized Chrétien's first romances, reverses itself in *The Knight of the Cart* so that the first-person homage to a patron takes rightful precedence over the author's third-person acknowledgement of his sources, which concludes the prologue.

In *The Story of the Grail*, Chrétien's final and unfinished romance, the third-person opening, "Crestïens seme et fet semance / d'un romans que il ancomance" (Christian sows and plants the seed of a romance he is beginning; lines 7–8), gives way at once to an extended eulogy to his later patron, Philip, Count of Flanders, who also provided the author with his source material. Like *The Knight of the Cart*, this romance begins with two relationships: Chrétien's professional devotion to Philip and his authorial dependence upon Philip's book. The long tribute to Philip is the exclusive domain of the first-person singular, and the prologue ends, as does the prologue to *The Knight of the Cart*, with the authorial third-person affirmation:

> Donc avra bien save sa peinne
> Crestïens, qui antant et peinne
> a rimoier le meillor conte,
> par le comandement le conte,
> qui soit contez an cort real:
> ce est li contes del graal,
> don li cuens li baille le livre,
> s'orroiz comant il s'an delivre.　　　　　(lines 61–68)

(Therefore Christian's labor will not be wasted when, at the

count's command, he endeavors and strives to put into rhyme
the finest tale that may be told at a royal court. This is the
Story of the Grail, from the book the count gave him. Hear
how he performs his task.)

The prologues to *The Knight of the Cart* and *The Story of the
Grail* never employ the first-person plural. Their alternation between the first-person and the third-person singular reveals a confident authorial third-person and a narratorial first-person voice
here used in affectionate tribute to honored patrons.

The first-person narrator of the prologues has a continuing
presence in the narratives themselves, where his reappearances
confirm, clarify, and even expand his position in the prologues.[21]
His presence continues to define his role as mediator between his
material and his audience and to develop the new bond between
himself and his audience.

The sole appearance of the first-person singular in the prologue to *Erec and Enide* gives way to forty-two appearances of
the pronoun within the narrative, by far the largest number in any
of Chrétien's romances. The longer and more interesting of these
appearances describe the narrator's desire for a straightforward,
indeed economical narrative devoid of tedious detail and repetition. The narrator will not, for example, describe the chamber
King Evrain prepared for Erec and Enide:

> Mes por coi vos deviseroie
> la pointure des dras de soie,
> don la chanbre estoit anbelie?
> Le tans gasteroie an folie,

---

[21]By reappearances or appearances I mean any occasion when the narrator uses
the first-person singular pronoun either for a few words or for an extended
duration.

et ge nel vuel mie haster;
einçois me voel un po haster,
que qui tost va par droite voie
celui passe qui se desvoie:
por ce ne m'i voel arester.   (lines 5523–31)

(But why should I describe in detail for you the silk embroi-
deries that adorned the room? I would waste the time in such
folly, and I do not wish to lose the time. Rather, I would
hurry along a little, for the man who adheres strictly to the
straight road passes the man following the indirect. For this
reason I do not wish to stop here.)

Nor will he describe the meal that evening: "Ici ne vuel feire
demore, / se trover puis voie plus droite" (I do not wish to delay
here if I can find a more direct route; lines 5534–35). While
Enide recounts Erec's complete history to Maboagrain's lady, the
narrator assures his audience that he will not repeat the story:
"por ce que d'enui croist son conte / qui deus foiz une chose
conte" (because the man who recounts the same thing twice
lengthens his tale in a tiresome way; lines 6273–74).

On other occasions the narrator avoids tedious detail by emphasizing the inadequacy of art to draw a full portrait. His initial
descriptions of both Erec and Enide end with the same question:
of Erec, "que diroie de ses bontez?" (What more can I say of his
good qualities?; line 93); and of Enide, "Que diroie de sa biauté?"
(What more can I say of her beauty?; line 437). The description
of Erec's coronation robe has a similar conclusion: "Que vos
diroie del mantel?" (What more can I tell you of the robe?; line
6742). Words are ultimately inadequate. Erec's coronation can be
suggested but not captured:

Donc voel ge grant folie anprandre,
qui au descrivre voel antandre;
mes des que feire le m'estuet,

436

et c'est chose qu'an feire puet,
ne leirai pas que ge n'an die
selonc mon san une partie.   (lines 6645–50)

(And so in my wish to attempt its description, I would be
embarking on an enterprise of sheer folly. But since I must
do it, and this is something feasible, I shall try to relate some
of it as best I can.)

The narrator's explicit concern with the form of his narrative
complements his constant emphasis on the credibility of his
material. He reminds his audience of his source, for example the
description of Erec's coronation robe is taken, he admits, from
Macrobius. At other times he confesses his own ignorance, which
is always a reflection of the incompleteness of his source: he does
not know what work Enide and her mother are doing in their
workroom (line 400), nor does he know if the Breton sculptor
sold his embroidered saddle (line 5304).

Reiterated words and phrases directed to the audience such as
"sachiez" (you can be certain; lines 300, 5886), "por voir vos di"
(I tell you honestly; lines 424, 5282), and "dire vos puis seüre-
ment" (I can assure you; line 2644) emphasize the narrator's
belief in his own material. Yet sometimes the belief is *seeming*,
for already in *Erec and Enide* the narrator introduces an implicit
skepticism towards some of his statements that awakens or confirms skepticism in his audience. He does not always expect his
audience to believe wholeheartedly in his details or descriptions,
and by drawing attention to his own *seeming* belief, he further develops the bond of trust between himself and his audience. Part of
his romance world is already make-believe, and some of the audience's enjoyment comes from the narrator's attempts to ensure
credibility while drawing attention to and even inducing possible
incredulity. As he describes King Arthur's scepter, for example,

the narrator affirms: "La verité dire vos os" (I dare tell you the truth; line 6814), then concludes that *every* kind of fish, wild beast, man, and bird was carved on the scepter. After the description, Arthur gazes on the precious object "a mervoilles" (with awe; line 6821); the narrator's audience no doubt felt awe too, but tinged with skepticism invited by the narrator himself. The romance ends with his similar call for incredulity under the guise of his call for complete credibility:

> mes ne vos voel pas feire acroire,
> mançonge sanbleroit trop voire,
> tables fussent mises a tire
> en un palés; ja nel quier dire.　　　　(lines 6861–64)

(I do not wish to make you believe—the lie would be too obvious—that the tables were placed in rows in one palace hall. My intention is not to say that.)

In all his appearances within the narrative, the narrator develops and defines his relationship with his audience, outlining some of his principles of narration, confirming his indebtedness to and dependence upon his source material, and confiding his attitude to it. On a few occasions, he even moves beyond his role as narrator and audience guide and becomes a commentator too. Enide is so attractive and beautiful

> que ne cuit pas qu'an nule terre,
> tant seüst l'an cerchier ne querre,
> fust sa paroille recovree,　　　　(lines 1649–51)

(that I do not believe her equal could be found anywhere, no matter where you sought or looked.)

Similarly, as the people lament Erec's departure from Carnant, the

438

narrator observes: "ne cuit que greignor duel feïssent, / se a mort navré le veïssent" (I do not believe they could have shown greater sorrow had they seen him fatally wounded; lines 2747–48). The narrator as commentator, a role Chrétien will develop in his later romances, locates the narrator as audience to his own narration, for the vividness of his response to details, descriptions, and incidents reveals his immediate contact with—but not involvement inside the world of—his story. The narrator is always, even in his commentaries, "present in the narration but absent from the story."[22]

The narrator's thirty-one appearances after the prologue in *Cliges* continue the patterns observed in *Erec and Enide*. Again the narrator advocates economy in narration; at the four-day tournament, he refuses to enumerate all those assembled:

> Cuidiez vos or que je vos die
> Por feire demorer mon conte:
> "Cil roi i furent, et cil conte,
> Et cil, et cil, et cil i furent?"   (lines 4588–91)

(Do not expect me to extend my tale by telling you such and such a king was there, and such and such a count, and there were these here, and those ones, and these others.)

He continues to draw attention to the inadequacy of art; Fenice, for example, cannot be described fully:

> Por ce que g'en diroie mains,
> Ne braz, ne cors, ne chief, ne mains
> Ne vuel par parole descrivre,
> Car se mil anz avoie a vivre
> Et chascun jor doblast mes sans,

---

[22]Grigsby, "Narrative Voices," p. 267.

Si perdroie gie mon porpans,
Einçois que le voir an deïsse.
Bien sai, se m'an antremeïsse
Et tot mon san i anpleasse,
Que tote ma poinne i gastasse,
Et ce seroit poinne gastee.   (lines 2695–2705)

(As I would render less than an adequate portrait, I do not intend to describe head, arms, hands, or body, for if I were to
live a thousand years, and my talent doubled every day, I
would waste my efforts and fail to capture the truth with my
words. I am certain that if all my talent I devoted, all my
labour I would lose. The attempt would be in vain.)

And the credibility of his material is emphasized not only in the
prologue but in the many reiterated words and phrases directed to
the audience that also occur in this romance.

Cliges, moreover, develops the figure of the narrator as commentator in two extended first-person passages. In the first, the
narrator, after his initial portraits of Cliges and Fenice, describes
their meeting and proceeds to reflect on his own language. Fenice,
he observes, has given Cliges her heart:

Doné? Ne l'a, par foi, je mant,
Que nus son cuer doner ne puet;
Autremant dire le m'estuet.
Ne dirai pas si com cil dïent
Qui an un cors deus cuers alïent,
Qu'il n'est voirs, n'estre ne le sanble
Qu'an un cors ait deus cuers ansanble;
Et s'il pooient assanbler,
Ne porroit il voir resanbler.
Mes s'il vos pleisoit a entandre,
Bien vos ferai le voir antandre,
Comant dui cuer a un se tienent,
Sanz ce qu'ansanble ne parvienent.

440

Seul de tant se tienent a un
Que la volanté de chascun
De l'un a l'autre s'an trespasse;
Si vuelent une chose a masse,
Et por tant c'une chose vuelent,
I a de tiex qui dire suelent
Que chascuns a le cuer as deus;
Mes uns cuers n'est pas an deus leus.
Bien puent lor voloir estre uns,
Et s'a adés son cuer chascuns,
Ausi com maint home divers
Puent an chançons et an vers
Chanter a une concordance.
Si vos pruis par ceste sanblance
C'uns cors ne puet deus cuers avoir,
Ce sachiez vos trestor de voir;   (lines 2780–2808)

(Gives? No, I swear I lie, for no man can give his heart. I must find a different expression.

I shall not talk as do people who speak of uniting two hearts in one body. That two hearts can lodge together in one body is not true, nor does it appear true. And if indeed they could come together, it would not seem to resemble truth. But if it be your pleasure to listen, I shall explain to you the true sense in which two hearts are one without coming together. They become one only insofar as the desire of each passes to the other. They have like desires, and because their desires are identical, some people are accustomed to saying that each possesses two hearts. But one heart is not in two places. Their desires may well be the same, but each has his own heart, just as many different men may sing verses and songs in unison. From this simile I present to you proof that one body is incapable of having two hearts. You may be absolutely certain of this.)

In this longest first-person commentary thus far in Chrétien's writings, the narrator returns to the credibility of his material. He begins and ends his reflections on love as a statement of concern for the verisimilitude of the narrative. Although it is possible to read these observations as a disparaging commentary on lyric poets who use fanciful expressions, and even on Guinevere herself, who told Cliges's father Alexander and his lady Soredamor:

> Qu'aparceüe m'an sui bien,
> As contenances de chascun
> Que de deus cuers avez fet un.   (lines 2256–58)

> (From the way you both behave, I am well aware that you have made one heart of two),

the narrator's commentary centers again on his relationship to his material and his own artistic concern for truth.

In his second extended commentary, the narrator considers the plight of lovers who lack the courage to confess their feelings to each other. Fenice's modesty when she is alone with Cliges prompts the narrator's extended meditation on the behavior of lovers:

> Mes volantez an moi s'aüne
> Que je dïe reison aucune
> Por coi ç'avient a fins amanz
> Que sens lor faut et hardemanz
> A dire ce qu'il ont an pans,
> Quant il ont eise, et leu, et tans.
>   Vos qui d'Amors vos feites sage,
> Et les costumes et l'usage
> De sa cort maintenez a foi,
> N'onques ne faussastes sa loi,
> Que qu'il vos an doie cheoir,
> Dites se l'en puet nes veoir
> Rien qui por Amor abelisse,
> Que l'en n'an tressaille ou palisse.   (lines 3813–26)

(But I long to offer some reason why true lovers happen to
lack courage and wisdom to tell their thoughts when they
have time, leisure, and occasion.

You who are learning about Love, who faithfully observe the customs and practices of his court, who have never
broken his law regardless of the consequences, tell if you can
see any pleasure from Love that does not cause trembling or
paleness.)

Here the narrator moves beyond his attitude to his sources and beyond his concern with verisimilitude. Now he assumes the role of
commentator, but not only on the credibility of his material, but
on the nature of love. Two centuries later the narrator of Chaucer's *Troilus and Criseyde* will portray himself as a disciple of
Love. Although Chrétien's narrator never offers a self-portrait, he
does present himself as an authority on Love and on the behavior
of those who fall under his spell. Whether his authority comes
from experience or from learning is a matter for speculation only,
for the narrator himself gives no indication. His few meditations
on love ultimately reflect his vivid response to his story.

The narrator's twenty-eight appearances within *The Knight
with the Lion* continue his presence as an artist concerned both
with economy in narrative and with the ultimate inadequacy of
words. Yvain's marriage to Laudine cannot be adequately described, the narrator assures his audience (lines 2161–65), nor can
the welcome she offers King Arthur (lines 2390–96). And when
Yvain departs from his new wife, the narrator confesses that such
a description would be tedious: "Trop i feroie de demore" (I
would spend too much time here; line 2635).

Many of the narrator's first-person observations attest to his
belief in his material. Yvain's sudden love for the widow of the
man he has just murdered leads the narrator to conclude: "n'ainz
mes ne cuit qu'il avenist" (I do not believe this could ever happen

again; line 1513). He assures his audience that Yvain was deeply afraid when he first approached Laudine (line 1952). And the hermit's homemade bread is almost inedible: "ne cuit que onques de si fort / ne de si aspre eüst gosté" (I do not believe he had ever tasted such hard, bitter bread; lines 2846–47). At the same time, the narrator interjects skepticism that unites him with his sometimes wondering audience. In his final description of the spring, he describes the torrent of rain, then assures his audience:

> Ne cuidiez pas que je vos mante
> que si fu fiere la tormante
> que nus n'an conteroit le disme.   (lines 6525–27)

> (Do not imagine I lie to you. The storm was so fierce that no one could relate the tenth of it.)

Obviously aware of his audience's disbelief, he accepts their attitude and further strengthens the bond of understanding uniting himself with them.

Three developments in the narrator are evident in this romance. First, he asserts more explicitly than in the earlier romances his knowledge of and control over the narrative. He intends to interrupt his narrative to tell his audience about the meeting between Gawain and Lunete:

> voel feire une brief remanbrance
> qui fu feite a privé consoil
> entre la lune et le soloil.
> Savez de cui je vos voel dire?   (lines 2398–2401)

> (I do want to say a brief word about a private meeting that took place between the sun and the moon. Do you know of whom I would speak to you?)

444

Even more assured is his refusal for the moment—and without the presence of the first-person—to explain the open space outside the walls of the baron's besieged castle: "Assez en orroiz la reison / une autre foiz, quant leus sera" (You will hear the reason for this later when the time comes; lines 3776–77). And he is rarely hesitant to admit his own ignorance: he does not know how many days it took Yvain and the lion to recuperate from their wounds (lines 4694–96); at the Castle of Most Ill Adventure, those who stabled the horses expected to keep them, but the narrator does not know if they were wise in their expectations (line 5350), nor does he know if the people were deceiving Yvain with their joyous welcome (line 5401); and he has no knowledge of the time Gawain spent away from the court (line 5866).

Second, as in *Cliges* yet even more so here, the narrator becomes a commentator on love. The long first-person passages have love and the behavior of lovers as their focus. The beautiful maiden at the Castle of Most Ill Adventure leads the narrator to speak of the God of Love. It is wrong for anyone to recover from Love's wounds, the narrator reflects, for such wounds never heal. His own society, he adds, does not know love (lines 5374–90). Still longer is his detailed analysis of the loving friendship between Yvain and Gawain (lines 5992–6099). Love is—and will be—the only subject, other than the narrator's relationship to his story and his audience, that commands his first-person commentary.

Even more significant are the passages where the narrator meditates on love without recourse to the first-person. The "nonprologial prologue" includes an extended elegy on Love's absence from contemporary society (lines 18–28); here is the first appearance of the narrator as commentator/elegist, a role he continues only in this romance and a role his Arthurian successors will develop. The assured and assertive voice of this passage, which is free of the first-person pronoun, reappears within the narrative.

When Yvain falls in love with Laudine, for example, the narrator comments at length on the various lodgings that become the dwellings of Love (lines 1379–1409).

Lastly, *The Knight with the Lion* returns within the narrative to a rare use of the first-person plural:

> Vers le chastel s'an vont molt tost
> qu'il ert si prés qu'il n'i ot pas
> plus de demie liue un pas,
> des liues qui el païs sont
> car a mesure des noz sont
> les deus une, les quatre deus.   (lines 2952–57)

> (They rode at once to the castle, which was within a half-league of the kind of leagues they have in that country. As compared with ours, two of their leagues equal one, and four equal two.)[23]

The narrator, who has carefully established his relationship with his audience, now moves effortlessly into the first-person plural, implying the kind of natural bond between narrator and audience of the epic tradition. And within the narrative of *The Knight of the Cart* are two similar first-person plural alliances with the audience. When Lancelot and Guinevere spend a night together in the prison cell, the narrator eschews a detailed description:

> mes toz jorz iert par moi teüe,
> qu'an conte ne doit estre dite.
> Des joies fu la plus eslite

---

[23]The only earlier appearance in Chrétien's romances of the first-person plural suggesting the bond between narrator and audience is the description of Guinguemar: "de cestui avons oï dire / qu'il fu amis Morgant la fee" (We have heard it said of him that he was a lover of Morgan le Fay; *Erec and Enide*, lines 1906–07). This use of the first-person plural does not appear in the narrative of *Cliges*.

et la plus delitable cele
qui li contes nos test et cele.   (lines 4680–84)

(But on this matter I shall always be silent. Every tale should
pass it over in silence. The choicest and most pleasurable
joys are those the tale keeps from us.)

And the arrival of the herald at the tournament leads to the narrator's observation:

Mostre mestre an fu li hyra
qui a dire le nos aprist,
car il premieremant le dist.   (lines 5572–74)

(Our master was the herald, who taught us the phrase, for he
was the first person to use it.)

In *The Knight of the Cart* the narrator employs the first-
person singular in twenty-six appearances within the narrative,
though half of them occur in the closing section written by Godefroi de Leigni.[24] The appearances continue the patterns we have
observed. If the narrator is ignorant of a matter, he will confess
his ignorance. When Gawain stands at the window with the young

---

[24]It is tempting to speculate that Godefroi de Leigni, perhaps Chrétien's assistant, was familiar with Chrétien's earlier romances and their more extensive use of
the first-person singular and did not notice that there was a significant decline in
the appearances of the pronoun, a decline quite evident in *The Knight of the Cart*.
For this reason, I cannot agree with Hult's contention that Godefroi is "a fiction of
Chrétien—a 'clerkly' author-figure allowing our devious first author the luxury of
two endings, two voices, and thus a highly nuanced, unlocalizable intentionality,"
especially since Hult posits Godefroi's frequent adoption of the first-person narrative voice as evidence of Godefroi and Chrétien being the same person; see David
F. Hult, "Author/Narrator/Speaker: The Voice of Authority in Chrétien's *Charrete*,"
in *Discourses of Authority in Medieval and Renaissance Literature*, ed. Kevin
Brownlee and Walter Stephens (Hanover, N.H., 1989), pp. 87–88).

lady, the narrator points out that he does not know what they said (lines 548–49). He remains committed to a straightforward narrative: he will not, he tells his audience, digress to meditate on good and evil (lines 3179–84). Other first-person appearances emphasize his bond with his audience. When Lancelot and the young lady come upon Guinevere's gilded ivory comb, he begins:

> Sor le perron qui ert iqui
> avoit oblïé ne sai qui,
> un peigne d'ivoire doré. (lines 1349–51)

> (Someone, I know not who, had forgotten a gilded ivory comb on the stone.)

But, of course, he does know the identity of the owner. When he describes the strands of hair in the comb's teeth, he warns his now skeptical audience:

> mes quel estoient li chevol?
> Et por mançongier et por fol
> m'an tanra l'en, se voir an di. (lines 1479–81)

> (But what was the hair like? You will, if I tell you the truth, think me a liar and a fool.)

Later, when Lancelot is armed and riding on his horse, he is so comely that "einz deïssiez, tant vos pleüst, / qu'il fu ensi nez et creüz" (you would have claimed he had been born and raised wearing the helmet; lines 2674–75). Then the narrator adds, "de ce voldroie estre creüz" (For this I would like you to take my word; line 2676), as though he knows and even shares his audience's inability to accept wholeheartedly this description.

Like *The Knight with the Lion*, this romance contains extended meditations on love, though in none does the narrator introduce

the first-person pronoun. When Lancelot hesitates to enter the
cart, the narrator contemplates the tension between Reason and
Love (lines 362–77). The lovesick Lancelot is proof that such a
patient seeks no cure (lines 1336–43). On one occasion, the third-
person commentator involves his audience directly in his meditation. Lancelot cannot sleep at the thought of his approaching as-
signation with Guinevere:

> Bien poez antendre et gloser,
> vos qui avez fet autretel,
> que por la gent de son ostel
> se fet las et se fet couchier.　　　　　(lines 4550–53)

> (Those of you who have done this can understand and explain
> why he pretended to be tired and went to bed because of the
> others in his lodging.)

Like the use of the first-person plural, this second-person address
confirms the intimate bond that now exists between Chrétien's
narrator and his audience.

The Story of the Grail, even in its unfinished state the longest
of Chrétien's romances, contains only twenty appearances of the
first-person pronoun. Many of these stress the need for an economical narrative. Even though he could, the narrator will not recount in detail the combat between Perceval and Clamadeu (lines
2678–79). The struggle between Perceval and the Proud Knight of
the Heath is only briefly recounted (lines 3909–11). And when the
narrator returns to the story of Perceval and his five years of
wandering, he has no wish to describe the grief at Gawain's
departure:

> ne d'ax ne del duel que il font
> rien plus a dire ne me plest.
> De mon seignor Gauvain se test

li contes ici a estal,
si parlerons de Perceval. (lines 6004–08)

(Of them and their grief, I have no wish to tell more. Of Sir
Gawain, the tale is silent here at this point. And so we shall
speak of Perceval.)

On some occasions, he does not even introduce the first-person
when he aims to avoid repetition:

Et il li conte
si com avez oï el conte.
Qui autre foiz le conteroit,
enuiz et oiseuse seroit,
que nus contes ce ne demande. (lines 1375–79)

(And he related the tale to him as you have heard it. It would
be pointless to tell the tale a second time, for no tale wants
repetition.)

The narrator's reliance upon his source is evident not only in
the prologue but also in three explicit references to his source
within the narrative (lines 707, 2805, and 7429); such references
do not occur in Chrétien's earlier romances. And there continue to
be the narrator's reminders of the incomplete nature of his source:
"Des mes ne faz autre novele, / quanz en i ot et quel il furent" (I
have no more details as to the nature of the dishes or their
number; lines 1562–63). The bond between narrator and audience
leads the narrator again to affirm the credibility of his material
while inviting and accepting his audience's skepticism. Perceval
leads his horse so close to King Arthur that the horse knocked the
king's cap from his head; this fact, he assures his audience, is
"sanz nule fable" (I am telling the exact truth; line 933). When
Gawain rides up to a castle so magnificent that no eyes of living
man ever beheld anything so splendid, the narrator begins his de-

scription: "ja ne quier que mantir m'an loise" (I have no desire to lie in this matter; line 6989). And the golden bed where Gawain later sleeps seems to invite incredulity so that the narrator cautions: "Del lit nul fable ne faz" (I am not making up an idle tale about the bed; line 7445).

The Story of the Grail contains no extended first-person meditations, perhaps because human love and the behavior of lovers are not central concerns in this romance. And this final poem underlines the comparative diminution in first-person appearances in the course of the five romances, as though Chrétien came to share the Aristotelian preference for an absent or almost-absent narrative voice.[25]

Between the prologues to the romances and the narratives themselves, there is complete consistency in Chrétien's presentation of his narrator. For the first time in medieval literature, Chrétien consciously and consistently creates a narrator who distinguishes and distances himself from the third-person author of the text. And this pioneering distinction between author and narrator accounts, to some degree, for those critics who either ignored or decried the presence of the narrator in medieval romance.

From the one use of a first-person singular in the prologue to *Erec and Enide*, Chrétien presents a first-person narrator whose first allegiance is to his source. Dependent upon the material for his knowledge or lack of knowledge, he never ceases to point out his narrative fidelity. Although his source is his most evident concern, his constant preoccupation is the forging of a bond with his courtly audience. Removed from the epic world with its shared communal identity between narrator and audience, the narrator de-

---

[25]It is interesting to note that the final fifth of *The Story of the Grail* does not have a single appearance of the first-person singular pronoun used by the narrator.

fines his own role in order to define his relationship to his audience. And as he assumes the role of his audience's guide to the story, he also defines the role of his audience as he shares with them his knowledge of and perspective on the material. The narrator envisions a dynamic relationship with his audience, for in these five romances he turns steadily to second-person address, even as his use of the first-person singular form decreases.[26]

In her book on *Cliges*, Michelle A. Freeman observes:

> By speaking of the poet-narrator in the third person, without naming names, Chrétien transforms himself into his narrator *persona* and, simultaneously, into a character of the romance. He poeticizes—that is, he draws into the textual world of romance fiction—the clerkly figure who forges the fiction.[27]

But this is precisely what Chrétien does not do: he never allows himself to become a character in the world of his fiction. Norris J. Lacy more accurately observes:

> The narrator, whether Chrétien or *je*, is a visible and indispensable inhabitant of his own poems. . . . The author's presence in his work thus draws our attention to the fact that we are dealing with fiction narrated by a story-teller whose primary objective is to excite and maintain our interest and who does all he can to assure that what we see is important,

---

[26]*Erec and Enide* has thirty-two appearances of the second-person address to the audience either in a second-person plural verb or in the use of the second-person plural pronoun, the latter usually in conjunction with the first-person singular pronoun; *Cliges* has seventeen; *The Knight of the Cart* thirty-one, including nine in the section by Godefroi de Leigni; *The Knight with the Lion* eighteen; and *The Story of the Grail* twenty-five.

[27]Michelle A. Freeman, *The Poetics of Translatio Studii and Conjointure: Chrétien de Troyes's Cligès* (Lexington, Ky., 1979), p. 32.

that we understand its function, and that we read the story as
he wants us to.[28]

Lacy's terminology, however, falsifies a crucial dimension of the
narrator, namely his place within the poem, for Chrétien's narrator
is not and never becomes an "inhabitant" of his romances. Unlike
narrators in later medieval literature, Chrétien's never moves into
the poem's universe; he never becomes a participant in any
dimension of the narrative's action. He has, as Lacy notes, "a
modified omniscient point of view."[29] He knows the thoughts of
his characters; sometimes he even reveals or suggests his knowledge of future events, and he can do this because his source offers
him this knowledge. He sees clearly, and so he anticipates what
lies ahead, reminding the audience that he is in full command of
his narration and its source. Chrétien's narrator, then, is not an inhabitant or a participant in the world of his fiction. He is an artist,
the *literary self* of Chrétien de Troyes as I would prefer him to be
called, frequently interjecting, but not interfering, in his own narration to assert his position and his relationship both to his source
and to his audience.

Self has a long history in regard to the figure of the narrator.
In 1959 Kathleen Tillotson re-introduced the nineteenth-century
term *second self* to designate the implied author of a literary text,
borrowing the term from a commentary on George Eliot.[30]
Second self implies a different self not necessarily related to the
real author. Martin Stevens' study "The Performing Self in
Twelfth-Century Culture" advocates the phrase *performing self* to

[28]Norris J. Lacy, *The Craft of Chrétien de Troyes: An Essay on Narrative Art*
(Leiden, 1980), pp. 36–37.

[29]Ibid., p. 40.

[30]Kathleen Tillotson, *The Tale and the Teller* (London, 1959), p. 22.

designate the implied author.[31] *Performing self* implies, however, a full portrait perhaps too consciously struggling to create a new self. And the phrase itself Stevens borrows from Richard Poirier's study of Robert Frost, Ernest Hemingway, and Norman Mailer.[32] Chrétien's narrator does not belong in such modern company, nor does he make himself such an active presence. Perhaps because of Chrétien's own reputation as the father of the novel, it has not been deemed inappropriate to apply to his narrator critical designations borrowed from studies of such writers as Proust and Mailer.[33] Peter Haidu goes so far as to invoke Joseph Conrad when referring to Chrétien's narrator:

> Most often, the author is a hidden power behind the articulated world of his fiction; when he comments directly to the reader, he tends to take on the *persona* of a narrator who may be quite distinct from the author; he tends to become a figure like Conrad's Marlowe.[34]

---

[31]Martin Stevens, "The Performing Self in Twelfth-Century Culture," *Viator* 9 (1978): 193–212.

[32]Following the terminology used by Stevens ("The Performing Self"), for example, Roberta L. Krueger regards the narrator of *The Knight of the Cart* as "a performer responding self-consciously to the *don contraignant* he has contracted"; see her "'Tuit li autre': The Narrator and His Public in Chrétien de Troyes' *Le Chevalier de la Charrette*," in *Courtly Romance*, ed. Guy L. Mermier (Detroit, 1984), p. 135. Jeanne A. Nightingale refers to the narrator of *Erec and Enide* as "the author in his role as performing *conteur*"; see her "Chrétien de Troyes and the Mythographical Tradition: The Couple's Journey in *Erec et Enide* and Martianus' *De Nuptiis*," in *King Arthur Through the Ages*, ed. Valerie M. Lagorio and Mildred Leake Day, vol. 1 (New York, 1990), p. 75.

[33]See, for example, Foster L. Guyer, *Chrétien de Troyes: Inventor of the Modern Novel* (New York, 1957).

[34]Peter Haidu, *Aesthetic Distance in Chrétien de Troyes: Irony and Comedy in Cliges and Perceval* (Geneva, 1968), p. 108.

And the introduction of such a term as *persona* with its mask-like connotations implies a complete other person or personality, a fully drawn figure far removed from the figure of the narrator Chrétien creates and develops in his romances.

Literary self accurately describes Chrétien's narrator, for, apart from his third-person enumeration of Chrétien's literary achievements and his brief reflections on his narrative art, he presents no self-portrait; even his few comments on love reveal nothing about himself. His narrating voice is akin to that of the epic narrator, for it too bears no trace of a distinct personality, and his first-person separation of himself from the third-person author reinforces the concept of the narrator as a voice without personality. Chrétien's narrator is always the *literary self* of its author, the public artist in contrast to the private person, the professional figure in contrast to the individual and his personality.

Chrétien's narrator or *literary self* occupies a seminal place in the history of narrative literature, situated as he is after the epic tradition and at the beginning of the romance tradition. Chrétien makes his narrator a self-conscious presence, acutely aware of the need to define his relationship to his audience, confirming the new role of a narrator in the new genre of romance. At the same time the narrator never enters the world of his fiction, remaining a non-participatory figure closer to the members of his own audience than to the characters of his fictional landscape.

In contrast to the twenty-seven appearances of *conte* in the five romances, the word *romanz* occurs seven times. In *Cliges*, it opens the narrative and appears again when the section on Cliges begins; in both cases, the word has the traditional meaning of a composition adapted from Latin. In his five other uses of the term, however, Chrétien gives it a new meaning as he applies it specifically to his own compositions. In the opening lines of *The Knight with the Lion* and *The Story of the Grail* and in the closing lines of *The Knight of the Cart*, he has *romanz* designate his own completed artistic creation. And in *The Knight with the Lion*, the maiden at the Castle of Most Ill Adventure is reading

> en un romans, ne sai de cui;
> et por le romans escoter
> s'i estoit venue acoter
> une dame.   (lines 5360–63)

> (from a romance—I do not know about whom. A lady had come to recline there and hear the romance.)

Here the narrator employs a word rarely used in the five romances and repeats it in two consecutive lines. Here is, I believe, Chrétien referring to his own literary genre of the romance; here is a moment of self-reflection through the words of the narrator.[35]

In each of the five romances, the narrator is the literary self of Chrétien de Troyes, the public artist aware of his calling and the need to define it. His is the voice of a conscious and conscientious artist of the latter half of the twelfth century, trying to establish his position in a romance world not too far removed in time from the third-person epic voice. His first-person voice is a solitary one, both a part of his audience in his responses to his story and yet also apart from his audience, for in the new world of romance, Chrétien is the first writer to distance his narrator from the author and place this literary self throughout his compositions but not inside the actual fiction he presents. The narrator is defining his position as his poems define *romanz*.

The literary self of Chrétien the author is a caring disciple, not, like the narrator of Chaucer's *Troilus and Criseyde*, of Love, but of the new world of romance in which he locates himself.

---

[35]Hunt, on the contrary, suggests the possibility that these lines "may be an ironic allusion to the *Charrete* which Chrétien abandoned to Godefroi de Leigni" ("Beginnings, Middles, and Ends," p. 112, n.16).

Barbarolexis Revisited:
The Poetic Use of Hybrid Language
in Old Occitan/Old French Lyric

ROBERT A. TAYLOR

About 120 medieval poems have been preserved in a language that is neither Old French nor Old Occitan but a variable mixture of the two. With a little historical and philological probing, it is generally easy to place these into two groups: some 17 are Old French poems that have been Occitanized to varying degrees; most of them may be placed alongside the full array of French manuscript copies in which they are preserved in their original form, and there is no mystery about their identification. The process of hybridization by scribal alteration has been examined with some precision by Gustav Ineichen.[1] His study indicates that there was a limited tradition of transmission of trouvère poems in the Occitan area and that this led to a scribal hybridization in which the Old French forms were progressively Occitanized. An interesting light is cast upon this process by the fact that the majority of the hybridized poems in question were copied in northern Italy, as were many of the extant troubadour poems. The linguistic situation here was more fluid than either the Old French or the Old Occitan traditions, and it is interesting to speculate that

---

[1]Gustav Ineichen, "Autour du graphisme des chansons françaises à tradition provençale," *Travaux de linguistique et de littérature* 7 (1969): 203–18.

the Italian scribes may have hastened the process of hybridization, simply because they considered Occitan to be the best language for lyric expression, and may have altered the Old French by habit because of the literary prestige of Occitan.

A much larger group of over one hundred poems is made up of troubadour songs, or supposed troubadour songs, which have been preserved in Frenchified form in northern French manuscripts. The corpus is an important one for a number of reasons. It gives evidence of a broad tradition of familiarity with Occitan poetry in the North. It preserves some of the oldest copies of a number of Occitan texts, even if they are in Frenchified form; it preserves many poems with musical notation, among the oldest of the chansonniers to do so, and in fact it includes some thirty unique melodies. Finally, it is important because it contains a number of mysterious, ambiguous texts that are not found elsewhere and that, in my opinion, give evidence of a highly-developed tradition of hybrid-language poetry practiced undoubtedly in the North, but utilizing both Occitan and French language in a unique mixture for their poetic expression. Manfred and Margret Raupach have recently documented a good deal of information on the whole corpus, and have made possible this closer study of the half-dozen remaining mysterious poems and of the phenomenon of hybridization as a whole.[2]

Some of these texts have been claimed for the northern French corpus, some for the southern Occitan corpus, some for both, and a few for neither. They have been seen as Occitanized French poems, Frenchified Occitan poems, or it has been suggested for one or two of them that they may be neither of these two

---

[2]Manfred Raupach and Margret Raupach, *Französierte Trobadorlyrik. Zur Überlieferung provenzalischer Lieder in französischen Handschriften.* Beihefte zur Zeitschrift für romanische Philologie, 171 (Tübingen, 1979).

things but may have been composed in a language that was hybrid from the start, and consciously so. Some are well-known poems, such as the dance-song "Tuit cil qui sunt enamourat / viegnent dançar, li autre non!" or the famous "A l'entrade del tens clar, eya." Several others appear to be admirable works of literature worthy of a continued effort to understand their message and the way in which they were created. Before returning to examine several of these works more closely, I believe that it would be helpful to speak briefly of the wider context of the literary family and climate to which they belong.

There has been in recent years a renewed interest in the phenomenon of linguistic pluralism, not only for its own sake as a linguistic force but also for its historical and social importance, and for its role in literary expression and in textual transmission.[3] Included in the notion of pluralism is a wide variety of contrasting language forms, used in literature for varied purposes, producing on the reader or listener a variety of effects. Many of these have still to be explored and understood (that is, bilingualism, translation, language interference, macaronic writing), but in all its manifestations it deals with the touching of two or more linguistic systems that have their own perceived identity and that create a dynamic tension when they are juxtaposed or mixed.

Bilingualism and multilingualism have been recognized as potent forces in the area of social, historical, and literary development. Macaronic poetry is being examined with more care and respect than in the past; a number of interesting studies have been made of intercalated languages or mixed languages in poems, ser-

---

[3]See the Montreal colloquium "Le pluralisme linguistique dans la société médiévale," 30 April–3 May 1986, proceedings to be edited by Pierre Boglioni; also the volume *Europäische Mehrsprachigkeit: Festschrift zum 70. Geburtstag von Mario Wandruszka*, ed. Wolfgang Pöckl (Tübingen, 1986).

mons, plays, moral treatises, and even fabliaux.[4] Paul Zumthor made one of the first attempts to analyze the stylistic use of bilingualism, that is, the conscious exploitation of linguistic oppositions for poetic effect.[5] Zumthor also recognized the value of what he called "registres," traditionalized sets of themes, vocabulary, forms, and rhythms that act as a characteristic generic base for certain literary forms. The registers that characterize, for example, the pastourelle or the epic or the "grand chant courtois" function almost as mini-language systems and can be juxtaposed or mixed in a manner similar to the mixing of Latin and the vernacular for conscious stylistic effect. When the notion of language choice is added to the list of items that can constitute a literary register, then the importance of language mixture can take on added depth; it becomes clear that nothing should be taken as unconscious or accidental in the history of lyric tranmission without very careful examination.

It was commonly felt by medieval society that certain languages were better suited to one literary genre than another.[6] In some of the theoretical treatises, and for Dante, Occitan was the language par excellence of the courtly lyric, while French was particularly suited to the narrative. Latin was the only appropriate language for serious philosophic or scientific discourse and was,

---

[4]See Ulrich Müller, "Mehrsprachigkeit und Sprachmischung als poetische Technik: Barbarolexis in dem *Carmina Burana*," in Pöckl, *Europäische Mehrsprachigkeit*, pp. 87–104.

[5]Paul Zumthor, *Langue et techniques poétiques à l'époque romane* (Paris, 1963), pp. 82–111; more detailed references are to be found in his earlier article, "Un problème d'esthétique médiévale: l'utilisation poétique du bilinguisme," *Le Moyen âge* 66 (1960): 301–36 and 561–94.

[6]See Ineichen, "Autour du graphisme," p. 218; and Zumthor, "Un problème d'esthétique," p. 590.

of course, the language of Church authority.

I shall refer specifically to a small group of texts that have been passed over too hastily as contaminated and bizarre, preserved in a hybridized French/Occitan language, and that have been thought to represent either faulty transmission by scribes who did not understand them or, perhaps, the product of a region lying across the linguistic boundary between *oïl* and *oc*, that is, reflecting the naturally hybrid language of the poet or of an intelligent scribe/adapter. I would like to demonstrate that some of these are neither contaminated nor spontaneously hybrid but are the result of a conscious literary effort on the part of the poet to exploit the dynamic of two opposing linguistic systems to attain specific effect.

Within the 120 or so poems preserved in hybridized form, most may be recognized as products of textual transmission and are not of particular interest to us here as indicating poetic use of language oppositions, except insofar as they may help us to perceive the traditions of hybridized poetry within which the more interesting poems developed. Virtually all of the French trouvère poems transmitted in Occitanized form may be compared with their established French formulation as found in a wider manuscript tradition in the northern French chansonniers. Their hybridization takes the form of a scribal Occitanization, due to a conscious or unconscious effort to adapt the texts to the norms of Old Occitan graphic, morphological, and lexical characteristics. There is no indication of a real effort to use the contrasting language forms for poetic purposes, although the process may have been helped along by the prestige of the Occitan language.

Hybridization in the other direction is not only more widely represented in the manuscript tradition, it is more interesting because of the variety of products it seems to have left behind. Among the more than one hundred poems that are called Occitan but are more or less hybridized in the direction of Frenchification,

most are clearly copies of Occitan troubadour poems that are
well-known in the standard troubadour chansonniers and that can
be examined and understood as regional variants of the original
Occitan texts. But some twenty of the poems are not found elsewhere, and, although some of these are obviously Occitan and
could, in theory, be reconstituted in their original Occitan formulation, there is a final stubborn group of poems that have continued to puzzle scholars by the difficulty of deciding whether they
are essentially Old French texts or Old Occitan texts.

The group has been a disquieting one for some time, although
no one has so far considered the poems important enough to be
studied closely as a group. Concerning one of them, part of a thirteenth-century motet "Li jalous par tout sunt fustat" (see Appendix,
poem 1), Paul Meyer had already revealed some doubt in 1872:

> On voit en effet du premier coup d'oeil que ce motet appar-
> tient à la langue d'oc, bien que le copiste l'ait un peu fran-
> cisé. Toutefois, il ne l'a peut-être pas autant francisé qu'on
> pourrait le croire, car notre motet peut avoir eu d'origine
> certaines formes plutôt françaises que provençales.[7]

Gaston Paris had gone further to state that the poem was composed by a northern French poet, who had added Occitan local
color to it. Not until 1954, however, was the definitive classification made by István Frank.[8] Frank based his conclusions on a
study of the rhyme words such as *frapat*, which does not exist in
Occitan, a final in *-ont* with supported *n* rhyming with two other

---

[7]Paul Meyer, "Mélanges de littérature provençale, II: Motets à trois parties," *Romania* 1 (1872): 404.

[8]István Frank, "'Tuit cil qui sunt enamourat'" *Romania* 75 (1954): 98–108; see also Frank, *Répertoire métrique de la poésie des troubadours*, vol. 1 (Paris, 1953), pp. xxii–xxiii.

forms with unsupported (mobile) *n,* and on the word *dançade,* which is just as unknown to Old Occitan as its hypothetical counterpart *danciée* would be to Old French. The poem cannot be restored to an "original" French state. The convincing explanation of István Frank was that the poem had been formulated from the start in a hybridized language, in which the underlying Old French was mixed with pseudo-Occitan *on purpose* by the poet.

The corresponding one-stanza rondeau "Tuit cil qui sunt enamourat" (see Appendix, poem 2) does not contain any obvious pseudo-Occitan or pseudo-French forms that would permit a sure conclusion, but it is highly likely that the same intentional mixture of the two languages characterized it from the start. These are literary pastiche poems, hybrid by their nature.

Other poems that were taken for Occitan texts at first because of some Occitan forms have now been shown to be entirely French. The poem "Mout m'abelist l'amouros pensement" (P/C 461, 170a) has an Occitanized first line because it is borrowed from a poem by Folquet de Marselha; the rest of the poem is entirely French.[9] A pastourelle that begins: "L'autrier m'iere levaz" (P/C 461, 148) has some rhymes that are clearly French (*pri:joi:cri:ci;* for which Old Occitan would be *prec, jauzic, crit, sai*); a scribe must have tried to Occitanize it a little, first by changing the French *levés* in the first line to *levaz,* but then following this, for the necessity of rhyme, with the rather bizarre rhymes *seraz, avaz, poteraz,* which could not have fooled many people, and in fact may have been intended to produce a humorous effect.[10] To these may be added two poems by Richard the

---

[9]See Raupach and Raupach, *Französierte Trobadorlyrik,* p. 50.

[10]See Frank, "Tuit cil qui sunt enamourat," p. 106, n.2; and Frank, *Répertoire,* introduction.

Lion-hearted, which were composed in French but are found with some Occitan coloration.[11] Many other Old French poems, in fact, have the occasional Occitanized form, but it is clear that this is due to the widespread contact with troubadour texts in the North and the prestige of the troubadour language rather than the conscious exploration of a rhetorical technique.

What of the famous *balada* that is in so many of the Old Occitan anthologies: "A l'entrade del tens clar, eya" (P/C 461, 12; see Appendix, poem 3)?[12] Certain forms in the poem are definitely French, such as the word *veillart*, but rhyming with it and with infinitives of the first conjugation is the word *par*, meaning "equal" or "peer" (Old French *pair*). This word can only be Occitan. Frank decided that the poem was basically Occitan, but Raupach remains doubtful, saying that its classification is not yet clear, and Van der Werf indicates that the poem "may not be of Occitan origin."[13] Its consciously hybrid nature makes it clear to me that it was composed by a French poet who chose to use Occitanized forms as part of its linguistic and literary register.

A religious poem beginning "Per vous m'esjau, done del firmament" (see Appendix, poem 4) is superficially Occitan, with graphic forms such as *laudar*, *podrie*, *voldrie*, *sap*, *aleujat*, and *jauziment*, but has some exclusively French words such as *vie* (line 29) and *guie* (line 30) in rhyme, *ja més* (line 27) and *pres* (line 28); and *lignie* (line 17): *rendrie* (line 18), which is a Picard rhyme.[14] Jeanroy edited the poem with Pierre Aubry for the sake

---

[11]See Ineichen, "Autour du graphisme," p. 206.

[12]See Frank, *Répertoire* 1:xxii.

[13]Hendrik Van der Werf, *The Extant Troubadour Melodies* (Rochester, N.Y., 1984), p. 23.

[14]For text see *Annales du Midi* 21 (1900): 67–71; also Frank, *Répertoire* 1:xxiii.

of its interesting melody, declaring that "sa valeur littéraire m'a paru absolument nulle." He concluded that the author was French, trying to write in Occitan, and that a scribe had made a mess of whatever the poem was like to start with. But Frank and Raupach have continued to include it in the Old Occitan repertory, with indications of doubt, perhaps because there has been no interest in claiming it for the Old French repertory. Within the framework of our larger group, it is obvious to me that it is a poem composed by a French author, with conscious use of hybridized Occitan forms.

Two final poems will lead us into unexplored territory, first because their Occitan identity has not until now been called into question and, second, because they both belong to what has recently been called the "contre-texte" tradition.[15] The first (see Appendix, poem 5) is a poem recently published for the first time by Gerald Bond.[16] It recounts the fabliau-like invitation to a more than willing lady to enter a monastery with eighty monks for purposes of illicit pleasure. In his brief comments on the language, Bond states that the base language is "clearly" Old Occitan, but with many Frankisms. There are phonemic forms such as *moines*, *maiso*, *cuilo*, and *oches*; lexical items such as *quintena* (line 17) which does not exist in Old Occitan but is common in Old French in the form of *quintaine* "target." The sense and the versification demand the Old French word *desor* in line 24 for the manuscript reading *dejus*. The unique hybrid form *irea* (line 16) is unknown in either language and represents a compromise between Occitan

---

[15]Pierre Bec, *Burlesque et obscénité chez les troubadours: Le Contre-texte au Moyen Age* (Paris, 1984); also René Nelli, *Les Ecrivains anticonformistes du Moyen Age occitan*, vol. 1: *La femme et l'Amour* (Paris, 1977).

[16]Gerald Bond, "The Last Unpublished Troubadour Songs," *Speculum* 60 (1985): 844–48.

irada and the French *iree*. Is this a poem in Frenchified Occitan or in Occitanized French? The French lexical items and the fabliau-like theme, along with an emerging pattern of similarities that are characteristic of several of the poems examined above, would lead me to lean toward the notion of composition by an Old French poet who knew a good deal of Old Occitan and who chose to formulate his poem in a hybridized language. There is no evidence to indicate that the literary climate that supported the use of Occitanized language by French poets existed for hybridization in the other direction, that is, for the use of Frenchified language by Occitan poets. Occitan was clearly the "prestige" language in the field, subject to mockery perhaps by Old French speakers, but is this not an admission of "superiority"?

The final poem (see Appendix, poem 6) is one that has appeared recently for the first time in critical edition, edited by Marie-Claire Gérard-Zai and also, independently, by myself, both editions in the second volume of *Studia Occitanica*.[17] It is listed as part of the Occitan repertory in Frank's *Répertoire métrique* and in the documentation of Raupach, but I believe that I have demonstrated that this text is also a pastiche, composed by a French poet in a hybridized language. There is a long list of superficially but highly visible Occitan forms, especially a number of endings in *-uda* in rhyme position, past participles in *-at*, and others. Against these are arrayed a number of forms with typically French phonemes such as *belisor*, *itan*, *cras*, *boisat*, and *oi*, and feminine *-e* endings (that would be *belazor*, *aitan*, *gras*, *bauzat*, *aic*, and *-a*). More important are a series of lexical items that are exclusively French, such as *enfat* (line 53) "poison," *pan mesalat* (line 54) "mouldy bread," *sorsemat* (line 56) "tainted" in speaking of pork, *vin cras et boutat* (line 58) "coarse spoiled wine," and a

[17]*Studia Occitanica in Memoriam Paul Remy*, ed. Hans-Erich Keller, vol. 2 (Kalamazoo, 1986), pp. 189–201.

cliché phrase *paupre et nuda* (line 5) "poor and shabby" applied to the peasant girls in the French popular lyrics. None of these words has any recorded usage in Old Occitan, but all are common in Old French, particularly in literature from the Picard area.

The poem is a lyric re-creation of a traditional misogynistic episode popularized by Ovid and represented directly in the thirteenth-century Latin *De Vetula*, upon which it is obviously based.[18] It expresses the lover's shock in discovering that he has been tricked into a rendezvous with a revolting old hag instead of his sweetheart, followed by a horrified description of her repelling qualities and a long curse, to which are attached the French expressions for poison, mouldy bread, tainted pork, and spoiled wine.

The textual history of the *De Vetula* is entirely confined to the northern French sphere, and it partakes directly of the fabliau tradition in the Northeast. The poem is, in my view, a culminating example of a text composed by a French poet using a hybridized French/Occitan language. The interesting question is: why? What might have impelled the composer to use this unusual linguistic form? The answer lies in the underlying literary traditions that had established Occitan as the most desirable language for the formulation of lyric poetry. The tradition was a long-standing and firmly based one, as we have seen through the extensive circulation of troubadour texts in the North, as well as in Italy, Sicily, Germany, Catalunya, Portugal, and Spain. The prestige of Occitan was, of course, so firmly established in Catalunya and northern Italy that it was used by poets from these areas instead of their own languages. The tradition did not become established to the same extent in northern France, but it was undeniably present, at least for a limited time, and will account for the phenomenon that

---

[18]*Pseudo-Ovidius De Vetula. Untersuchungen und Text*, ed. Paul Klopsch, Mittellateinische Studien und Texte, 2 (Leiden and Cologne, 1967).

I have presented. The use of Occitan forms as a sort of register of the courtly lyric mode, in order to validate the quality of the poems, may well account for the well-known acceptance of *amor* in an undipthongized Occitan form instead of the dipthongized form (*amour*) that would have been expected in northern France. The small number of genuinely hybrid poems that I have presented rapidly represent the brief flowering of a literary fad that may have passed quickly from favor. But while it was in effect, it motivated poets to add Occitan flavor to their poems, which they did to varying degrees and with varying success. The poems "A l'entrade del tens clar, eya" and "Tuit cil qui sunt enamourat" are almost perfect fusions of the two languages, while the others on my list are more transparently pseudo-Occitan. The religious poem "Per vous m'esjau" made a serious use of the register in an attempt to enhance the beauty of the pious content.

But the two contre-texte poems represent the highest point of the literary fashion, because they rely on its solid existence in order to make possible the parodic effect of their message. In these two cases, the Occitanized language is a part of the signal of the courtly register that is being turned on its ear for humorous effect. The Occitan coloring heightens the contrast and the shock value and the effectiveness of the message. In order to work, the pastiche must have been good enough to evoke the proper "Occitan" signal, but not complete enough to fool the enlightened audience, which had to realize what was going on. Unfortunately for the posterity of our poets, the fashion must have shifted after a short time. The audience was no longer enlightened and was, indeed, fooled into thinking that these were Occitan texts like the others in the collection where they are preserved. I hope to have demonstrated that they are not.

Poem 1: "Li jalous par tout sunt fustat," part of a motet, thirteenth century
Source: István Frank, "Tuit cil qui sunt enamourat," *Romania* 75 (1954): 100.

      Li jalous par tout sunt fustat
      et portent corne en mie le front.
      Par tout doivent estre huat:
      la Regine le commendat
5   que d'un baston soient frapat
      et chacié hors comme larron.
      Si en dançade veillent entrar,
      fier le du pié comme garçon!

Poem 2: "Tuit cil qui sunt enamourat," rondeau, thirteenth century
Source: Frank, "Tuit cil qui sunt enamourat," p. 100.

      —Tuit cil qui sunt enamourat
      —viegnent dançar, li autre non!
      La Regine le commendat
      —tuit cil qui sunt enamourat—
5   que li jalous soient fustat
      fors de la dance d'un baston.
      —Tuit cil qui sunt enamourat
      —viegnent avant, li autre non!

Poem 3: "A l'entrade del tens clar, eya," balada, thirteenth century
Source: Jean Deroy, "A l'entrade del tens clar—Veris ad imperia," *Mélanges Christine Mohrmann. Nouveau recueil offert par ses anciens élèves*, (Utrecht/Anvers, 1973), pp. 191–208.

    I.   A l'entrade del tens clar, eya
        pir joie recomençar, eya
        et pir jalous irritar, eya
        vol la Regine mostrar
5   k'ele est si amorouse.
        A la vi', a la vie, jalous.

Lassaz nos, lassaz nos
ballar entre nos, entre nos.

II. Ele a fait par tot mandar, eya
10   non sie jusq'a la mar, eya
pucele ni bachelar, eya
que tuit non venguent dançar
en la dance joiouse.
A la vi', a la vie, jalous.
15   Lassaz nos, lassaz nos
ballar entre nos, entre nos.

III. Lo reis i vent d'autre part, eya
pir la dance destorbar, eya
que il est en cremetar, eya
20   que on ne li vuelle emblar
la Regine avrillouse.
A la vi', a la vie, jalous.
Lassaz nos, lassaz nos
ballar entre nos, entre nos.

25 IV. Mais pir neient lo vol far, eya
k'ele n'a soig de viellart, eya
mais d'un legeir bachelar, eya
ki ben sache solaçar
la donne savorouse.
30   A la vi', a la vie, jalous.
Lassaz nos, lassaz nos
ballar entre nos, entre nos.

V. Qui donc la veïst dançar, eya
et son gent cors deportar, eya
35   ben puist dire de vertar, eya
k'el mont non aie sa par
la Regine joiouse.
A la vi', a la vie, jalous.
Lassaz nos, lassaz nos
40   ballar entre nos, entre nos.

Poem 4: "Per vous m'esjau, done del firmament," religious song, twelfth–thirteenth century

Source: A. Jeanroy and P. Aubry, "Mélanges et documents: une chanson provençale (?) à la vierge," *Annales du Midi* 12 (1900): 67–71.

   I.   Per vous m'esjau, done del firmament,
         Tres coralment
         Alumas et engres
         De vostre pres
5   Laudar tant com podrie:
         S'agrade a vous et Dé, mes non voldrie.

   II.   Quant Gabriel fist vous l'anonçalment,
         Tout erraument
         Se fu Diex en vous mes:
10   Cor a con gres
         Qui ben ne le credrie,
         Et sap que Diex en s'arme part n'aurie.

   III. Done, de qui tout paravis resplent,
         Per vous se sent
15   Aleujat de greu feis
         Et rege en peis
         Toute humaine lignie:
         Vide per mort vostre fius nous rendrie.

   IV. Douce done, de vous mont et descent
20   Lou jauziment
         per que de vous chantes.
         Done, marces!
         Prejas Dé que non vie
         Sobre poder de quelque dampnas sie.

25 V.   Mare au signar qui n'a començalment,
         Ne finament
         Non avra il ja més,
         Grans nous pres
         En iste mortal vie,
30   Et o ton fil en son regne nous guie.

Poem 5: "Ara lausetz, lauset, lauset li comandamen l'abbet," parody song
Source: Gerald Bond, "The Last Unpublished Troubadour Songs," *Speculum* 60
(1985): 844–48.

Ara lausetz, lauset, lauset
li comandamen l'abbet.

I. Bela, si vos eravatz   moina de nostra maiso,
a profit de totz los moines   vos pendriatz liuraso;
5   mas vos non estaretz, bela,   si totz jorns enversa no,
zo dix l'abbet.

II. Bela, si vos voliatz   en nostr'orden remanir,
gras capos ne grosses oches   no vos poirian falir;
mas a vos covenra, bela,   ab totz los monges a jazir
10   [e] ab l'abbet.

III. Er nos em .iiij. vint moines   tuit d'una religio,
e qan l'uns fa tort a l'altr[e]   ab grans verges nos batom;
mas vos no seretz batuda   si de colps de cuilos no,
zo dix l'abbet.

15 IV. "Si vos ez .iiij.xx. moines,   lo vulria mais de cen,
e serai ne fort irea   si no.us ren totz [. . .] tanz;
levarai vos la quintena,   firetz tuitx ardiamen
ab vostr'abet."

V. Bela, anui[t in]traretz   dinz en nostre dormitor;
20   de .L.iiij. moines   vos en farem cobertor;
non au[si]rez sein ne clotxa   si de vits sejornatz no,
zo dix l'abbet.

Aras n'intra nostr'am[ia]   ab los fraires el dormitor:
ja non exira la bela   tro qe dessus e desor
25   li don l'abbet.

Poem 6: "L'altrier cuidai aber druda," parody song, thirteenth century
Source: Robert A. Taylor, "'L'altrier cuidai aber druda' (PC 461, 146): Edition
and Study of a Hybrid-Language Parody Lyric," in *Studia Occitanica in
Memoriam Paul Remy*, ed. Hans-Erich Keller, vol. 2 (Kalamazoo, 1986), pp.
189–201.

I.	L'altrier cuidai aber druda,
	tota la meillor
	c'onques egusse veguda,
	et la belisor:
5	velle antiue, paupre et nuda,
	ben parlant d'amor.
	Trames per oc que·l saluda,
	et fac plaz gensor.
	Mais la trace malastruda!
10	Qu·eu per liei oi dat
	vels vin e troblat,
	peis et por salat.
	E l'oi calçada et vestuda,
	si me·n ab boisat.
15	Qu'en loc d'amige es venguda,
	en tens tenebror.
	Tint son pan en sor,
	et eu sus li cor;
	et trobai la piau cal[v]uda,
20	corde el col, espaulle aguda,
	memella pendant et viuda
	com borsa pastor,
	pis ossut et plat,
	e·l ventre ridat,
25	maigre rains et cuisse ruda,
	dur genoill et flat;
	et quant l'ai aperc[eg]ude,
	es me vos irat!
	Ab itant vir a la fuda,
30	non sui arrestat.
II.	Tan m'en es el cor creguda,
	rancune et gramor,

473

que continence ai perduda
d'amar per amor.
35 Que pensava la canuda,
que non ab calor?
Et volie essre batuda
subra son tabor!
Non ab tan langue esmoluda
40 qu'egusse acontat
demei la metat
del mal qu'ab pensat
dont deurie essre te[n]guda
per son lait peccat:
45 tos et gutta et mal qui suda
sanz aber retor;
freit et seif et plor
od fresche dolor,
ni ja·l tendre n'i paruda.
50 Que non sie a mort feruda,
de tal mal qui non la tuda,
ainz (la) teigne en langor.
N'el non ait d'enfat
for pan mesalat,
55 et carne de vella truda
ou (de) porc sorsemat,
pis de mar qui de loig puda,
vin cras et boutat.
Ja·n non es tant irascuda
60 que·m quidai (essre) vengat.